CLASS IN A CAPITALIST SOCIETY

A study of contemporary Britain

Class
in a
Capitalist Society

A study of contemporary Britain

JOHN WESTERGAARD

and

HENRIETTA RESLER

Basic Books, Inc., Publishers

NEW YORK

To Mike and Sue,
Wanda, Eric and Inger

Contents

Preface

The theme of this book is class inequality – its nature and extent in present-day Britain; its roots; the conflicts and tensions to which it gives rise, both overt and latent; the prospects of change to which such conflict may point. We have drawn on a wide range of sources in our attempt to map the patterns of class division. But the book is not, and is not intended to be, a catalogue of facts. Nor could it be so. Facts themselves can be selected, and put together to make some coherent sense, only within a perspective which sets criteria of relevance. Our perspective is Marxist. And our aim has been to present an interpretation of the class structure of Britain – as an example of contemporary Western capitalist societies – which is both Marxist and anchored in empirical fact.

One difficulty about writing such a book is that the record of events inevitably lags behind the events themselves. The point applies in one way especially to matters for which statistical documentation is relevant. We have made considerable use, for example, of statistics from official sources. But these are generally published well after the latest dates to which they refer. For the most part, moreover, they cannot be used simply as they stand, but need a good deal of subsequent work to be understood and presented in an appropriate form: continuous revision to take account of every addition to the record is not a practical proposition. Where we have drawn on quantitative material published by government offices at regular intervals, therefore, we have in the main been able to trace trends up to around 1971; sometimes not so far, rarely much beyond then. When the sources are special inquiries, whether undertaken by government or by others, we have often had to go further back for the most recent relevant information. Yet on these scores the lapse of time between events and publication matters relatively little, since the statistical evidence involved relates very largely to the basic facts of class incquality. As we try to show, the framework of inequality has remained remarkably constant for many years. There are no signs that it has recently begun to shift in any significant way which would elude us, because we are not able to carry the detailed documentation right up to date.

The difficulty of keeping abreast of time may be more noticeable when it comes to issues concerning, not the basic facts of class inequality, but political and popular reactions to them. Our discussion of those issues goes up to about the middle of 1974. But it may well seem outdated on a few points already by the time the book is published. That is inevitable during a period in which class tensions and class conflict have found more overt – and therefore also more changeable – expression in politics, public affairs and industrial relations than for a number of years earlier. It would have been no solution for us simply to ignore current events. The fact that class divisions are once again very visible in everyday political and industrial affairs is itself of large significance. We are forced to refer to events, particular details of which may have lost topical interest by the time this book is in print, in order both to illustrate general trends and to discuss their implications. But we think it unlikely that readers will feel more than a slight, occasional jar when they have an advantage of hindsight over us.

The sources on which we have drawn are indicated in footnotes. But we have not tried to give comprehensive references, beyond these, to the very large volume of literature and research material relevant to the subject. For a detailed bibliography on British social structure, interested readers are referred to *Modern British Society: a Bibliography*, by John Westergaard, Anne Weyman and Paul Wiles (Frances Pinter, 1974).

The bare bones of our interpretation may be familiar to some readers from a few earlier, short articles by John Westergaard. Our purpose here has been to put flesh on to these bones. Henrietta Resler joined John Westergaard primarily in order to help him assemble and analyse information from the extensive and widely scattered body of statistical and literary material that needed to be taken into account. But her contribution came in fact to very much more than that, extending to detailed discussion of themes and arguments and to comment on successive drafts at most stages of the work. Nothing short of inclusion of her name on the title page would be adequate to recognize her part in the book.

We have many and large debts to acknowledge. Our very warm thanks go to those who have read and criticized parts of the draft, from whose comments we have greatly benefited: to Ralph Miliband especially, and to Michael Burrage, Steven Lukes, Donald Pilcher, Angus Stewart and Paul Walton. There are others, too, who have helped us – sometimes more than they themselves may realize – because we have had the opportunity to discuss some of the issues involved with them, because we have learned from their understanding of the subject, or because they have given us guidance on source material. Among those to whom we are grateful on one or more of these scores are Meghnad Desai, Ruth and David Glass, John Griffith, Hilary Rose, Ian Taylor and Michael Zander; while we acknowledge the help received from some other friends and colleagues in footnotes at particular points of the text. Our special thanks are due to Karen Margolis, who helped for a month in extracting and analysing information, with exceptional commitment. ability and perceptiveness. We have a very great debt indeed to Isabel Ogilvie and Sheila Wright, who typed the drafts of the book with speed, punctiliousness and enthusiasm. We are grateful also to the London School of Economics, which gave John Westergaard sabbatical leave for a year, during which the major part of the work was done; and which provided the grant from which Henrietta Resler and Karen Margolis were paid.

Finally, we have personal debts to our families, which go well beyond those which are expressed in the dedication.

J.W.

H.R.

List of Tables and Diagrams

UNNUMBERED TABLES
AND DIAGRAMS

PART ONE

THEMES AND ISSUES

I

This book is about the class structure of contemporary Western capitalism. We focus on one particular society, Britain. All the detailed empirical material on which we draw relates to Britain, although from time to time we refer briefly to the situation in other capitalist countries. When we do so, it is in order to point to the essential similarity of condition between them and Britain, or to bring out certain distinctive features of the British example. But it is central to our approach that we take Britain as an example of a modern capitalist society. This is, in other words, not a book primarily about the 'peculiarities of the English'. It would have been possible to write a book – or several books – of that kind, quite different from this. It would not in our view, however, have made good sense to do so. For we believe, first, that the conditions of class and power which Britain shares with other capitalist countries, by virtue of the fact that they are capitalist, are overwhelmingly more significant than the differences among them. Second, we think that it is possible to discuss such differences sensibly only against the background of a detailed analysis of the dominant common features of capitalism. As we cannot carry out both kinds of analysis adequately at the same time, our main concern is with just those dominant features, illustrated by the British example.

We are not, therefore, following the view often suggested that Britain is a peculiarly 'class-ridden' society. When postulates of that sort are made they usually, for one thing, take 'class' in a narrow and trivial sense. The proposition then is that the British – perhaps the English upper and middle classes more specifically – are exceptionally obsessed with social ranking, and with the symbols of accent and manners that demarcate social rank. Whether the proposition is true or not, it concerns only one highly restricted feature of inequality: the sensitivity of people to gradations of prestige; the rituals and etiquette of inter-personal relationships within and across lines that divide the population in some sort of hierarchy of esteem. The concern is with what sociologists usually call social 'status'.[1]

Questions of this kind may have their own intrinsic fascination. And they have some significance beyond their impact on everyday life and their character as a ready-made target for ridicule. Status sensitivity, anxieties to be 'accepted' and 'to keep up with the Joneses', deference to 'superiors', are one form of response to inequality. And they may condition other possible forms of response – for example, by inhibiting consciousness of their common condition among the victims of inequality; by holding back collective protest against class power. Mr Pooter's agonized obsession with propriety and recognition by his 'betters' is not just a rewarding subject for satire.[2] It is also symptomatic of the kinds of aspiration for respectability which – now as around the turn of the century, in other countries as well as Britain – have helped to keep the socio-political loyalties of many low-paid office workers tied to the established order. The invidious distinctions of status-ranking – which in drawing-room conversation often seem to be regarded as the essence of class – are thus important enough when seen in a much wider context; but not otherwise. Taken by themselves, the gradations of social esteem tell one nothing about the concrete structure of inequality – the cleavages of economic position, power and associated chances in life – from which they derive, sometimes by complex and devious routes. It is those cleavages which are the hard core of class; and status sensitivity is only one form which consciousness of those cleavages may take.

Our first concern in this book, then, is with the hard core of class – with the substance and structural sources of inequality, irrespective of how people react to the experience of inequality; with what Marx

1. The term is usually attributed to Max Weber, who distinguished 'Stand' – translated as 'status' – from 'class': see his 'Class, status, party' in, e.g., H. H. Gerth and C. W. Mills, eds., *From Max Weber*, Kegan Paul, 1947. Weber's concept of 'class' was similar to Marx's, in so far as both saw class position as a matter of the place occupied by people in the system of production, and of the circumstances set for them thereby; while both also saw shared class position as a potential basis for recognition of common interests, and for collective class organization and action in consequence (see note 3, p. 3, below). The similarities end there. Marx emphasized, of course, the role of ownership of the means of production as crucial for class division; Weber more than Marx the part played by differences in the terms on which employees of different categories sold their labour. Above all, class and class division occupied a very much smaller place in Weber's social analysis than in Marx's.

2. G. and W. Grossmith, *The Diary of a Nobody*, 1st ed., London, 1895.

described as 'class in itself'.[3] Only after that can we take up the second major set of issues – those which concern responses to class division. The critical questions there are whether and how objective cleavages of power, wealth, security and opportunity give rise to groups whose members are conscious of a common identity. If so, moreover, does such identity take the form of some sense of common interest in opposition to others, providing a basis for collective organization in class conflict; or is it by contrast, for example, dissipated through factional fragmentation, and a predominance of individual anxieties about personal social status without political impetus? The focus of that set of questions is on how the victims of inequality respond. Active unity on the part of the beneficiaries of inequality is rarely necessary, except when their power is challenged. But the question is crucial about the unprivileged groups of the population: is their dependence in a condition of 'class in itself' translated into an active consciousness of 'class for itself'? For Marx, around the middle of the nineteenth century, the long-run prospects of capitalist society in answer to that question seemed plain: proletarians would eventually unite and throw off their chains. For many others, then and especially now, Marx's answer has seemed plainly wrong: proletarian unity is an illusion; and whatever chains there were have been worn away by reform. That view, we hope to show, is false. Wage earners are still enchained by capital, though the chains are suppler now than they were. Working-class unity has been and is a political reality – of a sort; but of a sort only. Fragmentation vies with unity. The labour movement is torn between pragmatic acceptance, with pressure for moderate reform, and so far ineffective rejection of the capitalist order. The outcome is still in the balance; and it may remain so for quite a time.

3. The distinction between 'class in itself' (the circumstances and mutual relationships set for people by their place in the system of production, by their positions in particular as owners or dependent labour) and 'class for itself' (consciousness of common interests by virtue of common class position, and collective organization and action in consequence) recurs in one form or another at several points in Marx's work. See, e.g., his *The Eighteenth Brumaire of Louis Napoleon*, 1st German ed., 1852: a work of central importance also because it contradicts the impressions conveyed by many critics of Marx, and by vulgar Marxists, that class divisions in his view could, already then, be summed up in the simplistic polar terms of a straight confrontation between capital and labour. (For a clear application of the distinction to analysis of a twentieth-century capitalist society, see T. Geiger, *Die soziale Schichtung des deutschen Volkes*, Stuttgart, 1932.)

II

Beside these issues, the niceties of status gradation which often loom large in discussions of class are hardly important. It is in any case by no means certain that sensitivity to the nuances and symbols of social esteem is exceptionally acute and pervasive in Britain. If distinctions of accent and U- and non-U manners were developed to a fine art in this country, so was elaborate use of occupational titles in Scandinavia and Germany, for instance. And in Scandinavia, too, to give another example, patronymic surnames – names ending in 'son' or 'sen' – are still often regarded as mildly shameful, because they suggest peasant or proletarian family origins.[4] Changes of name by deed poll to some grandiloquent invented surname, without the revealing tag, mark the socially aspiring as figures of fun there in much the same way as does the adoption of a 'refained' accent here. The symbols of status, in short, differ among countries, regions, groups and over time. That says little by itself. But even if top and respectable middle-level culture in Britain may have been especially obsessed with the subtleties of social ranking, a large part of the explanation would probably be found in a feature of British history that has had much wider and more significant consequences. That feature is the early emergence and slow development of capitalism in this country.

The process was drawn out over many centuries.[5] Agrarian and mercantile capitalism was translated into industrial capitalism some fifty to one hundred years before a similar transformation occurred

4. Cf. K. Svalastoga, *Prestige, Class and Mobility*, Copenhagen, 1951 (also *idem* and P. Wolf, *Social Rang og Mobilitet*, Copenhagen, 1961); G. Boalt, 'Family name and social class', *Theoria* (Lund), vol. 17, 1951.

5. The summary comments that follow on the character of capitalist development in Britain are derived from a wide variety of sources. Some more specific references are given at relevant points later in the book. But among general histories and commentaries see, e.g., B. Moore, *Social Origins of Dictatorship and Democracy*, Penguin Books, 1969 (ch. 1); M. Dobb, *Studies in the Development of Capitalism*, Routledge, 1946; H. Perkin, *The Origins of Modern English Society 1780–1880*, Routledge & Kegan Paul, 1969; G. M. Young, *Victorian England: Portrait of an Age*, Oxford Univ. Press, 1936; G. K. Clark, *The Making of Victorian England*, Oxford Univ. Press, 1960; E. J. Hobsbawm, *Industry and Empire*, Weidenfeld & Nicolson, 1968; E. P. Thompson, *The Making of the English Working Class*, Penguin Books, 1968; P. Anderson, 'Origins of the present crisis', in *idem* and R. Blackburn, eds., *Towards Socialism*, Fontana, 1965.

on any comparable scale elsewhere. At no time – not even in the seventeenth century, when economic, political and religious cleavages came together in civil war – did ascendant groups of the bourgeoisie climb to position and power, and remake economy and society in their own image, through a revolutionary displacement of former ruling groups. The typical process instead involved repeated inter-penetration of old and new strata, old and new interests. Members of the landed nobility and gentry themselves invested in new forms of enterprise at crucial periods of capitalist transformation; sent their younger sons into commerce and the professions; absorbed new entrants from finance and trade in each generation. It would not be surprising if one consequence of this process of social osmosis were a distinctive emphasis on the cultural symbols which – unlike crude wealth – could differentiate between established and outsiders, until the latter themselves were established. Elaboration of demarcations of language and life style by old élites, to protect their status against nouveaux riches, is a familiar phenomenon. Acceptance and imitation of these rituals by the newcomers, and transmission of similar pre-occupations further down the social scale, might then well be ex-pected, given that the newcomers could realistically hope to buy élite acceptance at least for their children or grandchildren.

Be that as it may, other consequences which followed – or prob-ably followed – from the early, slow and essentially non-revolution-ary development of British capitalism have been more important. Among them, not least, was the fact of Britain's industrial supremacy in the world until the late decades of the nineteenth century. When that supremacy faded, the heritage of capital equipment and organ-izational practices from the earlier phases of industrial capitalism was large. This coloured the adjustment of British business to foreign competition. It may have held back technological innovation and managerial initiative. And the adjustment itself, to a significant degree, took the form of a specialization in overseas finance and an associated revival of imperialism in rivalry with the new capitalist powers. The City of London, in this process, acquired or strength-ened its central place in the power structure of British business and as a major source of influence on economic policy. Educating a colonial élite to carry 'the white man's burden' added another thread to the ethos of the inappropriately named 'public' schools, which had been flourishing since before the middle of the nineteenth century in their dedication to raising the sons of the new and the old propertied classes in a common culture of gentlemanly self-assurance and respect for hierarchical order. That culture itself was a distinctive product of the interpenetration of landed, commercial and industrial interests at the top of the social structure. It probably contributed a characteristic note of disdain for technical expertise to styles of management in both government and business from the latter decades of the nineteenth century onwards, which was out of line with the innovatory enthusiasm of the earlier industrial bourgeoisie.

For labour, too, the early onset and comparatively slow pace of capitalist development had important consequences. Domestic industry had made large sections of the population effectively dependent on the sale of their labour power in an insecure commercial market well before the 'industrial revolution' of the late eighteenth and early nineteenth centuries. The 'cash nexus' had thus become the main bond that tied many people to the social order, even while the outward forms of independence in craftwork and small-scale agriculture might persist, and before mass migration to the mill towns and coalfields created by mechanized production got under way. Only the towns, however, provided the conditions – numbers, physical proximity, consciously and visibly shared experience – in which workers could effectively join together to make their own organizations and institutions for survival in, and opposition to, a hostile world. In Britain, moreover, they had to do so without foreign precedents for the most part. The markets in which they sold their labour were for long to remain separate and localized. The relatively slow rate of industrialization kept old trades tenuously alive over many decades, side by side with the growth of a factory and mining labour force with new conditions in common. The divisions thus built into the labour movement from its early days were stubborn, their effects long-lasting. All the more remarkable that attempts to create a single nationwide organization of the working class from the late 1820s to the 1840s – first in the abortive form of a General Union, then within the framework of Chartism – were made so early and went as far as they did. They failed nevertheless. And it was not until the last decades of the nineteenth century that militant and politically conscious organization directed to all levels and sections of the working class, the semi- and unskilled groups especially, again began to win through the barriers of quiescence and craft-exclusiveness which had characterized labour organization for thirty years after the collapse of Chartism. Marked traces of the old division have persisted for

much longer. Even militancy, moreover, has not been readily translated into effective political radicalism; and it has rarely been revolutionary. In the predominantly reformist line of British labour in
political action – mixed though that has long been with aspirations
for a society of equals without private capital – the historical absence
of a bourgeois precedent and ideology for revolution may, perhaps,
have played some part.

These are themes – some hard and fast, others speculative and uncertain – which will recur at various points in our discussion. They
relate to features of British experience that distinguish – or may
distinguish – our class structure, and responses to it, from the patterns
to be found in this and that other capitalist society. But it is the common features that are both central and logically prior. Among these,
one stands out above – and in a sense embracing – all others. That is
the crude and paradoxical fact that capitalism still survives. Perennially shaky though its foundations are, it has not been killed by its
internal contradictions. Not yet.

III

The survival of capitalism so far is indeed a paradox. There is, it is
true, something of the same puzzle about most societies except the
simplest: the stubborn continuities of social structure which they
maintain, despite their internal divisions. Contrary to the assumptions characteristic of 'functionalist' theorizing, complex societies are
not usually harmonious, blandly consensual, in stable equilibrium or
for ever on their way to it. It is far closer to the truth, if still too crude
and sweeping a generalization, to see them as perennially on the verge
of instability. The cleavages inside them are there all the time, as
potential triggers of change, even of collapse. Yet divided though
they are, they rarely plunge over the edge. That paradox – the common co-existence of cleavage and continuity – is at its most acute,
however, in the case of capitalist societies. For capitalism carried
with it a series of far-reaching promises which it cannot itself, by its
very nature, fulfil. The tension between promise and its practical
denial runs deep in all capitalist societies: it throws into sharp relief
the riddle of their resistance to revolution.

Capitalism promised material wealth and more: control over the
conditions of human existence, a release of mankind from the crude

constraints of want. It promised ceaseless innovation and a continuing rational critique of the order in being, on the premise that no
institutions were sacrosanct merely because they existed. It promised
freedom for individuals to follow their own fates: its ethos was a
creed of opportunity. It was just those promises which, in the nineteenth century and well before, provoked the fears of older ruling
strata in opposition to the spread of capitalist enterprise and power.
It was those promises, too – permeated by their own contradictions
though they were – which led Marx and Engels to write a suitably
qualified hymn of praise for the bourgeoisie into the Communist
Manifesto.[6]

Fundamental qualifications were certainly built into the promises.
The notion that no institution was sacrosanct could not be extended
to the institutions of private property: they were held to be exempt
from questioning. And once society had been recast in a capitalist
mould, the innovating impulse of capitalism was directed to technical and organizational innovation, and to defensive reform; not
to major changes of social structure. The freedom which capitalism
exalted was a freedom to be exercised in competition, with full success only for the few and supposedly guaranteed to none in advance.
Such competition, by its nature, proved impermanent. Its consequence would have been perpetual and pervasive insecurity. Those in
particular who achieved success through competition thereby also
acquired the power to curtail competition, and used it to safeguard
their success against insecurity. So 'perfect competition' in the
market became 'imperfect'; and the ethos of free opportunity was
never carried to the point of a challenge to those rights of inheritance
– de jure and de facto, economic and cultural – which keep opportunity firmly unequal. The capitalist conception of 'equality' was in
any case always and necessarily a limited one. Its goal, even in

6. To quote only a few snippets from the relevant passages: 'The bourgeoisie
. . . has accomplished wonders far surpassing Egyptian pyramids, Roman aque-
ducts, and Gothic cathedrals. . . . The bourgeoisie cannot exist without constantly
revolutionizing the instruments of production, and thereby the relations of
production, and with them the whole relations of society. . . . All fixed, fast-frozen
relations, with their train of ancient and venerable prejudices and opinions, are
swept away, all new-formed ones become antiquated before they can ossify . . . all
that is holy is profaned, and man is at last compelled to face with sober senses his
real conditions of life and his relations with his kind. . . . The bourgeoisie . . . has
created enormous cities . . . and has thus rescued a considerable part of the
population from the idiocy of rural life. . . .' (English translation of 1888, in
edition edited by S. H. Beer, Appleton-Century-Crofts, 1955: pp. 12–14).

abstract principle, was never equality of condition: only an 'equality of opportunity' which had substantive inequality as its logical corollary. The objective at best was to provide opportunities for enterprise, initiative and merit (however these might be defined and identified) to find their 'proper' level and reward in a society where levels and rewards remained markedly unequal. But even that limited ideal could not, within capitalist premises, be asserted so strongly as to lead to acceptance of the precondition essential for its fulfilment: the abolition of inheritance. For inheritance persists not just as a stubborn social fact; but as a right attached in law to the ownership of property.

Yet the promises were not easily contained within these fundamental restrictions. The qualifications were natural and self-evident in the eyes of the bourgeoisie who created and maintained the capitalist order. Not so in the eyes of the other new class of the population which capitalism brought into being: wage earners and their dependents who, with no property in the means of production, had only the market sale of their labour to rely on for livelihood and position. It is true that in one major capitalist society the bourgeois qualifications to the promises which accompanied the new order were never seriously challenged: at least until very recently, and even then very uncertainly. That was in the United States, where popular ideology has so far largely accepted the restricted definition of equality as equality only of opportunity. The notion of unceasing innovation has been enthusiastically embraced even by élite opinion there because, rarely directed to more than technological and organizational change in the interests of heightened efficiency, it has not usually been politically dangerous. The virtues of unbridled entrepreneurial competition have continued to be exalted in the American ethos, long after the reality of such competition vanished – though now at last, it is true, with more reservations. In the U.S.A., too, both lay and professional social philosophy has continued to identify industrialization with 'individualism', giving only limited and grudging recognition to the diverse new forms of collective organization and collective loyalties which industrial capitalism itself generated. But then America has been virtually unique among capitalist countries also in one other respect: its working class has not organized itself as a significant, separate political force.

Elsewhere, collective opposition from the labour movement gave an organized impetus to demands which took up the promises implied by capitalism, but rejected the qualifications attached to them. Capitalism in Europe engendered expectations among the new class of wage earners, and their organizations, which extended the ideal of equality of opportunity to one of equality of condition. Property, exempt from radical scrutiny in bourgeois social commentary, became a prime target of attack from labour. Labour opposition, of course, has often been fragmented. Its rejection of the restrictions on capitalism's promises, inherent in their origin, has been mixed with acquiescence. Yet nearly all European labour movements – social democratic as well as communist – have been inspired in part by a vision of a future society where the possibilities of human liberation suggested, and then denied, by capitalism would be realized. Capitalism thus gave birth, not only to a class of wage earners whose collective organization has threatened its own order; but also to widespread, if diffusely formulated, hopes which transcended the arbitrary limits set for them within that order. The clash was built into capitalism between promise and performance; between expectations and achievement; between pressures for equality and the persistent reality of inequality. The paradox is the stubborn capacity of capitalism so far to survive that clash: to institutionalize the class conflict inherent in the clash, containing it most of the time though never eliminating its sources.

The paradox is in some respects especially pointed in the case of Britain. For Britain pioneered industrial capitalism. And it produced, in Chartism, the first large-scale political movement of the working class – a movement which embraced a diversity of ideologies, despite a unifying practical concentration on achieving parliamentary representation and control; which in principle embraced all sections and levels of the working class, despite variations in its effective appeal. The collapse of that movement; the ascendancy within labour, for some three decades thereafter, of craft-based 'new model unions' concerned to secure the position of their members in the market without questioning the order of capital; the divisions by skill, trade, industry and region, as well as ideology, which accompanied the subsequent re-emergence of widespread militancy and the late formation of the Labour Party to represent the union movement in parliament – these all contributed significantly to the institutionalization of class conflict in Britain. But to describe them is not to explain them. And the predominant moderation and hesitancy of labour's opposition to capitalism in this country may seem particularly puzzling on one score above all. Whatever the restraints on the clash of class interest, those restraints have not here been reinforced by the kinds of division which in several other capitalist countries have cut across class lines to obstruct labour unity. Metropolitan Britain – excluding Northern Ireland, whose history as a settler colony has given it a socio-political structure quite different from the mainland's – shares with Scandinavia a freedom from deep cleavages of religion, language, regional culture or colour that might otherwise have divided the working class.

A pattern of cross-cutting allegiances – in which class interests are obscured by particularistic ties among those who speak the same dialect, were brought up in the same denomination, share similar disabilities or advantages in consequence of their ethnic origins – is certainly no guarantee of 'order'. The conventional assumption in many sociological textbooks that such 'pluralistic' fragmentation keeps overt tension low is plainly false. On the contrary, the co-existence of religious or colour cleavages, for example, with the perennial divisions of class is liable to produce a 'sub-proletariat' within the working class with a potential for explosive eruption into protest. Catholic workers in Northern Ireland, black workers in America, are doubly disenfranchised – by creed or colour, as well as by class. Their protest may be long delayed. But when it comes, it is all the more likely to take on a violence of despair, because there is no larger class movement to which 'sub-proletarian' protest can latch on. Particularistic fragmentation, then, is no recipe for 'order'. But it does, in its own highly effective way, help to maintain the wider order of capitalism, since it keeps divided the one force which, united, can challenge capitalism. In Britain and Scandinavia labour has not been cleft internally by divisions of that kind: there are contrasts here, not only with the United States and Northern Ireland; but also with Canada, Belgium and Holland, for example. But the very directness of the confrontation between classes then – unobstructed by cross-cutting divisions of loyalty – may perhaps itself have helped to encourage the tight institutionalization of conflict by which capitalism here has contained the threat to it engendered by its internal contradictions. If so, however, the paradox is all the more striking.

IV

Of course, there might be no paradox on certain assumptions. There would be none, if the kinds of inequality that mark our society were plainly functional, beneficial and inevitable in any society – or in any complex industrial society – whatever its economic and political arrangements; and if that rationale were then accepted by underdogs as well as privileged. There might be no paradox again if, alternatively, the inequalities of condition, power and opportunity in capitalist countries were steadily and significantly diminishing; if, in so far as some divisions remained, they followed quite separate lines in different areas of life, so that hardship in one field was countered by comfort or privilege in another; and/or if the only groups still sizeably handicapped relative to others were isolated minorities. In fact, commentary on the subject teems with suggestions of these sorts. Most of them have a long history. But they acquired fresh impetus in and around the 1950s especially: a period, significantly, of relative internal quiescence, conservatism and repression of dissent in Western countries; of cold war politics.

American commentators led the field. An old defence of inequality as necessary and socially efficient, for example, was refurbished in tune with a growing predominance of 'functionalist' interpretations in professional sociological analysis.[7] A hierarchy of privilege, it was argued, was essential if people possessing scarce skills and initiative were to be enticed into undertaking key functions, which were indispensable for society at large and required such rare personal qualities. The pattern of inequality as it was, so it was implied, neatly fitted the bill. No more and no less was necessary; the pattern would otherwise adjust in some automatic fashion until it did meet the bill. What exists exists because it must exist. The argument, of course, is familiar from classical and neo-classical 'liberal' economics, though it was dressed up here in sociologese.

7. See especially K. Davis and W. Moore, 'Some principles of stratification,' *Amer. Sociol. Rev.*, April 1945; and also T. Parsons, 'A revised analytical approach to the theory of social stratification', in R. Bendix and S. M. Lipset, eds., *Class, Status and Power*, Free Press, 1953. Among the many criticisms of the paper by Davis and Moore, see, e.g., those by M. M. Tumin, *ASR*, vol. 18, nos. 4 and 6, 1953; W. Buckley, ibid., vol. 23, no. 3, 1958 (reply by Davis, vol. 24, no. 1, 1959); D. H. Wrong, ibid., vol. 24, no. 6, 1959.

We do not want to spend time rebutting it in detail. That has been well done by others before; and the central weaknesses of the argument in any case are glaring. The image which it invokes, of a society where privileges are no more than the necessary rewards for essential services of manifest public benefit, is patently unreal. First, rewards accrue automatically to property ownership that require no services in return. On the contrary, the more property an owner has – quite regardless of how he acquired it – the more immune he is from the need to render any service of substance at all. And in a capitalist society like ours, as we shall try to show later, private property is the prime source of concentrated inequality. Second, the functionalist defence of inequality implies that wealth and high status confer no accompanying advantages of power on their beneficiaries. But if this assumption is false – if power in fact cannot be thus dissociated from other privileges – there is then a crucial circularity in social affairs to which the functionalist argument is blind. Privilege then carries with it power to shape the contours and character of privilege itself. The interests of those who already have wealth and high status will play a central part in determining prevailing definitions of what 'functions' (such as property ownership) are to be deemed so essential as to merit special rewards; in setting the nature and size of such rewards; in keeping scarce 'skills' scarce, and the effective supply of 'qualified' candidates for top positions short, in order to preserve monopolies for the privileged. It is, to put the point at its mildest, prima facie implausible that concentrated riches and honour in any society should not carry just some such power with them. That likelihood can be ruled out only if it is plain that power is shared equally among all – among rich and poor, propertied and propertyless, capital and labour alike; that inequality is the outcome of a model process of democratic agreement in which no voice carries further than any other. The assumption is rarely stated quite as baldly as that; but it needs to be if the functionalist defence of privilege is to stand up. Part of our argument in this book will be concerned to demolish the conceptions of a 'pluralist consensus' in which that assumption has typically been wrapped up.

A variant of the functionalist thesis gathered support especially as the cold war turned into deadlock, and then into institutionalized accommodation between the Atlantic and Soviet blocs. The postulate in this version was that the management of an industrial economy requires essentially the same sort of pattern of inequality – of division of labour and authority, of fairly sharply graded incentives – whether the society in question is nominally communist or capitalist. The same logic of technological and organizational necessity would impose itself on industrial societies of both faiths, the more advanced and complex their economies. So Western capitalism and East European communism were converging upon the same path. Within both, power was an outcome of bureaucratic organization: in the Soviet bloc openly so; in the West, through a process of managerial usurpation behind a continuing façade of private property. The thesis at this point incorporated a theme common in much other commentary: the postulate that economic and political control no longer derives from the private ownership of wealth; that ostensibly capitalist countries are therefore no longer capitalist. The concentrated bureaucratic power seen from this perspective to be increasingly characteristic of all advanced industrial societies was sometimes condemned: set as a new target for radical opposition. But often the conclusion, expressed or implied, was that something much like the existing pattern of inequality – or 'stratification', to use the anodyne term favoured by sociologists – was inescapable: a 'functional' necessity for any complex industrial economy.[8]

Comparisons between Western capitalism and the state-owned economies of Eastern Europe are outside the scope of this book. But even a superficial consideration of the thesis of 'convergence' between the two is enough to expose its fundamental flaws. Leave aside the point that its adherents assume a crude technological determinism – the organization of high industrial production is said to generate an essential identity of social structure everywhere, however veiled by differences of outer form – that comes oddly from com-

8. See especially C. Kerr et al., Industrialism and Industrial Man, Harvard Univ. Press, 1960 (also, e.g., J. K. Galbraith, The New Industrial State, Hamilton, 1967). Cf. the criticisms made of this thesis by, e.g., J. H. Goldthorpe, 'Social stratification in industrial society', in P. Halmos, ed., The Development of Industrial Societies, Sociological Rev. Monograph no. 8, 1964; D. Lane, The End of Inequality: Stratification under State Socialism, Penguin Books, 1971; F. Parkin, Class Inequality and Political Order, MacGibbon & Kee, 1971 (ch. 5: see also idem, 'Class stratification in socialist societies', Brit. J. Sociology, Dec. 1969). There are, of course, several left-wing condemnations of East European 'state socialism' (or 'state capitalism') which have features in common with the thesis of 'convergence', but do not draw the conclusion that inequality is functionally necessary. For another radical version of the thesis, which – with intellectual roots not least in Max Weber – emphasizes a similarity of centralized bureaucratic oppression and irresponsibility in both the U.S.A. and the U.S.S.R., see C. W. Mills, The Causes of World War Three, Ballantine Books, 1960.

mentators of a school who have often ascribed to Marxism, their *bête noire*, an economic determinism which they have then pilloried for its alleged blindness to the causal complexity of reality. The crucial weakness of the thesis of convergence is its bland indifference to the significance of private property. It is plain that state ownership of economic resources in the countries of Eastern Europe has not eliminated inequality there: far from it. Power is concentrated still, because state ownership has not been translated into effective public ownership: access to control remains privileged. But the economy is not, as in Western countries, governed by a pursuit of market profit on the part of separate private corporations. State policy is the prime economic motor, even when enterprises have been given partial autonomy and market criteria are followed in some sectors. Above all, whatever the range of incomes from top to bottom, it excludes the component which contributes most heavily to concentrated privilege in capitalist countries like Britain: income from private ownership of the major means of production. Privilege in that crucial and distinctive form is plainly not a necessity in industrial societies. Beyond that, comparisons between Western capitalism and East European state ownership are a poor guide to any 'functional imperatives' of industrialism. For to draw lessons of that sort from such comparisons requires the highly questionable assumption that the two blocs between them represent the only possible alternatives for the organization of industrial societies.

These theories dispose of the paradox by asserting that inequality is indispensable. Others have done so by asserting that inequality is, or fairly soon will be, a thing of the past as a phenomenon of much significance. This was a constant refrain of social commentary in the 1950s. Though the voices that proclaimed it became a good deal less strident and self-confident in the 1960s, the thesis that class is gradually withering away is still widely assumed to hold good. Only the pace of the process is taken now to be slower than once believed, and the route it follows perhaps a little more devious. The substantive inequalities of earlier capitalism, in this view, are fairly steadily diminishing. Income, wealth and security become progressively more evenly spread. Individual movement up and down the social scale becomes easier, in consequence particularly of widening educational opportunities. Jobs in the middle ranges of skill and reward are growing in number and importance; that reinforces these changes, and contributes to a recasting of the structure of Western societies in a mould of 'middle class' conditions and life styles. Power and influence are more widely diffused: throughout society at large, or among a multiplicity of different élites and pressure groups representing diverse interests and competing against each other with none in a position of durable dominance. In so far as power retains some degree of concentration, it no longer derives from the accumulation of private wealth; but from control over bureaucratic organizations, in public at least as much as in private enterprise. Property and power thus no longer go together, it is argued. State activity has grown enormously, and on the whole has been directed to protection of those who were formerly weak, to helping labour against capital: so much so, in some versions of the thesis, that the power wielded by organized labour is a new source of tyranny. So, on all scores, the old class structure of capitalism is being eroded. The working class is less and less a distinctive group: no longer a majority marked off by its condition of dependence. In the new 'post-capitalist' society that is emerging quietly from the ruins of the old order, a succession of 'strata' only marginally distinct from each other in economic standing, influence and esteem, all sharing a common citizenship, are replacing the classes of yesterday.[9]

If capitalism were thus changing its spots, this would resolve the paradox of its continued survival. Its internal contradictions would be dissolving: its promise, long withheld, in process of fulfilment. The basis of protest would be steadily crumbling. But that, then, would point to a paradox of a different kind: the persistence of signs of class conflict, however moderated by institutionalized compromise, despite the erosion of its foundations. One explanation has relied on time-lags. Comments have been legion that the class mould in which party politics and industrial relations have been set is outmoded. 'Modernization' is said to be the solution. And that, from this perspective, means the creation of new institutions, practices and

9. See, e.g., C. A. R. Crosland, *The Future of Socialism*, Cape, 1956; J. Strachey, *Contemporary Capitalism*, Gollancz, 1956; T. H. Marshall, *Citizenship and Social Class*, Cambridge Univ. Press, 1950; D. Butler and R. Rose, *The British General Election of 1959*, Macmillan, 1960; M. Abrams *et al., Must Labour Lose?*, Penguin Books, 1960; F. Zweig, *The Worker in an Affluent Society*, Heinemann, 1961; R. Dahrendorf, *Class and Class Conflict in Industrial Society*, Routledge & Kegan Paul, 1959 (German ed., 1957); J. K. Galbraith, *American Capitalism*, Houghton Mifflin, 1956; D. Bell, *The End of Ideology*, Collier Books, 1961; K. Mayer, 'Diminishing class differentials in the United States', *Kyklos*, vol. 12, no. 4, 1959; R. A. Nisbet, 'The decline and fall of social class', *Pacific Sociol. Rev.,* Spring 1959.

habits of thought 'freed' from class concerns: a dedication to 'efficiency' and economic growth as if these were objectives resting in themselves, capable of definition without reference to conflicts of interest over the allocation of resources and rewards. There are, on this interpretation, no 'two sides' in industry, except in consequence of inherited attitudes which have no contemporary justification. There is instead an essential harmony of interests between all and sundry: the barriers to progress are barriers only of communication. Another explanation, which incorporates time-lags in a different way, has postulated a residual survival of inequality in one 'dimension' despite its progressive extinction in others. Manual workers, now allegedly 'middle class' in economic condition, are still denied social recognition by the old middle classes; and they resent it. Status tensions, by this argument, take the place of clashes of collective economic interest: a theme that recurs in varying form in much of the debate.

V

Much of our argument will be designed to demonstrate that class inequality is not withering away. To anticipate, modifications of its range and form have been quite limited, despite a background of generally rising affluence for the population at large. Property, profit and market – the key institutions of a capitalist society – retain their central place in social arrangements, and remain the prime determinants of inequality. The vast expansion of state activity; the consolidation and institutionalization of labour's counter-pressure against capital; the diversity and complexity of influences that bear on policy in public and private enterprise; the deliberate direction of education to widening individual opportunity and tapping resources of individual talent – all these and related developments in this century have so far done little to shift the balance of power and unequal life prospects significantly between classes. Their impact has been within boundaries largely fixed by the maintenance of private property, profit and market as the key institutions controlling the conduct of society's affairs.

The point that inequalities persist in Western societies is a good deal more familiar now than it was ten or fifteen years ago. The simple equations current earlier are no longer taken for granted so readily as they were. It is not now seen as unmistakably self-evident that technical innovation and economic growth lead to transformations of social structure; that affluence produces mass quiescence and an 'end of ideology'. This change in perceptions did not come about because the bedrock of inequality shifted, or even mainly because it came to be mapped very much better. Inequality was there all the time, and visible enough if one took the trouble to keep one's eyes open. But it became much more difficult to ignore, because domestic tensions within Western societies came into focus once more in the 1960s. There was a multiplicity of forces at work, with no clear single source, no very coherent direction, but evident cumulative impact. The cold war between Western and Soviet blocs waned, and with that also some of the pressures for internal conformity. The hot war in South East Asia escalated. With no sign that the U.S.A. could impose its own settlement by fire-power, this evoked mounting dissent within America and throughout the West. In the U.S.A., too, came the long delayed black protest: first moderate and directed to 'civil rights'; then, by stages, showing a sharp edge of violence against violent rearguard repression, with desperate attempts to assert 'black power' against ameliorative reform. Student militancy spread wide; and its eruptions set off panic anxiety, even where there was none of the fire to them which there was at times in France, most notably, and in Germany and Japan, for example. Less dramatic, but likely to be more durable and far-reaching in effect, were the signs that the central, tightly institutionalized pattern of control over industrial conflict was breaking up in Britain and some other countries. To this could be added a recurrence of sporadic 'direct action' – such as 'squatting' by homeless families, rent strikes, worker occupation of factories – outside the limits of conventional political and industrial opposition. So the climate of social interpretation changed, as rising tension exposed the bedrock of inequality for all but the most rigidly averted eyes to see. In turn the change in climate encouraged production of new evidence to dispel at least the simplest versions of 'post-capitalist' theory.

Yet recognition of the fact that inequalities persist has not, on the whole, been coupled with recognition of the common root of those inequalities in capitalism. Marxist theory, it is true, has shown a revival on the radical flank of Western social science. But much of that has been directed to rediscovery and hotly debated interpretation and re-interpretation of earlier Marxist work, in a style whose scholasticism and obscurity sometimes rival conservative American 'grand social theory'; rather than to a face-on confrontation with 'post-capitalist' analysis, using hard facts as ammunition.[10] The sterility of much conventional empirical research in the social sciences has led to something of an indiscriminate castigation, by radicals, of all factual inquiry as 'mindless empiricism'. Marxism – in Marx's own hands a theory steeped in fact – has been weakened in its revival by its new adherents' frequent distaste for 'positivism'. They have tended – with many individual exceptions – to leave the concrete exploration of class reality today to others. Partly in consequence of that, much of the rediscovery of inequality since the 1960s has been a rediscovery of inequalities in the plural, as apparently separate and discrete phenomena, their links and common source in the primary institutions of property, profit and market left unexposed.

'Poverty' has been rediscovered, for example. But to single out 'the poor' for special attention in practice runs the risk of emphasizing the specific to the neglect of the general. The spotlight picks out the variety of particular circumstances – old age, sickness, large family size, single parenthood, unemployment, especially low pay – which push working class people under an arbitrarily defined poverty line. It leaves only dimly lit the wider structure of inequality, and the over-all condition of dependence which exposes workers at large to the risk of 'poverty' in such circumstances. Remedies proposed tend to be correspondingly discrete, directed separately to each set of par-ticular circumstances. Again, the multiple hardships suffered by black and brown people by virtue of their skin colour have attracted a great deal of research effort and liberal indignation. But offensive as colour labelling is, these handicaps are only one special set in the general series of impediments to life chances in a class society. They presuppose, and operate within, the wider inequalities of property

10. There are, of course, a number of exceptions where Marxist theory and per-spectives have been applied recently in concrete institutional analysis of contem-porary capitalism. Among the most notable of these, see R. Miliband, *The State in Capitalist Society*, Weidenfeld & Nicolson, 1969, and P. Baran and P. M. Sweezy, *Monopoly Capital*, Monthly Review Press, 1966 (Penguin Books, 1968). See also, to give just a few more examples, M. Kidron, *Western Capitalism since the War*, Penguin Books, 1970; A. Glyn and B. Sutcliffe, *British Capitalism, Workers and the Profits Squeeze*, Penguin Books, 1972; H. Frankel, *Capitalist Society and Modern Sociology*, Lawrence & Wishart, 1970; N. Birnbaum, *The Crisis of Industrial Society*, Oxford Univ. Press, 1969; A. Gorz, *Stratégie ouvrière et néo-capitalisme*, Editions du Seuil, 1964.

and market which liberal ideology takes for granted. Privileges and disabilities in educational opportunity, to take a third example, have also been extensively documented and are a prime target for reform. Understandably so, since they result in 'wastage of talent'; and since individual anxieties increasingly have focused on education, as qualifications acquired at school and college have come to play a more and more important part in setting the limits to individual prospects in the labour market. But however much social circulation through the educational system may be accelerated, and talents matched to jobs thereby, that by itself will not alter the structural principles that determine inequality of condition in our society. Those are the principles that property confers wealth and power without work; that earned incomes are sharply graded by the market pull of the jobs with which they go; that people who retire without property are the nearer poverty the lower their former earning power in the market. We shall take up these themes later in this book. What matters here is the fragmentation of diagnosis which has typically accompanied the accumulation of research on inequalities in this and that area of life. Each of these topics – poverty, 'race relations', educational opportunity – has attracted an industry of specialized research, with its own academic entrepreneurs, tycoons and itinerant international experts. Specialization is unavoidable and necessary. But it has had a high price, in so far as it – the organization of the business of research itself – has helped to maintain a fragmented view of inequality.

The rediscovery of inequality has been accompanied by a revival of notions which share with the functionalist defence of privilege a postulate that inequality is unavoidable. One argument runs that, since taxes and welfare provision have apparently done little to change the larger pattern of distribution, further attempts in that direction may as well be abandoned. The facts of life set tight limits to what policy can achieve. The premise here, that policy has been directed to radical redistribution, is false. There is point to the argument nevertheless, though a point to which its adherents themselves are usually insensitive. The facts of life that set limits to policy are the facts of power in a capitalist society: they are contingent, not eternal.

We shall try to explore those facts of power in some detail. We shall be little concerned, by contrast, with another newly re-emerged variant of the thesis that inequality is inescapable. This is an argument that occupational groups at different levels of reward, power and esteem are marked off from each other by roughly corresponding differences in average intelligence; and that intelligence is largely inherited by genetic transmission.[11] The hierarchy of privilege thus reflects a hierarchy of natural endowment. There is ostensibly wide scope here for an inference that class division is a necessary outcome of genetic inequality, even when the initial thesis has not been taken to that conclusion. The central assumption of fact in this argument is very fragile. There is no way in which the relative shares of 'nature' and 'nurture' in measured intelligence can be assessed to produce a ratio of durable validity. For the component of 'nurture' is itself variable, and dependent on societal arrangements. So, therefore, are also the limits – if there are any – to its impact on the component of 'nature': to the extent to which, in changed social conditions, poor or average genetic endowment might be enhanced by human action. Leave that aside, however; and also other doubts which critics have voiced on technical grounds. The point remains that no plain political conclusions would follow even if the assumption were correct. There is no self-evident law of either morality or social necessity that intelligence, natural or nurtured, must be rewarded with privilege. A capitalist society certainly follows no such law. For its greatest privileges go to those who have no need to demonstrate intelligence in order to obtain them: as a return on property ownership, however the property was acquired. The biological plea for 'stratification', like the functionalist plea, closes its eyes firmly to the fact that capitalist inequality is the product, not just of occupational differentiation – the workings of the labour market; but especially of the division between those who have and those who do not have capital.

Characteristic of these various reactions to the rediscovery of inequality in and since the 1960s has been, in summary, a recurrent reluctance to recognize the common source of class division in economic institutions. That is not surprising, since it is a main feature of the conventional ideology of a capitalist society to deny or veil the force of economic relations in shaping the totality of social structure. This is evident again in yet another line of diagnosis which has gained currency in recent years. That is the notion that poverty is a cultural

11. Cf., e.g., R. Herrnstein, *IQ in the Meritocracy*, Allen Lane, 1973. See also the application of similar arguments to differences among 'races' and ethnic groups, in H. J. Eysenck, *Race, Intelligence and Education*, Temple Smith, 1971, and *idem*, *The Inequality of Man*, Temple Smith, 1973.

condition: the product of an accumulation of collective incompetence and lack of initiative at the bottom of the social pile. There is a close parallel here with nineteenth-century conceptions of pauperism as reflected, for example, in the 1834 Poor Law and in the Charity Organization Society's later condemnation of the 'undeserving' as distinct from the 'deserving' poor. In the current version, it is true, poverty is not the result of individual sin. But it is the result of culturally conditioned ineptitude and apathy. The causal sequence implied is the same. Cultural reinforcement of individual weakness is the source – not an outcome – of poverty; and it is that which keeps the poor poor. Remedies must then be sought in therapeutic measures: in attempts to 're-educate' the poor, or at least their children, to enable them to escape from the cultural trap in which they are said to be caught. Structural economic change is seen as neither relevant nor feasible.

The notion, of course, is familiar from the inter-war years, when the unemployed were often described as 'unemployable'; and echoes of that convenient diagnosis came to be heard once more as deflationary policies by government stepped up unemployment in the 1960s. It is part and parcel again of conventional social welfare ideology. The problems of 'problem families' are defined as problems of their own making: what can be done at best is to help them to unmake them. But this set of everyday stereotypes has now been dressed up in academic theory, and as a philosophy for social policy. In that crystallized form, it is true, the conception of a 'culture of poverty' is today essentially American. The ideological air in Europe has been too far influenced by a critique of economic institutions, with organized support from the labour movement, to absorb this kind of diagnosis unresistingly. But there have been some undertones of a perception of poverty as a cultural condition behind the programmes of special aid to 'educational priority areas' in Britain. And there are similar undertones in recent, and highly fashionable, research that has begun to explore the cultural differences between classes with which inequalities of educational opportunity are associated. Those undertones remain, so long as the research stops short of probing in any extensive way into the structural conditions by which distinctive patterns of 'subculture' may be explained. The inference then is close to the surface – even though it is not drawn by the research workers themselves – that inequality is an outcome of working-class cultural incapacity; not of economic institutions. As so often, and whether by default or design, the blame for inequality falls neatly on its victims.[12]

VI

So, the rediscovery of inequality may be neutralized in interpretations which trace its sources to its victims; which take it as an unalterable fact of life; which identify it only as a diversity of separate phenomena, the outcome of unconnected or no more than loosely connected causes. The facts may thus be fitted to perspectives which see nothing drastically wrong with the established order. Even so, none of these interpretations has the comfortable simplicity of the belief that class divisions can be ignored because they are gradually vanishing, more or less of their own accord. Once post-war complacency on that score had given way to doubt, the paradox of capitalism's survival despite its breach of promise came into sight again. Interest revived in the old question 'Why no revolution?', though the question was not usually put in just those words.

It was, clearly, no longer good enough to dismiss the paradox with an assertion that a progressive erosion of inequality was turning workers 'middle class'. If 'embourgeoisement' were dousing working-class opposition, the processes at work had to be fairly complex. There had been no very substantial and continuous shift in class inequality to explain any such shift in class perspectives. Nor, indeed, was it obvious that workers were identifying themselves more with their 'betters', and moving from dissent to consent in doing so. Certainly, the British Labour Party in the 1950s and 1960s, like many of its continental counterparts, put its right foot firmly forward. This was associated with an argument that workers were turning bourgeois in outlook. And the party's claim to office in 1964 – when it won the election by a hair's-breadth, after thirteen years out of government – was in essence a plea that it could run the capitalist

12. For a recent American contribution which argues a version of the 'culture of poverty' thesis, see E. C. Banfield, *The Unheavenly City*, Boston, 1970. C. A. Valentine, *Culture and Poverty*, Chicago, 1968, is a sharply pointed critique of this thesis in its various guises. The British studies of class cultural differences relevant to educational opportunity, to which we refer, are those which have focused on linguistic patterns, directed by B. Bernstein. See especially his *Class, Codes and Control*, vol. 1, Paladin, 1973 (some of the essays in which show Bernstein to be conscious of the risk on which we comment here) and W. Brandis and D. Henderson, *Social Class, Language and Communication*, Routledge and Kegan Paul, 1970.

economy more efficiently than its Conservative rivals. But the connection between party policy and grass-root sentiment in the labour
movement was far from clear. And even before the unions clashed
with their own government in the late 1960s, there were signs of rank-
and-file worker militancy which were not easily reconciled with a
hypothesis of widening working-class docility. Mild reformist policies
and sentiments of ostensible acquiescence in any case have a long
history in the labour movement. There was no 'golden past' of solidary radical defiance with which labour conservatism in the mid-
twentieth century could be neatly contrasted, frequently though such a
contrast was implied in conventional commentary of both right and
left.[13] The mixture of defiance and conservatism is present as well as
past, in varying ratios at different times. No attempt to explain how
capitalism has so far survived its class contradictions – here and elsewhere – can be persuasive unless it recognizes the continuing contribution of both ingredients to labour ideology and practice.

Frequently, such attempts have failed to do just that. They have
posited influences, old or new, which have tamed working-class
opposition and diverted it from direct confrontation with capitalism.
They have skated more lightly over the resistance of working-class
opposition to those influences; its resilience; its capacity at times to
transcend its own limitations and to maintain, though in diffuse form,
the vision of a fraternal society without private capital and without
classes. For the rest, interpretations of labour's response to capital in
Britain differ considerably in approach and emphasis. Among those
which have caught on in the debate of recent years – leading by different routes to a common conclusion that there is little effective impetus in the working class to overturn the order of capital – at least
three distinct themes can be traced.

One is an assumption that the predominant 'moderation' of
British labour derives from certain persistent peculiarities of the
cultural climate in this country. Some American commentators, for
example, have revived a long-standing notion that deference to
authority and rank is at the core of a cluster of 'central values',
common in one form or another to all classes in Britain.[14] The

13. Cf. R. Miliband, 'Socialism and the myth of the golden past', in *idem* and
J. Saville, eds., *The Socialist Register 1964*, Merlin Press, 1964.
14. See, e.g., S. M. Lipset, 'The value patterns of democracy', *Amer. Sociol.
Rev.*, August 1963; H. H. Hyman, 'England and America: climates of tolerance
and intolerance', in D. Bell, ed., *The Radical Right*, Anchor Books, rev. ed. 1964;
E. A. Shils, *The Torment of Secrecy*, Heinemann Educational Books, 1956; G. A.

political tone of these interpretations has been conservative or mid-Atlantic 'liberal'. But a notable left-wing diagnosis – while far more compelling in range and depth – shares with them an emphasis on the key role of national idiosyncrasies of ideology. By this analysis, to summarize it crudely, the failure of the British labour movement to free itself for a frontal challenge to capitalism can be attributed especially to the absence of a preceding model of bourgeois revolution.[15]

A second theme picks out an inhibiting effect on labour radicalism of constraints rooted in 'traditional' working-class culture. Class divisions are also the boundaries of distinctive 'sub-cultures'. In one of these interpretations, the boundaries of working-class culture – even today, still more in the past – act as limits on aspirations, ceilings to horizons. Workers have demanded relatively little of the world, because they have set their standards by reference in the main only to their own, their neighbours', their workmates' and their fathers' circumstances.[16] Another interpretation, with much the same outcome, highlights the sense of fellowship engendered within working-class communities of early and mid-industrialism: in communities with a small range of occupations and industries, where the relationship of work life and home life intertwined – mining settlements, textile towns, dockside and railway communities, iron and steel towns. Here par excellence, it is argued, were the roots of labour solidarity. But such solidarity of locality and trade is too parochial to carry within itself the seeds of the vision and far-reaching loyalties necessary to sustain a class movement with socialist objectives. This, at least, must be inferred from the accompanying conclusion that labour unity tends to fragment, as working-class communities of this multi-bonded character die out.[17] And in one significant recent contribution to the debate, the inference is made explicit. The radical, socialist, extra-parochial strand in labour movement ideology is identified there as essentially an import, carried into the movement by

Almond and S. Verba, *The Civic Culture*, Princeton Univ. Press, 1963. Walter Bagehot's *The English Constitution*, first published in 1872, can be seen as holy writ for this school of thought.

15. P. Anderson, op. cit. (note 5 above).

16. W. G. Runciman, *Relative Deprivation and Social Justice*, Routledge & Kegan Paul, 1966.

17. D. Lockwood, 'Sources of variation in working class images of society', *Sociol. Rev.*, vol. 14, no. 3, 1966; J. H. Goldthorpe, D. Lockwood *et al.*, *The Affluent Worker*, 3 vols., Cambridge Univ. Press, 1968–69. Cf. also F. Parkin, 'Working class conservatives', *Brit. J. Sociology*, Sept. 1967.

intellectuals and professional politicians: without firm roots in working-class culture and without the capacity, therefore, to sustain itself once the leadership jettisons it to engage in the politics of compromise.[18]

The third main theme in recent commentary on this subject leads on from the second. The emphasis here is on a postulated increasing isolation of workers from one another; a realignment of their aspirations towards individual and family goals rather than to collective and class objectives. This has sometimes been interpreted as involving a growth of 'status' ambitions. Workers, it is acknowledged, are now setting higher aims for themselves and their children than they did; yet any political punch which this might carry is dissipated because their new hopes centre on personal success.[19] But the authors of the contribution which has made the greatest impact, along a similar line of argument, see no signs of a progressive incorporation of manual workers into a 'middle class' pattern of life styles and status identification. Workers remain workers; but of a new kind. Industrial work increasingly offers no intrinsic satisfactions – and generates no durable ties between workmates. Its compensation is of one sort: money. Aspirations focus on the pay packet and its expenditure: they are essentially private. And although new demands for common services and public reforms may arise out of them, such radical potential as there might be to this is likely to find no way of expression, because the established labour movement is too enmeshed in bargaining and institutionalized compromise to listen.[20] There is explicit recognition here of a tension between increasing working-class demands on life and their frustration as inequality persists. But the prognosis is still that an effective challenge to the established order is unlikely to result.

These various theories do not exhaust the attempts which have been made to account for the practical predominance of policies of accommodation in labour's response to capital. But it is these theories, in particular, which have set the tone of much of the debate in recent years. They have, in the main, two significant features in common. One is a preoccupation with the role of cultural patterns, seen as persisting over long periods of time or as embedded in the 'micro-structure' of local conditions of community and workplace, in

18. F. Parkin, *Class Inequality* . . ., op. cit. (note 8, above), especially ch. 3.
19. Runciman, op. cit. (note 16 above).
20. Goldthorpe, Lockwood *et al.*, op. cit. (note 17 above).

shaping working-class consciousness and allegedly inhibiting its radical potential. The point does not lend itself to simple statement in summary form. But the consequences of this kind of preoccupation have been a relative neglect of the part played by larger forces of market and politics, at a national and international level, in forming and changing labour's response to capital. The second feature, as we have already said, is a common tendency to highlight the restraints on working-class opposition while neglecting the no less striking fact of its persistence. Labour ideology and action show a continuous and significant streak of subversion, side by side with the predominant line of reform. Conflict has been largely institutionalized. But there is a perennial risk to capital that this institutionalization may break down: a risk which began to loom a good deal larger again from the 1960s than it had done in the 1950s. To turn one's eyes away from that is to foreclose a question which in fact remains open: whether capitalism can continue to survive its internal class contradictions. It is the persistence of those contradictions, and our argument that the question remains open, which are the main themes of this book.

VII

We shall not tie ourselves to rigid definitions of class groupings and their boundaries, fixed in advance. To recognize the force of class division implies no commitment to an arbitrary assertion of particular lines of division from the outset. We start with the view that class 'in itself' is manifest as a set of closely related inequalities of economic condition, power and opportunity. The more closely related those inequalities, and the sharper the divisions in life circumstances which they entail, the more firm then is the structure of class 'in itself'. That is so irrespective of how people themselves – victims or beneficiaries of inequality – see and respond to their class situations: questions concerning the activation of class 'for itself' which can be explored only after the contours of class 'in itself' have been mapped. We start also with an assumption that property and property relations play the key part in forming the contours of inequality. But we take that, not as a self-evident proposition, but as a highly plausible and theoretically well-grounded hypothesis, to be demonstrated by concrete evidence. To the extent that private ownership and associated control of the productive apparatus prove to be the crucial source of inequality – directly, and through the workings of market mechanisms and state policies shaped by a predominance of private capital – to that extent the force behind class division is capitalism; and the prime line of division in the web of inequality is that between capital and labour. Yet there are other lines of division, too. There are gradations within labour, for example, arising from differences in market position and security. There are groups whose members, while formally employees, sell their labour at so distinctive a premium, so control their own markets and have shares in property and societal power, that they are much closer to capital – even part and parcel of it – than they are to labour: top professionals, high state officials, above all central management in private corporate enterprise. Conversely, there are business entrepreneurs, in formal terms their own masters, whose ownership is nominal and whose market dependence on big business such that their condition may be little different from that of labour: small shopkeepers, for example, if they are not already hired employees of chains and combines whose branches may still trade under individual names.

But divisions and gradations of this kind are matters for inquiry and demonstration; not for specification in advance by preconceived definitions so inflexible as to preclude inquiry. So too – and still more so – when it comes to the question how and where those lines of division fall which people themselves recognize: which mark their response to class inequality. In practice, however, the possibilities of inquiry are often limited by the ways in which the population is categorized in the sources on which one has to draw. Routine clerical workers and the like, for instance, are frequently bracketed with managers and professional people – of all levels – in a blanket 'non-manual' category. This is so although there is evidence to show that, in some crucial respects at least, much low-grade 'white collar' labour is increasingly subject to market conditions on a par with those of semi-skilled or even unskilled manual labour; and although, just for that reason, the reactions of this traditional 'buffer group' to a changing class situation acquire new interest. Again, petty entrepreneurs are rarely separately distinguished in sources of information. Above all, 'class' classifications as adopted in the great mass of relevant research are usually based exclusively on occupation. It is then impossible to single out for direct attention those whose class position derives essentially from the possession of substantial capital. They are in any case, of course, a tiny group in purely numerical terms, and cannot be picked out by ordinary sampling procedures on the normal scale of operation. It is one·of the ironies of a complex society, where power and wealth are tightly concentrated, that the concentration itself helps to keep the privileged hidden from the spotlight, because they are so few in number.

So the common tendency in research to accept a conception of class condition as most conveniently summarized by reference to occupational position – relevant enough though it is in respect of the mass of the population – significantly obscures the nature of capitalism, because it veils the pinnacle of power and wealth from clear sight. Similarly, the ordinary terminology of class – frequently professional as well as lay – also hides reality in one crucial respect. 'Middle class' is often used as an umbrella term of startling elasticity to describe all sections of the population who are not manual workers: from routine grade office labour, increasingly indistinguishable in market position from manual workers, to the very top. If an upper crust is distinguished, it is as likely to be defined by traditional criteria of social esteem, or by way of indiscriminate occupational bracketing, as by those criteria of economic position and power which are relevant for a diagnosis of class 'in itself'. But in many instances, 'middle class' covers the whole span beyond 'working class' (itself usually conceived as embracing only the mass of manual workers): nonsensically 'middle' between a lower group and a vacuum. The terminology is conservative by implication: partly because the word 'middle' suggests a structure of inequality in which status is the predominant basis of distinction; but above all because the notion entailed of a vacuum above the 'middle' implicitly denies any significant concentration of privilege at the top.

Thus the common language of class covers up the most central feature of class. For it is, as we shall try to show, the concentration of power and property in a very small section of the population on which the whole ramified structure of class inequality turns. For all that late twentieth-century capitalist societies like ours are complex in their detail, they are very simple in that essential respect.

PART TWO

INEQUALITIES OF CONDITION AND SECURITY

1 Affluence and inequality

I

When social commentators in the 1950s and early 1960s postulated a progressive transformation of capitalism into 'post-capitalism', the centrepiece of that diagnosis was an assumption that economic inequalities were steadily diminishing. Other important assumptions were built into the more sophisticated versions of the thesis. The nature of power, it was said, had changed drastically through its detachment from private property, and through the emergence of a complex network of pressures and interests resulting in diffusion of influence over the shape of society into many hands. Increasing social mobility was taken to be unfreezing fixed positions which individuals and families had previously occupied over their lifetimes, and to be forging new ties of personal acquaintance, experience and identity between the different strata of the population. But the touchstone of the 'affluent society' was a postulated reduction of economic inequalities to little more than frills. Capitalism, so it was at least implicitly acknowledged, had not in the past matched its creation of wealth by a fair and tolerable distribution of wealth. It was now doing so, through a more or less silent process of transformation from within.

Two sets of changes were thought to be at work, closely related to each other. First, and most simply, inequalities of income, property and security of life were assumed to be growing steadily smaller, and less significant in their impact. Second, so the argument ran, such economic inequalities as remained were much less class-tied than they had been before. They arose now far less from ownership and non-ownership of capital and from pressures of the labour market – from the relations of production – than from conditions unrelated, or only loosely related, to class. Residual poverty was seen as the product of old age, physical and mental handicap, high fertility, social incompetence – also, it was added later, of discrimination against women, against coloured people, against other minorities. As such it was remediable by some combination of improved welfare measures and socio-cultural therapy. No radical changes in the economic foundations of society would be needed. In so far as they might have seemed necessary earlier, such changes had now occurred or were occurring – quietly, almost surreptitiously, without fuss. Capitalism, in its new 'post-capitalist' form, was fulfilling the promise which it had long withheld.

The evidence adduced for this erosion of economic inequalities was very sketchy, and would have been highly vulnerable to criticism in a period less coloured than the 1950s by socio-political complacency. But there were at least some signs from the decade before which might seem to give support to the thesis. Explanations, on the other hand, were usually quite rudimentary. Some relied on assumptions about the consequences of taxation and welfare measures. In fact, attempts to measure the real impact of public policy on distribution were rare and little known, but already then underlined the need for caution in assuming that state action was spreading wealth much more evenly. Other explanations looked to changes in industrial and occupational structure – to a relative contraction in the numbers of unskilled and casual workers and to a concomitant expansion in the numbers of non-manual workers, in particular. There was inferred from these changes, on their own or in conjunction with crude data on money incomes, a transformation of the structure of jobs and incomes from the shape of a pyramid or cone to the shape of a diamond or lozenge, bulging affluently in the middle. This kind of geometric description was dramatic, but both inaccurate and mis-leading. It was inaccurate because it attributed to the shape of income distribution in the post-war years a degree of simplicity and novelty which it did not have, while ignoring the continuing pyramidical shape of property ownership.[1] It was misleading beyond that because

1. Earned incomes have long shown some of the features of a normal distribution curve – that is, a shape more like a diamond than a pyramid. *All* incomes – earned and unearned together – do not in fact show that shape today, but are bimodally distributed: the numbers bulging at two points, the first of which is accounted for mainly by pensioners. (For a diagrammatic representation from unadjusted Inland Revenue figures for 1966, see J. Ryder and H. Silver, *Modern English Society*, Methuen, 1970, p. 202.) Property distribution has a pyramidic

it exaggerated the changes in occupational structure, and misinterpreted their significance, in ways that we shall discuss later.

In general, explanations of the postulated process of economic equalization did not go beyond assumptions of these kinds, and brief references to reduction of unemployment and of earnings differentials by skill as well as by sex and age. Nor did they need to. For the thesis was borne less by evidence and explicit argument than by faith. A theory of automatic progress has a long history in both popular and academic thought. It received fresh support in the 1950s – as a prognosis for the future, not as a characterization of the past – both because some real, though quite limited, changes had occurred during the previous decade; and above all because the socio-political climate was hostile to the implications of any diagnosis that those changes had run their course.

II

Such as they were, these changes had indeed run their course by the early 1950s. But the point was obscured not only by the reluctance of most commentators to look at the signs; not only by the fact that the signs in any case were complex and took time to read; but also by a conceptual confusion so elementary that its persistence as a feature of the debate about capitalism and 'post-capitalism' seems wilful. No clear distinction was drawn between the question of absolute levels of living and security – the 'average' conditions of life – and the question of distribution, the range of inequality around the average. 'Affluence' reflected in rising overall levels of living for the population at large was, and still often is, equated *ipso facto* with a reduction of relative inequalities. If that equation were correct, then there would be nothing new by itself in the erosion of inequality alleged to mark the transition from capitalism to 'post-capitalism'. For increasing average 'affluence' has been a long-standing trend in Britain and other industrial capitalist societies – intermittent, it is true, and slower for many decades in Britain than in countries which industrialized later; but in the long run so far a pronounced upward trend nevertheless.

To take just a few estimates, net national income per head of

shape since very large numbers of people own no property sufficient to be recorded in official data.

population in the United Kingdom has been calculated as more than doubling in real terms between the early 1920s and the middle 1960s. The trend was uneven. It had been downward in the preceding period around World War I; it was more or less flat during the depression years around 1930; it turned down again between the early and the late 1940s. But the long-term trend was upward both before and after World War II. By the early 1940s the index of *per capita* national income stood about 50 per cent above its level twenty years before; by 1965 it was some 50 to 60 per cent higher than in the early 1950s. The rates of increase during the periods of fastest expansion were much the same – 16 or 17 per cent over five years – both pre-war and post-war: from the early 1930s to the early 1940s, and again from the 1950s.[2] Industrial productivity and real gross wages have been estimated for the United Kingdom as growing by an annual average of about 2 per cent per head over the period from 1871 to 1895; as stagnating with even some decline in real wages, from 1895 to 1913; as rising again, by an average of about $1\frac{3}{4}$ per cent per year from the early 1920s to 1938, and by more than 2 per cent a year from 1949 to 1960. Comparisons with corresponding estimates for the U.S.A., Sweden, Germany and France show the U.K. lagging behind these other countries in the two decades before World War I, and again in the years after World War II; it was behind the others for which data are available during the inter-war years, too, in terms of growth of industrial productivity, though not in terms of growth of real wages.[3] The 1960s were marked by rising unemployment and increasingly uneven rates of economic growth. But the overall trend in real gross incomes from employment was still upwards. After discounting for price increases, average wage and salary earnings in the U.K. rose by about 3 per cent per year, or even slightly more, over the period 1960–70.[4]

The issue here is not the slower rate of growth in output and real incomes in Britain by comparison with a number of other industrial capitalist countries for much of the time since the 1890s, relevant

2. S. Pollard and D. W. Crossley, *The Wealth of Britain 1085–1966*, Batsford, 1968 (p. 258).

3. E. H. Phelps Brown, with Margaret Browne, *A Century of Pay*, Macmillan, 1968 (pp. 170, 312).

4. Calculated from official series (*Department of Employment/Ministry of Labour Gazette*) of earnings of male manual and male administrative, technical and clerical employees in manufacturing and certain other industries, with adjustment for increases in the general retail price index.

though the variety of explanations suggested for that are to other questions concerning the nature of British capitalism and its class structure. Nor is the point to argue that long-run economic growth – slow or fast – is an inherent and necessarily continuing feature of capitalism. To make that assumption would be to beg the questions raised by recent signs of a possibly deep-rooted economic crisis – by a conjunction of uneven growth rates, high unemployment and accelerating inflation with falling rates of profit, from the 1960s, long after Keynesian techniques of economic management were presumed to have mastered the major tendencies to recurrent stagnation characteristic of earlier capitalism.[5] The point for the moment is a much simpler one. Increases in average levels of living are in no way a new phenomenon. The rates of increase which have prevailed since World War II have long historical precedents. Indeed the kinds of figures quoted earlier exaggerate recent trends of growth in disposable income – the real value of earnings in hand – because they are gross measures taken without regard to the effects of direct taxation. As more and more earners have been brought within the range of income tax, and as effective rates of direct taxation have been raised in the lower reaches of the range especially, net earnings have risen progressively slower than gross earnings. Those of male manual workers, for example, rose by an average of only about 1 per cent a year in the 1960s compared with about 2 per cent a year in the earlier period after World War II, although the rate of growth in gross earnings was faster in the 1960s than before.[6]

There is, therefore, no magic or novelty attaching to the rising 'affluence' of the post-World War II epoch. It may of course be argued – it has certainly often been implied – that there is some qualitative difference between recent and earlier increases in real income: that prosperity in the 1950s and 1960s has raised the condition of the bulk of the population over some threshold between 'poverty' and 'affluence', above which inequalities of condition relate in the main only to inessentials. That argument, however, raises a series of questions about the criteria by which, and on whose judgment, 'essentials' are to be distinguished from 'frills'; we shall discuss these later. The argument does not dispose of the fact that generations of

5. See especially A. Glyn and B. Sutcliffe, *British Capitalism, Workers and the Profits Squeeze*, Penguin Books, 1972; also Jackson *et al.*, note 6 below.
6. D. Jackson, H. A. Turner, F. Wilkinson, *Do Trade Unions Cause Inflation?*, Cambridge University Press, 1972 (pp. 65–8 ff.).

ordinary earners before the 1950s had experienced substantial improvements in their conditions in absolute terms. Merely to note the fact of such improvements, then and now, throws no light whatsoever on the critical question of trends in the range of relative inequality around the rising average.

III

It has now, by the early 1970s, become almost part of conventional wisdom to dismiss the faith of the 1950s in a progressive erosion of economic inequalities as either nonsense or at least glibly over-optimistic. The recognition of reality which that implies is welcome. But the very assurance with which this dismissal tends to be expressed carries at least two dangers with it.

The first is the risk of adopting a vulgar version of the theory 'plus ça change, plus c'est la même chose'. Such a theory, projecting the experience of the 1950s and 1960s backwards without qualification, is blind to those periods in which special circumstances have produced some genuine shifts in distribution. As we shall show, shifts of that kind have been moderate in extent, and the product of exceptional conjunctions of events. But they have given an impetus to reformist social policies which goes well beyond their actual achievements: they have helped to create illusions that evolutionary adaptations of policy are sufficient to spread income, wealth and security much more evenly within a continuing capitalist framework. The exceptional and limited character of such shifts in distribution has to be shown in order to dispel those illusions. That in turn entails recognition of their historical reality – not their dismissal by a crude theory that nothing ever changes.

The second danger arises from the way in which the rediscovery of inequality in the 1960s replaced the rival faith of earlier post-war years. It was the social turbulence of the 1960s which opened many eyes to the persistence of inequality, much more than an accumulation of factual evidence. Facts to question and refute the complacency of the 1950s were available well before they were generally used for that purpose. But they did not come into public and professional consciousness until mounting unrest – of different kinds and from a variety of sources – pointed to a partial dissolution of that 'consensus' about the established order which had been taken widely for granted in the 1950s. So the 1960s saw a change in fashions of social observation and commentary. But fashions can change again. Resistance to changes of fashion requires, among other things, a solid knowledge of facts. It is for this reason, not least, that a fairly detailed examination of the record with regard to trends in economic equality is essential, even though the outcome now – unlike ten years ago – is not likely to be much of a surprise.

2 Trends in income inequality

I

The record is not simple to piece together and summarize; and there are gaps in it. There are two main sources of information: data compiled by government in the process of tax collection; and data from sample surveys. Both suffer from weaknesses: a principal effect of these is to understate the degree of inequality. Tax records do so because devices to evade taxation within the letter of the law are effectively available mainly to those who have much money to lose by taxation and who, by the same token, can afford to pay for the advice and services needed to reduce their losses on that score.[1] Sample surveys on this subject are also normally liable to suffer from considerable inaccuracies, and to understate income and property, especially at the top end of the economic scale. For the very rich are a small and reticent group of the population. Their financial affairs, moreover, are highly complex by their very magnitude, and do not lend themselves to examination by standard survey questionnaire of a

1. For a detailed analysis and discussion of tax-evasive devices in and around the 1950s, see R. M. Titmuss, *Income Distribution and Social Change*, Allen & Unwin, 1962 (especially chapters 5–8). There are later though rather more light-weight accounts in, e.g., J. Todd, *The Conjurers*, Lawrence & Wishart, 1966; and O. Stanley, *Taxology*, Weidenfeld & Nicolson, 1972. In respect of death duties, see, e.g., A. B. Atkinson, *Unequal Shares*, Allen Lane: the Penguin Press, 1972. Tax-evasive devices are liable to rapid change in response to counter-measures, and accounts may therefore quickly get out of date on matters of detail. Stanley, for example, underlines the point that he was writing before new devices had been elaborated to replace a number which had been stopped by the Labour Government in the late 1960s. There is, of course, no hard information on the amount of tax evasion. And we have come across no data on matters which might give hints of its scale – e.g., the number of professional tax consultants and the extent to which they are recruited from among people initially trained as Inland Revenue inspectors.

kind tolerably suitable for the majority of people. For these reasons – and because this small minority on any evidence accounts for a very substantial share of total wealth – sample inquiries in this field require large sampling fractions and exceptionally elaborate questioning so far as the very rich are concerned. The results otherwise take quite inadequate account of just those sources of wealth which, because they are carefully wrapped up to minimize taxation, are also under-stated in official records. But few surveys are, and indeed can readily be, designed to reduce this problem.[2] These points do not exhaust the difficulties involved in income and wealth estimation: the subject is a minefield of technical problems. But the points mentioned are crucial in kind, because they relate directly to the question of distribution. Inequality by its own nature sets up obstacles to its proper description.

II

So the evidence produces something of a patchwork. But the main features of the patchwork look much the same from whatever angle they are seen. The crucial period is that of the last thirty odd years. This is so for two reasons. It is for that period that the decisive emergence of capitalist affluence has been claimed; and information for the same period is better than it is for earlier years. Table 1 gives a rough preliminary view of trends in the distribution of personal income from the late 1930s to the late 1960s. Incomes are shown as recorded in Inland Revenue data after deduction of direct taxes: to show them before tax would, of course, be to ignore whatever redistribution may occur through direct taxation. Leaving all qualifications aside for the moment, the main features are clear.

First, there is evidence of a distinct shift of income away from the top – a reduction in the range of inequality – between 1938 and 1949. The richest 5 per cent of 'income units' – married couples and individuals – were estimated between them to take nearly one-quarter of the total value of post-tax incomes just before World War II, but only about one-sixth of the total in the late 1940s. The share of the richest 10 per cent, to take another example, was reduced from one-third of the total to a little over a quarter over the same period.

2. For a rare example of a special survey among the wealthy to supplement a representative national sample survey, see L. R. Klein *et al.*, 'Savings and finances of the upper income classes', *Bulletin Oxford Univ. Inst. Statistics,* November 1956.

Second, however, that trend towards greater equality slowed down markedly from 1949 to 1954, and thereafter virtually ceased. Indeed, the relative position of the very poorest may have worsened from the 1950s. No significance, it should be added, can be attributed to very small and inconsistent changes in the figures from one year to another, given the nature of the data.

TABLE 1

Distribution of personal allocated income after direct taxes, 1938–67 (unadjusted)

Groups of 'income units' (percentages expressed cumulatively—i.e., the richest 5% include the richest 1%, etc.)	Estimated percentage share of total value of all personal allocated income received by the groups of 'income units' (couples and individuals) shown on left					
	1938 %	1949 %	1954 %	1957 %	1963 %	1967 %
Richest 1% received	11½	6½	5½	5	5	5
Richest 5% received	24	17	15½	14½	15½	15
Richest 10% received	33½	27	25	24	25	24½
Richest 20% received	46½	42	42	38	*	*
Richest 40% received	*	64	65½	63	64½	64
Poorest 50% received	*	26½	25½	27½	*	*
Poorest 30% received	*	14½	11	13	12	11½

Sources: Estimates from Inland Revenue data by H. Lydall, 'The long-term trend in the size distribution of incomes', J. Roy. Statist. Soc., Series A, 122 (1), 1959, and by J. Utting (ibid.); by R. J. Nicholson, 'Distribution of personal income', Lloyds Bank Rev. January 1967; and by A. J. Walsh, 'Tax allowances and fiscal policy' in P. Townsend and N. Bosanquet (eds.), Labour and Inequality, Fabian Society, 1972. (There is some overlap between the time series presented in the two first sources, and a few small discrepancies between some of the figures in the two. Where necessary we have taken a figure between those of the two series in such cases, but the discrepancies are in any case insubstantial.)
Note: 'Income units' are as defined by the Inland Revenue authorities – i.e., married couples when taxed jointly, and individuals separately taxed. For other notes and qualifications, see text and table 2.
* No data given in sources.

Third, despite the redistribution of the 1940s, the degree of inequality even by these crude measures remained pronounced during the 1950s and 1960s. Thus at the end of the period, the richest 1 per cent still turned up with five times the share which they would have had if income had been equally distributed – that is, merely according to their numbers in the population; the richest 5 per cent three times their 'parity share'; the richest 10 per cent two-and-a-half times their parity share; while the poorest 30 per cent got little more than a third of what would have been theirs if there had been equality. On this record alone, a minority of one in twenty between them took a larger share than went to the third of the population with the lowest incomes. Yet these figures understate the real extent of inequality.

There are two main kinds of deficiency associated with the estimates. One arises from the fact that information is presented for 'income units', as defined for tax collection purposes. Inland Revenue's practice of regarding married couples as effectively 'joint spending units', and therefore jointly taxable, is by itself reasonably realistic. But shifts over the years in marriage and divorce rates, in the composition of households, in the extent of employment among wives (at possibly different rates of increase at different income levels) as well as other changes are all liable to reduce the extent to which the data for different years are genuinely comparable over time. A conjunction of changes of this sort may, for example, have produced an exaggerated picture of the redistribution which appears to have occurred during the 1940s, though this cannot be accurately determined.[3] Separate information for households of different composition can help to reduce these problems; and some such material for recent years will be referred to later.

The other, and overridingly important, set of deficiencies arises in connection with the definition and measurement of income. Not only do the figures shown necessarily incorporate rough estimates of income for those sections of the population too poor to pay income tax at a given time. But a variety of sources of income are either excluded or inadequately covered. Among these are benefits in kind (from state services, for example, and significantly also business and professional privileges in the form of expense-account living); employers' contributions to life insurance and private health schemes; and not least various forms of untaxed property income (e.g., capital gains, which were entirely free from tax until 1963 and after that were still taxed at a rate in practice generally lower than income tax; as well as undistributed profits, which accrue as a gain to shareholders for the future). Finally, the taxes deducted in the estimates are direct taxes only. No allowance is made for the impact of indirect taxation – taxes on housing, goods and services which, as we shall show later,

3. See R. M. Titmuss, op. cit. (note 1 above), especially chapter 3.

fall heavily on wage earners and the poor. The significance of these limitations is crucial. For, except in respect of state benefits, their consistent effect is to understate high incomes and overstate lower incomes. So the sharpest edges of inequality are blunted in the picture so far drawn.

Attempts to adjust for some of these omissions indicate the nature of this understatement of inequality, though not its precise magnitude. What is more, they also give a strong hint that such compression of the range of inequality as occurred in the 1940s was a good deal less striking than would appear from the first series of estimates. The adjusted figures shown in table 2 are illustrative rather than comprehensive. No revised calculations are available for the whole range of incomes; only for top incomes. And the estimate for 1959/60 cannot be fully compared with those for the earlier years, since the basis of adjustment differs somewhat between them. With those qualifications, two conclusions nevertheless stand out plainly.

TABLE 2

Share of top income recipients in personal income after direct taxes, 1938–1959/60, before and after adjustment for certain omissions

Groups of 'income units'	Estimated percentage share of total value of all personal income received by the richest 1 per cent (5 per cent, 10 per cent) of all 'income units'				
	1938 %	1949 %	1954 %	1957 %	1959/60 %
Before adjustment (as in table 1): The richest 1% received	11½	6½	5½	5	5
After adjustment (see notes below): The richest 1% received	15	10½	9½	9	10
The richest 5% received	*	*	*	*	20½
The richest 10% received	*	*	*	*	30

Sources: (*a*) For 1938–57, H. Lydall, loc. cit. (table 1): the adjusted figures are estimates to allow for undistributed profits, certain benefits in kind and employers' contributions to life insurance.

(*b*) For 1959–60, estimates derived from calculations by J. E. Meade, *Efficiency, Equality and Ownership of Property*, Allen & Unwin, 1964 (pp. 29, 78–81) of the probable incidence of untaxed property income in 1959, applied to the figures for 1960 presented by A. J. Walsh, op. cit. (table 1) with appropriate translation from pre-tax to post-tax basis. The unadjusted figures for 1960 are virtually identical with those shown in table 1 for 1963.

* No data available from sources.

First, the share of the very rich – here the top 1 per cent – fell substantially less between 1938 and the beginning of the 1950s than was suggested by the unadjusted figures, which took no account of undistributed profits, certain benefits in kind and employers' contributions to life insurance. Without allowance for these things, the share of this tiny minority was apparently halved during the 1940s (from 11½ per cent to about 6 per cent). After adjustment, the cut is reduced to one of roughly a third (from 15 per cent to about 10 per cent). The difference on this score between the two sets of figures reflects, of course, a rise in the estimated proportion of real income that escaped taxation among the very wealthy during this period. That is not surprising. Profits, for example, were increasingly held back for re-investment or in reserve, rather than distributed. And it is quite plausible that tax evasion in general became more institutionalized and effective in response to so-called 'penal' rates of taxation during those years especially. In an economy dominated by private business and property the elaboration of tax-evasive devices becomes an industry in itself, with whose activities the tax authorities have to live by negotiation and accommodation as much as they may try to curb them by cracks of the whip and intermittent legislative alteration of the rules.

Second, the degree of continuing inequality indicated by the adjusted figures is now very marked. It can thus be inferred (from comparison of tables 1 and 2, with some simple interpolation of a few missing figures) that the 10 per cent share of total post-tax income which went, around 1960, to the richest 1 per cent of the population was much the same as the share going to the poorest 30 per cent of the population. The richest 5 per cent then took between them not very much less than did the poorest half of the population: each of the two groups, the small minority and the low-income half, had about one-quarter of total adjusted income after tax. There are, moreover, no signs in these or other figures of any substantial change since then.

The point is crucial. For that degree of inequality – roughly similar shares for the top 1 per cent as for the poorest third or so, for a privileged 5 per cent as for the millions in the bottom half of the population – simply does not square with the glib assertion, so commonly made, that any sizeable redistribution must cut mainly into middle-range incomes, the incomes of skilled and other 'comfortably-paid' workers, because there is little surplus to take from at the top.[4] In so far as there is any point to that assertion, it is only that it reflects the assumptions of those who make it about the limits of the 'politically possible'. To transfer the bulk of real income now enjoyed by the very rich to, say, the poorest half of the population could not be done through taxation within an economy whose tone is still set by private business and property. The intense concentration of income at the top arises, as we shall show, from a concentration of profit-bearing ownership among a tiny minority, and from the operation of market mechanisms necessarily associated with the continuing pre-dominance of private enterprise in economic affairs. Any policy of redistribution which is to cut drastically into the wealth of the few must therefore involve public appropriation of the means of produc-tion. A socialist programme of that sort is, quite simply, ruled out of consideration by those who argue that the funds to lift low incomes have to come mainly from the pockets of wage earners. Their con-ception of what is practicable, in short, makes sense only if their implicit premise is accepted: that private capital remains the prime economic motor. But they are plainly wrong – and either ignore or deliberately falsify fact – when they claim that there is no sizeable wealth at the top. There is plenty, in very few hands.

III

The conclusion so far – the persistent stability of overall income inequality in the 1950s and 1960s, following some moderate redistri-bution during the 1940s – can be sharpened in several ways: by taking the story right up to the beginning of the 1970s; by bringing into account a larger range of items relevant to the balance sheet; and by distinguishing the situations of households of different composition. Since the early 1960s official estimates have been published of the incidence of taxes and social service benefits.[5] The basic data of these

4. For a recent version of this assertion, see Roy Jenkins, *What Matters Now*, Collins 1972 (inter alia, pp. 20–22, 117–18), e.g., '. . . the comfortable majority will have to make their contribution. It is an illusion to imagine that the gap between rich and poor and the rest of us can be closed solely at the expense of the rich.' 'We have to persuade motor car workers . . . that they have an obligation to low-paid workers in the public sector.' '. . . The gulf between majority and minority now cuts across class lines.' '. . . many manual workers are to be found on the "haves" side of the barricade.'
5. 'The incidence of taxes and social service benefits in . . .,' *Economic Trends*, at intervals from November 1962. (Tables 3 and 6 below have been calculated

estimates come from nationwide sample surveys – the regular series of Family Expenditure Surveys – not from the tax authorities. For reasons already discussed, they are subject to deficiencies which also result in understatement of inequality. But they have the advantage of taking into account the effects of indirect as well as direct taxation, and of welfare benefits in both cash and kind. Sample surveys provide the only practical basis for attempts to allocate losses and gains on these scores to households of different composition and income. Accuracy and coverage are not, of course, complete. There are errors in the record of income, which involve inadequate allowance for property income, income from self-employment and employer-provided 'fringe benefits'. Social service benefits include all state payments in cash, and estimates of the value to households of health, education and welfare food services and of subsidies to public housing. But they do not include, for example, the benefits derived from tax concessions in respect of private insurance and pension schemes, mortgage and other interest payments; nor do they include the full effect of differences in the kinds and costs of education received by children of different social classes. All of these omissions understate public benefits in the upper range of the economic scale. Provided such qualifications are kept in mind, however, the survey estimates are a valuable addition to the crude information assembled in the course of tax collection.

We shall use these data later to trace the separate effects of tax and welfare benefits on income distribution. For the moment, our purpose is to follow the overall trend in that distribution over the years, taking into account these estimates of individual losses and gains through the activities of the 'welfare state'. Table 3 uses a simple summary measure of the trend in 'net income' distribution from 1961 to 1970 – the spread of post-tax-and-benefit incomes between top and bottom 'quintiles', expressed in relative terms in order to abstract from the effect of changes in actual money values over the years. The higher the figure, the greater the degree of inequality. The ratios do not express the full range of disparity in incomes right from top to bottom – only the relative distance between the lowest income among

from data in the issues of February 1970 and February 1972.) For an early application of estimates of this kind to analysis of overall income distribution, see J. L. Nicholson, *Redistribution of Income in the UK in 1959, 1957 and 1963*, Bowes, 1965 (and his contribution to C. Clark and G. Stuvel, eds., *Income and Wealth*, Series X, Bowes, 1964).

the richest fifth of the population and the highest income among the poorest fifth. So inequality is more acute than the figures show. But what matters here is the trend – the movement of the ratios over time.[6]

TABLE 3

Summary measures of inequality in income after all taxes and social service benefits, direct and indirect, 1961–1970

Households comprising –	Households of this composition as per cent of all households, 1970	Top (i.e., fourth) quintile income expressed as percentage of bottom (i.e., first) quintile income			
		1961	1965	1968	1970
1 adult only	17	233	216	221	216
2 adults only	30	214	197	209	238
2 adults, 1 child	10	178	174	175	186
2 adults, 2 children	12	182	178	178	180
2 adults, 3 children	5	164	174	167	174
2 adults, 4 children	2	167	168	158	158
3 adults only	9	179	171	186	188
3 adults, 1 child	3	168	171	168	178
3 adults, 2 children	2	152	171	172	159
All other households	10	*	*	*	*
All households in samples	100	270	275	282	295

Sources and definitions: See text and footnotes 5 and 6, pp. 44–46. The effect of a reallocation, from 1969, of employers' contributions to national insurance, from original income to indirect taxes, is probably small for the purposes or comparability over time in this table. The exclusion of certain tax concessions from benefits, referred to in the text, does not matter here in so far as they are counted as part of original income instead.
* Full data not published.

There are again no signs of any general narrowing in the range of inequality. On the contrary, by these measures it widened during the 1960s – overall, for all households taken together; and for six out of the nine distinct types of household listed (comprising more than two-thirds of the population). Only among single-person households

6. The top quintile is the income of the unit (household) at the boundary between the richest 20 per cent and the rest of the population; the bottom quintile is the income of the household at the boundary between the poorest 20 per cent and the rest. Thus 60 per cent of all households fall between the two. Data were not published, for the period as a whole, to allow the use of alternative measures – e.g., the range from top to bottom decile – to supplement this measure.

and the few couples with four children was there any trend – and that an irregular one – for income inequality, post-tax-and-benefit, to diminish during the decade; while the range of inequality among households with two adults and two children remained substantially unchanged. An analysis of the movement of upper and lower quintile incomes in relation to median incomes – not shown in the table – suggests that the overall tendency for income inequality to widen between 1961 and 1970 arose more from a relative acceleration of top incomes than from a relative deceleration of low incomes, although both processes were at work. The rich and the fairly rich, in other words, became disproportionately richer; while the poor just about – though not quite – managed to maintain their position in relation to a slowly rising average.

Special interest attaches to the second half of the 1960s, after a Labour government had come into office in 1964. The earlier period of moderate 'income equalization' in the 1940s had overlapped with the administration of the first Labour government ever to have a majority in the House of Commons – although the redistribution of income in that decade set in earlier, in association with the special pressures and policies of the war economy, and was petering out already before Labour left office in 1951. When the next Labour government came to power in 1964, its programme gave top priority to 'modernization' and overall economic growth: to a claim, in effect, that Labour could run the capitalist economy of Britain more efficiently than the party of capitalism itself. In practice, the priority for 'modernization' and economic growth was translated into one for restraint on earnings, a large surplus on the external balance of payments, and until late 1967, rigid maintenance of the exchange value of sterling. Even before that translation, however, redistribution had been pushed well into the background as a policy objective. Despite some Labour reforms ostensibly directed to 'fairer shares', therefore, it is not surprising to find here no evidence of any general change in trends between the early and the late 1960s. Indeed, income inequality widened more overall while Labour was in office than during the first part of the decade, though the detailed pattern – household type for type – was somewhat more varied than earlier. In those years, too, as throughout the decade, the widening of inequality seems to have been associated mainly with disproportionate increments in wealth for those already well off.

Given the nature of the data, a single set of measures is not fully conclusive. But the signs are clear that overall income inequalities certainly were not reduced in the 1960s, and probably increased. Other calculations underline the point. For example, despite a continuing decline in the ratio of corporate profits to wages and salaries before tax, the ratio *after* tax rose in the late 1960s as it had done earlier – to 30 per cent of aggregate wages and salaries in the second half of the decade, compared with 28½ per cent in the earlier part of it and 25 per cent around 1950. Direct taxation in fact shifted further from profits on to employment income during the period of Labour government. And the effects both of changes in rates of taxation on earnings, and of the fact that more and more people on relatively low earnings were caught up in the tax net over time, were regressive. The result was largely to neutralize the impact of successful union pressure, during the last couple of years of Labour government, for higher wages especially for low-paid workers.[7] Unemployment rose substantially from 1967 on. At the bottom of the economic scale, it is true, increases in rates of payment under National Insurance and in respect of Supplementary Benefits exceeded the average rise in wage earnings higher up the scale during the Labour period. But the main increase in state allowances came early in the government's period of office, and thereafter earnings tended to rise faster than benefits.[8]

7. For these points see Jackson *et al.,* op. cit. (note 6 ch. 1, p. 35, above), especially pp. 70, 76–81. Broadly similar conclusions about the constancy of income inequality during the late 1960s were reached by several of the contributors to P. Townsend and N. Bosanquet, eds., *Labour and Inequality*, Fabian Society, 1972 (e.g. chapters, 2, 8, 9, 11, 12, 16). By contrast, M. Stewart ('The distribution of income', in W. Beckerman, ed., *The Labour Government's Economic Record: 1964–1970*, Duckworth, 1972) cautiously concluded that there appeared to be some reduction of income inequality during the Labour years. He attributed this mainly to increases in public benefits which indeed occurred (see note 8 below and table 6 of text). But the conclusion seems to have taken insufficient account of regressive features of taxation, including the 'tax trap' for low earned incomes as described by Jackson *et al.* (see above). And although it drew in part on the same material, the overall assessment did not involve – and was not consistent with the results of – measures of income dispersion between constant proportions of households as shown here in table 3 of the text. Given the inadequacy of information there cannot be ultimate certainty about possible minor changes in distribution; disputes about these acquire something of the character of theological debate. Stewart's optimism in the end does not rest on a claim that the Labour period saw any major change; but on the dubious assumption (often advanced by the Labour Party in self-defence) that the 'measurable improvement' of which he saw signs *might* have been substantial had overall growth of output not been so 'deplorably slow'.

8. The real value of a single pension rose by about 14 per cent from 1963 to 1969 (from the last Conservative increase to the last Labour increase); that of

Some of these matters will be discussed again later, when the forces making for persistent and marked inequality of income are examined. Here the point is the fact of inequality and its broad stability over the past twenty years.

IV

Long-term trends in income distribution over the century as a whole are very difficult to establish; impossible, indeed, except in the crudest of terms. One tentative attempt to do so found no signs of any substantial changes in distribution during this century, other than those associated with the special circumstances of the 1940s; at most a very slight curtailment of inequality before that.[9] Broadly similar conclusions have sometimes been drawn from the apparent stability of the aggregate share of wage earnings in total income from the 1860s to the 1960s, at a ratio of some 38 or 39 per cent of gross national product. In fact, the stability of this ratio might rather suggest some narrowing of inequality during those hundred years. For the proportion of wage earners in the working population – broadly speaking, of manual workers – declined over the same period. If their aggregate earnings remained constant as a share of all wealth produced, their *average* earnings must then have increased somewhat relative to other shares. But the inference is uncertain, and the magnitude of any such long-term shift to wage labour unknown, since the data are crude. For one thing, they take no account of the impact of taxes and public benefits. For another, there are ambiguities in the definitions of 'wages' and 'wage earners'. The distinction between 'wage' and

unemployment benefit for a man with wife and three children by 16 per cent; that of the average male manual manufacturing worker's take-home pay by about 10 per cent only. But the major part of the rise in benefit rates came early in 1965, and later increases were not proportionate in scale. (A. B. Atkinson, in Townsend and Bosanquet, op. cit., note 7 above.) These are post-tax estimates. Measured only pre-tax, benefit rates just about kept pace with earnings of adult male manual workers in manufacturing. As a ratio of the latter, Supplementary Benefit (with estimated provision for rent and rates) amounted to 38 per cent after the 1963 increase, 39 per cent after the 1969 increase, for a pensioner couple; 58 per cent after both increases, for a couple with three children. (A. B. Atkinson, *Poverty in Britain and the Reform of Social Security*, Cambridge University Press, 1969, pp. 19–20, 203–204; with additional calculations by us for 1969.)

9. H. F. Lydall, 'The long-term trend in the size distribution of incomes', *J. Royal Statist. Society*, Series A, 122 (1), 1959 (pp. 31–35).

'salary-earners' – wherever it is drawn precisely – is in any case artificial, because salary-earners have conventionally included large numbers of routine white-collar employees whose earnings, from other evidence, are fairly low and have been falling relative to those of many others.

One study in the 1960s focused, by contrast, on the share of employment income of all kinds (wages, salaries and the non-profit component of income from self-employment) versus that of property income. The indications to be derived from that are still necessarily tentative. The relevant estimates again do not take account of taxes and public benefits (though the impact of these even today, as will be shown later, is much more limited than usually assumed); and they count as 'labour' income the salaries of all employees, including those of company directors and managers whose rewards as controllers are more akin to profit than to earnings from employment. With those qualifications, the results nevertheless offer some clues about long-term trends. Three main measures were used: the respective shares of 'labour' and 'property' over time in gross national product, in gross domestic product and in net domestic product. The differences between them are not important in this context, because the trends in respect of all three are virtually identical. The share of 'labour' rose during the sixty years of this century covered; that of 'property' fell. But that shift occurred almost entirely as the result of changes in two periods only: around the time of World War I (when the share of 'property' in gross national product, for example, fell from 45 per cent in 1910–14 to 33 per cent in 1921–24); and around the time of World War II (with a further fall from 33 per cent in 1935–38 to 27 per cent in 1946–49). Both between the wars and from 1950 to the mid-1960s, no shifts of any substance took place.[10]

Hazy as the signs are from this and other evidence about long-term trends, they reinforce the lessons of the much more detailed record of the last thirty years or so. There are no indications of an inherent and continuing trend towards substantial redistribution of

10. C. H. Feinstein, 'Changes in the distribution of the national income in the U.K. since 1860', in J. Marchal and B. Ducros, eds., *The Distribution of National Income*, Macmillan, 1968 (especially pp. 119–20, 126–9). We have ignored a fourth measure used by Feinstein, which excludes rental income of dwellings from 'property'. Feinstein shows, as have others, the stability of 'wages' at around 38–39 per cent of gross national product from 1860 to the early 1960s. But it is worth noting that the ratio had fallen to 35 to 36 per cent by 1969 (after Feinstein's paper), since when data for its calculation have not been published.

income within the capitalist economy of Britain. There has been some redistribution; but that has been confined to limited periods and exceptional circumstances – those of the two world wars. Outside those special periods, overall income disparity appears to have remained remarkably stable; at particular times even to have increased. Inequality today plainly cannot be dismissed as a matter of 'frills', when the richest 1 per cent of the population take as much of all income as the poorest third or so.

3 Determinants of income inequality

I

The range and shape of income inequality in Britain reflect the fact that the economy is still, in all essentials, capitalist. Three main forces determine the pattern of distribution. The first – and the overwhelmingly important one – is private ownership of capital. The second is the complex of pulls and pushes in the labour market. The third is the activity of the state – central government, local authorities and publicly owned industry – in collecting taxes and distributing benefits, as well as through attempts to influence the economic climate. The central role of private ownership in shaping the pattern of distribution arises in two ways: directly, because it is the concentration of private property which has the major part in explaining the continuing accumulation of a very large share of national output in few hands; indirectly, because the workings both of the labour market and of state economic activity reflect the prevailing influence of business views and interests in the assumptions by which everyday economic affairs are conducted in a capitalist society. We shall try to show, in the rest of Part Two of this book, the ways in which each of these three forces contributes to the pattern of income distribution. We shall reserve to Part Three an attempt to draw out the implications of that analysis for an understanding of the distribution of power; and in that connection to show the central part played by private capital in shaping both the conscious decisions, and especially the implicit assumptions, of private and public enterprise which determine social conditions.

Our emphasis on the critical importance of capital ownership, indirectly as well as directly, already implies that the distinction between the three forces is made for convenience in analysis only, while the three in fact are fairly closely related. The private ownership of capital, the institutions of property and the principles of profit-making with which it is associated, colour the ways in which the labour market and the state in its economic role work. There is over-lap among the three forces on other scores, too. Government, for example, influences the labour market; and it has set out to do so more and more directly since World War II, in successive efforts to impose 'wage restraint' and 'incomes policies'. The rise of large-scale corporate enterprise, which has made for a partial and formal separation of ownership of capital from control over it, has helped to veil the distinction between property income and employment income. Directors and senior managers cannot in real terms be seen as deriving their salaries and other rewards primarily from the sale of their labour in the market. They are able in large part to determine their own remuneration – within flexible limits, and collectively rather than individually – because they occupy positions of control. Their rewards, in considerable measure, are a claim on profits – in effect, though not in form: a point which we shall take up again later. Finally, there are other factors involved in the determination of income distribution which cannot be subsumed under the three headings. Among these, for example, are differential movements in the prices of goods and services, which may favour some income groups at the expense of others and thus redistribute real purchasing power. For all these qualifications, the broad threefold distinction between property ownership, labour market pressures and state activity provides a practical framework for assessing the forces behind the persistent inequality of income.

II

All three elements were involved in the shift of income distribution that occurred during the 1940s.

The share of distributed income from property – company dividends, interest, rent and so on – in total personal income before tax fell from about 22 per cent in 1938 to about 11 per cent in 1949. It has fluctuated closely around the latter level since then.[1] These figures

1. Calculated from *National Income and Expenditure* reports for 1965, 1970 and 1972 (for the period 1938–1971).

exaggerate the significance of the change in the 1940s. They do not take account of the rise in undistributed profits. Nor is it possible to adjust them to allow for the likelihood that some increasing part of profits may have been translated into salaries, 'perks' and expenses for the controllers of corporations. There was almost certainly a real decline in the share of property income at that time nevertheless.

In the labour market, wages increased over the decade around the war more than salaries. This suggests some further redistribution between classes, though part of this change may reflect a decline in the position of routine clerical workers, wage earners in all but name. Skill differentials in wages were reduced; and so were differentials between the earnings of men, women and young people. But these shifts, it should be noted, clearly involved redistribution within, rather than between, classes: a tendency to levelling among manual wage earners, not a shift from capital or high salaries to ordinary labour.

Again, although estimates from official records as usual cannot be taken at their face value, the incidence of direct taxation became more progressive in the course of the 1940s. The result was to reduce the share of top and middle incomes in the post-tax total more than had been the case before the war. Moreover, the basic framework of the present state welfare system – national health, pensions and other national insurance benefits, as well as free secondary education – was established during the same decade. This was supplemented after the end of the war by a building programme which, until some years into the 1950s, concentrated very largely on public housing. The equalizing effects of state welfare provisions are, as will be shown, a good deal more limited than usually assumed. They make for redistribution within classes at least as much as between classes. Even so, the establishment of the welfare system, compressed within a few years, still made a real contribution to 'fairer shares' by comparison with pre-war conditions; and it did so more than is shown in figures confined to cash income, which exclude public benefits in kind and by way of subsidies to council housing.

Finally – as a further factor not taken into account in conventional estimates of the distribution of disposable income – the movement of prices during and immediately after the war favoured those on low and moderate incomes. The cost of necessities – food, housing and fuel in particular – rose less than that of other goods and services, in consequence of deliberate government control.[2] Since then, by contrast, price levels have increased a good deal more for these things than they have in general. The effect of this reversal of trends is to sharpen the contrast between the equalizing tendencies of the decade of war and post-war 'social reconstruction', and the stability or accentuation of income inequality from around 1950.[3]

The shift in the 1940s was thus the outcome of an unusual conjunction of circumstances. There was first the mobilization of the economy for war, accompanied by acute shortages of labour. In association with that came the special measures for rationing, price and rent control, restraints on profits and greater equity in increased taxation, which were politically agreed as essential for class co-operation in the war effort. Moreover, for much the same reasons, new health and welfare services were initiated already during the war; and they were extended in far more comprehensive form during the years immediately afterwards – by Labour, but with Conservative opposition generally confined to detail rather than principle.

It is not possible to assign exact responsibility for the redistribution – in any case measurable only in rough terms – between 'natural' pressures of the war economy, deliberate measures of policy taken during the war, and the post-war institutionalization of the welfare system. What is important, first, is that the shift was not radically reversed once it came to an end. The Labour victory in 1945; the wider support for 'social reconstruction' which this reflected, in Britain and elsewhere, until cold war pressures helped to bring about a standstill; the policies put through in consequence until the late 1940s – these certainly played a significant part. But their effect may have been much more to prevent a reversal, to consolidate the redistributive trend set in motion during the war, than substantially to

2. For most of the points in this and the preceding paragraphs see D. Seers, *The Levelling of Incomes since 1938*, Blackwell, 1950 (probably the most comprehensive examination of the 1940s shift, including the different trends of 'working class' and 'middle class' costs of living). Seers was early to note the levelling off of the 'equalizing' trend by the late 1940s, and signs of some regression in the early 1950s. See his 'Has the distribution of income become more unequal?', *Bulletin Oxford Univ. Inst. Statistics*, February 1956. He did not deal in any detail with the overall net effect of taxes and benefits; but see A. M. Cartter, *The Redistribution of Income in Postwar Britain*, Yale, 1955, as the first major post-war study on that point.

3. The general index of retail prices rose by a little under 160 per cent from 1948 to 1971, but the cost of food and housing both by about 200 per cent and that of fuel by nearly 240 per cent. (Calculated from *British Labour Statistics*, H.M.S.O., 1971 and *Monthly Digest of Statistics*, Sept. 1972.)

extend that trend. What is important, second, is the simple fact that the shift did come to an end, sometime around 1950. The timing cannot be accurately established; but the fact itself is firm. The 1940s were a watershed in the social history of Britain as of many other countries – not a period in which continuing trends were merely writ larger than at other times. And though the shift in social structure which the redistribution of that decade involved has not been radically reversed, some of its features were showing signs of erosion by the 1960s and the early 1970s – a period which may prove another watershed in our class history, though in different and more complex ways.

III

To understand the subsequent persistence of inequality largely in the mould set for it by the end of the 1940s, we have to examine again the influence of capital ownership, labour market forces and state activities – and to do so this time in a fairly detailed way. As we have already stressed, and shall use concrete evidence to show, the order of importance among these three elements is as we have listed them. The concentration of private capital in a small minority of the population is the prime factor in giving the few so large a share of income as they have. The effect of state action on the distribution of income as initially determined by property ownership and labour market forces is, by contrast, very modest.

In the mythology whose central thesis is the erosion of class inequality, however, the order of importance among the three forces is commonly reversed. Crucial significance is attributed to taxation and state benefits as instruments of redistribution. To this is sometimes added an assumption that some steady process of diminution in pay differentials in the labour market – whether through union pressures or otherwise – is helping to trim the sharp edges of inequality between classes. Property ownership in any case is assigned a much curtailed significance as a source of economic inequality; and it is often left almost entirely out of account in popular and political debate on the subject, except where property in urban land is concerned.

Just because this mythology has been and is still so powerful, it is essential to dispel the illusions which it has generated. We shall therefore start by looking at the role of the state in shaping the ultimate pattern of income distribution, in order to clear away the common notion that taxes and public benefits play a major part in shaping – or reshaping – the economic hierarchy of class. Only after that shall we take up the influence of labour market forces and, finally, of private ownership of capital: the latter last, because by virtue precisely of its central significance it leads on to the issues of power to be discussed in Part Three. We move, in other words, from the least to the most influential of the three main determinants of income patterns.

4 Taxation and welfare provision

I

Redistribution through taxation and welfare provision is quite limited. The reasons for that are straightforward. First, there is very little progression in taxation when all kinds of tax are put together: the proportion of income taken in taxes is much the same over very large ranges of the income scale. Second, although public welfare provision is progressive – it helps the poor proportionately more than the rich – in absolute terms the gains involved for people with low incomes are very modest; and the redistributive effect of state benefits is further reduced by public support for private welfare provision. Government benevolence in that respect is directed mainly to those who are already well off.

The first point will seem startling and unbelievable to many people, although it has been firmly established at least since the early 1960s.[1] Misconceptions arise partly because the impact of indirect taxation is commonly forgotten. But even direct taxes on income rise much less steeply up the scale than is usually assumed. For one thing, progression in the proportionate rates of income tax up the scale of income, to the 'standard rate', was abolished by the Labour government in the 1960s. For another, direct taxes include national insurance contributions which, despite a small 'graduated' element, throughout the 1950s and 1960s on balance constituted a regressive tax, levied at a more or less flat rate irrespective of income and falling therefore proportionately most heavily on the shoulders of the low-paid.

Moreover, tax concessions – for dependents, expenses, privately or employer-arranged insurance, mortgages and other interest payments – reduce the progression of 'normal' income tax in several ways.

1. See especially Nicholson, op. cit. (ch. 2, note 5, above).

They do not benefit those too poor to pay income tax at all. And in so far as rates of income tax rise progressively with increasing income, the real value of tax concessions increases the higher the marginal rate of tax – that is, the higher the income of the individual or couple concerned. (A taxpayer with too low an income until the late 1960s to pay more than, say, one-tenth at the margin would gain only a tenth of a pound for each pound deducted from his taxable income as a duty-free allowance. The taxpayer paying one-third at the margin would benefit by a third of a pound for each pound deducted as an allowance.) Finally, dependent allowances apart, the arrangements for which tax concessions are available are ones used mainly, and most effectively, by people on comfortable to high incomes. Ordinary wage earners and the poor do not set expenses against income from fees. They are either not enrolled in private insurance schemes set up by their employers, or they are enrolled on comparatively unfavourable terms. They are not usually in a position to take advantage of covenants with tax reliefs attached. They either cannot afford to buy homes at all, or have only relatively small mortgages for house purchase. They do not on the whole finance expenditure beyond their immediately disposable incomes from bank loans and overdrafts, but have to rely on hire purchase and savings clubs at high rates of interest and without tax concessions. Working-class credit, in short, is very expensive, both because high rates of interest have to be paid, and because tax concessions are not generally available to reduce the effective cost. Upper- and middle-class credit is much cheaper on both scores.

The mix of tax concessions and the rules governing them have varied from time to time. So have rates of income and surtax, and the levels of income at which they take effect. It is not our purpose to trace these permutations over time. The essential point is very simple. Regardless of particular variations, even direct taxation is, and was throughout the 1950s and 1960s, only moderately progressive in its incidence across the range of incomes. The point can be seen from the columns headed 'Direct tax' in table 4 below, for 1970. Of course, the impact of direct taxation is negligible at very low incomes. And it is greater than appears from the table at very high levels in income: the top income bracket, £60 a week or more, is open-ended, and cannot be sub-divided because numbers in the sample above that level are too small. But the lower margin of that top category represented an income over twice the average earnings of male manual workers in 1970 (about £28). Yet households in the £60 plus category as a whole paid on average no more than about 20–25 per cent of their incomes in direct taxation – only 5–10 per cent more than those with half as much money. The progression in effective rates of direct tax for families with two children rose only from 14 per cent to 19 per cent over the long range from £23 a week (around the average earnings of unskilled manual workers) to solid 'middle class' incomes of £60 or more per week.

TABLE 4

Incidence of direct and indirect taxes, 1970: all households and selected household types

Original income	All households			Households with 2 adults*			Households w. 2 adults, 2 children*		
	Taxes as % of original income plus cash benefits			Taxes as % of original income plus cash benefits			Taxes as % of original income plus cash benefits		
(£ per week)	Direct tax	Indirect tax	All taxes	Direct tax	Indirect tax	All taxes	Direct tax	Indirect tax	All taxes
Under £5	0	25	25	1	33	34			
£5 –	2	25	27	1	22	23			
£6 –	3	23	26	1	27	28			
£7·3 –	4	22	26	2	22	24			
£8·8 –	7	24	31	6	30	36			
£10·7 –	9	21	30	7	22	29			
£13 –	9	24	33	10	26	36			
£15·7 –	11	23	34	12	23	35	5	24	29
£19 –	12	24	36	15	21	36	8	26	34
£23 –	15	22	37	18	21	39	13	22	35
£28 –	15	23	38	16	23	39	14	22	36
£34 –	16	21	37	17	21	38	15	20	35
£41 –	17	19	36	19	19	38	15	18	33
£49·5 –	19	19	38	20	17	37	19	16	35
£60 –	22	16	38	25	14	39	19	16	35
All incomes	16	20	36	19	19	38	16	19	35

Source: Central Statistical Office, 'The incidence of taxes and social service benefits in 1970', *Economic Trends*, February 1972. (Data from the 1970 Family Expenditure sample survey.)

Notes: * The two household types selected for illustration include only 'non-retired' households – i.e., they exclude households in which the combined income of members aged at least 60 and retired makes up half or more of total household income.

Direct tax includes income tax, surtax and national insurance contributions, (Taxes on capital – i.e., on capital gains, undistributed profits and inheritance – are excluded, just as the corresponding forms of capital are excluded from income.)

Indirect tax includes local rates; duties on drink, tobacco, betting, etc; purchase tax; licence fees (radio, television, driving); motor duties and stamp duties; import duties; selective employment tax; employees' contributions to national insurance; etc.

No figures are shown for cells of the sample with fewer than 10 households. Cells with small numbers, though ten households or more, may produce chance fluctuations in the pattern of results, which therefore needs to be considered overall without regard to isolated deviations.

The incomes shown are ranges – e.g., '£5 –' = £5 to under £6. They are the ranges of annual incomes used in the source, divided by 52 to give weekly figures. These income ranges relate to original incomes only; but the incidence of taxation is calculated as a percentage of original income *plus* cash benefits.

II

Politicians concerned to defend their record, the mass media and the public relations machinery of private business seem to have been remarkably successful in persuading people that the incidence of direct taxation is more progressive than it is. One reason why so many have been persuaded to believe this may be, paradoxically, the very fact that it is not so progressive. The impact of income tax is therefore relatively heavy on moderate incomes – especially on those of wage earners who get caught up in the tax net, after previous immunity, by a nominal rise in their money earnings. People on moderate incomes may for that reason be all the more open to persuasion that the impact of income tax on themselves represents the 'tail end' of a burden still very much heavier further up the scale.

Be that as it may, the ideological apparatus of 'post-capitalism' has had yet more remarkable success in keeping a veil drawn over the limited contribution made by income tax to all state revenue. Income tax accounts for less than half of all taxation. Other forms of taxation are regressive in their overall incidence; they hit the low-paid proportionately hardest. In fact, direct taxation with some specific progression in its impact – income tax, surtax, death duties and more recently capital gains tax – made up only a little more than 40 per cent of all tax revenue in the years from 1950 to the early 1970s: some 43 per cent in 1971 (of which 40 per cent came from income tax and surtax), the ratio fluctuating between 39 per cent and 44 per cent over the years. National insurance contributions – mildly regressive, though a direct tax according to conventional classification – rose from 10 per cent to about 14 per cent of the total. Taxes on expenditure, imposed by central government and local authorities, made up the remainder.[2] It is such taxes on expenditure, in particular, which are regressive – which fall relatively hardest on the weakest shoulders.

Not all indirect taxes do so, it is true. To take the estimates for 1970, purchase tax and the duties on drink and oil – together rather less than two-fifths of all indirect taxes – were progressive in incidence. But the effect of the rest – including local rates, despite

2. Calculated from *National Income and Expenditure* reports for 1960, 1970 and 1972 (for the period 1950–1971). (The ratios of direct to indirect tax indicated in the last line of table 4 of the text are not directly comparable, partly because they exclude taxes on capital.)

means-tested rebates introduced after a government report in 1965[3] –
was generally regressive. And the overall impact of indirect taxes is
plain from table 4 (columns two, five and eight): the burden in relation to income falls the higher the income of the household.

When the effects of all taxes are combined (table 4, columns three,
six and nine) it is therefore not surprising to find that the cut taken by
the state shows little variation as a fraction of income over most of the
range. Such progression as appears in the figures for all households –
from a total tax cut of 25 per cent at the lowest income level to one of
38 per cent at the highest shown – is misleading because households
of widely varying composition are here lumped together. The incidence of all taxation for households of two adults only, for example,
shows some unevenness, but very little overall progression. Most of
these households pay out rather more than a third of their incomes in
taxes, whether they have, say, £60 plus a week, £30 or £15 – sometimes even when they have less. So too in the case of couples with two
children. Much the same is true for other household types not shown
in the table, with the general exception only of 'retired households'
with one or two adults. In their case, effective rates of overall taxation
rise from around 25 per cent at very low incomes to about 40 per cent at
income levels of £16 to £19 per week; but above that level the tax rate
again appears to remain roughly constant, so far as there are figures
available. Even at its most generous, in short, the state at the beginning of the 1970s exacted a series of levies amounting to one quarter
of income: that on the incomes of the very poorest, mainly working-
class pensioners. For the rest, the proportion of income taken in taxes
rose quickly to a third or rather more – and stayed around that ratio,
with virtually no distinction between small wage earnings and very
comfortable salaries well into the executive and professional range.

III

One arm of the 'welfare state' is therefore practically crippled so far
as redistribution is concerned. The other arm – that which hands out
benefits – does in a sense work roughly as it is assumed to: handing
out more to the poor than to the rich. But its effects are fairly puny, if
redistribution is the yardstick. The first three columns of table 5 show

3. *The Impact of Rates* (Allen Report), Cmnd. 2582, 1965. Rates on property –
in effect paid by occupiers, whether owners or tenants – are the only tax raised by
local authorities, who have no power to impose income taxes.

a marked progression in the proportionate incidence of social welfare benefits, direct and indirect. The *relative* additions to income at the bottom of the scale are very large, those at the top of the scale very small. Indeed, the pattern could hardly be different, for a quite simple reason. Incomes at the bottom of the scale are so low in absolute terms that welfare benefits make a sizeable addition to them when calculated in proportionate terms; by contrast, incomes at the top of the scale are so high that even considerable benefits add only a small fraction to the total. In that sense the marked progression in the incidence of benefits, measured proportionate to income, in large part reflects the sharp initial inequality in distribution of income.

In *absolute* terms, the progression is very much less impressive. The estimated monetary value of all benefits – from figures in the original source not shown in the table – came to averages per household of about £490–£550 for the four lowest income categories of all households in 1970. It fell gradually to a little over £400 for households with £16–£19 per week; and then to amounts varying between £320 and £350 over the rest of the income range, with no further drop in the average. Households with £60 a week and more gained as much, in absolute terms, as those with £23–£28 a week, and more than those with £19–£23 a week. In fact, the 'large' amounts received by households at the very lowest income levels came mainly in the form of cash payments: pension, unemployment and sick pay, supplementary benefits. Benefits from the national health services were estimated, in terms of their cash value, to be much the same across the range of incomes. Some others – from use of state educational services in particular – increased with income, not only because many of the poorest households comprise pensioners with no young children; but also because middle-class children stay longer in education, and have easier access to its more expensive sectors, than do working-class children. Indeed, the latter kind of differential is understated in these estimates.

Moreover, the benefits shown, it needs to be repeated, include only those which are provided by central and local authorities in the form of cash payments, direct services, and subsidies to public housing. They do not include any of those benefits which the state supports by the negative device of abstaining from tax demands which it would otherwise impose. The tax concessions involved are as much publicly financed benefits, in effect, as they would be also in form if Inland Revenue were to abolish the concessions and provide for direct cash payment of their value instead. The nature of these concessions, disproportionately more effective and valuable the higher up the socio-economic scale one goes, has already been indicated. Their effect has been to establish two systems of welfare.[4]

One is the 'public system', officially recognized, and taken into account in estimates of gains and losses through redistribution of the kind summarized here. This operates in large part on the basis of 'bedrock provision' – a more or less effective guarantee of subsistence at a low level in old age, ill health and unemployment. Parts of the public system, however, are directed to provision at a much higher level, ostensibly equally available to all. That is true of national health and education. Public housing is in a highly ambivalent position, and has been increasingly confined to a residual role as a service for those who cannot 'fend for themselves'.

The other system is one of provision which is formally private, but financed in part by the state through tax reliefs. That system embraces, notably, employer-provided pension, sick pay and supplementary health service schemes; and also the private provision and purchase of housing, aided by direct grants to owners for improvements and especially by tax concessions for mortgages. The division between the two systems is essentially one of class. The inequalities of the society have been built into, and are reinforced by, this bifurcation of welfare. Some detailed features of the cleavage in provision, and new developments in policy which will accentuate it, will be discussed later. The point which is essential here concerns the overall effect of 'dual provision': the real incidence of publicly financed benefits is a good deal less progressive in relation to income than appears from table 5.[5]

4. R. M. Titmuss was the first to emphasize this point and demonstrate it comprehensively. See his *Essays on the Welfare State*, Allen & Unwin, 1958 (especially chapter 2).

5. Fringe benefits attracting tax relief are discussed in the following chapter on the labour market. Subsidies to public housing, which are taken into account in table 5 of the text, amounted to just over £400 million in 1970/71. Tax relief on mortgages (together with improvement grants to private owners), which are *not* taken into account in the table, came to some £315 million: an average of £61 per owner occupier getting tax relief, compared with only £53 for each tenant of a new council house or flat. (*Social Trends*, no. 3, 1972, p. 143.) One tentative estimate put tax relief for owner occupiers around the mid-1960s at averages ranging from just over £50 a year for the relatively few such households with under £10 a week to nearly £130 a year for those with incomes of £40 and more: an overall average in this estimate a good deal higher than indicated by the official data quoted before. (C. Crouch and M. Wolf, in Townsend and Bosanquet, op. cit., ch. 2, note 7 above.)

TABLE 5

Incidence of direct and indirect benefits, and of all taxes and benefits combined, 1970: all households and selected household types

Original Income (£ per week)	All benefits, direct and indirect, as per cent of original income plus cash benefits			Income after all taxes and benefits, as per cent of original income		
	All households	Non-retired households with –		All households	Non-retired households with –	
		2 adults	2 adults, 2 children		2 adults	2 adults, 2 children
Under £5	114	110		726	409	
£5 –	81	77		227	245	
£6 –	69	68		189	190	
£7·3 –	67	67		178	184	
£8·8 –	57	53		141	129	
£10·7 –	51	46		130	124	
£13 –	43	33		113	97	
£15·7 –	37	27	43	104	91	117
£19 –	26	17	27	89	78	93
£23 –	23	13	25	86	72	89
£28 –	20	10	20	81	69	83
£34 –	16	6	17	78	68	81
£41 –	14	5	15	78	66	81
£49·5	12	3	13	74	66	77
£60 –	8	2	8	70	63	73
All incomes	21	10	18	84	71	83

Source: As for table 4.

Notes: Benefits (in the first three columns) are calculated as percentages of original income *plus* cash benefits. Final net income (in the last three columns), after all deductions and additions in tax and benefits, is calculated as a percentage of original income only. The income ranges shown relate, for *both* sets of columns, to original income only.

Direct benefits include all cash payments (family allowances, pensions, supplementary benefits, etc.) and the estimated value of health, education and welfare food services. Indirect benefits comprise only the estimated value of subsidies to public housing. They exclude, e.g., tax concessions in respect of children and other dependents, mortgage repayments, contributions to private pension schemes, etc. (so that the effective incidence of benefits is understated in the first three columns at higher income levels especially, though the last three columns are not affected).

For other notes, see table 4

Even without allowance for that, the modest nature of the redistribution to which public benefits – but hardly taxes – contribute is evident from the fact that the absolute value of those benefits in 1970 was no higher on average for households with incomes at the level of an unskilled manual worker's earnings than for those in the top income category. When the effects of both taxes and public benefits are taken in conjunction (table 5, last three columns), net gains were confined to households with incomes up to about £16 per week. Net losses above that level, moreover, were not sharply proportionate to income, though the gradient was progressive. The combined effect of taxes and public benefits, in the case of households of all types, was to cut the incomes of households at the average manual worker's level of earnings (about £28 a week) by some 20 per cent, and the incomes of households in the top category (£60 and more a week) by only another 10 per cent more than that. As things are, in fact, the 'welfare state' provides for wage earners to finance the bulk of their own social security. Redistribution between classes is very limited.

IV

There were no signs of a reduction in overall inequality of income during the 1960s, measured after allowance for all taxes and public welfare benefits. If anything inequality widened. (Table 3, p. 46.) It is still possible that redistribution through the activities of the state may have increased during the same period, while the results were insufficient to outweigh a simultaneous acceleration of inequality in original incomes. To some extent, in fact, this seems to have been the case. Table 6 suggests that, for all households taken together regardless of differences in their make-up, the balance of gains and losses through welfare benefits and taxes shifted in the course of the 1960s to favour the poor at the expense of the well-off. The balance moved from 'neutral' to 'net gain' for those with low incomes (the bottom quintile); while the net proportionate loss for the well-to-do (the highest quintile) increased a little.

The result, however, needs to be interpreted with caution. For that overall pattern of change was similarly evident only in the case of two out of the nine separate types of household distinguished in the body of the table: households comprising single persons and two adults on their own. 'Retired' households make up a high proportion of these – and a proportion which evidently increased during the decade, since average money income before tax and benefits actually showed a fall in these two categories between the two samples.[6] The proportion of pensioners in the population had indeed been rising fairly steadily. So, in the course of the 1960s did the proportion of unemployed people. On both scores the consequences, other factors apart, would be to increase the numbers on very low incomes; to reduce the rate of growth in original money incomes at the bottom of the pile to a rate lower than the average; and to produce an actual fall of average original money incomes in those household categories with a high concentration of pensioners. This is just what appears to have happened. At the same time, cash benefits to people at the bottom of the pile – pensions, supplementary benefits, unemployment pay – were raised during the 1960s: in the early period of Labour government especially, and on a scale that exceeded the effective rate of increase in earnings, though part of that advance was eroded over the later years.

These trends – increased state aid at the bottom of the socio-economic scale, during the 1960s, counteracting a growth in poverty measured by original incomes – explain the heightened impact of redistribution on the types of household most affected, those with one and two adults only.[7] Even in their case, however, only the poor in single-person households gained enough on the swings and roundabouts for the final income gap among households of this composition to be narrowed (see table 3). For all other household types (except the small group with four children), the net balance of taxes and benefits shifted in ways that either hit poor and rich more or less equally hard, or – as in the case of households with three adults and one or two children – hit the poor but not the rich.

In general, it is a very striking feature of the figures for 1970, as for 1961, that the combined impact of taxes and state benefits varies little between poor and wealthy households of the same composition. There are marked differences on that score, it is true, in the case of one- and two-adult households: the poor among these (the lowest

6. This increase in the proportion of 'retired' households among those with one and two persons cannot be shown directly from the data which, for 1961, do not distinguish between 'retired' and others.

7. The same trends explain the increased impact on all households taken together (table 6, last line); for, when all are lumped together, one-and-two-person households make up a high proportion of those at and below the bottom quintile.

quintile) clearly gain from the activities of the state, those who are well off lose. But in the case of most other types of household – the great majority of which have one or more children – the ratio of final income to original income is not so very different between poor and wealthy. On the whole, of course, the poor lose rather less from the balance of taxes and state benefits than do the wealthy; or they gain rather more. But these differences in the impact of the 'welfare state' up and down the income scale (evident when one reads the figures of table 6 horizontally across the table) are a good deal smaller than the differences to be seen in the impact of taxes and benefits on households of similar income but different composition (evident when the figures are read vertically). The 'welfare state' does redistribute income. But, as the pattern of the data here confirms, this is redistribution between households at different stages of life far more than it is redistribution between households at markedly different levels of income. It is redistribution within classes far more than it is redistribution between classes.

TABLE 6

Changes in the combined effects of taxes and benefits at low and high income levels, 1961–1970

Households comprising –	Income after all taxes and benefits, direct and indirect, expressed as per cent of original income			
	For bottom (first) quintile		For top (fourth) quintile	
	1961	1970	1961	1970
1 adult only	186	390	80	74
2 adults only	97	170	76	70
2 adults, 1 child	85	79	80	75
2 adults, 2 children	93	87	89	81
2 adults, 3 children	107	102	101	90
2 adults, 4 children	122	126	110	109
3 adults only	88	83	74	69
3 adults, 1 child	92	87	80	80
3 adults, 2 children	103	101	86	87
All households in samples (including those not listed above)	98	128	83	79

Sources: As for table 3. (See footnote 5, p. 44 ; and for explanation of quintiles, footnote 6, p. 46.)

V

It is not yet possible to show, in a similar way, the exact consequences of the series of changes in taxes and benefits introduced by the Conservative government which came into office in 1970. But there is no doubt about their general direction: an accentuation of inequality. There were two main purposes to these policies. The first, as it was presented to the public, was to alleviate poverty while attempting to ensure that funds to that end were concentrated more effectively on the people most in need of them. The second was to increase 'incentives' for the managerial groups especially, and to provide for faster growth of capital. So, in principle, there was to be more help for the poor, though the 'poverty line' was defined in different ways in different policy measures. But above this low threshold, inequality was to have more freedom of rein: a good deal more, in fact.

Among the measures to alleviate poverty were increases in the rates of existing cash benefits; the introduction of a scheme to supplement low family incomes; and a proposal to replace the latter scheme later in the decade by a system of 'tax credits', through which many people with incomes below a certain limit (but not the very poorest) would automatically receive some supplementary payments from the state, without needing to make special application. With the exception of the tax credit scheme, however, the receipt of welfare benefits was made still more dependent on prior application and proof of 'need' than it had been before. Milk, for example, was no longer provided free of charge to children at school, unless hardship could be shown. Rent rebates made available for private as well as public tenants under the Housing Finance Act 1972 were to be given only to tenants who applied and demonstrated their need under the relevant formulae. The result was to guarantee that far fewer people would actually receive these forms of state aid than were entitled to them on paper. For, as we shall show later (see especially Part Three, ch. 3), very high proportions of those who are eligible for means-tested services do not – and often do not even know that they can – apply for them. To require special application and proof of need before state support is given is a device whose effect, in a class-divided society, is to exclude many of the poor from relief. It does not concentrate benefits effectively on those with the greatest claim to them. It does save money – or will do so, unless the administrative costs of public inquisition into private circumstances outweigh the economies achieved because so many eligible people do not apply.

The policies designed to increase managerial incentives and provide for faster growth of private capital indeed required economies in public expenditure, since they involved a wide range of tax concessions and cuts in tax rates, at high levels especially. The withdrawal of certain general services, and their provision instead on a selective basis, made for some such savings. So, not least, did the changes in the form of government support for council housing under the Housing Finance Act 1972. The rents of local authority housing were now universally to be raised to 'fair rent' levels – in effect to levels set by market forces, though with an element of public regulation. General subsidies to local authority housing were withdrawn, and replaced entirely by a centrally fixed scheme providing income-related rent rebates for council tenants – on application only. The extension of the rebate scheme to tenants of private landlords reduced the savings involved. But it was clear that, on balance, state expenditure on housing for rent would be sizeably cut in the long run in consequence of the Act; and market mechanisms would be given much looser rein in this crucial field than before. Government concern to rely more on market forces and private provision, above a threshold of bedrock provision by the state, was reflected again in proposals to introduce a two-tier system of retirement pensions intended to encourage private occupational pension schemes, with the state responsible only for pensions at a minimum level. The effect of this would be to extend and further institutionalize the class divisions in welfare provision to which we have referred earlier.

It was clear already before the Conservative programme was implemented that its consequences would be to widen overall inequality.[8] Its impact cannot be calculated in precise terms for some time. But a

8. C. V. Brown, 'The impact of tax changes on income distribution', *Planning* (PEP), no. 525, Feb. 1971. The conclusion of this attempt to calculate in advance the effect of Conservative proposals for changes in taxes and transfer benefits (which did not, however, take account of suggestions for negative income tax – later 'tax credits' – or other measures specifically directed against poverty) was that overall inequality would widen, and losses be concentrated among ordinary wage earners and lower-paid salary earners. For general analysis of the Conservative government's measures of tax relief and proposals for pensions and tax credits, see J. C. Kincaid, *Poverty and Equality in Britain*, Penguin Books, 1973 (especially pp. 116–18 and pp. 249 ff.). This book is a valuable and hard-hitting examination of the system of taxation and public welfare as a whole.

broad hint of the effects of these policies can be obtained from an estimate that the measures introduced by the end of 1972, together with the tax credit proposals due to come into force later, would be likely to produce net gains on average of over £2,000 per person for the minority of people with incomes of £5,000 or more – but only about £80 per person for those with annual incomes of £1,000 or less.[9] There is considerable room for argument about the assumptions on which estimates of this kind are based: the figures are therefore no more than indicative. But the general nature of the redistribution involved was in no doubt. State provision for those on low incomes might be improved, in relative as well as absolute terms, by the measures introduced in the early 1970s. But inequality would be substantially widened above the 'poverty line', and the range of disparity in incomes as a whole significantly extended. That indeed was the intention of a programme inspired by a concern to allow the 'natural' forces of a capitalist economy more free play.

9. M. Meacher, 'The rich and the poor', *Labour Monthly*, 12 (54), Dec. 1972. See also A. Harrison, 'Where the money's gone', *Poverty*, no. 23, Summer 1972. This set the aggregate net gain by 1972 for the £5,000 a year income group at about £450 million, compared with £500 million as estimated by Meacher. It also pointed to a widening in the gap, from 1969 to 1972, between the real post-tax value of an initial £2,500 a year 'middle class' income and that of public benefit provision.

5 The labour market: occupational earnings

I

Long-run changes in job structure which have been at work in all advanced industrial economies are often assumed to have contributed to a progressive diminution of inequality through a spread of 'middle' and higher salaried incomes. In fact these changes have commonly been exaggerated; and their impact on income distribution has been by no means clear-cut.

Some of these occupational shifts were part of the process of the growth of industrialism, rather than of its subsequent internal transformation. Agriculture and related activities declined as industry expanded; but in Britain, where industrialism set in early, there was little scope for further change on that score in this century. Farmers, farmworkers, fishermen and the like accounted for only $7\frac{1}{2}$ per cent of the labour force already by the end of World War I; for just under 4 per cent by the early 1960s.[1] The main features of the changes in occupational structure in this country during the past half-century and more have, of course, been the growth of non-manual work, and the decline of domestic service and unskilled manual work. But the first of these shifts, to which commentators often assign outstanding social significance, has affected men far less than women. It makes little sense to emphasize the overall increase in non-manual jobs – to a figure approaching half the labour force today, excluding agriculture and the armed forces – when non-

1. See Part Four, chapter 1, for details of the figures on occupational composition in this and the following paragraph. (We have counted all 'personal service' jobs – generally low-paid – as manual.)

manual workers still make up little more than a third of the male labour force, and when the class structure is still shaped by the economic positions of men far more than by those of women. Moreover, many of the new non-manual jobs for which labour had to be recruited during this century have been low-level clerical and sales jobs. Routine white-collar work of this kind accounted for well over one in every three men with non-manual jobs both in 1921 and in the 1960s: and for a far higher, and rising proportion of the women in non-manual jobs. These in effect are wage-earning jobs; and those of male clerks in particular have progressively lost the modest premiums which they once enjoyed in the labour market. (See section II below of this chapter.) Their expansion can certainly not be counted as contributing to a spread of well secured salary incomes.

It is true that the share of unskilled work and casual labour among manual occupations has fallen – from about one in four to one in eight of all manual jobs for men, over the period from World War I to the 1960s, for example. So, of course, has the number of domestic servants. But there are more people employed now in other kinds of personal service work, usually poorly paid; and the number of semi-skilled manual jobs has grown as production processes in manufacture have become more highly mechanized. The share of skilled workers in the male manual labour force did nevertheless show a rise from 1921 to the 1960s, though a fairly modest one – from some 53 per cent to about 60 per cent (and the census classifications on which these figures are based are rather generous in their designation of 'skill'). But the proportion of manual workers classified as skilled dropped drastically over the same period in the case of women – from one-third to no more than a fifth. There is no simple way of characterizing this complex set of changes. But it is plainly false to postulate a major shift towards 'middle' and higher-paid jobs, when the bulk of the labour force are in essentially wage-earning jobs, however those jobs are conventionally designated; and when many white-collar employees are now merely semi-skilled operatives in the world of office work.

II

With one or two significant exceptions, moreover, the broad pattern of inequalities in earnings between different occupational groups has remained remarkably constant over long periods. Table 7 summarizes data from the only study to have attempted a comprehensive series of estimates of occupational pay in Britain from just before World War I to well after World War II. Scattered and uneven in quality though the original sources are, the results can be taken to give a reasonably accurate picture of overall trends, so far as men are concerned. The position of women in the labour market is left, in the main, for discussion in the next chapter.

TABLE 7

Changes in relative earnings of main occupational groups, 1913/14–1960:
male earners only

Occupational group (men only)	Indices of earnings – occupational group average expressed as a percentage of average for all men in the same period				
	1913/14	1922/24	1935/36	1955/56	1960
Higher professions	357	326	341	244	253
Managers and administrators	217	269	237	234	230
Lower professions	169	179	165	97	105
Foremen	123	150	147	124	126
Clerks	108	102	103	82	85
Skilled manual workers	108	101	105	98	99
Semi-skilled manual workers	75	70	72	74	72
Unskilled manual workers	69	72	70	69	67
All non-manual workers	142	158	152	144	145
All manual workers	88	83	85	83	82
All men	100	100	100	100	100

Source: G. Routh, Occupation and Pay in Great Britain 1906–60 (Cambridge Univ. Press, 1965): summary data, p. 107, recalculated to provide indice sfor men only; with additional computations in respect of figures for all non-manual and all manual workers.

There was some compression of the range of earnings from professionals at the top to unskilled workers at the bottom, over the five decades taken as a whole. But the shift in that respect was confined to the exceptional time around World War II, from 1935/36 to 1955/56. And the results again are consistent with other evidence in showing some widening of differentials thereafter, though the last period covered by these figures – the late 1950s – is only short. Despite the long-term compression of the range from top to bottom, moreover, average earnings in the higher professions (with those of the very heterogeneous category of managers and administrators only a little way below) exceeded average unskilled earnings by a factor of about four in 1960. The relative gap between the non-manual and the manual groups, taken crudely as aggregates, was then if anything rather wider than it had been half a century earlier. And the rank order of the various occupational categories was much the same as before.

There had, however, been two striking changes. First, the 'lower professions' – a mixed bag including school teachers, vets, librarians, but also draughtsmen and laboratory assistants – had dropped to a point on the earnings scale only a little way above the arithmetic average, the level of skilled manual workers. The second change is one which we have already referred to in general terms. In a less precipitate but socially no less significant fall, clerks had dropped from a position of parity with skilled manual workers to a point well below the overall average, midway between the skilled and the semi-skilled. Indeed, although later data are not directly comparable with those up to 1960, the decline in relative earnings of clerical workers may have been resumed in recent years. To go by the information and definitions of some new large-scale official sample surveys, male clerks on average by 1971 had earnings now lower than those of semi skilled manual workers in a wide range of industries. (See table 8 below.[2])

The particular changes in the position of these white-collar groups may well have helped to foster a notion that a general long-term trend towards equalization has been at work across the board; and that manual workers in the process have enjoyed a significant advance of their position in the overall hierarchy of earnings. In fact there has been no such general trend. And manual workers, as is clear from table 7, have not ascended the earnings scale relative to the average. If anything they have come down it a step or two. What has happened, by contrast, is something more like a 'proletarianization' of large sections of the petty bourgeoisie. The position especially of low-grade office and sales employees as workers who live by the sale of their labour power has been accentuated – whether or not they

2. Data from official series (*Department of Employment/Ministry of Labour Gazette*) reinforce this conclusion. Average earnings for different categories of male employees rose as follows from 1960 to 1970:
    Clerical and related workers in public sector work, insurance and
      banking – by 72 per cent.
    All administrative, technical and clerical staff in the same indus-
      tries – by 89 per cent.
    Manual workers in manufacturing – by 91 per cent.

themselves recognize this – by their loss of the wage advantage from which they previously benefited by comparison with non-skilled manual labour. In terms of earnings, the gap has opened up wide between 'small' white-collar workers and the managers, administrators and 'established' professionals at the top of the tree – whose recorded earnings understate their total incomes, and whose at least partial control over their own terms and conditions of work puts them outside the market in which rank-and-file earners sell their labour. There is no refutation of capitalism involved in these changes, but a confirmation of its divisions.

TABLE 8

Earnings of male clerks in relation to manual workers' earnings,
1913/14 – 1960 and 1971

Occupational group (men only)	Indices of earnings – occupational group average expressed as a percentage of average for all male manual workers in the same period					
	1913/14	1922/24	1935/36	1955/56	1960	1971*
Clerks	122	122	122	99	102	96
Skilled manual workers	122	121	124	118	119	(106)
Semi-skilled manual workers	85	85	83	89	87	(99)
Unskilled manual workers	78	86	82	83	80	(87)
All manual workers	100	100	100	100	100	100

Sources: G. Routh, op. cit. (see table 7 above) for 1913/14 to 1960.
　　Dept. of Employment Gazette, December 1971 (pp. 1141–42) for 1971: data from New Earnings Survey of April 1971, with additional computations in respect of average earnings of clerks.
* Note: No direct comparison can be made between the 1971 figures and the earlier ones, for reasons relating to definitions of categories and coverage of the data.

III

It has been part of the postulate of progressive equalization that the earnings of occupational groups previously quite distinct now overlap to a large extent. The data just presented show no general movement in that direction: only the specific trend of petty bourgeois proletarianization, with quite different implications. But those data relate to average earnings. A fuller examination of the argument requires information about the range of earnings within different occupations; and about variations in earnings by age and stage of life. Reasonably comprehensive data of that sort have become available only very recently. Since 1968, a continuing series of official nationwide surveys has been instituted, using samples large enough (an effective total of 170,000 employees in 1971, for example) for the relevant kind of information to be provided for occupations distinguished in considerable detail. Table 9 summarizes some of the results of the 1971 survey for an illustrative selection of male occupations.

There is more disparity in earnings than is visible from these data, which have to be read with certain points about their nature in mind. The figures relate to gross pre-tax earnings of employees in their sole or main jobs. Any earnings from subsidiary work are excluded. Overtime pay, regular bonuses and commissions, and payments in kind when these are made by statutory regulation, are taken into account. But other 'fringe benefits' are omitted, as are irregular payments received outside the week or month of pay covered by the survey. The ranges of earnings are therefore understated; and more so at the top of the socio-economic scale than at the bottom, since sizeable fringe benefits are a common feature of the pay of business executives especially. The figures for professional occupations need also to be taken with a large pinch of salt – because they relate only to salaried employees, not to fee-paid professionals who are their own employers; and because even salaried professionals may often have significant additional earnings from fees, which are ignored here. Finally, the categorization of occupations is necessarily so summary that, on this score too, the full range of inequality finds inadequate expression. 'Company chairmen and directors' and 'general and divisional managers', for example, are very heterogeneous groups. The overall data for them here give no hint of the magnitude of pre-tax earnings among the minority of top businessmen, as shown by other information. From an official report for 1968, the gross pay of the average 'main board member' in private sector companies with net assets of £11 million or more ranged, already in that year, from over £12,000 per annum in the smallest-size category of these companies to nearly £19,000 in the largest; that of the 'highest-paid executive' within each similarly from almost £17,000 to £32,000.[3]

3. National Board for Prices and Incomes, *Top Salaries in the Private Sector and Nationalized Industries*, Cmnd. 3970, 1969 (p. 51).

TABLE 9

Gross weekly earnings of adult full-time male employees in selected occupations, 1971

Occupational groups (male full-time employees only, pay not affected by absence)	Median gross weekly earnings (£)	Percentages (cumulative) of employees in each occupational group having gross weekly earnings of:						
		Under £20	Under £25	£35 and more	£40 and more	£50 and more	£60 and more	£70 and more
Managers – general and divisional	69·6	—	2	92	88	75	63	50
Company chairmen and directors	66·5	3	5	85	79	64	55	43
Medical and dental practitioners	58·4	—	—	91	82	62	48	40
University academic staff	57·7	2	2	88	80	66	47	29
Managers – marketing, advert., sales	52·7	—	2	83	75	56	35	21
Managers – personnel and training	47·1	1	1	81	68	40	25	17
Architects and planners*	47·2	2	3	81	69	44	24	11
Solicitors*	46·2	15	22	58	54	44	29	12
Teachers in further education	44·8	1	3	84	67	33	10	2
Accountants*	43·4	9	16	65	56	35	21	12
Managers – works and production	42·8	1	4	74	57	33	18	9
Engineers, scientists, technologists	41·4	1	5	71	54	28	13	6
Managers – office	40·9	2	9	65	51	32	17	9
Foremen – senior, higher level	38·1	—	3	65	41	9	2	1
School teachers	37·1	4	14	59	34	11	3	1
Office supervisors	35·1	2	10	51	23	7	2	1
Foremen and supervisors – other	33·5	2	11	43	24	7	2	1
Technicians, including draughtsmen	33·2	4	15	42	24	7	2	1
Sales supervisors	32·4	6	18	41	25	8	3	1
Clerks – senior grade	32·1	3	17	38	23	8	2	1
Sales representatives, travellers	31·4	9	25	37	24	10	4	2
Welfare workers	30·3	9	23	33	18	5	—	—
Manual workers – skilled**	29·8	6	25	28	15	4	1	—
Manual workers – semi-skilled**	27·7	12	36	20	10	2	—	—
Clerks – intermediate grade	25·0	16	50	10	4	1	—	—
Manual workers – unskilled**	24·3	25	54	12	5	1	—	—
Clerks – routine and junior	21·4	39	73	4	1	—	—	—
Catering, domestic, service workers†	21·1	44	68	7	4	1	—	—
Shop salesmen and – assistants	20·4	47	81	2	1	—	—	—
Agricultural and related workers†	19·9	51	81	2	1	—	—	—

Source: Department of Employment Gazette, December 1971 (pp. 1150/52, 1157/59): data from New Survey of Earnings, April 1971. (This table does not list all occupations shown in the source, but an illustrative selection from all parts of the range.)

Even those figures, moreover, were averages. They took no account of additional earnings from subsidiary directorships, consultancy and the like or, of course, of income direct from property. And they must have risen considerably between then and 1971, the year to which the data in table 9 relate.

Even as the figures of the table stand, they show some fairly clear breaks in the hierarchy of occupational earnings. The broad mass of manual workers of all skills and none, of service workers, shop assistants and clerks below the senior grade, stand out at the lower end of the scale. Very few of these men earned as much as £40 a week in 1971, despite common assumptions to the contrary – even among the skilled only 15 per cent. Proportions ranging from about three in every four to nearly all had less than £35 a week before deductions. Large numbers were on very low pay, but with marked variations between groups – from 6 per cent in some occupations to 40 or 50 per cent in others falling under the £20 a week line, for example.

Earnings as low as that were rare in the next main block up the scale – foremen, supervisors, technicians, senior clerks, as well as school teachers; with another 'semi-professional' group, welfare workers, on the lower borderline of that block together with sales representatives. Here, generally, between two and three in every five men earned at least £35 a week; from a quarter to over a third, £40 a week or more; but only small proportions reached the £50 mark.

All these were still below what appears as a major line of division in the hierarchy. Above that line were managers of all levels, directors and professional employees. There was a wide range of variation within this group: some managers and technical personnel belonged only marginally to it. But never fewer than half – generally between two-thirds and four-fifths or more – earned £40 a week at least; from one to over two in every three, more than £50 a week. The fact that the proportions were not still higher reflects among other things an averaging out, in these aggregate data, of earnings for men at quite different stages of their careers. Managerial and professional salaries rise substantially in the course of the normal career: typical

---

Notes: — = less than one half per cent.
* Figures for employees in professions where considerable numbers of members are fee-paid, and thus excluded, are shown in italics.
** Figures for the different grades of manual skill relate to workers in a wide range of selected industries and trades, but exclude some manual workers.
† Earnings include allowance for value of payments in kind made under statutory regulation.
For other notes see text.

earnings in middle-age and later are well above the figures shown here.

Clearly, there are overlaps between these major groups – of a kind. The fact that both routine and intermediate-grade clerks, as well as shop assistants, are now among the lowest-paid men highlights doubts about the contemporary relevance of the conventional distinction between 'manual' and 'non-manual'. And it adds fuel to the fire of old questions about the response, or lack of response, of white-collar workers to their class situation. But it needs to be stressed again that these are old questions. They do not arise from, or point to, any process of embourgeoisement of manual workers, whose earnings have remained constant relative to the average. They arise from the reinforcement over time of the long-standing 'proletarian' – *de facto* wage-earning and dependent – position of large sections of the petty salariat in the market. The same questions are also relevant in the case of the intermediate block of supervisors, technicians and some low-paid professionals further up the scale. These do, however, enjoy a premium in the market by comparison with ordinary wage earners. And their position with respect to features other than crude earnings – their share in authority and fringe benefits, for example, and the pattern of their careers – distinguishes them from manual and clerical workers, and helps to tie many of them more to the minority above them than to the majority below them.

Yet there is no support in these figures for a notion that earnings now overlap significantly right across the occupational scale. There is little even ostensible overlap of earnings between the broad mass of manual, lower clerical, sales and service workers – bunched overwhelmingly in aggregate under the £35 a week line in 1971, and ranging far down into the region of subsistence wages – and the managers, executives and established professionals who are concentrated on the other side of that line and stretch well above it. Even such overlap as there is at the margins between these two blocks is not only overstated, by omissions from the data of the kinds mentioned earlier. It is also largely confined to one stage of life.

The last point is plain from the chart (on p. 81) and from table 10. (Both use the same information – data from 1970, because the 1971 survey on which table 9 was based did not provide information in the relevant form. But the chart shows median earnings at different ages in money terms, whereas these are converted in table 10 to percentages of the median earnings for each occupation at ages 21–24.)

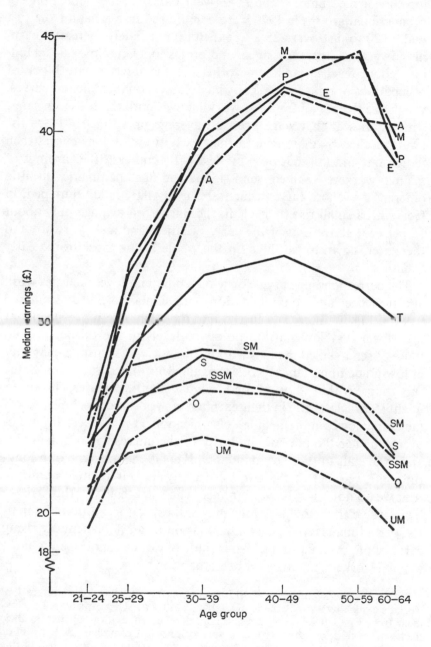

For key, see table 10, page 84

Most men earn much the same early in working life, whatever their jobs: median earnings of the 21–24-year-olds over the whole range of occupational groups in 1970 were compressed into a band from just under £20 to just over £25 a week. But immediately thereafter earnings diverge sharply. Managers and professional employees – including school teachers and some others in the intermediate block of occupations of table 9 – typically have careers on incremental curves, which rise steeply during their working lives until the forties or later, with salaries at that stage even on average up to nearly twice the levels reached by these men in their early twenties. The curves then flatten out and fall, but only modestly. By contrast, the earnings of manual workers – skilled, semi-skilled and unskilled men with little difference – follow curves which are nearly flat: mildly humped, in fact, with a small rise to levels in the thirties on average only about 15 per cent above that of the early twenties; and a slow, steady fall thereafter, down to earnings on the whole below those of the early twenties.

The corresponding curves for white-collar employees in sales work and in 'offices and communications' are similar to those of manual workers. They differ only in the fact that they rise more steeply at first, from very low starting points to levels in the thirties around those of semi-skilled manual workers. So the wage-earning character of low-grade non-manual work is again clear in general terms. Some subgroups within those broad white-collar categories, however, might show a later rise in their earnings curves – as do technicians – if the data allowed more detailed classification. It is not certain, moreover, whether the present similarity of the curves for routine office and sales staff to those of manual workers is the outcome of a long-run shift, parallel to the overall decline in their relative earnings. And we do not know how often men who start their working lives in low-grade clerical and sale jobs may still expect promotion to supervisory and managerial posts, and thus on to an incrementally rising curve of life-cycle earnings.[4] That route of escape is not open to most manual workers, and has not been for a long time.

4. Calculations from unpublished information for 'office and communication' workers (which was kindly made available to us by the Department of Employment from its 1970 survey) suggest a considerable net outflow of men in their thirties from clerical into other jobs involving a net loss of perhaps 30 per cent or more of clerks in that age group. There is no means of saying how much of this may result from promotion. There also appears to be a net inflow (proportionately perhaps on a similar scale) into clerical work at higher ages – of men in their

It is, in short, not clear exactly how far the process of 'market proletarianization' experienced by the petty salariat over time has gone. But there is no doubt about the sharp contrast, in the pattern of income over the typical life cycle, as well as in overall earnings, between manual workers on the one hand and managers, executives and professionals on the other. This contrast, which is reinforced by other features of their respective 'market situations', is a crucial one. And it almost certainly plays a large part in differences of approach to the management of everyday life, and of responses to the social order, between the classes.

IV

The contrast in career prospects, moreover, is only one of a series of class differences in the terms of employment which add to those shown by data on gross cash earnings.

Non-manual workers work fairly short hours. This goes for all or most of them – including clerical employees, whose low earnings in the routine grades are associated with relatively short hours of work, and therefore with a considerably smaller handicap in respect of hourly rates of pay than in respect of gross earnings. By contrast, manual workers work long hours. Their average working week in 1971 ran to about 45 hours – only a small reduction from the post-war

fifties. (These could be people finding, or pushed into, clerical jobs as a preliminary to retirement: the ratio of routine to all clerical jobs rises in this age group.) Our calculations are based on the differences between the actual age composition of the male clerical labour force, and that to be expected on some rough assumptions about past patterns of recruitment if undisturbed by in-and-out movements in the course of working life. They are too uncertain to do more than suggest possibilities. In general, of course, the patterns of life-cycle earnings shown in the chart and table 10 take no account of occupational mobility – of promotion and demotion from one 'curve' to another in the course of working life: a subject discussed in Part Four. They also give only a snapshot picture of age differences in earnings at one moment of time – not a moving picture of changes in the earnings of individuals followed up over time; nor do they therefore take account of general increases in earnings and levels of living through increasing production. An earlier study of 'The life cycle in income, saving and asset ownership' (H. Lydall, *Econometrica*, April 1955) also used snapshot data from a national survey, but did not distinguish clerical workers as a separate group. Class differences in life-cycle earnings, of course, contribute substantially to the fact that overall inequality of income rises steeply from younger to older age groups. (See, e.g., A. R. Prest and T. Stark, 'Some aspects of income distribution in the UK since World War II', *Manchester School*, September 1967.)

TABLE 10

Variations in median gross earnings by age, for full-time men in selected occupations, 1970

Age group	Median earnings at each age expressed as per cent of median earnings in the same occupational group at age 21–24											
	M	E	A	P	T	O	S	SM	SSM	UM	All non-manual*	All manual*
18–20	—	56	—	52	60	70	66	63	72	85	63	70
21–24	100	100	100	100	100	100	100	100	100	100	100	100
25–29	128	132	130	145	122	123	124	110	110	108	130	110
30–39	166	157	179	175	140	138	139	114	114	113	157	116
40–49	180	171	188	144	137	135	113	112	110	163	114	
50–59	180	165	193	194	136	125	127	105	105	101	155	105
60–64	162	155	192	171	130	114	114	98	97	92	132	95
All ages	166	146	176	155	123	119	119	104	104	101	133	105

Source: Department of Employment Gazette, January 1971 (pp. 51–55): data from New Earnings Survey of April 1970.
Notes: — = insufficient cases for separate presentation.
* For lack of space, data are shown only for selected main occupational groups. The totals for non-manual employees include groups M to S and other non-manual workers not listed here; those for manual employees, groups SM, SSM and UM and other manual employees not listed here.

Occupational groups
M = managers
E = prof. engineers, scientists and technologists
A = academic staff and teachers (especially school teachers)
P = other professional and technical
T = technicians
O = office and communications workers
S = sales workers
SM = skilled
SSM = semi-skilled
UM = unskilled
manual workers in a wide range of selected industries and trades

peak of around 47 hours in the late 1940s, or from the slightly lower average of the late 1930s.[5] Even that reduction may well in part reflect the trend of economic recession in the 1960s. The notion that ordinary workers have much more leisure time at their everyday disposal than before the war is a gross misconception. It may in part derive from the fact that the 'standard working week', over and above which manual work is paid at overtime rates, has been substantially reduced by collective bargaining. The actual working week has been cut only minimally. Over one in every five manual workers in full-time work in 1971 worked more than 50 hours a week; the same was true of only three in every hundred non-manual workers. (See table 11.)

Working long hours is in fact almost the only way in which

5. Department of Employment Gazette, November 1972 (pp. 1069, 1071); G. S. Bain et al., 'The labour force', in A. H. Halsey, ed., Trends in British Society since 1900, Macmillan, St. Martin's Press, 1972 (p. 120).

manual workers – and then still only a minority – can reach the high earnings which they are so often wrongly assumed to get as a matter of common experience. No more than 11 per cent of all full-time manual workers earned £40 or over before deductions in 1971. Of these seven in every ten worked more than 45 hours a week; over half, more than 50 hours. Far more non-manual workers had earnings at least of that level. Very few worked comparable hours in the process. By and large, above the conventional line of division between manual and non-manual – the real line of division can be seen from other information to fall somewhat higher up the scale – earnings vary very little with the actual hours of work. Below the line they do – in both directions. Long hours give a bonus; short hours – whether preferred by the worker or forced on him – a penalty in loss of wages.

TABLE 11

Hours worked by full-time manual and non-manual workers, 1971: all men and women, and those earning £40 and more (men) or £20 and more (women)

	FULL-TIME MEN				FULL-TIME WOMEN			
	All Men		Men Earning £40 and More		All Women		Women Earning £20 and More	
	Manual	Non-manual	Manual	Non-manual	Manual	Non-manual	Manual	Non-manual
% of men with £40 and more: % of women with £20 and more:	11	34	(100)	(100)	11	37	(100)	(100)
% working following hours per week:								
Up to 35 hours	5	15	} 19	} 84	23	26	4	34
Over 35, up to 40 hours	35	63			58	58	51	50
Over 40, up to 45 hours	20	13	11	7	13	15	20	14
Over 45, up to 50 hours	19	5	17	4	4	1	} 25	} 2
Over 50, up to 60 hours	16	3	30	3	2	—		
Over 60 hours	5	1	23	2	—	—		

Source: Department of Employment Gazette, January 1972 (pp. 43–46): data from New Earnings Survey, April 1971.

Fines for loss of working time, though not formally so described, are in fact still among the normal contingencies of life for manual workers. In 1970, for example, one in every six men and one in every four women, among manual workers in full-time employment, lost pay for working fewer than the basic hours set during the week or fortnight covered by the official survey.[6] The main reasons were sickness; late arrival or early finish; and voluntary absence, whether approved or not. Direct and indirect involvement in industrial disputes accounted for little of the total. Employers may regard deductions of that kind as reasonable forfeits, and necessary for 'discipline', although loss of pay for sickness could be so described only if sickness were equated with shirking. But non-manual workers, paid typically on a more regular basis, are not usually subject to similar penalties. During the same period less than 3 per cent of the men among them, and 5 per cent of the women, lost pay in comparable ways. The proportions were little higher in the case of the poorly paid routine-grade white-collar groups included in the totals. On that score as on some others, even low-level office and sales work still offers at least marginal advantages.

Paid holidays of at least two weeks a year are now universal for manual workers whose terms of employment are union-negotiated or regulated by statutory order. Roughly one in every two has a basic entitlement of more than two weeks, if usually only by a few extra days. Before World War II, by contrast, over half the manual and low-paid white-collar labour force were estimated to have no regular provision at all for annual consecutive holidays with pay.[7] So there has been a genuine creation of leisure on this score. But holiday provision is still marked by sharp class differences even in terms of formal entitlement, let alone if one asks who can afford to take the full holidays for which they are given time. In 1970 the proportion of men entitled to at least sixteen working days off on pay – over three weeks a year, taking week-ends into account – ranged from around two in every three for most grades of managers to less than one in four, one in eight and one in ten, respectively, among skilled, semi-skilled and unskilled manual workers. Clerks were generally in or near the 'managerial region' by this measure, though without the very long holidays enjoyed by some managers. Shop assistants were in much the same position as skilled manual workers.[8]

6. *DE Gazette*, February 1971 (pp. 133, 141 ff.: New Earnings Survey of April 1970). On this and a number of other class differences in conditions of employment discussed in the following paragraphs see also the publications by Dorothy Wedderburn referred to in note 18 below.
7. Department of Employment, *British Labour Statistics*, HMSO, 1971 (p. 91).
8. *DE Gazette*, loc. cit., see pp. 134, 147 ff. See note 6 above.

V

A catalogue of broad class differences in conditions of employment soon becomes tedious, because the patterns repeat themselves with only small variations. But it needs nevertheless to be extended to one other and critical field: that of welfare benefits paid under private arrangements by employers. Fringe benefits generally increase sharply with employment status and income. One estimate for the mid-1960s showed the tax-free advantages obtained by company executives rising steadily up the scale, from an effective addition of 11 per cent to junior salaries at the £1,000-a-year mark, to one of 31 per cent – nearly a third extra – for executives with salaries of £7,000 and more.[9] This estimate included some allowance for expense account living, such as the use of company cars. But the major ingredient in fringe benefits that are more commonly available is entitlement to welfare payments under employers' schemes – sick pay, superannuation and life insurance in particular. It is here that the class-tied character of the dual system of welfare – public, and employer-run but state-aided – shows itself transparently. Access and benefits under employers' schemes show marked occupational contrasts, especially across the conventional non-manual/manual dividing line. In addition, women face discrimination under these schemes, as in so many other respects. And employees of public authorities are more likely to have some coverage than those working for private employers.

In 1970, over 90 per cent of adult male non-manual employees in full-time work were covered by employers' sick pay schemes. There were only small variations in this ratio between one level and another of office staff, even down to the lowest-paid white-collar groups. But the proportion covered was around an average of no more than 65 per cent among male manual workers, with some differences by occupation and industry. Membership of occupational pension schemes at the same time ranged from an overall enrolment of just about four in every five non-manual workers – with near-universal coverage in some professions and government service, though rather less than two-thirds coverage for sales staff – to an average of only about 50 per cent among manual workers as a whole, with enrolment of around

9. A. J. Merrett and D. A. G. Monk, *Inflation, Taxation and Executive Remuneration*, Hallam Press, 1967 (pp. 46, 47).

a third or less in the case of unskilled, personal service and agricultural workers.

Coverage on both scores, and especially in respect of pensions, was poorer for women in full-time employment. This is to be expected in a society where women suffer from a whole range of handicaps. What needs to be noted especially is the class gradation in the pattern of sex discrimination involved. The exclusion of women from sick pay and pension schemes provided by employers is far more marked in the lower than the higher reaches of the occupational hierarchy.[10] Class and sex differentials reinforce each other here. So they do in several other respects, as we shall show in the next chapter. It is working-class women who have to face sex discrimination in the labour market in its sharpest form.

Enrolment in employer-provided occupational pension schemes grew substantially from the 1950s to the late 1960s, though at a declining rate. It then showed signs of falling off – from an estimated coverage of 51 per cent of the employed labour force in 1967 to one of 49 per cent by 1971. The effect of this levelling out and subsequent slight fall in the trend was to accentuate class divisions in provision. Enrolment of non-manual employees remained roughly constant from 1967 to 1971. That of manual workers fell, to widen the gap. (See table 12.) A similar process of increasing class bifurcation seems to have been at work already earlier in the 1960s, in respect of private welfare payments of all kinds with superannuation and pension schemes as their main component. It follows from what we have already said that employers spend far more for these purposes on the average member of their administrative, technical and clerical staff than on the average operative in their manual labour force. The ratio of expenditure between the two categories of employees in fact rose still further, to the advantage of 'staff', between 1964 and 1968 in manufacturing and in some other industries. By 1968, employers in manufacturing were spending well over five times as much in payments of this sort, per head, on their non-manual as on their manual employees. The corresponding ratios were no less than eight to one in construction, five or six to one in government service, mining and insurance and banking, though only three to one in public utilities.[11]

10. *DE Gazette*, loc. cit., pp. 155–6, see note 6 above.
11. Calculated from data of surveys by Department of Employment, *Labour Costs in Britain in 1964* and . . . *in 1968*. See also, for 1968, *DE Gazette*, January 1971 (pp. 13–17).

TABLE 12

Estimated coverage or occupational pension schemes in firms and organizations with such schemes, 1967 and 1971

Per cent of employees (in firms and organizations with schemes) who were members of schemes		1967			1971		
		Private firms	Public sector	Total	Private firms	Public sector	Total
Non manual	Men	75	90	78	75	94	81
	Women	40	70	51	36	60	45
	All	62	80	68	60	78	66
Manual	Men	60	65	61	45	68	51
	Women	15	15	15	19	25	20
	All	44	51	46	37	61	42
All employees		51	65	56	47	71	53

Sources: Calculated from data in the Government Actuary's surveys of *Occupational Pension Schemes, 1967* (pp. 7–9) and *1971* (pp. 6–8). Percentages are in the main only approximate since, except for certain categories in 1967, the raw data are in the form of figures rounded to the nearest 100,000.

Note: Only firms and organizations with schemes are included – estimated to comprise about 92 per cent of all employees in the UK in both years. It is not possible to revise the estimates in the table to allow for the omitted 8 per cent, and these will have been largely employees of small private firms.

Inequalities of that magnitude cannot, of course be explained only by the fact that access to membership of fringe benefit schemes is unequal. It is not just that manual workers are far less often covered by employers' welfare schemes than are non-manual workers – commonly for no other reason than that their jobs are classified as ineligible, or because they have been in their jobs for too short a time to qualify. It is also that, when they are admitted to schemes of this kind, they join on terms which are usually much less favourable than those for non-manual workers. The point is plain, in summary form, from the following estimates of manufacturing employers' annual expenditure on superannuation and pension provision for their employees in 1968.[12]

12. Estimate from application to 1968 survey data (note 11 above) of percentage

	(1) Operatives	(2) Admin. tech., cleri- cal staff	(2) as cent per of (1)
Per cent of employees covered	37%	56%	151
Average expenditure per employee:			
Overall (incl. those not covered)	£14·4	£79·1	549
For those covered, only	£43·6	£141·3	324

In other words, employers paid into their pension funds more than three times as much money on behalf of each staff member of the funds as they did on behalf of each manual worker who was also a member. The advantage which non-manual employees enjoyed in this respect over manual workers – even when the comparison excludes those, mainly manual workers, who were not enrolled at all – shows a sharp contrast in the terms on which staff and operatives eligible for membership were admitted to these schemes. Taken proportionately, the gap in this respect between the two broad categories of employees was very much larger than the gap in cash earnings between staff and workers. For non-manual employees as a whole – a very mixed group – got on average only some 20–35 per cent more cash than manual workers (according to whether one looks at the earnings of all or only those of men). But they got well over 300 per cent more money per head paid into 'private' pension funds on their behalf. Welfare provision from employers – aided by the state – does more than just complement class divisions in cash earnings. It accentuates them.

Some of the ways in which this happens are evident from the official survey of occupational pension schemes carried out in 1971.[13] The report on that drew a line between 'staff schemes' (those either confined to non-manual employees or admitting both categories) and 'manual schemes' (comprising only manual workers). Rather more

---

coverage for full-time manual and non-manual workers in manufacturing in 1970 (*DE Gazette*, August 1971), with adjustment from 'all industries' figures to include part-time employees. (Coverage probably did not change sufficiently from 1968 to 1970 to affect the estimate sizeably.)

13. Government Actuary, *Occupational Pension Schemes 1971*, HMSO, 1972 (especially pp. 5–6, 27–44, 47–9).

than half of all manual worker members were enrolled in one of the latter kind. These are schemes which usually provide only flat rate benefits and do not, like most staff schemes, relate pensions to terminal earnings. When they do so, they generally pay out smaller fractions of terminal earnings than staff schemes; and far more rarely than the latter do they allow at least part of the pension to be commuted to a lump sum. They commonly make no, or only relatively poor, provision for early retirement on grounds of ill health. They are a good deal less likely than staff schemes to make pensions available for widows of men who retire before their death; and to provide for augmentation to meet at least part of those increases in costs of living that occur after retirement. Moreover, they allow refund of contributions for those changing jobs on less generous terms than staff schemes. This is only a summary list. And it does not show how far, in addition, manual workers enjoying membership of 'staff schemes' are bunched into the schemes with the least favourable terms of their species, as seems likely. The pattern of institutionally established class differences is still clear enough.

Over and above this, there is considerable doubt about the effectiveness with which most schemes – staff or manual – will in practice provide pensions of any substance for the majority of their members. Only an insignificant proportion of those members who change jobs – about 8 per cent of them in 1971, and also earlier, as shown by an inquiry in 1966[14] – carry their accrued pension rights with them, in full or part, for transfer to another scheme. The effect of this over time must be to concentrate the eventual benefits from accumulated private, tax-concession subsidized pension funds disproportionately on a fairly small fraction of all those who were once members. They will go to those most favourably placed to transfer rights from one job to another, and to those who have stayed longest in the jobs from which they eventually retire.[15] These are people in executive and professional jobs, rather than ordinary workers. So the outcome must be to reduce effective overall coverage to levels well below those

14. Ministry of Labour, National Joint Advisory Council, *Preservation of Pension Rights*, H.M.S.O., 1966 (pp. 19, 20).

15. We are grateful to our colleague, Michael Reddin, for drawing our attention to these points. As implied in the next comment in the text, job turnover rates are fairly high overall (over two in every five employees changed employer at least once over the ten years 1953–63); and they rise down the occupational scale. (A. Harris and R. Clausen, *Labour Mobility in Great Britain 1953–63*. Government Social Survey, 1966.)

indicated in survey data reporting current enrolment; and to do so still more in the lower than the upper reaches of the socio-economic scale. Real provision will prove much less than it seems, its associated class inequalities in relative terms still sharper than appears already.

VI

So practically every step in a documentation of the divisions in the labour market shows up merely another aspect of the same overall pattern. There is much complexity of detail. But now, as in the past, two major lines of cleavage stand out.

One line separates a small group of directors, managers, established professionals and high officials – perhaps 5 to at most 10 per cent of the working population, even on a generous definition – from the rest. Nominally now in the main salary earners, their position is ill-described by the term. They are not dependent on the markets in which they sell their labour in anything like the way that other earners are. The top business executives among them are able to set their own pay, in effect, within broad limits. Members of the established professions – especially those in the senior ranks – have a share through their organizations in shaping the conditions of their own labour markets: in control over entry, as well as in considerable influence over the nature of their work and the demand for their services. Doctors, for example, are in a powerful position to set the standards of medical care; and to block potential competition from less qualified people in auxiliary medical jobs who might otherwise take over part of their work. There is no parallel here even with the numerically atypical cases in which manual workers have been able to establish fairly tight control over entry to their jobs. Dockers, for instance, have not in recent years been able to prevent the erosion of their quasi-monopoly by container firms employing much cheaper labour outside the dock areas; typographers have resisted, but cannot in the end prevent, the use of new printing techniques which cut the demand for their labour.

Nor is this all. Just because high executives and professionals are at the top of the economic hierarchy, they are also close – in ways to be discussed later – to those who administer state power. They are tied by a variety of bonds of affinity to – indeed they include – ministers, senior civil servants and members of policy advisory bodies. They can count on official sympathy and support for their interests. They are thus helped to maintain professional monopolies. They are in a good position to ride lightly through the restraints of government 'incomes policies' – as the doctors did in a spectacular way in 1970. Incomes policies do not in any case apply effectively to salaries and fees that are negotiated individually; and the regular annual increments characteristic of salaries at this level, and in 'middle class' jobs lower down the scale, are exempt from control. Businessmen and professionals at the top of the tree, moreover, have the resources, advice and contacts needed to make full use of tax loopholes and the concessions available from the state in support of 'private welfare'. All of this happens as a matter largely of routine, without special pressures or conspiracies, because the privileges of the privileged are taken for granted in the ordinary run of affairs. Above all – as we shall show in chapter 7 – individual ownership of capital is firmly concentrated in this small cluster at the top, especially among the controllers of private business. Their property holdings are a major source of income and security, as well as of power.

At the other end of the scale is the broad mass of ordinary earners – those who are entirely dependent on the sale of their labour, in a market in which the only power they can exercise is the essentially defensive one associated with collective organization in unions and on the shop floor. They comprise some three-quarters or more of the working population. But the line that divides them from the intermediate group above them is blurred, and has been shifting. There are fairly marked differences in market position between subgroups of rank-and-file labour: differences, within the wage-earning class, between various grades of skill; between those in expanding and those in contracting industries; between small sections which may be able, at least for a time, to establish union closure in a little corner of the labour market, and the rest; between manual and low-grade office and sales workers; between men and women. Such differentiation is in the main an inevitable accompaniment of the common dependence of these people on the sale of their labour in the market – or in what, in effect, is a series of different markets, only partly overlapping. It is also a familiar source of weakness in collective organization. For it produces a duality of interests: contradictions between the interests that may divide workers from each other, and those that unite them across the network of fissures in the wage-earning market. As major inequality breeds minor inequalities, so the critical cleavage of interest associated with the former can be obscured by subsidiary clashes of interest associated with the latter.

Yet from a distance, certainly, it is the common features in the situation of ordinary earners that stand out. Those common features embrace far more than the range of earnings within which they have to live. An element of insecurity and unpredictability is still an inherent component of their lives. The manifestations of that include, of course, the risk of unemployment. Unemployment has been a good deal lower since than before World War II. But the rate rose from the 1960s to a recorded, and understated, figure of over $3\frac{1}{2}$ per cent for the labour force as a whole in 1972, and 5 per cent for men. And while it began to fall again in 1973, government curtailment of the working week to three days in early 1974, in response to a ban on overtime by the miners, sharply increased the real incidence of unemployment, and once more demonstrated the exposure of manual workers to drastic fluctuations in their means of livelihood. In general, the risk of having to go without a job has probably spread to some categories of white-collar and even executive workers; but it is still far more of a hazard for manual workers than for others.[16]

Insecurity and unpredictability go well beyond that. They arise also from the normal dependence of a manual worker's earnings on the number of hours that he works – on the availability of overtime; the risk of short-time work; the penalty in loss of wages to which he is liable if he is sick, or late, or takes time off. They are evident again in the composition of his wage packet. Only about two-thirds of the average male manual worker's pay is accounted for by his basic wage. The rest comes from overtime earnings, from payment by results, from premiums for shiftwork at awkward hours and the like. These are all elements which are at least partly unpredictable; and which, in the case of both overtime and shift premiums, involve a sacrifice of leisure hours that are taken for granted by most white-collar workers.[17] His exclusion from employer-run security schemes, either alto-

16. The official statistical series (*Department of Employment Gazette*) do not record unemployment according to occupation. The Labour Mobility Survey 1953–63 (note 15 above), however, showed marked occupational differences in rates of dismissal and redundancy, with a much higher incidence for manual than non-manual workers.

17. *DE Gazette*, August 1969 (p. 727: New Earnings Survey of September 1968). The dependence of manual workers' earnings on the number of hours worked was brought out sharply by the reduction of the working week to three days in early

gether or from those with the more favourable terms, is part of the same package.

Insecurity in some other respects was reduced, from the 1960s, by legislation to extend the notice due before termination of a contract of employment; to give some protection against unfair dismissal; to provide compensation on redundancy; to raise state benefits for sickness and unemployment closer to basic earnings for a limited period. But there were qualifications attached in practice; and it is uncertain how far those improvements, real in absolute terms, have diminished the gaps in these respects between manual and non-manual workers, whose conditions are also not fixed.[18] Above all, the contrast remains striking between the 'life cycles' of ordinary workers and those of managers, executives, professionals and some sections of the salariat below these levels. There is no evidence of any substantial change on that score. This contrast – between the flat life cycle of workers, descending into or near poverty in old age, and the incremental and promotional curve which the bourgeois life cycle typically follows – underlines the insecurity of working-class life. And it points in particular to the conclusion that it is not possible for workers to 'plan' individually for, and 'invest' in, the future on the assumption of an upward progression through life. Such bourgeois virtues of domestic management are solidly grounded in the privileges of bourgeois existence.

The existence of an intermediate cluster of people between wage earners and directors, managers, high officials and members of the established professions is, and for long has been, of crucial significance. For they form a social and political buffer group; and their position provides a goal on which the individual aspirations of people further down the scale may focus. The people in these intermediate jobs depend no less essentially than rank-and-file earners on the sale of their labour. But they sell their labour at a premium which puts their earnings some way above those of ordinary workers. They

1974, when some sections of the manual labour force must have had their incomes cut to *less* than three fifths (given the premium rates at which overtime work is paid). Salaried employees, by contrast, were in the main immune.

18. See Dorothy Wedderburn, 'Inequality at work', in Townsend and Bosanquet, op. cit. (ch. 2, note 7 above). To the legislation referred to there should now be added, for the 1970s, the *Industrial Relations Act 1971* (sections 19–33), and similar provisions in subsequent legislation to repeat that Act. See also *idem* and Christine Craig, *Men in Manufacturing Industry*, Cambridge University Press, 1969, for a general survey of conditions of employment.

share, if only on a modest scale, some of the fringe benefits enjoyed as a matter of course by their economic superiors. Their life cycles follow at least in part an upward, incremental curve, rather than the low hump and downward slope of most manual and other routine workers. For these reasons there is some element to their lives of the kinds of security, predictability and opportunity for individual 'investment' in the future which are much more firmly established among those above them in the hierarchy. These as well as other features of their situation – their prospects of promotion in addition to increments of salary, for example, and the share in minor authority which many members of the intermediate strata enjoy – modify the nature of their dependence on the sale of their labour. The result is a characteristic marginality of position, which has widely ramified consequences for their everyday culture, social loyalties and perceptions of political interest. Low-level managers and supervisors, technicians, members of the 'junior' and 'auxiliary' professions – all of these probably come into the intermediate cluster, though there are both differences and uncertainties of situation among them sufficient for the label 'group' in the singular not to be appropriate to describe them.

Routine-grade clerks and sales workers, though they used to be part of this intermediate cluster, at least at its lower margin, are no longer so. They retain some of the special advantages that went with that position. A line drawn by criteria relating to access to moderate fringe benefits, relative security of employment, regularity of earnings and hours of work, will still separate most clerical workers – shop assistants not so clearly – from manual workers. But in terms of earnings – sheer cash as well as its distribution over the life cycle – male clerks and shop workers are now firmly among the broad mass of ordinary labour; and indeed often well down towards the bottom of the pile. Their descent to this position over time poses, in an especially acute form, the classical series of questions which concern the response of white-collar workers to their class situation. The answers to those questions may well, at least in part, turn on the answer to another question, on which there is little up-to-date information available. This is how far promotion may still offer white-collar earners some real route of escape from their low pay and routine work.

6 Women in the labour market

I

Two reasons dictate some special consideration here of the position of women in the labour market. First, it may be argued that overall inequalities of earnings throw a distorted light on economic inequalities between classes, in so far as they include a considerable element of inequality ostensibly unrelated to class: namely, wage and salary differentials between men and women. It is to take account of that possibility, and because the socio-economic position of men is still far more important than that of women for the character of the class structure, that our discussion of the labour market has so far focused on men. Nevertheless, if earnings differentials among women followed quite different patterns from those among men, the effect could be to alter the picture of class inequality, and perhaps to blur its sharpest edges. Second – and related to the latter point – married women today far more commonly have jobs than they did earlier in this century. The contribution of wives' earnings to family budgets in the working class especially is often assumed to have blunted the impact of class inequality as measured by household incomes.

II

Contrary to popular belief, female employment in general has increased very little during this century, until quite recently. The overall proportion of women recorded in census data as having paid work remained roughly constant, at about one-third of the female population aged 15 and over, from before World War I to well after

World War II. Not until the middle 1960s was the rise in employment among wives sufficient to outweigh the various factors working in the opposite direction – a long-term shift in age structure, later entry into work, earlier retirement, earlier marriage and more marriage. Only then did the overall proportion show a rise to over two in every five.[1] But married women have indeed increasingly taken on jobs outside their homes, from World War II onwards. The percentage of those with paid jobs among all wives went up from 10 in 1931 to 23 in 1954, and to about 40 by the late 1960s. The figure was then around 50 per cent in the case of married women in the economically most active age groups, between the mid-thirties and the mid-fifties.

It is true that the pattern for long was one in which those wives who had jobs were drawn predominantly from the working class. If that pattern still prevailed, the effect of the increase in numbers of married women entering the labour market would, by itself, certainly be to raise working-class family incomes proportionately more than those of families higher up the socio-economic scale. In fact, however, there are signs that married middle- and upper-class women are now progressively abandoning the ideal of 'marriage as a career' to which they long conformed, and demanding work outside their homes. The class-linked persistence of conformity to that ideal was still visible to some degree in figures from the 1961 census. About one-third of the women married to men in each of the occupational grades from unskilled manual to 'intermediate' non-manual were then at work; but the proportions among wives of established professional men, employers, managers and senior administrators were only around one-quarter. Those class differences were already fairly limited, however; and they had apparently been reduced to quite negligible proportions by 1965.[2]

The notion of marriage as a career may have been shared by the working class as an ideal; but it was never a really practical proposition in their case. Working-class wives had, and still have, relatively

1. Unless otherwise stated, statistical data in this section derive from the censuses of population (usually for England and Wales rather than Great Britain or the UK). Female employment may well be understated in those figures, but probably not more so now than in the past.

2. Audrey Hunt, *A Survey of Women's Employment*, Government Social Survey, 1968 (Vol. I, p. 120). The proportions in paid work among all housewives, from this 1965 survey, were about 50 per cent for both manual and non-manual households; with a range from 45 per cent in households headed by professional and administrative workers to 55 per cent in unskilled households, exceeded only in the case of service worker households (70 per cent).

little choice in the matter. It has long been quite common for them, out of simple need, to try to get some form of paid work to supplement family income, in so far as they could. Their deliberate limitation of family size, and the increased demand for labour from the 1940s by comparison with the inter-war years, have made it easier for them to do so. By contrast, marriage and employment continued to be seen – and to be treated usually in practice – as incompatible alternatives for middle and upper-class women, for long after child-rearing had been limited to only a fairly short span of their lives in marriage. Wives in these classes have therefore had, and are still having, to assert a demand for the right to work against an ideal which denied that right. The likely elimination of this ideal as a point of practical differ- ence between the classes will reinforce class inequality as measured by family income. The result is not so paradoxical as it may seem at first sight. It represents a shift of inequality from leisure into money earnings from work. And it is only one among several examples of the ways in which erosion of old differences of orientation between the classes, through the spread of what in some respects resembles a 'common culture', may in other respects accentuate class divisions.

III

It is again true, of course, that women's earnings are much lower than men's. This is so both because women at each main level of the social hierarchy are concentrated in the poorer paid, the less skilled, the auxiliary occupations; and because, within similar occupations, they still generally get paid a good deal less than men. Measures directed only against the latter form of discrimination – the Equal Pay Act 1970, for example – do nothing to deal with the first form of discrim- ination. There are signs, indeed, that they stimulate an increase in its practice.[3] But none of this means that sex inequalities in earnings 'negate' or 'cut across' class inequalities. On the contrary.

The occupational cleavages of earnings found among men are re- produced among women in terms that are proportionately in fact still sharper. Moreover, the range of inequality in pay on the female side of the labour market has tended to widen over time. As among men, the lower-level professions – teachers and nurses in the main – have slid down the scale of relative earnings. The position of clerical

3. See, e.g., Sheila Rowbotham, *Woman's Consciousness, Man's World*, Penguin Books, 1973 (pp. 98–9).

TABLE 13

Relative earnings of full-time women in main occupational groups, 1922/24–1960

Occupational group (women in full-time work)	Indices of earnings: occupational group average for women expressed as percentage of –					
	– average for all women in the same period		– average for unskilled women in the same period		– average for men of the same occupation in the same period	
	1922/4	1960	1922/4	1960	1922/4	1960
Higher professions	—	(327)	—	(510)	—	(70)
Managers and administrators	155	228	217	356	33	54
Lower professions	208	139	291	217	67	72
Forewomen	148	138	209	215	59	62
Clerks	103	97	145	151	57	59
Skilled manual workers	85	91	119	141	49	50
Semi-skilled manual workers	95	78	134	122	79	59
Unskilled manual workers	71	64	100	100	57	52
All women (full-time)	100	100	140	156	58	54

Source: as for table 7.

Notes: (a) No data for higher professions in 1922/24 (and estimate uncertain for 1960).

(b) In general, greater caution is needed in evaluating figures of this kind for women than in the case of the figures for men in table 7 – partly because the basic data in some respects are less certain; partly because sizeable changes in the composition of the female labour force over time affect interpretation of the indices used. For these reasons, 1922/24 has been taken as the starting point, instead of 1913/14 as in table 7; and a second measure of occupational differentials in earnings (an index using unskilled earnings as the base) has been added to supplement the measure from table 7 (which takes average earnings as the base).

workers has hardly changed, however. And there is as yet, despite slight overlap at the margin, a line among women that divides manual from non-manual work in terms of normal earnings. In addition, more women have managed to get into fairly high level occupations – although these are only a small minority still, and they are very rarely to be found in top positions. Partly in association with that process, the earnings of women in managerial and executive jobs have risen substantially, to widen the gap from top to average and top to bottom. (Table 13, first four columns.)

Today, while full-time working women even in the moderately well-paid job ranges as senior nurses and school teachers have median earnings no more than around those of skilled and semi-skilled manual men, the steps down the scale from that level are, relatively speaking, if anything steeper in the female than in the male labour market. (Table 14, first six columns.) So the class pattern of inequalities in women's pay complements that in men's pay; and it even extends it. On the whole, the gaps between men's and women's earnings within similar occupations are smallest in the higher paid groups, and widen down the scale of jobs and pay. Women school teachers, welfare workers and nurses, for example, are paid on average only about one-fifth less than their male colleagues; women clerical workers about a third less than men in similar jobs. But women manual workers get little more than half as much in gross earnings as men in manual work of comparable levels of skill. (Table 14, last two columns.) This class linkage in the pattern of labour market discrimination was not visible before the war, and even in 1960 did not appear as clearly as later. (Table 13, last two columns.) It was quite plain by the end of the 1960s; and it was not noticeably altered by a tendency in recent years – as seen from 1968 to 1971 – for the gaps between male and female earnings in a number of occupations to narrow slightly. Sex inequality in pay, to put the point summarily, reinforces class inequality: it strikes hardest at the lowest levels of the occupational hierarchy.

So too in other respects. We have already shown, for example, that discrimination against women in access to employer-provided welfare benefits is more acute in manual than in non-manual work. More remarkably still: a general tendency for women by comparison with men to be pressed more firmly over time into lower grades within the main occupational groupings has been particularly striking at the bottom of the socio-economic scale, while only marginally visible at the top. (Table 15.) Women especially, of course, have shifted away from manual and service work into non-manual work. But now as in the early 1920s, professional women are heavily concentrated in the 'minor' and 'auxiliary' professions; non-manual women as a whole in routine clerical and other low-grade 'white-blouse' jobs; manual women workers in jobs requiring little or no recognized skill. (And even those who do skilled manual work do not on average earn a premium in pay for it.) What is striking, first, is that the occupational status of women relative to men within each main 'band' has

TABLE 14

Median weekly earnings before tax of full-time women compared with men in selected occupations, 1971

Occupations (including some for which comparable data not available for men)	Median gross weekly earnings		Indices of occupational differentials – median for occupation as per cent of:				Women's earnings as per cent of men's earnings	
			Overall median		Unskilled median		(These data)	(For comparison)
	Women (£)	Men (£)	Women	Men	Women	Men	1971	1968
Professional, semi-professional								
Nursing matrons, sisters	30·3	—	183	—	208	—	—	—
School teachers	28·4	37·1	171	125	195	153	77	79
Welfare workers	25·8	30·3	155	102	177	125	85	—
Medical auxiliaries	22·8	—	137	—	156	—	—	—
Nurses – all (incl. matrons, etc.)	20·0	23·5	120	79	137	97	85	70
Laboratory technicians, etc.	18·4	30·0	111	101	126	123	61	62
Office and sales workers								
Office supervisors	26·4	35·1	159	118	181	144	75	65
Clerks – senior grade	19·6	32·1	118	108	134	132	61	65
Secretaries, shorthand typists	19·4	—	117	—	133	—	—	—
Clerks – intermed grade	18·0	25·0	108	84	123	103	72	66
Retail, shop –, dept. managers	17·2	26·4	104	89	118	109	65	—
Office machine operators	16·9	—	102	—	116	—	—	—
Sales supervisors	16·4	32·4	99	109	112	133	50	49
Copy-, audio-typists	16·3	—	98	—	112	—	—	—
Clerks – routine, junior	15·7	21·4	95	72	108	88	73	68
Shop-, sales assistants	12·1	20·4	73	68	83	84	59	53
Manual and service workers								
Manual – skilled*	14·7	29·8	89	100	101	123	49	49
Manual – semi-skilled*	15·6	27·7	94	93	107	114	56	52
Manual – unskilled*	14·6	24·3	88	82	*100*	*100*	60	57
Cooks, chefs	14·3	25·5	86	86	98	105	56	54
Cleaners, charwomen	13·0	19·8	78	66	89	81	65	60
Waitresses, waiters	12·0	16·4	72	55	82	67	73	—
All employees, full-time (incl. those not listed above)	16·6	29·3	100	100	114	123	56	53

Source: Dept. of Employment Gazette, December 1971 (pp. 1157–1161, 1152); and for 1968, *Gazette* May 1969 (pp. 408–409): data from New Earnings Surveys of April 1971 and Sept. 1968. There were too few women in occupations higher up the scale for the sample to yield separate figures for these.

Notes: — No data available.

* Figures for the different grades of manual skill relate to workers in a wide range of selected industries and trades, but exclude some manual workers.

Differences of definition prevent direct comparison with the figures of table 13.

actually worsened since 1921 – an outcome, at least in part, of the much increased share of married women in the female labour force. Second, this deterioration has itself been noticeably class-linked: very marked in respect of manual work, comparatively negligible in respect of the professions. So much for the twin notions that the gaps in status at work between men and women have generally narrowed; and that in the process sex handicaps have been reduced more in the lower than in the upper reaches of the occupational scale. The reverse is the case.

TABLE 15

The concentration of women in lower grade jobs within broad occupational bands, 1921, 1961 and 1966

	1921	1961	1966
Professional jobs			
Per cent of all professional WOMEN in 'minor' professions	93	93	93
Per cent of all professional MEN in 'minor' professions	46	42	40
All non-manual (incl. professional) jobs			
Per cent of all non-manual WOMEN in routine grades	51	70	72
Per cent of all non-manual MEN in routine grades	38	40	40
All manual (incl. personal service) jobs			
Per cent of all manual WOMEN in non-skilled jobs	64	80	78
Per cent of all manual MEN in non-skilled jobs	47	45	39

Sources: Computations from data from censuses (England & Wales) of 1921 and 1961, and sample census of 1966. The figures for 1921 and 1961 derive from a special analysis using a classification of occupations devised in that connection to provide comparability over the intervening years (see footnote 1, page 72). The occupational classification used for 1966 is based directly on the published socio-economic group classification and is not fully comparable with that for 1921 and 1961.

IV

Add to all this the facts that about one in every two working wives has only a part-time job; that this is one sign among several of the relatively variable and non-dependable character of married women's contribution to family budgets;[4] and that the incidence of part-time

4. On this, and the limited availability in general of subsidiary earnings for major items of household expenditure, see Centre for Urban Studies (Ruth

work rises as one descends the occupational scale.[5] The conclusion is then plain that the inequalities of the female labour market – internally and in relation to the male labour market – in no sense take away from or cut across the general pattern of class inequality. On the contrary, they sharpen class divisions.

That conclusion might need modification if there were complex cross-currents in the recruitment of married women into different levels of occupation: if, for example, the wives of manual and low-paid clerical workers found jobs in the higher reaches of women's work, while managers' and professionals' wives often took low-grade manual work. The proposition is absurd on the face of it, though there is surprisingly little information on the precise nature of the relevant patterns of job recruitment. A nationwide sample survey as far back as 1949 showed, as one would expect, that the level of jobs held by married women was strongly associated with the socio-economic level of their families. The proportions of working wives with manual jobs thus ranged from 86 per cent when both husband and father were themselves manual workers, and 69 per cent when the husband but not the father was; to 62 per cent in the reverse case, and as little as 31 per cent only when both were non-manual workers.[6] The proportions taking non-manual jobs have no doubt risen in all four categories since then, as 'white-blouse' work has grown. But, in relative terms, the general pattern is unlikely to have changed much.

Women in manual work are almost certainly still recruited practically exclusively from working-class families; women in non-manual work above the routine grades no doubt very largely from middle- and upper-class families. The two streams meet in routine-grade non-manual work – as typists, secretaries, saleswomen – and presumably more so now than in the past, although there are no figures available to show this. There may well be consequences of

Glass et al.) Housing in Camden, Vol. 2, London Borough of Camden, 1969 (p. 42).

5. See, e.g., Hunt, op. cit. (note 2 above), Vol. II. pp. 20–21, 36.

6. R. K. Kelsall, Sheila Mitchell, 'Married women and employment in England and Wales', Population Studies, July 1959 (survey data from 1949). Among working mothers of young children, in a longitudinal survey at about the same time, the proportions in manual and domestic service jobs ranged from 70–80 per cent for those with husbands in manual work, through less than 50 per cent for wives of 'black-coated' workers, to 11 per cent for those with 'professional and salaried' husbands. J. W. B. Douglas and J. M. Blomfield, Children under Five, Allen & Unwin, 1958, p. 120. We have found no later data in surveys concerned with women's employment.

some social significance arising from that meeting: from the fact that increasing numbers of wives, and especially daughters, of manual workers get a foot inside the world of non-manual work. But the social implications are probably limited by a number of other factors. It is likely that working-class women are concentrated disproportionately in the most routine grades of clerical and saleswork, with the least opportunities for promotion and for contact with their superiors. Moreover, these low-level non-manual jobs may be increasingly separated from the rungs above them, even though that process of assimilation of clerical routine to manual work – very marked in the male labour market by the yardstick of earnings – has not as yet gone far in the female labour market. The limited and intermittent character of women's engagement in work, compared with that of men, may also reduce the significance of such contact as working-class wives and daughters have through their jobs with the white-collar world.

There are many unknowns here; and the balance among them is quite uncertain. There is no such uncertainty about the fact – evident from one point after another – that the special exposure to exploitation in the labour market to which women are subject strengthens the impact of economic inequality between classes.

Women in all classes are the victims of handicaps associated with their sex. But those handicaps take different forms at different levels of society. Middle- and upper-class wives, as we have stressed, are still having to stake a claim for liberation by asserting a right to work in conflict with an ideal of marriage as a career, by which many women themselves in these classes are influenced even today. The right to work is not, and has not for long been, a real issue for married working-class women – though practical opportunities to do so are. They have often taken work of some kind, because they have needed to – when they could. Work in their case, moreover, is commonly not a source of positive satisfaction and psychological enrichment – as it is often conceived by middle- and upper-class women who seek their own liberation – any more than it is for working-class men. Manual work has few such intrinsic satisfactions to offer, if any; low-grade clerical work, probably fewer than in the past. Again, a demand for career opportunities on a par with those of men makes little sense so far as women limited to manual, and probably now also routine-level office work, are concerned. Men in rank-and-file wage-earning work do not have careers anyway: they have jobs, with at best only a short run of regular increments and few prospects of promotion. What matters for working-class women, as for working-class men, is cash in first place. It is on that score, especially, that they experience discrimination against their sex in employment. Their handicaps are a particular and acute expression of the dependence of labour in a market economy. And class divisions, to repeat, are accentuated by the heavy incidence of sex discrimination in the lower ranges of the labour market. There is no neutralization or contradiction here of one form of inequality by another: the two are linked.

7 Capital: the ownership of property

Private ownership of capital is the key to class division in Britain as in other capitalist countries. Taxation and public welfare provision have done little to alter the broad pattern of material inequality between classes, because the objectives and effects of public policy are limited – though they are not rigidly fixed – by the needs and influence of business in an economy where private enterprise continues to play the predominant role. Inequalities in earnings between jobs of different kinds remain marked, in much the same mould over long periods of time, because they are still – even with public employment of a substantial fraction of the labour force, and with increasing state intervention to counter inflation – determined principally by market demands in an economy directed to make capital yield a secure profit to its owners. Private capital, in other words, carries power: we shall discuss those issues in more detail later. But capital ownership has an immediate significance for material inequality – irrespective of its power over policy and in everyday affairs – which is the subject of this chapter.

Possession of property – of capital in the means of production in particular – remains the crucial source of wealth, and the most potent cause of inequality of income. Top salaries and the fringe benefits that go with them share something of the character of income from property. They derive in part from control over economic resources, and from the influence which their beneficiaries themselves have over the specialized markets where they 'sell' their labour. In fact, high business and professional earnings from work go hand in hand with large incomes direct from property ownership, to make up the wealth of the rich. And the higher the total income of an individual, the larger the contribution to it direct from property.

Investment income comprises an apparently quite small fraction of the aggregate of incomes of which the tax authorities take note: no more than 6 to 7 per cent of the total assessed as taxable in 1969/70, for example.[1] But it makes up very much more of the incomes of the well-to-do and the wealthy, even when no account is taken of understatement. Income from investment accounted for 15 per cent of the aggregate taxable incomes of those in the £3,000–£4,000 bracket in that year; for nearly 25 per cent in the case of those with £5,000–£6,000 a year; for over 40 per cent of the total among those with £10,000 and more – a steady and progressively steeper rise up the scale for each step after the threshold of moderately comfortable 'middle class' incomes has been crossed. And its distribution is very strongly concentrated at the top. At an estimate, nearly five in every six 'income units' (married couples and single persons) in 1969/70 had no recorded investment income at all. But 10 per cent shared two-thirds of the total; 5 per cent alone, three-fifths of it; 1 per cent only, well over a third. Those who comprise that last tiny minority – over two-fifths of whose taxable income comes from investments – are those who, as shown earlier, between them have as large a slice of income after tax as the poorest 30 per cent or so of the population.

II

Figures of this sort are indicative rather than precise – for the usual reasons. One method of estimation is, as here, to start with data on investment incomes as reported to the tax authorities. Other deficiencies apart, this is to ignore forms of property which do not yield immediate income by way of interest, dividend and rent. An alternative approach (and one used for a long time in this country, in the continuing absence of any general tax on capital) is to take, in effect, the dead as a skew sample of the living. What this involves is to use the distribution of property among those who die leaving estates subject to death duty as a guide, after appropriate adjustments for

1. This and the following estimates are based on data in *Inland Revenue Statistics 1972* (p. 77), with a rough allowance for 'income units' excluded there because they were below the tax limit.

patterns of mortality, to the distribution of property in the population at large. There are weaknesses here too. First, the bases of
adjustment for mortality are imperfect, and may differ between one
estimate and another. Second, some property escapes death duty;
and there can be disagreement anyway about what constitutes
'property'. The most comprehensive recent study of the subject, for
example, presents two alternative estimates of the distribution of
private wealth in the middle 1960s (1963–67), both by application of
the estate duty technique. Between them, these estimates attribute to
the richest 1 per cent of the adult population (25 years and over)
from 22 to 29 per cent of all private property; to the richest 5 per cent,
from 41 to 54 per cent; to the richest 10 per cent between 52 and 67
per cent of the total. The lower series include the expected future
value of both state and private pensions in 'wealth'; the higher series
only that of private pensions. The inclusion of either is debatable.
Their exclusion would raise the figures throughout. Even aside from
that, the twin estimates as they stand are acknowledged to understate
concentration. While they make allowance for some devices available
to reduce duties – 'settlement' of property by discretionary trusts and
otherwise – none is made for the fact that the market values by which
company shares are assessed for death duties fail, in aggregate, to
express the full value of net company assets.[2]

These uncertainties of estimation are not too important, however,
by comparison with two outstanding facts. First, there is heavy concentration of private property however the exact figures come out.
The share of all personal wealth owned by just the richest 1 per cent
of the adult population was probably near 30 per cent around 1970.
This rough figure excludes the value of formal entitlements to
pensions: reasonably so, in our view, since even the benefits of
private occupational pension schemes are uncertain – as we have
pointed out earlier – while state pensions are determined by changing
public policy and involve no rights that can be sold or passed on to
others. The estimate, too, makes some allowance for understatement
of the value of income-yielding property in the data available –
hardly full allowance, when it is remembered that well over a third of

2. A. B. Atkinson, *Unequal Shares: Wealth in Britain*, Allen Lane: the Penguin
Press, 1972 (pp. 10–14). We have drawn on this invaluable study at several points
in the following discussion. But we should emphasize that the choice, in the next
paragraph, of some 30 per cent as the most likely share of the one-per-cent
minority in all wealth is ours, and unlike Professor Atkinson's estimates excludes
formal pension rights from 'property'.

all income from property reported for tax in 1971 was in the hands of a 1 per cent minority. Ownership of small property which yields no taxable income – owner-occupied housing, motor cars, household goods and personal effects, for example – is spread much more widely of course, though still unevenly; and the limit in value below which these things can hardly rate as 'property' is debatable. But whatever the precise share of the 1 per cent minority – above or below some 30 per cent – it is very large. And with 5 per cent of the adult population holding something like half the total in their hands, the concentration is enormous. Except in so far as many now own – or are buying – the homes they live in, considerable sections of the salaried groups, as well as the mass of wage earners, are excluded from property ownership of any substance.

The second outstanding fact is the limited degree to which private wealth has become more widely diffused over time. On the face of things, it is true, there has been a long-term trend towards a greater spread of property ownership. The share of the 1 per cent right at the top fell quite sharply between 1911 and 1960, a period for which estimates calculated on a comparable basis are available. (Table 16.) But first appearances here are deceptive. Set the threshold a little further down the scale of wealth, and the impression of diffusion becomes much weaker. The share held by the richest 5 per cent fell only very moderately over the same half-century; that of the richest 10 per cent still less. By the measures used here to trace the long-term trend, the latter group – only one in ten of all adults – still held some four-fifths of all private property in their hands in 1960; the remaining 90 per cent hardly one-fifth of the total between them. These measures probably exaggerate the concentration at each date. But since they allow comparison from one date to another over the period, they point to the nature of the trend. The richest 1 per cent yielded some of their wealth to the people a little way below them – to the next 4 or 9 per cent. But the share of the rest – the great majority – rose little in the process. It is not possible to carry the story forward in a way that directly links the trend until 1960 with the trend since then. Figures for the period after 1960 (also shown in table 16) understate the continuing extent of inequality by comparison with those for the half-century up to 1960. Yet the pattern of the trend from 1961 to 1971, taken by itself, is similar to the pattern over the fifty years before: a continuing drop in the share held by the very richest, though their part remained massive by 1971; a proportionately milder decline in the share of the wealthy people just a step or two below them on the ladder. There was no radical shift of property ownership in the 1960s: reports to that effect were misleading.[3] House and car ownership became more common; and the value of household goods and personal effects in the hands of ordinary people no doubt increased. But any spread of wealth beyond that was negligible. Significantly, as we shall underline again later (section IV below),

3. Official estimates thus appear to show a recent, more general decline in property concentration, with noticeable effects beyond the 5 or 10 per cent minority at the top. (Cf. *Inland Revenue Statistics 1973*, pp. 130–131; and summary analyses of the same data in *Social Trends* – e.g., for 1972, p. 86.) These data derive from information about death duties; and the estimates have the merit of taking account of class mortality differentials. But they exclude nearly half the adult population – those with so little property that they are not covered in the original sources of information. If these people were included, the concentration of property ownership would prove greater than appears in the published figures. The point is explicitly acknowledged in the appendix notes to the main tables (e.g., *Inland Revenue Stats. 1973*, p. 171), though not in the tables themselves. Moreover, inclusion of that part of the population left out of account would reduce the apparent trend towards greater diffusion of property over time, and almost eliminate it on one assumption. The overall degree of inequality is measured, in the Inland Revenue estimates, by the 'Gini coefficient': total concentration of property in one pair of hands would give a coefficient of 100, total dispersal equally among all a coefficient of 0. The figures presented in the main tables – confined to 'owners' excluding the poorer half of the population – show a decline in the coefficient from 72 in 1961 to 64 in 1971. But an alternative calculation in the appendix notes, which takes into account the people otherwise excluded on the assumption that these had no property, produces a change over the same period only from 87 to 84. The assumption is extreme. But it is clear that a realistic estimate would show a much gentler decline than the 72–64 trend presented in the main tables of the official publication. We have made the assumption (table 16) in our estimates for 1961 to 1971 from the same data that the people left out of account in the original material held about 5 per cent of all property – an assumption in line with the information available for the population covered in the official data. Another set of estimates, from the same Inland Revenue material, has also been published with a conclusion that ownership of wealth became markedly more widely dispersed in the course of the 1960s: A. Day, 'The nation's wealth: who owns it?', *The Observer*, 20 Jan. 1974. It is not clear how these estimates were brought up to 1973, when the raw material for that year could not yet be available; but the figures shown for 1973 do not differ substantially from our estimates for 1971 in table 16. However, Professor Day's table showing a trend of diffusion from 1911 with marked acceleration in the 1960s is misleading, because it puts together the earlier estimates for 1911 to 1960 with figures for 1965 to 1973, without indicating that these are two separate series, calculated on different bases and assumptions. His figures for 1965 are quite similar to our estimate for 1961. Had he used the 1961 data (as we do in table 16), the juxtaposition of the estimate for that year with the estimate for 1960 from the 1911–1960 series would have made it clear that the two series are not comparable, and that the apparently startling shift between 1960 and 1965 in *The Observer* article is in large part an artifact of differences in methods of estimation.

ownership of capital in private enterprise remained as intensely concentrated among a tiny minority in 1970 as it had been fifteen or twenty years earlier.

TABLE 16

Long-term trends in distribution of private property, 1911–1960 and 1961–1971

Groups within adult population (aged 25+) owning stated proportions of aggregate personal wealth	Estimated proportion of aggregate personal wealth						
	Period 1911–1960 (common basis)					Period 1961–1971 (common basis)	
	1911/13 %	1924/30 %	1936/38 %	1954 %	1960 %	1961 %	1971 %
Richest 1% owned	69	62	56	43	42	32	26
Richest 5% owned	87	84	79	71	75	55	47
Richest 10% owned	92	91	88	79	83	*	*
Hence:							
Richest 1% owned	69	62	56	43	42	32	26
Next 2–5% owned	18	22	23	28	33	23	21
Next 6–10% owned	5	7	9	8	8	*	*
95% owned only	13	16	21	29	25	45	53
90% owned only	8	9	12	21	17	*	*

Sources: J. R. S. Revell, 'Changes in the social distribution of property', *International Conference of Economic History*, vol. I, Munich, 1965: for period 1911–1960.

Calculations from *Inland Revenue Statistics 1973* (table 92), with figures of population aged 25 and over in Great Britain from *Annual Abstracts of Statistics*: for period 1961–1971.

Note: The series for 1911–1960 cannot be compared with that for 1961–1971. Though the two series are both derived from information on death duties, the coverage and assumptions used differ between the two. As comparison between the 1960 figures of the first series and the 1961 figures of the second series suggests, the second series is likely to understate the degree of concentration of ownership while the first series probably overstates it. See also footnote 3 to text.

* We have not calculated the proportions of property owned by the richest 10 per cent and the remaining 90 per cent for 1961 and 1971, as the data are in such a form as to make estimates of those figures more uncertain than the other estimates shown for these years.

In short, much of the apparent diffusion of wealth has been confined to those already well-to-do. The process has been carried beyond their ranks in so far, especially, as owner-occupation of housing has spread – encouraged by government policy which, through concomitant restrictions on the role of public rented housing, has compelled even many people who initially could ill afford it to buy their homes. The increase in home ownership sets up new divisions within the wage-earning population: between those who thus acquire a small stake in the rising value of land and those who, as council or private tenants, are the victims of this inflation. We discuss the point again later. But there is nothing here to affect property ownership in its crucial form: ownership of the means of production. And the retention of a massive share in all wealth by the top 5 or 10 per cent of the population is very striking. The reason for the shift *within* their ranks – from the richest 1 per cent to those just a little way down the scale from them – is plain. That shift represents, primarily or even exclusively, the measures taken by the very rich to safeguard their wealth against taxation.

Property which is transferred to relatives, or others, some time before the death of the original owners has not been liable to death duty. Protection of private wealth has therefore required – and produced – earlier division of large holdings of wealth among kinsfolk, with little effect on the social distribution of capital. There is no other inference to be drawn from the pattern of the shift; and there is positive evidence to strengthen the inference. Rates of estate duty have, in general, been raised steeply since the nineteenth century. They are now – even after substantial reliefs to the wealthy by the Conservative government in the early 1970s – at levels often described by the rich as 'penal': rising, for example, to more than 70 per cent on estates of $2\frac{1}{2}$ million or more. Yet for all this, the yield from this form of taxation has declined in proportionate terms – both as a fraction of all revenue from taxation; and in relation to the yield which would be expected, given the rise in rates, had evasion not become more widespread and effective. Relevant estimates point to a fairly continuous increase – throughout the century, and carrying on steadily during the 1960s – in avoidance of death duties through 'gifts *inter vivos*'.[4] Though the subject of bitter complaint by the privileged – such complaints are a pervasive and significant accompaniment of 'welfare capitalism' – estate taxation on death has contributed practically nothing to a liberal objective of 'wider ownership'. Practically nothing at least, unless 'wider ownership' is taken to mean only that merchant bankers, industrialists and top professionals hand over

4. C. T. Sandford, *Taxing Personal Wealth*, Allen & Unwin, 1971 (especially pp. 52–6, 63–9, 86–9); Atkinson, op. cit. (note 2 above), especially pp. 126–38.

part of their wealth to wives and children a little earlier than they would have done otherwise.

Inheritance in fact continues to play a major part in the maintenance of property concentration. About one in every two men who died in the late 1950s leaving estates of £100,000 or more, for example, had himself inherited at least £50,000 from his father. Two in every three had inherited at least £10,000. And there were no signs by such measures of any substantial change in the contribution of inheritance to wealth since before the war.[5] These facts are a simple reminder of some significant features of capitalist social structure. They underline the resistance inherent in the institutional framework of capitalism to implementation of the notion of 'opportunity', though that notion is part of the ideology which has accompanied the development of capitalism. They point to the central and actively conservative role of links of kinship within the bourgeoisie in the maintenance of inequality, for all the neglect of this in sociological fashions obsessed with the defensive and much less securely buttressed kinship relations of the working class.

III

Two common arguments are advanced to dismiss the significance of the continuing concentration of property ownership. Neither can stand up to scrutiny.

The first is that little more is involved than a 'natural' accumulation of wealth in the hands of middle-aged and elderly men. Ownership, it is said, is in the main a male prerogative; and it takes a good part of a lifetime to build up wealth. If the resulting concentration is unfair, the inequalities at work are those of sex and age, not of class. Quite apart from what is known about inheritance, other facts too bluntly contradict this thesis. For one thing women have a large, though still not quite proportionate, share in ownership: about 40 per cent of all private wealth in 1970.[6] For another, the argument requires that

5. C. D. Harbury, 'Inheritance in the distribution of personal wealth', *Economic Journal*, December 1962. Even a modest inheritance, by the standards of the very rich, provides of course a good basis for further accumulation of wealth through investment in rising assets. Cf. G. Z. Fijalkowski-Bereday, 'The equalizing effects of death duties', *Oxford Econ. Papers*, June 1950.

6. *Social Trends 1972*, p. 86. (Women's share in wealth has been rising, no doubt in part in association with the process of intra-family diffusion to reduce death duties.)

wealth should be more or less equally distributed among people – men and women taken separately – of the same age. In fact it is not: concentration of ownership is almost as marked age for age as it is overall.[7] Property does not separate old from young to any sizeable extent: it separates the rich from the rest, at each stage of the life cycle.

The second argument is that property ownership, concentrated though it is, contributes little to overall economic inequality: hypothetical redistribution on an equal basis would not add much to the resources of ordinary people. This view, often airily stated with no supporting evidence, is false. It is unambiguously refuted by an estimate in the most recent major study that, split equally, the income yielded by private property would have provided every married couple in 1971 with over £9 a week – corresponding to about a quarter of average gross income in households with married couples – and very substantially change the overall distribution of income.[8] The postulate thus exploded is one version of the more general thesis that 'soaking the rich' can do little to make incomes more equal: any redistribution to the poor must hit the 'middle ranks' of affluent and not so affluent workers hard. This thesis is patently untrue, as we have stressed before. It is a highly significant feature of the character of contemporary capitalist society that the thesis is nevertheless so readily asserted, so rarely challenged, and so commonly accepted as a guiding assumption in policy.

IV

The point is, of course, that radical redistribution would require the dissolution of private property and therefore of capitalism itself. 'Liberal' proposals – including policies suggested by the Labour Party – fall very far short of that. They are designed, through such measures as direct taxation of capital and the revision of death

7. See especially Atkinson, op. cit. (note 2 above), pp. 49–52, a vigorous refutation of the 'accumulation through life' argument. For earlier data on property ownership by age and sex, relevant to the same point, see e.g. H. F. Lydall, *British Incomes and Savings*, Blackwell, 1955; and *idem* and D. G. Tipping, 'Distribution of personal wealth in Britain', *Bull. Oxford Univ. Inst. Statistics*, February 1961.

8. Atkinson, op. cit. (pp. 37–8); supplemented by the *Family Expenditure Survey 1971* (p. 82).

duties, merely to moderate the effects of private ownership; not to abolish it. Nationalization of economic enterprises of the limited kind practised in Britain may or may not affect policy control. It does, and has done, practically nothing to reduce the concentration of private wealth, so long as the original owners receive 'fair compensation'. We shall take up this point again later. Significantly, no proposals have been given effective political voice for the abolition of inheritance – only for its modification. Yet inheritance has no logical place in that part of the capitalist ethos which has paid lip service to the ideal of the self-made man: to a right, and duty, of each individual to make his own way in the world. Inheritance is in flagrant breach of pretensions to equality of opportunity. Its maintenance reflects the interests and influence of those who already have property, or are in a good position to acquire it – a small minority, so far as substantial ownership is concerned.

TABLE 17

Concentration of main types of private property, 1954

Groups within adult population owning stated proportions of the aggregate value of property of the kind indicated	Share of total within each of following categories owned by percentage of population specified on left				
	All net private capital	Cash and bank deposits	Land, buildings, trade assets	Govt. and municipal securities	Company stocks and shares
	%	%	%	%	%
Richest 1% owned	43	23	28	42	81
Richest 5% owned	68	48	58	71	96
Richest 10% owned	79	64	74	83	98

Source: H. F. Lydall, D. G. Tipping, 'The distribution of personal wealth in Britain', *Bulletin Oxford Univ. Inst. Statistics*, February 1961. (Estimates derived by application of data from a national sample survey in 1954 to overall property distribution as indicated by 'death duties' technique.)

The concentration of property – of private capital – involves also a concentration of power: power to preserve or change the shape of economy and society. This set of issues needs separate and detailed examination. But it is important to note, already here, that ownership is by far the most strongly concentrated precisely in the case of that form of capital which, in packages sufficiently large, confers potential power over policy: shareholding in private economic enterprise.

Petty property takes the form predominantly of cash – in banks and savings deposits – and of owner-occupied housing. The larger the capital owned, the higher the proportion invested in securities and shares of all kinds and, as one goes up the scale of ownership, in company stock especially. (See table 17.) The result is an accumulation of stock in the hands of a tiny fraction of the population. Some 93 per cent of all adults in 1970 held not even a single share or, for that matter, any government bond. Most of the 7 per cent or so who did had only small or modest holdings. A minority of 1 per cent owned about four-fifths of all capital of this kind in personal hands. There is massive concentration even within the ranks of the small group of shareholders.[9] And there has been very little change on that score. It was much the same in 1950. Then, too, the highly privileged 1 per cent of the adult population owned more than four-fifths of the total net value of company stock; the richest 5 per cent little short of the whole lot. (Table 17.)

The conception of Britain as a 'property-owning democracy' – even if taken only as a realizable aspiration – has little enough meaning so far as property in general is concerned. It is laughable so far as property in the means of production is concerned. The private enterprise which dominates the economy is in the hands of a tiny group with massive holdings of wealth. Only a small proportion of the population outside that circle have even a nominal share in corporate business. The vast bulk of the population have none at all – only their common dependence on selling their labour in the market. These facts of capital concentration are elementary; but they are all-important.

9. Calculated from estimates of stock holding (*Inland Revenue Statistics, 1972*, pp. 122–124) and of the population aged 25 and more, or aged 18 and more – the choice making little difference in this connection (*Annual Abstract of Statistics 1972*). Detailed figures of shareholding are presented in table 19 (Part Three, chapter 2). We are grateful to our colleague, Tony Fielding, for help with these calculations. (Although these estimates derive from information about estates liable to death duties, and therefore exclude the section of the population owning little or no property, they are consistent with estimates from other sources that some 2–2½ million persons – some 6 to 7 per cent of the adult population – then owned ordinary shares. (Cf. J. Moyle, *The Pattern of Ordinary Share Ownership 1957–1970*, Cambridge Univ. Press, 1971, p. 8.)

8 Conclusions and implications

I

There is, in summary, a clear pattern to what might seem at first a tangle of facts. Rising levels of living for every man have gone hand in hand with a marked persistence of economic inequality in relative terms. Exceptional circumstances at times compressed the range of contrasts in income and wealth. Those shifts had lasting effects. But they were confined to the periods around World War II and probably World War I. They formed no part of a continuous trend towards equalization, and they entailed only modest redistribution. Disparities may indeed have widened since the 1950s. They certainly did not narrow significantly, from the early 1950s to the early 1970s, under governments of either political shade.

Postulates to the contrary – strident for many years after the war, though they then became more subdued – have commonly attributed to the 'welfare' activities of government a benevolence that is not matched by reality. Proportionate to their incomes, the poor and the mass of ordinary wage earners carry hardly less of the weight of taxation than do the rich. State benefits add more to the resources of the poor than to those of the rich – in relative terms, just because the poor have so little money to start with. But they add little more to low incomes in absolute terms, in actual cash and services. Wage earners pay for their 'welfare state' largely out of their own pockets; and they do not have the influence, the proximity to those who make policy and execute it, the sheer self-assurance of privilege, which enable businessmen and high professionals to tap the resources of the state to boost 'private' welfare arrangements for themselves and colleagues close to them in the hierarchy.

For the mass of the population, material conditions of life –

improving more or less regularly though they have been for a long time – are still governed primarily by the terms on which people sell their labour during their working lives. And for most of them – for manual workers, and many low-grade white-collar workers who have lost the advantage in the labour market which once supported their claims to modest 'middle class' status – the life cycle usually follows a curve fairly close to a flat line. It rises to a low hump in early adulthood, improvements over time in the average level of living apart; and slopes downwards through middle into old age. The contrast is clear with the upward, incremental and promotional life cycles characteristic of members of the middle-range salariat – run-of-the-mill executives and officials, the lower and auxiliary professions. There is a still sharper contrast with the life cycles of people at the top, who share control of the dominant institutions of economy and society or enjoy the security of the established professions.

Economic position and power at the top, moreover, are firmly buttressed by property ownership. Private capital is massively concentrated in the hands of a small minority, though it is now more dispersed within the families of the wealthy than in the past, as a protection against taxation. Some 1 per cent of the adult population have as large a share of all income after tax as the poorest 30 per cent or so. Two-fifths or more of their income comes from investments: a matter of little surprise, since they alone own about 30 per cent of all private wealth, and four-fifths of all company stock in personal hands. Private property, individual and corporate, is the pivot of a capitalist economy, as much in its 'welfare' form as before. It is for that reason above all that, despite its expansion of production, capitalism can make no claim to a steadily more equal spread of wealth. Inequality is entrenched in its institutional structure.

II

Britain is no odd man out among capitalist countries in these respects. True, rates of economic growth have been relatively slow here since the late nineteenth century. But there is no evidence to suggest a connection between that and the fact that the range of material inequality has changed so little. Overall trends seem to have been very similar in other Western capitalist societies for which there

is information. International comparisons are beset by special difficulties. Differences in tax and benefit systems, in accounting procedures and definitions of relevant aggregates and categories, mean
that cross-national comparisons of the magnitude of inequality are
hazardous at best. They are certainly more difficult still to make than
are estimates of trends over time in individual countries, each
considered separately. Even the latter estimates commonly suffer
from weaknesses of a kind familiar from the British data. Inequality
everywhere sets up obstacles to its own description. And the information is often poorer in range and technical quality than recent
British material. Income distribution after direct taxation is much
harder to get at than pre-tax distribution, for example; and systematic attempts to assess the net impact of all taxes and public benefits,
direct and indirect, have so far been rare. Nevertheless the patchwork picture which can be sketched from the more readily available
sources comes out in much the same configuration as the more detailed portrait of Britain.

Both in the United States and Western Europe, incomes and earnings generally showed a shift towards smaller disparities during or
just around the 1940s. But, as in Britain, that trend was not subsequently maintained. With one or two exceptions – Norway and possibly West Germany – inequality of income either stayed fixed or
marginally increased from the 1950s on into the 1960s. This was so
with incomes measured before direct taxation; and also after tax, so
far as the restricted data on the latter score go.[1] As in Britain too, net

1. See H. F. Lydall, *The Structure of Earnings*, Clarendon Press, 1968, and
Secretariat of the Economic Commission for Europe, *Incomes in Post-War
Europe* (Economic Survey of Europe in 1965, Part 2), U.N. 1967: mainly pre-tax
figures, but with some reference to tax effects in the latter source (chapter 6).
For the U.S.A. see, e.g., Mary Henson, *Trends in the Income of Families and
Persons in the US 1947–1964*, Bureau of the Census (Tech. Paper No. 17), 1967
(pp. 2, 188–90: pre-tax); S. Kusnetz and E. Jenks, *Shares of Upper Income Groups
in Income and Savings*, National Bureau of Economic Research, 1953 (e.g.,
pp. 33, 46: post-tax, 1919–1946); G. Kolko, *Wealth and Power in America*,
Praeger, 1962 (e.g., p. 34: post-tax, 1947–1955). For Sweden, of special interest as
a 'prototype social democracy', see R. Bentzel, *Inkomstfördelningen i Sverige*,
Industriens Utredningsinstitut, 1942 (especially chapter 6: post-tax, 1935–1948);
Finansdepartementet, *Ägande och inflytande inom det privata näringslivet*, S.O.U.
1968: 7 (pp. 189–203: mainly pre-tax but with some reference to tax effects,
1948–1964). We are grateful to Mrs Lena Daun, of the Swedish Institute in
Stockholm, for providing us with a large amount of relevant published Swedish
material; to Richard Scase of the University of Kent at Canterbury for his comments and advice about information for Sweden; and to Donald Pilcher for
advice on American material.

redistribution through the 'welfare state' appears to be very limited in effect, where attempts have been made to measure it. Indirect taxation everywhere makes up a high proportion of government revenue – generally one-third to one-half of the total. The incidence of taxation in all forms taken together is likely to be almost flat in relation to income, or even regressive – a point for which there is direct evidence in the case of the U.S.A. and Western Germany. Public benefits are probably progressively distributed in relative terms, though with considerable variations. But such redistribution as results from tax-and-benefit systems as a whole seems again to be mainly within classes rather than between them – from wage earners to retired wage earners, for example, much more than from property and high salaries to ordinary earners.[2]

Changes in the pattern of labour market pressures differ from one country to another, as can be expected not least because the chronology of industrialization varies from one to the other. But there are crucial common features among those countries now more or less highly industrialized. There are marked similarities in their case in the general pattern of occupational inequalities of earnings; and similarities again in the trend towards market proletarianization of male clerks, which has been visible at least in recent years in Western Germany and the U.S.A. The reinforcement seen in Britain of class inequalities by sex inequalities, through widening of the disparity between men's and women's earnings as one descends the occupational scale, is confirmed by evidence from Germany and, though less markedly, from France. The contrast of 'life cycle earnings' between manual workers and executives, professionals and the like is plain again from French and American data, though with some differences of detail from the corresponding patterns in this country.[3]

The range of overall income inequality from all sources obviously varies to some extent. It is probably rather less in Sweden, for example, than in Britain and the U.S.A. It appeared to be much the same around 1960 in the latter two countries, according to one set of estimates; but these did not take full account of the more extensive

2. See especially E.C.E., op. cit., chapter 6 (note 1 above); C. Clark and G. H. Peters, 'Some international comparisons', in Clark and Stuvel, op. cit. (ch. 2, note 5 above); Sweden, Finansdepartementet, op. cit. (note 1 above).

3. For relevant calculations or raw data, see E.C.E., op. cit. (chapter 5); Henson, op. cit. (note 1 above, pp. 247–55); H. P. Miller and R. A. Hornseth, *Present Value of Estimated Lifetime Earnings*, U.S. Bureau of the Census (Tech. Paper No. 16), 1967.

apparatus of public welfare in Britain, limited though its redistributive effects are within its own terms. Relative poverty, and above all insecurity, are without doubt especially acute in the richest of all capitalist societies, the United States. The concentration of property ownership, on the other hand, appears to be still more striking in Britain than in America and probably many other capitalist economies. This may be so, however, mainly because the trend towards erosion of small-scale enterprise in agriculture and business has gone furthest in this country; and because owner-occupation of housing – irrelevant in any case to property for power – is less widespread here than in the United States.[4]

Yet none of these differences between one country and another are sufficient to obscure the major similarities of economic inequality across the Western capitalist world. The predominance of private enterprise and property imposes tight restraints on social democratic 'welfarism' – in Sweden as in Britain, for all the contrasts between these and the United States. Almost everywhere disparities of income have remained constant, or have even grown rather wider, since the shift of the 1940s. Britain on these scores is not a deviant case, but one moderately well documented specimen of late twentieth-century capitalism.

III

The persistence of inequality came to be recognized, during the 1960s and early 1970s, in public debate about 'the condition of England' as of other capitalist countries. This recognition in turn has prompted a series of diagnoses and prescriptions for reform which, in effect and often also by design, are conservative in character. Responses of that kind characteristically turn on an explicit or implicit description of the key issue as a problem of 'poverty'. Poverty – dismissed as an increasingly residual phenomenon in the 1950s – was rediscovered with a vengeance in the 1960s. It has become part of the verbal stock in trade of politicians and commentators of nearly all

4. See especially H. F. Lydall and J. B. Lansing, 'A comparison of the distribution of personal income and wealth in the United States and Great Britain', *Amer. Econ. Review*, March 1959; R. J. Lampmann, *The Wealth Share of Top Holders in National Wealth 1922–1956*, Princeton, 1962; J. D. Smith and S. K. Calvert, 'Estimating the wealth of top wealth-holders from estate tax returns', *Amer. Statist. Assoc., Proceedings Business and Economic Statistics Section*, 1965 (pp. 248–65).

shades of opinion; and the subject matter of a major growth industry in social and economic research, especially in the United States. This preoccupation with poverty is liable to obscure reality; and for that reason, in our view, it is on balance politically retrogressive in impact. In drawing an arbitrary line (or series of lines) to distinguish the 'poor' from the rest, it diverts attention from the larger structure of inequality in which poverty so defined is embedded. That is often not the intention. On the contrary, much of the research on poverty – typically undertaken by radical rather than conservative social scientists – has started from an explicitly 'relative' definition of poverty. The 'poverty line' is set by reference to contemporary standards of expectation; it moves upwards over time as absolute levels of living improve; and it is acknowledged to be only one arbitrary line among many that could be drawn at different levels of the hierarchy of inequality.[5] The effect for all that is to focus on what goes on below the line. The risks associated with that are twofold.

The first risk is to encourage false diagnosis. This is manifest in the assumption – often made by politicians, welfare workers and journalists, more rarely by the professionals of poverty research themselves – that the causes of poverty can be read off from the characteristics of the poor. A line drawn anywhere near what can be regarded as a 'subsistence level of living' at a particular time is bound to cut off, below it, a minority of the population embracing a high proportion of non-earners and specially handicapped people. (The fact that it is bound to do so is itself a commentary on the public philosophy of a society which takes it for granted that property ownership and market sale of labour must be the prime determinants of livelihood.) True, one of the merits of recent poverty research has been to emphasize – in refutation of earlier complacency – that the lower limit of labour market earnings is well below such a poverty line. Even so, very many – usually most – of 'the poor' will be state pensioners, sick people and invalids, families with many children, and families with only one parent.[6] The spurious equation that identifies

5. See for Britain especially the work of Peter Townsend and his colleagues – on this point, e.g., P. Townsend, ed., *The Concept of Poverty*, Internat. Cttee. on Poverty Research, 1970; for the United States the work, among others, of S. M. Miller and his colleagues – e.g., S. M. Miller and Pamela Roby, *The Future of Inequality*, Basic Books, 1970.

6. By the criterion of minimum subsistence as allowed in the official scale of benefits, some 5 per cent of all households ($3\frac{1}{2}$–4 per cent of all persons) were 'in poverty' in Britain in 1960 and in 1967. With a line set alternatively 40 per cent

characteristics of the poor with causes of poverty then leads to the conclusion that poverty is in large part the result of old age, physical and mental handicap, high fertility, family dissolution and child-bearing outside marriage. The 'causes' so diagnosed are individual conditions, ostensibly unconnected with each other and unrelated, or only incidentally related, to class. The remedies often proposed are correspondingly discrete, directed to this or that particular condition by itself, whether they involve only financial assistance or also include measures of 'preventive therapy'. They are not designed to produce wholesale change in the general structure of inequality.

That sort of diagnosis is a commonplace of public debate and policy; and it lends support to the notion that inequality now cuts across class divisions.[7] It is false precisely because it closes one eye firmly to the total pattern of inequality, only the bottom end of which is visible under the poverty line. Subsistence poverty is indeed common among old people, the sick, the handicapped, and so on; but only because the majority of the old, sick and handicapped have previously been dependent on jobs that provided them with few or no other resources to fall back on than meagre benefits from public

---

above that level, 18 per cent of all households (14 per cent of all persons) were 'in poverty' in 1960. The composition of the 'poor' populations in 1960 according to their primary source of income was as follows:

| Primary source of household income | Persons in households with household incomes – | |
| | Below subsistence | Below line 40% above subsistence |
	%	%
Pensions	37	35
Other state benefits	44	23
Other income, mainly earned	19	42
Total persons in 'poverty'	100	100

Sources: B. Abel Smith, P. Townsend, *The Poor and the Poorest*, Bell, 1965 (pp. 40, 45–6); Atkinson, op. cit. (ch. 2, note 8 above), p. 36.

7. To take just one example of this sort of diagnosis: an official Swedish enquiry deduced, from the large number of non-earners and part-time earners among people with low incomes, that low income was relatively independent of occupational status. It ignored, in this conclusion, the point that among those with low incomes, earners and non-earners alike were, in the main, manual workers or small farmers – then or in the past – or came from families of that socio-economic level. (Inrikesdepartementet, *Den svenska köpkraftsfördelningen 1967*, S.O.U. 1971: 39, pp. 10, 72–6 ff.)

funds. Rank-and-file wage earners – manual and routine non-manual – live with the risk of poverty over their heads. They face a likely prospect of poverty on retirement. And they face a threat of poverty even before that: on redundancy and if forced to work short-time; on transfer to low-paid work in the later years of working life; in sickness, in widowhood, and through loss of subsidiary household earnings.[8] The risk of poverty at two stages of the working-class life cycle – in childhood and the child-rearing phase of working life – has been markedly reduced during this century: this for the simple reason that families are now much smaller than they were, and child-bearing is compressed within a short span of years. But poverty in old age is more common than it was, because more workers live on to experience it. To the bourgeoisie, by contrast, the risk of subsistence poverty is remote. High earnings, fringe benefits, greater job security, the incremental rise of the typical life cycle, the consequent relative ease of individual 'planning' and saving – all these confer relative immunity. And property ownership gives total immunity.

So, even when not intended that way, preoccupation with 'poverty' runs a constant risk of encouraging a distorted image of society. In that image 'the poor' – or a series of separate categories of poor – are singled out from the mass of wage earners from which they are recruited. And the division is ignored between the wage-earning class – in or out of poverty – and the secure though differentiated ranks of the 'middle and upper' classes. It is this sort of image which in turn leads to the second risk: the risk of false prescription. Precisely that image of society is implied when, for example, a prominent and representative Labour politician argues that sacrifices by workers are the main prerequisite of redistribution.[9] It is implied again when a

8. As emphasized already in British poverty surveys around the turn of the century, far more working-class families will be 'in poverty' at some time during a period of years than are in poverty at any one moment. A suggestion by T. Stark (*The Distribution of Personal Income in the United Kingdom 1949–1963*, Cambridge University Press, 1972, p. 58) that conventional studies exaggerate inequality, in so far as they count among the poor those who are only temporarily in that condition, is odd – at least if one is concerned with the social significance of poverty and inequality. For then it is the *risk* of descent into poverty that is important. Many with average incomes, over a period, above the poverty line will spend some time below it. (Stark's study uses an index of inequality of which the main ingredient is a measure of 'poverty'. It shows some *decline* in inequality on that score over the period, but within an irregular pattern of fluctuation. We have not drawn on it in our general analysis, for technical reasons: mainly because it deals only with pre-tax incomes.)
9. See ch. 2, note 4 above.

Conservative government's counter-inflationary 'incomes and prices' policy attempts to saddle unions with a moral responsibility to help lower-paid at the expense of higher-paid workers, but provides for no transfer from capital to labour; and when that policy then is presented – and almost universally hailed by the press – as 'fair', and a welcome return to 'consensus politics'.[10] Examples could be multiplied almost without end – not least from the various versions of incomes policy adopted by governments of both parties. They represent a common response to the rediscovery of inequality, masked and tamed as a rediscovery of 'poverty'.

IV

The 1960s and early 1970s saw a series of proposals – and in Britain, at least, several policy measures – aimed at greater 'selectivity' in the distribution of public benefits. That aim was to be achieved in part by making more benefits conditional on application to show 'need'; in part by the introduction of 'negative income tax' or 'tax credits'.[11] Ostensibly directed towards fairer shares, the target of these proposals

10. For example, the White Paper, *The Programme for Controlling Inflation: The Second Stage* (Cmnd. 5205, January 1973) and the Act following from it provided, inter alia, for pay increases over 12 months of up to £1 per week plus 4 per cent of the previous year's pay bill per head (to a limit of about £5 per week). This was to be taken as an average for any settlement, with the distribution between lower- and higher-paid to be settled by negotiation. Quite apart from the fact that, as always, salaries negotiated individually would not be effectively subject to control, the scheme allowed profit margins to be set at the average level of the best two years in the previous five. These and other measures of the programme (e.g., some increase in rent allowance scales), had to be seen, moreover, in the context of overall government policy. This provided for selective aid at the bottom of the scale, but was coupled with large tax reliefs and increases in rental income and property values at the top, as referred to earlier. It was these 'distributive' questions in the package of government policy taken as a whole (including also the exclusion of imported food from price control) on which the trade unions focused in their attack at that time on the incomes policy. See also notes 24 and 25 below.

11. One of the chief spokesmen in Britain for 'selectivity', negative income tax and associated policies has been the Institute of Economic Affairs: see, e.g., A. Christopher *et al.*, *Policy for Poverty*, I.E.A., 1970. For one of many American examples of this sort of prescription (strongly reminiscent in this case of the philosophy of the British 1834 Poor Law and the later Charity Organisation Society), see E. C. Banfield, *The Unheavenly City*, Boston, 1970. Proposals for 'selectivity' and related measures are critically examined and attacked in, e.g., P. Townsend *et al.*, *Social Services for All*, Fabian Society, 1968; David Bull, ed., *Family Poverty*, Duckworth and Child Poverty Action Group, 1971; Atkinson, op. cit. (ch. 2, note 8 above).

in practice was redistribution only in a very special sense. They would, if they worked as they were said to be intended, give greater help to the 'poor' below one or more arbitrarily drawn lines of special need. But they would also, and that deliberately, extend the range of inequality above this threshold, through some combination of direct tax reliefs, shifts to indirect taxation, and wider scope for the operation of 'free market' forces. Their effect therefore would be, and has been, to accentuate the primary characteristics of existing tax-and-benefit provisions as mechanisms for redistribution within classes, while increasing inequality between classes.

The public appeal of proposals for greater 'selectivity' in any form has been strengthened by the fact, and misinterpretation of the fact, that redistribution through government action has so little effect. The poor, it is argued, could be helped more, if less help were given to those who are not so poor – including people earning 'good' wages. Selectivity in the form of 'negative income tax' or 'tax credits', more-over, has additional appeal, because it would offer an indisputable advantage to people on low incomes. It would provide for automatic, rule-bound and anonymous payment of cash benefits, requiring neither knowledge of legal entitlement nor specific appliontion on the part of potential recipients. Payments, in a consistently applied negative tax scheme, would be made as a matter of course to those people whose tax returns showed incomes below the subsistence limits set. Indeed, such a scheme *could* be one arm of a policy of overall equalization; but only if it were coupled with a transformation of the total tax system, to make the incidence of taxes continuously, markedly and effectively progressive up the entire scale of income and wealth. This, it is clear, has not been intended by any of the actual proposals for benefits to be linked to taxation.[12]

One major criticism of these proposals – including the tax credit measures which were scheduled for introduction by a Conservative government in Britain by the mid-1970s – is that they make for very steep progression of effective rates of tax in the bottom reaches of the income scale. The poor are caught in a 'poverty trap' with possibly strong disincentive consequences. If their earned incomes rise, they lose benefit – or pay tax on the increase – at a high rate.

12. The Conservative government's green paper, *Proposals for a Tax-Credit System* (Cmnd. 5116, October 1972), left a crucial gap of £1,300 million for the financing of the scheme unexplained. If that were met largely from increased indirect taxation – as seemed quite probable when the proposals were published – the effect would be regressive.

Whatever the disincentive effects, the real force of this criticism lies in the contrast to which it points between steep progression of taxation at low incomes and the concern of businessmen and many politicians to moderate progression higher up the scale. An alleged need for financial incentives to managers and professionals is invoked to justify both tax concessions to the wealthy, and a further release of market forces to extend the range of inequality upwards. But the relevance of incentives is, at the same time, denied in application to people on low incomes. Sauce for the bourgeois gander is not sauce for the working-class goose.

Even a tax credit system which was joined with other changes in taxation to produce some positive redistribution right across the board – hypothetical though that prospect is – could make only a very limited contribution to greater equality by itself. No alteration of taxation conceivable within the continuing context of a capitalist economy – given business demands for 'incentives' and business needs to maintain profit – could be expected to do more than rather mildly moderate the present inequalities of money income and wealth. Short of public appropriation of private property, and subsequent policies to equalize incomes according to need, more effective redistribution would require the maintenance and extension of public services provided equally for all, as a 'right of citizenship', irrespective of income.[13] Health and education are the services which, in Britain today, come nearest to that description. Neither comes fully within it, it should be added: partly because a private sector has been retained in each case; partly because the practical operation of class divisions makes for inequalities in the availability of services and their effective use within the public sector. If these services were privately run; or if use of their 'public parts' were, in law or practice, restricted to people of 'limited means' – then, whatever devices might be adopted to ensure minimum provision for all, the result would be a dual or hierarchical system of provision. The divisions within this system would correspond to the continuing divisions of income and wealth in the population.

It is just that sort of duality or hierarchy which is at work, and was extended under policies adopted in the early 1970s, in respect of pensions and housing. Selective provision once more is redistributive

13. See T. H. Marshall, *Citizenship and Social Class* (Cambridge University Press, 1950) for the concept of 'citizenship' embodied in services provided on a universal basis.

in effect only in the lower ranges of the scale of income. The effect above the threshold is to 'let inequality rip'. Full nationalization of provision on the other hand – though often attacked as indiscriminate and ineffective in redistribution, because the wealthy benefit as well as the poor – has an egalitarian thrust right across the board. This is so not only symbolically, because all users are treated as citizens with equal rights of access. The result also contributes materially to more equality, by taking a whole area of consumption out of the market in which inequalities of income and wealth determine use. Within the tight constraints of an essentially capitalist economy, greater efficiency in overall redistribution is not helped by more 'discriminate' provision of services. It requires, on the contrary, the removal of wider areas of consumption from the market through universal provision, coupled with more discriminate – more progressive – taxation up the entire range of income and wealth.

Of course the constraints are tight. The structure of power and the profit orientation of economic enterprise make for strong resistance to any policies of even modest positive redistribution beyond mitigation of 'poverty'. Moreover, inequality breeds further inequality, and cumulatively strengthens the public ideology which takes inequality for granted. Examples come easily to hand. If incomes in working life are unequal, it is argued in both Labour and Conservative policies, then pensions must be so too, to reduce problems of 'personal adjustment' on retirement for managers and professionals no less than for ordinary wage earners.[14] The gradation of authority in private and public business must, we are told, be marked by a clear corresponding gradation of salaries: so the peak must be high to accommodate all the steps below it. Moreover, top earnings in the public sector must be nearly competitive with those in the private sector, even if it is difficult to make them wholly so. (Both these arguments were advanced and implemented under a Labour incomes policy, the general direction of which was otherwise to freeze the structure of inequality in the interests of counter-inflation.)[15] It is said, again, that financial incentives at the top need to be large because, the higher the basic

14. Cf., e.g., T. H. Marshall, *Social Policy*, Hutchinson, 1970 (pp. 102 ff.). See also pp. 172–92, where the author argues in general for a moderate 'maximization of welfare' objective for social policy, in contrast to a pursuit of equality.

15. N.B.P.I., op. cit. (ch. 5, note 3 above). For general analyses of Labour incomes policies, see Joan Mitchell, *The National Board for Prices and Incomes*, Secker & Warburg, 1972; C. Balfour, *Incomes Policy and the Public Sector*, Routledge & Kegan Paul, 1972.

income, the smaller the psychological effect of a given increment as encouragement to enterprise. (The corollary of this argument, if correct, is that any special incentives which might be needed could be quite small if there were near-equality of incomes and no private property. But the argument is not, of course, usually taken to that logical conclusion.) Correspondingly, at the bottom of the scale, low earnings in the labour market are assumed to require a still lower level of public benefit in unemployment – a 'wage stop' – to discourage 'scrounging'. The latter term itself deftly attributes blame to the victims of inequality. And the assumption illustrates the inexorable pressures to define 'incentives' in financial terms in a market economy. Even critics of inequality are caught up in those pressures when they argue against 'tax credit' schemes on the ground that such schemes have a heavy disincentive effect at the lower end of the income scale.

Last, but not least, wage bargaining in the unequal labour market inevitably acquires something of the character of inter-union, inter-worker rivalry. And so long as profits remain elusive as a practical target of union demands, success of one union may indeed be bought at the expense of others. The immunity of profit in the process is often obscured – with the dedicated aid of politicians and journalists – by the apparent competition among workers for shares in that 'pool of wages' to which union demands are seen, as a rule, to be effectively confined. The beauty of this, for maintenance of the order as it is, is to assist in working-class fragmentation; and again to encourage allocation of blame for inequality on its victims. In fact the resilience of working-class solidarity to these contrary pressures is in many ways remarkable. But that resilience is clearly under heavy strain when politicians, businessmen and those who direct the mass media, from their little-publicized positions of affluence and security, single out the 'greed' of electricians, car workers, dockers, railway drivers or miners for near-unanimous and often venomous attack.

Inequality, in short, is a vicious circle. As such it is difficult to reverse. But it can be broken.

V

Should the circle be broken? One answer is to say: 'No – in the end it all amounts to very little.' Forced to acknowledge the persistence of inequality in Western societies, some commentators have taken refuge in this sort of defence of contemporary capitalism. Inequalities remain, in relative terms, much as they were: that may be conceded. But their moral and social significance is vastly reduced by comparison with the past, it is argued, because they operate at much higher – and more or less steadily increasing – levels of living. Inequalities relate now in the main to 'frills': everyone has cake, but some have more icing than others.

The extension of the average span of life itself provides the simplest illustration of this argument. Class differences in the risk of death are still marked, in relative terms. Indeed, the gaps have recently tended to widen. Holding age constant, death rates among adult men in 1930/32 ranged from 10 per cent below the average in the case of high professionals and administrators, to 11 per cent above the average in the case of unskilled workers. There were signs, by the end of the 1940s, of the emergence of an uneven gradient of class mortality, even though the overall range had widened. But by 1959/63 – the period of the latest series of figures – there was again a consistent inverse relationship between class and death rates, and a noticeable widening of the gap in relative terms. The range was now from a level nearly 25 per cent below the average for men of the top class, and a figure little different for those in intermediate grade non-manual jobs; through death rates close to the average for clerical, sales and skilled manual workers and for the semi-skilled; to a rate no less than 40 per cent above average in the case of the unskilled. Comparison over the years is distorted by changes in definitions of the occupational categories, and in their size and internal composition. The unskilled, for example, are a smaller group than they were; and unskilled work may possibly be more of a 'dumping ground' for men in ill health and special difficulties than before. Yet it is clear that such changes can be only part of the explanation: there has been some real widening of the relative class gaps in adult risks of death.[16] So too, the proportionate class differentials in infant mortality remained remarkably constant from 1921 to 1950 – with deaths before the first birthday over twice as common among children of the unskilled as among children of fathers in high professional and administrative jobs. These differentials were maintained again into the middle 1960s; while those relating to stillbirths and to

16. Registrar General, *Decennial Supplement, England and Wales, 1961: Occupational Mortality Tables*, H.M.S.O., 1971.

perinatal mortality actually widened during that, or roughly the same, period.[17]

Even so – and here is the crux of the argument in question – these are all relative differences. Absolute class differences in the risk of death have narrowed, as the overall risk of death before completion of the 'natural span of life' has been greatly reduced. The expectation of life at birth today is about 69 years for men, 75 for women. Since about the mid-nineteenth century, 30 years or more have been added to the life expectation of the average child born: not, incidentally, because old people live much longer than they used to, but because far more people survive to old age. In the 1840s, over 15 out of every 100 children born died within their first year of life; so still in the 1890s. But by the second decade of this century, the rate was down to about 13 in every 100; and it was less than 2 per 100 by 1970.[18] How much does it really matter, runs the argument applied to this example, that for every infant death to parents in the top class there will be proportionately twice as many to parents in the unskilled group? For, in any case, over 97 in every 100 infants of the unskilled group survive.

One rejoinder is in direct terms of moral principle. It matters, because inequality itself is objectionable: an affront to human dignity. It involves a denial of the common value of human life to assert that, as a matter of arrangements within society's power to control, some should have a greater claim than others to livelihood, welfare and the conditions of a good life. Inequality is therefore all the more objectionable in societies which have the wealth, the potential capacity and self-knowledge to eliminate it. But forceful as it is to us, the weight of that reply in the end hangs on acceptance or rejection of the egalitarian axiom on which it is based. That is not true of another answer, which starts by challenging the realism of the crucial premise on which the argument to 'frills' relies: the assumption that there is a fixed and fairly clear threshold to divide essentials from inessentials.

In some respects there is a threshold of that sort. Life itself is an

17. Registrar General, *Decennial Supplement, England and Wales, 1951: Occupational Mortality*, Part I, H.M.S.O., 1954; J. N. Morris and J. N. Heady, 'Social and biological factors in infant mortality', *Lancet*, 12 February–12 March, 1955; C. C. Spicer and L. Lipworth, *Regional and Social Factors in Infant Mortality*, H.M.S.O., 1966; N. R. Butler and D. C. Bonham, *Perinatal Mortality*, Livingstone, 1963. (Perinatal mortality is the technical term for stillbirths and deaths during the first week of life, taken together.)

18. Registrar General, *Statistical Review for England and Wales 1970: Part I, Tables, Medical*, H.M.S.O., 1972.

essential; and there is a finite limit to improvement, for example, in rates of infant survival. The limit is reached when 100 out of every 100 infants survive; and even the unskilled are now not very far from that point, slow though recent progress on that score has been. But the analogy has very restricted application. There is no obvious, and certainly no fixed, limit to improvements in respect of most goods, services and uses of time; in the quality of life itself. So too there is no obvious point, before that, at which improvement passes from essentials to frills. On the contrary: in real social terms the threshold moves constantly upwards. As levels of living and security rise, yesterday's luxuries become necessities today: supply creates its own demand. Indeed contemporary capitalist economies are geared just to that – if possible, in fact, to keep demand ahead of supply.

So, as old wants have been met, new ones emerge or are deliberately promoted. It ill becomes the privileged to dismiss new popular wants as concerned only with frills, when they themselves would never dream of giving up their privileges. In the process of rising popular demands, moreover, many old class differences in expectations and aspirations are gradually eroded. Ordinary workers are likely increasingly to set their definitions of need by 'middle class' standards. In that sense, there is 'class assimilation', of a formal and superficial kind. But because the concrete inequalities of income and wealth persist at new levels, the gap between workers' aspirations and their achievement widens. The implications are that discontent is likely to increase; not to decrease.

VI

Housing provides one obvious example of the rise and partial 'class assimilation' of expectations. By fixed standards, housing conditions have greatly improved, and are still improving. But standards are not fixed. Official criteria – of overcrowding, of unfit dwellings, of deficiencies in facilities that require improvement, and so on – have become generally more demanding over time. There can be no doubt that popular expectations have risen at least correspondingly. When, for example, by the mid-1960s well over 60 per cent of all households had a full set of four 'standard' domestic facilities for their exclusive use – W.C., bath or shower, basin and hot water – this marked a considerable improvement over time, of course. But the fact that more than one household in every three – far higher proportions of the poor, the unskilled and semi-skilled, the old and the young, small households and households renting private accommodation – did *not* have the full combination for their own use, was all the more striking just because facilities of this kind were now regarded as basic. They had become an element in minimum housing requirements. And the class contrasts in deprivation on this score – one in every two households without the full set among the unskilled and semi-skilled, for example, as against only one out of seven in the top and intermediate non-manual groups – were critically significant, just because substantial numbers of working-class households nevertheless *had* now achieved that level of comfort: council tenants in particular.[19] Council housing – in general of slightly better quality than owner-occupied housing by this criterion – has played a major part in raising housing standards, especially since World War II. In that process, working-class expectations in particular have been raised, popular demands increasingly assimilated to current 'middle class' norms. When such expectations are frustrated, denied by the persistence of inequalities in provision, the impact is all the sharper.

In fact, since the 1950s, policy shifts have joined market pressures to deepen the divisions in housing provision. This was not so in the years immediately following the end of World War II. New housing was then made available on lines closer to the principles of 'social service' provision than at any time before or since. The supply of new housing was, in large part, taken out of the commercial market; and it was allocated according to need, irrespective of income. The great majority of all new houses and flats were built by public authorities – five in every six until the early 1950s, three in every five still by the middle years of that decade. Development values in the land, moreover, had been nationalized by the Town and Country Planning Act 1947. This public take-over of future increases in the value of land was designed to secure the financial benefits of new development for the community at large, instead of for those who happened to own the land; to allow planning control without continuous compensation to private interests; to enable public authorities to acquire land for housing and other purposes at no more cost than its value in existing use. Rents in private housing were then also controlled.

It is true that none of this amounted to – or was intended as a step

19. Myra Woolf, *The Housing Survey in England and Wales, 1964*, Government Social Survey, 1967 (pp. 78–81).

towards – the designation of housing provision in general as a full social service. There was no long-term design behind it to remove housing *en bloc* (in the manner of health services) from the market and from the influence of inequalities of income and wealth. A radical policy of that kind would require, among other things, ultimate public ownership of all housing – with, for example, the conversion of both owner-occupier freeholds and tenancies of local authority housing into new forms of public leasehold. Housing up to at least a high basic standard would need to be allocated without regard to income. Rents might be replaced by income-related tax charges. Full-scale nationalization of land would certainly be an essential prerequisite. Nevertheless the germ of such a possible designation of housing as a social service across the board – unrealistic only on the assumption that housing allocation must, by some divine ordinance, generally follow the gradations of income and wealth – was present in the policies of the 1940s.

The picture has changed completely since then. The right to increases in land values arising from development was handed back to private owners during the 1950s; and public authorities were compelled from 1959 to pay 'full market value' for land which they acquired. The inevitable result, in conjunction with other pressures, was a rapid escalation of land prices and housing costs, especially in and just after the late 1960s. The costs of acquiring land for local authority housing, for example, rose by as much as 40 per cent per dwelling in one year, 1970/71, over the country as a whole, bringing them to a level two-and-a-half times as high as in 1964. The corresponding increases were still faster in Greater London.[20] Rent control in private housing was loosened in successive legislation. By the 1970s – following an earlier Labour measure in the same direction – it was being entirely replaced by a system of rent 'regulation', with the effect of edging rents up to 'market levels'. Far more drastically, the same system, with the same effect, was applied also to public housing from 1972. Rent rebates and allowances adjusted to income – on a scale a good deal more generous than in the case of other cash benefits – were introduced as part of that package. But they were made

20. Department of the Environment, *Housing and Construction Statistics*, No. 2, 1972 (on which we have also drawn at several other points in this paragraph). For a sharp general commentary on the effects in London of the denationalization of development values, and of other changes in policy and planning practice from the 1950s on, see Ruth Glass, 'The mood of London', in D. Donnison and D. Eversley, eds., *London: Urban Patterns, Problems and Policies*, Heinemann, 1973.

available only on application – a feature known from extensive past experience to reduce 'take up' far below its ceiling; and they could be expected in general to meet only a limited part of the long-run cost to tenants arising from the shift to market rents.

The role of public housing had in any case already been considerably curtailed over the years. Its contribution to all new housing fell to under 40 per cent by the early 1960s; rose again during the Labour years, and immediately thereafter, to around 50 per cent; and was then reduced even more. Subsidies for 'improvement' of private housing were considerably extended, from the late 1960s especially, with little public control. These in practice gave substantial aid to private landlords, as well as to owner-occupiers; and they gave leeway for further increases in private sector rents. Governments of both parties encouraged owner-occupation, applying and extending a system of subsidies by way of tax reliefs which rise, in effect, with increasing income. That was regressive enough. But the wider consequence of increased owner-occupation – taken still further by sale of council housing – was to drive a thick, and steadily thickening, wedge between those who thus acquire a share in rising land values and those who suffer from them.

That division, and its repetition up the scale between small and large owners, accentuates existing divisions of income and wealth. But it no longer coincides neatly with the main line of separation between ordinary earners on the one hand, the 'intermediate salariat' and those above them on the other. Increasing numbers of working-class households have been tempted, or forced, into the owner-occupation market at its lower end. This process was encouraged by successive cuts over long periods in the share of public housing in new building; by rises in basic council rents even before 1972, often in association with local rebate schemes designed to reduce subsidies and concentrate them on poorer tenants; by the tax reliefs available for house purchase.[21] The effect of the Housing Finance Act 1972

21. By 1970, in Great Britain as a whole, nearly one half of all households lived in owner-occupied homes, while one third were local authority tenants. Three in every five owner-occupiers were still paying off mortgages, and of these one third were headed by a man or woman earning less than £30 a week (though mostly at least £20 a week). (*Source:* see note 20 above, p. 90; from 1970 Family Expenditure Survey.) Relevant data from the 1971 Census were not yet available at the time of writing. But (taking figures for England and Wales) already in 1966 about 40 per cent of skilled manual households, 33 per cent of the semi-skilled and 24 per cent of unskilled households were owner-occupiers. The proportions were much higher, of course, among managers and professionals (around 70–75 per

would clearly be to accentuate the trend. The Act was designed to expose municipal housing to the blast of market forces as never before. It put the public sector of housing on all fours with the private rented sector, though with the additional refinement that council tenants might, out of their higher rents, have to finance part of the allowance scheme to support larger rent payments to landlords in the private sector.[22] The impact of the 1972 Act on individual households would be mitigated in both sectors by provision for rent relief – but to an uncertain extent in practice; and with net redistributive gains confined, and even that patchily, to households in the lowest range of the income scale. The consequences for the role of local authority housing at large would be to exacerbate the shift into owner-occupation, divisive as that institution is; and to put a large question mark against the long-term future of the public sector.

VII

Housing is thus one of the focal points of the clash between rising demands and continuing inequality. Education is another, though the inequalities at work there are less directly economic in character and the great bulk of services in that case are in public ownership. But the most straightforward manifestation of the clash is in the pattern of wage claims and union demands since the late 1960s.

When the unions and the T.U.C. then abandoned their reluctant co-operation in Labour 'incomes policies', wage claims thereafter were framed in terms a good deal more ambitious than before. Their sheer magnitude often implied, and they sometimes directly expressed demands for a cut in profit shares and management rewards. They reflected, on the part of unions and workers on the shop floor, a more overt impatience with continuing inequalities, even though

cent) and in the intermediate and junior non-manual groups (65 and 54 per cent respectively). The share of owner-occupation had risen rather more, however, in the manual than in the non-manual groups since 1961. There are indications from the same data that, against a background of overall improvement, *relative* class differences in overcrowding may if anything have widened a little between 1961 and 1966, overall and within each type of tenure. But changes in the Census definition of habitable rooms rule out precise comparison between the two dates. (Calculations from *1966 Housing Tables*, Part I: pp. 15–34, and *1961 Household Composition Tables*, pp. 7–27, both for England and Wales.)

22. R. A. Parker, *The Housing Finance Bill and Council Tenants*, Child Poverty Action Group, 1972.

this impatience was not translated into clear political statements.[23] Earlier collaboration in incomes policies had not only accentuated the incompatible duality of roles acquired by the unions, which had increasingly come to act as agents of government and employers in enforcing discipline on the members whom they were supposed to represent. But it had also, by the same token, undercut union criticism of the structure of economic inequality. For the essence of counter-inflationary income policies – Labour and Conservative – was to accept the existing share of labour in general as fixed, if not actually too high. These policies paid some lip-service to a need to raise the lowest incomes. But they offered no effective means even to that end – whose achievement, it implied, required sacrifices by the more 'affluent' groups of wage earners, not by those whose high incomes escaped control. They made no provision, as we have emphasized before, for redistribution from capital and management to labour. This is hardly surprising, since a prime purpose of these policies was to secure profits against mounting economic uncertainty.[24]

The first prerequisite for a revival of union opposition to the overall pattern of inequality was therefore withdrawal of support for incomes policies of this kind. In taking that step against a Labour government – still in form and tradition their own government – the unions did not make the point explicitly. They did so a good deal more overtly – all sorts of qualifications aside – when they refused to support Conservative incomes policies during the early 1970s. For union opposition was then explicitly directed against the general

23. For a well-documented, 'new style' wage claim see *The Ford Claim 1973*, Ford National Joint Negotiating Committee (Trade Union Side), December 1972.

24. To give one illustration of the immunity of capital from measures, under prices and incomes policies, claimed to be designed in part to give a special boost to low incomes: the Conservative government's Price Commission (*Report for the period 1 June to 31 August 1973*, pp. 14–19) sharply refuted business claims that profits had suffered, or would suffer in future, in consequence of restrictions during the various phases of counter-inflationary policy. The Commission's evidence and arguments pointed in the opposite direction. *The Times* in a leader (17 October 1973) commented that 'the tears now being shed by the Confederation of British Industry . . . are those of an exceptionally brazen crocodile.' And it added its own estimate that profits would continue to rise as a proportion of national income, if the policy were successful. As another illustration, the Pay Board's later report on *Problems of Pay Relativities* (H.M.S.O.; January 1974, Cmnd. 5535) – a document of monumental vacuity – discussed only differences in pay among groups of 'employees'; not between labour and capital or, for all practical purposes, between labour and salaried management.

thrust of government policy with regard to the distribution of income and wealth in society at large.[25]

The effect of these more ambitious union pressures on overall inequality was still negligible. The numbers of the old and the unemployed were rising at the same time, to lengthen the tail of poverty from those sources. Wage increases for those at work – including relatively larger rises for many low-paid groups in the late 1960s, as a result of new pressures from below and union response to those pressures – were partly nullified when they were caught in the tax net.[26] It is true that rates of profit then were declining. The contribution of union and shop-floor worker demands to that decline is still an unsettled – perhaps an irresoluble – question. Measured pre-tax, the fall in rates of profit can in any case be traced back as far as the early 1950s, though its effect on rates of profit post-tax was not visible until the 1960s.[27] Its impact on ultimate distribution of income was nevertheless nil, or virtually so. For the *share* of profit in total income – though falling more or less steadily since around 1950, when measured before tax – actually increased consistently over the same period, when measured after tax.[28] The owners and controllers of private enterprise, it appears, were able to draw good advantage from the tax system to protect their stake in wealth against the decline in its business profitability.

There are no answers in these facts themselves to the far wider-reaching issues which they raise. One question is whether a continuing decline in profits could eventually force a limited redistribution of wealth within a capitalist framework, despite all protective barriers. The crucial question, however, concerns the capacity of

25. See, e.g., the T.U.C.'s policy paper in criticism of the Conservative government's 'Phase Two' incomes policy in early 1973 (*The Times*, 2 February 1973). Cf. also note 10 above.

26. Jackson *et al.*, op. cit. (ch. 1, note 6, and ch. 2, note 7 above). On the rise in low-paid workers' earnings around the end of the 1960s, see also J. Hughes, 'The low paid', in Townsend and Bosanquet, op. cit. (ch. 2, note 7 above); and data from the official New Earnings Surveys. According to the latter, unskilled men's earnings rose by 27 per cent from September 1968 to April 1971 compared with 25 per cent for all manual men; and (see table 14 of the text) women's earnings rose generally faster than men's over the same period.

27. Glyn and Sutcliffe, op. cit. (ch. 1, note 5 above), p. 66. It was this book, and an earlier paper by the same authors (*New Left Review*, No. 66, March–April 1971), which drew attention to the decline in profits and the wide-ranging issues arising from it. See also the debate between the authors, W. Beckerman and others in the *New Statesman*, 8 December 1972 to 5 January 1973.

28. Jackson *et al.*, op. cit. (ch. 1, note 6 and ch. 2, note 7 above), p. 81.

capitalism itself to survive. The signs of a crisis in capitalism, of which the squeeze on rates of profit was part, became increasingly evident during the 1960s and early 1970s. They were evident in the rising though frustrated demands of labour; in the attempts of successive governments to curb labour by legislative and other means; in the confrontations between government and a reluctant union movement to which these attempts in turn gave rise.

It could be that all this points to the prospect of an increasingly overt clash over the very principles of contemporary capitalist social structure. The possibility cannot be ruled out of such a clash between, on the one hand, a surge of radicalism against the foundations of the present order, on the part of a working class increasingly pressed into consciousness of the incompatibility of its demands with the institutions of contemporary capitalism; on the other, a dictatorial elaboration of the apparatus of state and business control, appealing to the 'common interest' in stability and restraint of inflation, to enforce industrial and political 'discipline', restore business profitability, and freeze distribution in a still more unequal mould. On the face of it, resentment and impatience in the wage-earning population – certainly more visible than before – may still seem diffuse, unfocused, fragmented; the forces for extension of 'discipline' clearly stronger. Business and government in the early 1970s were a good deal more ready to diagnose labour militancy as signs of incipient rebellion and conspiracy for revolution, and to take measures accordingly, than were unions and workers to translate their demands into an explicit political challenge to the dominance of capital. Yet these issues acquired a new salience in the years around 1970, as class conflict became more overt and persistent. Even tentative answers to the questions about prospects for the future, however, require a close look at other features of the total pattern of class division, class organization and class consciousness.

PART THREE

INEQUALITY OF POWER

1 Power – anonymous, routine and institutionalized

I

To discuss inequalities of material condition before inequality of power, as we have done, may seem to be putting the cart before the horse: putting effects before cause. So it is in a way. But there is good point in doing so, for two reasons. The first is practical. The advocates of 'post-capitalism' – especially of those versions of the thesis which have had the widest circulation – have taken as the keystone of their argument the postulate that material inequalities are now much less significant than before. Their voices have been loud and profoundly influential. Exposure of the continuing features of capitalist class structure therefore requires the demolition of their case. It is practical to start that demolition job by knocking out the keystone.

The second reason is more fundamental: it relates to the concept and nature of 'power'. The persistence of acute inequalities of material condition and security is indeed, so we argue, a product of the persistence of capitalist power. But to assert a clear distinction here between source and product, cause and effect, is easier to do in the abstract than it is to apply and demonstrate that distinction in concrete terms. Causes, to be recognized as such, can be seen only by their effects. So, too, power is visible only through its consequences: they are the first and the final proof of the existence of power. The continuing inequalities of wealth, income and welfare that divide the population are among the most crucial consequences – the most visible manifestations – of the division of power in a society such as Britain. Those inequalities reflect, while they also demonstrate, the continuing power of capital – the power, not just of capitalists and managers, but of the anonymous forces of property and the market. They also both reflect and demonstrate the orientation of state power. But 'reflection' and 'demonstration' are not easily separated. In practice, one cannot describe inequality of power without first describing the inequalities of condition which are among its main consequences. It is they, not least, which show the presence of power.

Power 'in itself', in other words, is a rather elusive phenomenon. Its effects are tangible. But power as such is something of an abstraction. It certainly cannot be measured in the way, for example, that the distribution of wealth can be measured. And just because it is not hard and fast, there is no simple and agreed definition of what it is. Clearly, the notion of a capacity to determine events and conditions is involved. But quite apart from the problems which arise because nobody, anywhere, ever, has an absolute and unqualified capacity to determine events and conditions – 'control' shades into 'influence' as soon as one starts looking into it – there are other problems too. One concerns the question whether only people – individuals, groups, organized bodies – can be seen as exercising power.

That is often assumed to be so. Many social scientists talk about power – or control, influence and so on – as if these necessarily involve action by individuals or groups. On this view it is indeed only people – individually or collectively – who wield power; and their power is recognizable by their actions. So, to find out where power lies in a society, one must identify an 'élite', or several élites, who make decisions. It is certainly relevant to do that. But it is hardly enough. For that sort of approach, on its own, neglects the point that individuals or groups may have the effective benefits of 'power' without needing to exercise it in positive action. We have more in mind here than just the fact that some people are able to pull strings behind the scenes: string-pulling is still an active exercise of influence, even though it is difficult to detect. What we have in mind is a passive enjoyment of advantage and privilege, obtained merely because of 'the way things work', and because those ways are not exposed to serious challenge. In any society, the pattern of people's lives and their living conditions take the forms which they do, not so much because somebody somewhere makes a series of decisions to that effect; but in large part because certain social mechanisms, principles, assumptions – call them what one will – are taken for granted. Typically, of course, those mechanisms and assumptions favour the interests of this or that group *vis-à-vis* the rest of the population. The favoured group enjoys effective power, even when its members take no active steps to exercise power. They do not need to do so – for much of the time at least – simply because things work their way in any case.

In a capitalist society the social mechanisms and assumptions which are generally taken for granted in this way are those, in the first instance, of private property and the market. It is they which largely determine the living conditions of the people and the use of resources. And they clearly favour the interests of capital: they confer power on capital in a very real and tangible sense. But the proof of that power is not to be found only, or even chiefly, in the fact that capitalists and managers make decisions. It is to be found in the fact that the decisions which both they and others – including government – make, and the sheer routine conduct of affairs even without definite decision-making, in the main have a common denominator: an everyday acceptance of private property and market mechanisms. It is taken for granted, 'in the way things work', that profit should be the normal yardstick of investment in most areas of activity; that the living standards of the propertyless majority should be set primarily by the terms on which they sell or once sold their labour; and so on.

To put the point in general terms, there is power inherent in anonymous social mechanisms and assumptions – in 'social institutions' – not just in individuals and groups. There are two practical consequences which need to be underlined. First, the power of capitalists and managers in a capitalist society is itself circumscribed by the mechanisms from which these people benefit. They are not normally free, for example, to abandon long-run profit maximization as the guiding criterion of their activities. And much of the internal transformation of capitalism over the last century or so – the continuing concentration of business, the consequent emergence of monopolistic competition and oligopoly, the extension of state activity – can be ascribed in part to the efforts of capitalists and managers to protect themselves against the circumscribing uncertainties of the market. Secondly, the point of emphasizing the place of anonymous social mechanisms in power is to draw attention to the controlling role of assumptions which are often not stated, simply because they are taken for granted in practical affairs. The power of capital, to repeat, is revealed much less in positive acts of decision-making – involving conflict and choice between alternative policies – than in the everyday, for much of the time unquestioned, application of those assumptions which give priority to private capital accumulation and market exchange in the use and distribution of resources. Power is to be found more in uneventful routine than in conscious and active exercise of will.

II

Much academic work on the subject has neglected this point from the outset, simply by defining power in such a way as to exclude the power that goes with uneventful routine. This is the case, for example, with one very common definition which stipulates that, for power to be exercised, there must be some opposition to be overcome: power then is a capacity to determine events and the lives of others *despite* resistance. This notion in turn is often linked with a distinction between 'power' and 'authority'.[1] The latter phenomenon, by contrast, implies control which is not opposed, but accepted as right and proper by those who are subject to it. Their acceptance of it 'legitimizes' it. There is certainly an important distinction here; and it may seem scholastic hair-splitting to squabble about the words by which to describe it. Yet there is a risk of real confusion if the term 'power' is reserved for dominance which evokes and overcomes opposition, while dominance 'legitimized' by a lack of opposition is designated 'authority'. The reasons for that risk are worth setting out, because they can help to throw a little more light on the nature of power.

First, the conventional labels fail to distinguish between two issues that are logically separate. One concerns the general character of domination in a given society: the interests which it favours and the mechanisms through which it works. The other concerns the way in which the subordinate population reacts to its subordination. Of course the two issues are connected. If the ruling group finds itself opposed, it may take measures to subdue the opposition: resistance will then have provoked a change in the mechanisms of domination.

1. The distinction is usually attributed to Max Weber (see note 2 below). The theoretical literature in sociology and political science on power is enormous and much of it, in our view, sterile. But for a short recent debate which goes over some of the main issues, see the papers by M. Spencer, R. Martin and J. P. Scott in *Brit. J. of Sociology*, June 1970, September 1971 and March 1973.

But that need not happen. Whether it does or not depends, in large part, on how far the rulers feel seriously threatened. In any case, the central features of the pattern of social domination are likely to remain the same, whether or not resistance provokes the ruling group to take special measures. For example, an escalation of worker militancy in a capitalist economy may – as in Britain at the turn of the 1970s – threaten business profitability and lead to a more vigorous use of law and state force against organized labour. The established order has lost some of its former 'legitimacy'; its maintenance depends more than before on measures to subdue resistance. So dominance shows more features of 'power', by the conventional definition, and fewer of 'authority'. Yet that shift throws little light on the workings of property and the market. They are the mechanisms which are central in the pattern of domination; and they continue to determine conditions of life and the use of resources in much the same way as earlier. The effects of property and market are much more powerful and continuous than are the effects of any specific measures of enforcement (such as legislation to restrict union organization and strike activity) which mark a shift away from 'authority' and nearer to 'power'.

Secondly, the word 'authority' may convey a misleading notion of a dominance both less absolute and more beneficent than 'power'. Perhaps no such notion is intended. And many theorists who use this terminology would certainly claim that, when they talk about the 'legitimacy of authority', they imply no moral approval, only a sociological description. Yet the words have a moral colouration which is liable to be misunderstood.[2] In fact no control could be firmer and more extensive than one which embraced the minds and wills of its subjects so successfully that opposition never even reared its head. A few extreme examples show how the vocabulary glosses over this simple point. In the conventional usage, the label 'power' would be withheld from the domination exercised, say, by slave-masters over docile slaves; by paternalist employers over a passive and unorganized labour force; by a fascist government which had exterminated all effective opposition. Yet the label would be brought back into play the moment domination in any of these cases was potentially weakened by some stirring of protest, some questioning

2. As others have noted, Weber's term 'Herrschaft' would have been more appropriately translated as 'domination', rather than 'authority' with its ambiguous connotations.

of the legitimacy of 'authority'. Unchallenged strength attracts the milder label, its weakening the harsher one.

The examples are unreal: and on just that hangs a third point. It is doubtful whether any body of slaves has ever been entirely docile; any labour force entirely passive; any government successful in extinguishing all opposition. So an element of 'power' would be present in all these situations. The converse is still more important. It is difficult to imagine any kind of power which is sustained entirely without a degree of acceptance by its victims, if only because they have to adapt to make everyday life practicable. So an element – indeed a large element – of 'authority' is always present, even when 'power' is at its strongest. Reality is mixed; and the conventional distinction throws only a dim light on the ambiguities which the reality of mixture involves. When 'conflict' and 'consensus' co-exist, as they typically do, each is shot through with the effects of the other. Much of what may pass for consensus is liable to be something short of positive acceptance: pragmatic conformity, sullen resignation, even latent rebellion. And conflict will be in large part institution-alized: kept within bounds both by agreed restrictions on the means and forms of conflict and, not least, by the fact that the issues effec-tively disputed are confined within a fairly narrow, 'realistic' range.[3]

This latter feature of conflict institutionalization is crucial for an understanding of power in a society such as this. For example, many trade unions in Britain maintain a formal commitment to the establishment of socialism in the future; and that long-term goal still has emotional force at least as a symbolic expression of opposition to the established order. But it has, of course, very little practical force in day-to-day affairs: in the business of collective bargaining and of recurrent industrial conflict between shop floor, unions, employers and government. And this for one reason above all others. It appears – at least most of the time – to serve no practical purpose for the unions to attempt to widen arguments about wages and working conditions into arguments about the total structure of economy and society. So rejection of capitalism's moral legitimacy co-exists with pragmatic acceptance of its continuation. Realism seems to require

3. The term 'institutionalization of class conflict' was used by T. Geiger in his *Klassesamfundet i Støbegryden*, Copenhagen, Gad, 1948 (German ed. 1949), and taken up, e.g., by R. Dahrendorf, *Class and Class Conflict in Industrial Society*, Routledge & Kegan Paul, 1959 (German ed. 1957). But the notion, in various forms, has of course a much longer history: cf., e.g., R. Michels, *Political Parties* (first English ed., 1915).

the latter; and once this definition of what is realistic has been adopted, that itself tends to cripple even the abstract expression of socialist goals as so much 'pie in the sky'. The containment of opposition in this way, by the sheer weight of assumptions about the limits of 'practical politics', is the essence of conflict institutionalization. The terms on which conflict is institutionalized – usually unstated, because they are taken for granted by men 'with their feet on the ground' – are the crucial parameters of power. To try to fit them into some kind of continuum between 'authority' and 'power' in the conventional sense is to miss the point. It would be an arid terminological exercise.

III

Three closely related themes run through these preliminary comments. First, there is power inherent in anonymous social mechanisms as well as in identifiable groups or individuals. Second, power derives more from the routine application of effectively unchallenged assumptions than from the manifest dominance of one faction, group, interest or policy over others in open conflict. Third, the institutionalization of conflict involves just that kind of unspoken adoption of key assumptions, behind which there is pragmatically dictated agreement but no legitimation through positive consensus. The effect is to restrict the policy alternatives about which there is practical dispute to a much narrower range than would otherwise be the case. So, many crucial decisions are not 'made', because they are built in from the start. Power lies closest to the interests that benefit most from this predetermination of the boundaries of conflict.

The importance of 'non-decisions' has indeed been underlined in some of the recent literature on power.[4] But more is involved than the capacity of a well-placed group to 'mobilize bias' or 'pre-empt decisions' – as the point is often seen – by actively preventing particular policy alternatives from being considered. That description certainly applies, for example, when officials or executives without formal powers of policy making – civil servants, say, or middle-level managers in business – are in a position so to prepare the ground that they present their 'masters' with no choice, or only quite a

4. See especially P. Bachrach and M. S. Baratz, *Power and Poverty*, Oxford Univ. Press, 1970.

limited choice, between different courses of action.[5] This entails more
or less direct and deliberate manipulation. It does not cover the
situation of which the essential feature is common acceptance of
certain basic premises, which nobody directly engaged in dispute,
bargaining or advice considers it realistic to challenge and which
automatically rule out a wide range of alternative policies. This is a
foreclosure of options without manipulation. None is needed here,
on or off stage, so long as the unspoken agreement about premises
holds. But such agreement cannot be equated with common approval.
Nor can it be assumed that the balance of agreement has been struck
at a point that somehow favours all interests 'equally', 'impartially'
and with neat symmetry.

Yet it is precisely that kind of assumption which has coloured a
mass of research, interpretation and commentary, directed to the
conclusion that the structure of power in Britain and other Western
societies has been fundamentally transformed. Put schematically,
there are three basic views of which that conclusion is the outcome.
All three are brothers under the skin. All postulate that an earlier
concentration of power in capitalist society has given way to a
diversity of competing pressures among which none is supreme. All
suffer from the same constitutional weakness: they fail to distinguish
between the core assumptions which make up the 'parameters of
power' on the one hand, and the conflicts among competing interests
which take place inside those limits on the other. But they differ in
taking different routes to the same destination.

The first is the familiar theory of 'managerial revolution', which
argues that the power of private business has been tamed from within,
by a divorce between ownership and control and an emergence of a
'responsible' managerial class. The second is less easily identified.
But is not badly described in shorthand as the theory of the 'welfare
state', though the usual connotations of that term are too restrictive.
The postulate here is that the power of private capital has been tamed
from without, by the growth of the state as a kind of third force,
exercising control in response to a diversity of pressures reconciled in
new conceptions of the 'public interest'. The third is a variation on the
same theme, that business has been tamed from without. But in this
version there is less emphasis on the role of the state; more on an

5. Cf., e.g., R. E. Pahl and J. T. Winkler, 'The economic elite: theory and
practice', in P. Stanworth and A. Giddens, eds., *Elites and Power in British
Society*, Cambridge Univ. Press, 1974.

alleged general diffusion of power among a multiplicity of competing groups and interests, none of them predominant, all engaged in a polygon of forces in which alignments shift from issue to issue and from time to time. This, the theory of 'pluralism', is the least specific of the three; and the most elastic. It can embrace the other two, yet does not wholly stand or fall by them. But it expresses most clearly the theme which is common to all three: that the former link between property and power has been severed, and power itself has been converted into a plurality of countervailing pressures.

2 Private business and 'managerialism'

I

The notion that private business power has been tamed from without is, on the face of it, a plausible one. The elements of the argument, after all, are part of everyman's knowledge of the social history of this century: the growth of the state and its increasing involvement in economic affairs; the elaboration of a network of public services for social security, education, housing, health and so on; the rise and recognition of the trade unions; the establishment of labour on the political scene. The notion that business has been tamed from within – in consequence of changes in its own structure and organization, irrespective of outside constraints from government, labour and other sources – has none of the same surface plausibility. On the contrary, many obvious signs point in the opposite direction. Greater concentration of business resources in few hands must, other things being equal, strengthen the power of business in society. In fact the concentration of private capital, by a variety of indices, has steadily increased; and it is still increasing.

A small number of giant corporations hold the keys of the economy. Fifty of them alone accounted for a seventh of the total manufacturing labour force of the United Kingdom in the mid-1930s, a fifth by 1958, a quarter in 1963.[1] By the latter date, they and the next fifty or

1. M. C. Sawyer, 'Concentration in British manufacturing industry', *Oxford Economic Papers*, Nov. 1971. For another measure of increasing concentration, see J. Moyle, *The Pattern of Ordinary Share Ownership* (Cambridge University Press, 1971, p. 11): the 100 largest companies with quoted shares accounted for 51 per cent of the aggregate market value of all quoted share capital in 1963 and for 60 per cent only six years later, in 1969.

so on the list – a total of just under a hundred business enterprises, each employing at least 10,000 people – took up a third of the entire labour force in private sector manufacture; produced still more of the total output; and contributed well over two-fifths of all new investment in that field. (Table 18.) Small businesses still predominate in one sense – if they are counted firm by firm. But a count of that kind

TABLE 18

The growth in scale of enterprise – private sector manufacturing industry, UK, 1935–1963*

Size of enter-prise: no. of persons em-ployed in each enterprise	Enterprises of size shown accounted for following shares of the private sector manufacturing industry's total –						
	Labour force			Net output			Capital ex-penditure**
	1935 %	1958 %	1963 %	1935 %	1958 %	1963 %	1963 %
1–24	⎫	5·9	5·7	⎫	5·2	4·3	3·1
25–99	⎪	9·9	7·9	⎪	8·4	6·5	4·8
	⎬ 50·5			⎬ 47·4			
100–199	⎪	8·0	6·1	⎪	6·9	5·1	4·3
200–499	⎭	12·1	9·4	⎭	11·0	8·3	6·8
500–999	8·9	9·2	7·7	8·6	8·6	7·4	6·2
1,000–1,999	9·1	9·1	8·2	9·3	9·4	8·0	7·1
2,000–4,999	10·4	11·5	12·2	11·3	12·3	12·8	12·3
5,000–9,999	7·4	9·5	10·4	8·6	10·1	11·6	11·8
10,000–19,999	6·0	7·5	10·7	6·1	8·2	11·8	13·5
20,000–49,999	5·9	10·0	12·2	7·3	11·6	13·0	14·5
50,000+	1·8	7·3	9·5	1·4	8·3	11·2	15·6
Total	100·0	100·0	100·0	100·0	100·0	100·0	100·0
Summary							
Under 500	50	36	29	47	32	24	19
500–1,999	18	18	16	18	18	16	13
2,000–9,999	18	21	23	20	22	24	24
10,000 and over	14	25	32	15	28	36	44

Sources: A. Armstrong and A. Silverston, 'Size of plant, size of enterprise and concentration in British manufacturing industry, 1935–58', *J. Royal Statist. Society*, Series A, vol. 128, no. 3, 1965 (from Census of Production data); and *Census of Production 1963, Reports 131–132*, HMSO, 1970. (Publicly owned iron and steel companies are included.)

Notes: * Relevant data from the 1968 Census of Production had not yet been published at the time of writing.
** Capital expenditure *less* disposals.

makes no sense, for it ignores the insignificance of their impact on the economy. Enterprises employing fewer than twenty-five people numbered 70 per cent of all manufacturing enterprises in 1963 (the giants with 10,000 or more, by contrast, less than a fifth of 1 per cent). But their combined share of the total labour force in manufacturing was under 6 per cent; of aggregate net output, little more than 4 per cent; of all new capital expenditure, only 3 per cent. There are two immediately obvious implications of the trend to increasing scale and concentration of productive industry. First, the industrial labour force is predominantly employed by, and dependent for its livelihood on, big business: over 70 per cent of employees in manufacture in 1963 worked for organizations with at least 500 people on their payroll. Second, the markets in which business sells its output are increasingly dominated by a few large enterprises. In 1963 again, the five biggest in each manufacturing trade accounted for an average of nearly 60 per cent of all sales within the trade. This was a 4 per cent increase over the average only a few years before; and in many trades of course, concentration was well above that level.[2] Outright monopoly is rare; restricted, monopolistic competition, the general rule. Indeed, the weight of considerations of market control and security over sheer economies of scale in production, among the factors making for concentration, is evident from the fact that concentration is a good deal further advanced when measured, as here, in terms of the size of enterprises – business organizations – than when measured in terms of the size of physical establishments, production plants. Big business is much bigger than technology alone requires.

The scale of enterprise, it is true, is much smaller in the non-manufacturing sector of private industry than in manufacture; and that sector is expanding faster than manufacture, as the economy continues to shift more resources into 'tertiary' activities ancillary to direct production. But there, too, scale is increasing.[3] And in recent years a boom of business mergers – involving companies engaged in distribution, property and finance especially – has accentuated the trend to concentration.[4] Figures showing the increasing predomin-

2. Sawyer, ibid.

3. E.g., enterprises employing 500 people or more increased their share of the non-manufacturing private sector labour force from 26 per cent in 1958 to 29 per cent in 1963, their share of net output from 31 per cent to 32 per cent. (*Census of Production 1963, Reports 131–132*, H.M.S.O., 1970.)

4. The number of companies acquired by merger in the manufacturing sector rose from 525 in 1967 to 631 in 1968, the expenditure involved in the process from

ance of a few large firms in the sales markets for particular products tell only part of the story. Another part involves extension of power by individual corporations and their affiliates along the whole line of control, from raw material supply through production to distribution. Yet another, and newer, trend is the emergence of large 'conglomerates' that look for security against market uncertainties in a wide spread of activities over different fields. The organization of private business, moreover, increasingly transcends national boundaries. In 1963 already, subsidiaries of foreign corporations – nearly four in every five of American origin – accounted for 7 per cent of the United Kingdom's labour force in private sector manufacture; 11 per cent of net output; 13 per cent of new investment in that field; and 25 per cent of manufacturing exports.[5] Many British companies, too, have subsidiaries overseas; and the two-way links between British and foreign capital play a large part in the country's export trade. In the mid-1960s, British companies with foreign affiliates and British subsidiaries of foreign corporations between them produced five-sixths of the total value of exports; and nearly one-third of all exports went to associates of these companies abroad, as transactions from one pocket to another of the same international combine.[6] An estimate for 1968 set the aggregate assets of 'multinational producing enterprises' outside their countries of origin at a figure of $94 billion: over half the total owned by enterprises of American parentage, those of British parentage next in line with one-fifth.[7] The biggest of the multinational mammoths control assets which rival the total productive capacity of the smaller European nations. The sales turnover of General Motors in 1967, for example, marginally exceeded the gross national product of Belgium; Standard Oil (New Jersey) was next on the list, at a figure roughly equivalent to

£756m. to £1,666m. The boom subsided subsequently so far as manufacture was concerned. But the number of acquisitions rose to 334 in 1971 in the case of distribution (as against 267 in 1970 and an earlier peak of 315 in 1968); and to 203 in 1971 in the case of commerce and finance (as against 185 in 1970, with no figures available before 1969). See *Annual Abstract of Statistics 1972*, p. 368.

5. *Census of Production 1963, Report 132*, H.M.S.O., 1970; J. H. Dunning, *The Role of American Investment in the British Economy*, P.E.P. Broadsheet no. 507, February 1969.

6. D. Lea, 'Multinational companies and trade union interests', in J. H. Dunning, ed., *The Multinational Enterprise*, Allen & Unwin, 1971. (Data from a Board of Trade survey in 1966.)

7. J. H. Dunning, 'The multinational enterprise: the background', in *idem*, ed., *The Multinational Enterprise* (note 6 above).

Switzerland's or Denmark's G.N.P.; Ford next again, with a turn-over above the G.N.P. of Norway.[8]

II

Yet it is, paradoxically, on just this increase in scale and concentration that the postulate of private capital's 'civilization by internal transformation' rests. That thesis – the theory of 'managerial revolution' or, perhaps better, of 'managerial infiltration' – in outline runs like this.[9] Growth in scale has necessarily entailed the rise and pre-dominance of joint stock enterprise. Large business is typically owned, not by single individuals, families or partners who them-selves run the enterprise, but by a multitude of shareholders. The shareholders are far too many and too scattered to exercise control. Though collectively owners in law, they become no more than creditors in fact. So, in the place once occupied by owner-entrepre-neurs, there is now a power vacuum. Or there would be, were it not filled by those who *are* in a position to exercise control: the 'manag-ers'. Constitutionally only salaried officials – agents responsible through the board to the legal owners – in fact they acquire real power. There has been no agreement – and indeed little clarity – among proponents of the thesis as to where, within management, the locus of power is then to be found. Some versions argue that it drifts downwards, to middle and technical levels of management, because their role as expert advisers gives managers at these levels power to limit the alternatives which they present for consideration

8. L. Turner, *Invisible Empires: Multinational Companies and the Modern World*, New York, Harcourt Brace Jovanovich, 1971 (pp. 135–6).

9. The classic formulation was A. A. Berle and G. C. Means, *The Modern Corporation and Private Property*, New York, 1932; the famous extension of the argument, the title of which caught on, J. Burnham, *The Managerial Revolution*, Penguin Books, 1945 (American ed., 1941). The most sophisticated British ex-ample of the 'optimistic' current version of the thesis is still C. A. R. Crosland, *The Future of Socialism*, Cape, 1956, the theme of which was taken up in cruder form in the Labour Party's policy statement, *Industry and Society*, 1957. Among later variants on the optimistic 'post-capitalist' theme – expressed with or without reservations – see A. A. Berle and C. Kaysen in their contributions to a symposium in *Quarterly Journal of Economics*, Feb. 1965; and J. K. Galbraith, *The New Industrial State*, Hamilton, 1967. For two recent general, and critical, reviews of these and many other formulations of the thesis, see T. Nichols, *Ownership, Con-trol and Ideology*, Allen and Unwin, 1969; and J. Child, *The Business Enterprise in Modern Industrial Society*, Collier-Macmillan, 1969 (chap. 3).

higher up, and thus to 'pre-empt' the decisions of their superiors. Be that as it may, the crux of the argument is that power is divorced from ownership.

To Burnham, whose book in the early 1940s gave the thesis its popular name, the implications were disturbing. The new class of managers threatened, through their control of increasingly giant enterprises in both public and private sectors, to wield unprecedented, practically unchallengeable and irresponsible power. Later versions of the theory have taken, almost uniformly, a much happier view of the prospects. By and large, it is now argued, managers of private corporations can be trusted to exercise their control 'responsibly'. Since their power derives from office not from ownership, the pursuit of profit will be only one among a variety of their goals of policy; and quite possibly a subordinate one, defined in minimum practical terms. The interests of shareholders will rank no higher than the interests, say, of employees, of customers, of suppliers, of 'the public' at large perhaps. Overriding all will be the 'interests of the firm' as such – of its maintenance and growth as ends in themselves. That reorientation of policy criteria will be encouraged, moreover, by an increasing recruitment even of top-level management from among professionals and technical specialists. For they *par excellence* can be expected to be job-, product- and growth-oriented rather than dedicated to profit maximization.

So, on these assumptions, two crucial dimensions of class no longer coincide: power has been split off from wealth. The main burden of the socialist case for public ownership has been dissipated, the argument continues. For ownership no longer confers power. If there are still risks of an abuse of concentrated power, these are risks common to public and private enterprise; and indeed perhaps serious only in the former. They derive from the impermeability of bureaucracy and large-scale organization, not from the private ownership of capital. The devils in the demonology of this faith are bureaucrats, not capitalists. And the bureaucrats of private industry – the managers – are exempt according to the newer interpretations: if not quite angels yet, they are at least well on their way to redemption. Business management, increasingly professional and property-less, becomes socially responsible: it can be relied on to look after the interests of us all. Corporate private enterprise has acquired a conscience; or even if it has not, it will behave as if it had. The growth in scale and concentration of capital has resulted in its 'socialization'.

There is a curious parallel here with the process anticipated by Marx – but with a difference. He saw the trend to concentration, and its accompanying formation of an army of managers, officials, technicians and supervisors, as involving a partial, subterranean socialization of the means of production. This process would help to prepare the ground for full socialization through public appropriation; but it would not come to fruit without that last revolutionary stage, in which socialism would supplant capitalism. By contrast, the post-war theory of managerial infiltration claims the achievement of a new moral order, while neatly dispensing with Marx's last and crucial stage. Private ownership of capital can safely be allowed to continue, and to yield private profit as before. Its legitimacy, oddly, is taken to be confirmed by the postulate that it no longer has any active part to play in the running of business.

III

Clearly the crucial issue here is how corporate business acts; not how it is organized. However striking the contrasts in administrative structure, funding and processes of decision between capitalist industry today and yesterday, the point in the end turns, not on the question *who* makes business policy, whether owners or managers; but on *what* business policy is – what are its objectives, its yardsticks of success and failure, its effects on the use and distribution of resources. The thesis of benevolent managerialism provides an object lesson in how not to tackle issues of this kind, the central issues of power. The evidence which it calls in support focuses almost entirely on the question 'who?'; hardly at all on the question 'what?'. For answers to the latter, the thesis relies on no more than inferences from its answers to the former. And those inferences are neither plausible on their own terms nor supported by fact.

The managerial school is right, if we just count heads, that most of those who share in the ownership of the means of production do not control them. People who hold stock in private corporate enterprise – whether directly or through investment trusts and the like – are a tiny minority of the population: barely 7 per cent of all adults aged 25 years and more in this country in 1970; about 15 per cent in the United States, where share ownership is rather more widely diffused. Yet even these people usually have holdings which – though they look sizeable in a society that excludes the great majority from ownership altogether – are far too small to give an effective part in direct control. Over half of all individual shareholders in Britain in 1970 had less than £1,000-worth of stock each; over three in every four, holdings of under £5,000 each. Shareholdings of that size, a minority privilege though they are, are flea-bites in relation to the aggregate volume of private corporate capital. Even when added together, they amount to very little as a fraction of the total. The 1·7 million people who, with holdings of under £5,000 each, made up more than three-quarters of all individual share-owners in 1970, between them still mustered only 11 per cent of the total capital value of personally held stock in private companies. (Table 19.)

Such overall figures illustrate the pattern one finds, on a reduced scale, within most of the large corporations that dominate the economy. To take one example – among the very biggest – Imperial Chemical Industries alone had 575,000 shareholders in 1969, the great majority of them 'smallholders'.[10] Fragmentation of this nature clearly rules out participation in active policy-making for most share-owners. Fragmentation in this sense, moreover, is increasing. It is most pronounced in the case of the largest corporations; and it is they which point the way to the future, so long as capitalism survives. Fragmentation of share-ownership has also grown over time *within* the largest corporations. The share of the twenty biggest single holdings in the value of all vote-carrying stock in the average giant British corporation declined substantially – from 35 to 22 per cent – between the mid-1930s and the early 1950s, with a concomitant diffusion of stock in the hands of a multitude of owners with small- and medium-sized holdings. On top of that, many shares do not carry even formal rights of voting; and these are more common in the mammoth corporations – the pointers to the future – than in others. In legal, as well as in factual terms, the trend is towards increasing disenfranchisement of the 'average' share-owner. Controllers, conversely, often own only small fractions of the capital which they direct; and increasingly so again. To take the directors of the ninety-two largest industrial and commercial companies in Britain, the average board in this group between them had personal holdings of voting stock in their own corporation amounting to only 3 per cent of the company's total vote-carrying capital in 1935; still less – 1½ per cent – by 1951, the latest year for which figures of this kind are

10. J. Moyle, op. cit. (note 1 above), p. 3.

TABLE 19

Individual ownership of shares and debentures in companies with quoted stock, Great Britain 1970

Value of shares and debentures owned by individuals (total held by each individual, whether in one or more companies)	Persons with shareholdings of this value –		
	– numbered the following percentage of all adults aged 25 years and more	– numbered the following percentage of all individual shareholders	– held the following percentage of the total value of all individual shareholdings
	%	%	%
£1–£199	1·6 ⎫	24·7 ⎫	0·3 ⎫
£200–£499	0·9 ⎬ 3·4	13·2 ⎬ 52	0·6 ⎬ 2
£500–£999	0·9 ⎭	14·2 ⎭	1·3 ⎭
£1,000–£1,999	0·7 ⎫ 1·7	11·0 ⎫ 26	2·3 ⎫ 9
£2,000–£4,999	1·0 ⎭	14·9 ⎭	7·0 ⎭
£5,000–£9,999	0·5 ⎫ 0·9	8·0 ⎫ 14	7·4 ⎫ 20
£10,000–£19,999	0·4 ⎭	6·0 ⎭	12·5 ⎭
£20,000–£49,999	0·4 ⎫	5·2 ⎫	24·2 ⎫
£50,000–£99,999	0·1 ⎬ 0·6	1·9 ⎬ 8	17·7 ⎬ 69
£100,000 and more	0·1 ⎭	0·9 ⎭	26·7 ⎭
Total ⎫ Per cent ⎬ Persons ⎭ or value	6·6 (2,212,000)	100·0 (2,212,000)	100·0 (£14,990 million)
Persons with no shares at all (25 years+)	93·4	—	—
Total population 25 years and more Per cent Persons	100·0 (33·4 milion)	—	—

Source: Calculated from estimates in *Inland Revenue Statistics 1972* (p. 122) derived from information on death duties. (Our calculations for the third column are based on average values for the different size categories which assume that the distribution is log-normal, though with an average value for the last, open-ended category of the original data (£200,000+) of £350,000. But variations in the assumptions made produce very little change in the pattern shown. See also Part 2, note 9, p. 117.)

available.[11] So indeed, on these scores, it would look as if capital ownership is more and more divorced from capital control. Most owners, on a crude count of heads, are in no position to exercise active control; and top controllers own only very small proportions of the capital they administer.

IV

So far so good for the thesis of managerial infiltration. But that is also as far as its valid case goes. The inference of a disinterested detachment of business policy from considerations of profit maximization simply cannot be drawn from these facts of joint stock organization. To start with, the fragmentation of shareholding is a double-edged phenomenon: it is linked with overwhelming concentration. Most share-owners are smallholders. But most share *capital* is tightly bunched in few hands. And it is capital that carries weight, not heads. People owning shares to the tune of £20,000 and more in 1970 were a small minority among a tiny minority – no more than 8 per cent of all individual shareholders; about one half of 1 per cent of the entire adult population. But they disposed of nearly 70 per cent of all corporate capital in personal hands (Table 19.)

Overall concentration is still greater than these figures indicate. For they omit the holdings of company stock which are owned, not by individuals, but by other companies and institutions in turn. And such corporate holdings are large: only about 5 per cent of the *number* of ordinary shareholdings in 1970, they made up some 50 per cent of their total *value*.[12] Big corporations are in fact often closely interlocked with others of their kind and with financial institutions, through interpenetrating stockholding and overlapping board membership.[13] True, the implications of corporate ownership depend on

11. For the evidence on increasing diffusion or fragmentation of shareholding referred to above, see P. S. Florence, *Ownership, Control and Success of Large Companies*, Sweet & Maxwell, 1961 (especially pp. 68–9; 57, 61, 64, 66; 90–1, 105).

12. Calculated from Moyle, op. cit. (note 1 above), pp. 7, 9, 18.

13. E.g., over half the 90–odd largest industrial and commercial companies in 1951 had at least one director in common with one or more other companies in the same group; two in every five had such links with at least two of its peers. (Florence, op. cit., note 11 above; pp. 88–9). M. B. Brown has shown that merchant bankers (who are not included in Florence's figures unless they have seats on the boards of more than one of the giants) are strongly represented as

the nature of the policies pursued by corporation controllers, the very issue in debate. But the overwhelming concentration of individually held stock alone, measured by its value, is enough to dispel the notion that ownership in general is too fragmented to carry significant weight in control. It is only small ownership that is fragmented; large ownership is highly concentrated. The same diffusion of shareholdings which marks the disenfranchisement of small owners in fact gives added weight to the large holdings of the few. The more other stock is scattered, the smaller the fraction of the total needed by the few to make their influence felt. Influence, moreover, does not require active participation in control. The power to change top management or to sell a large block of capital can be enough – *if* clashes of policy between major shareholders and company directorate should occur.

They will and do occur from time to time. That in itself is no indication of clashes of interests and overall objectives: there are always liable to be differences of view about the best means to achieve profitability. But the thesis of benevolent managerialism postulates an inherent conflict of interests over the very definition of business goals: between owners concerned with high profit, and controllers

---

part-time directors on the boards of industrial and commercial companies. Members of the boards of the major merchant banks were thus also on the boards of four in every ten of the 150 largest home industrial companies in 1966 ('The controllers of British industry', in K. Coates, ed., *Can the Workers Run Industry*, Sphere 1968, p. 56). Given the interlocking both of capital and directorates among large corporations, the proportion of total capital *represented* on the boards (by directors associated with shareholder companies as well as by directors with personal holdings) must be very much greater than the proportion of total capital owned by directors individually. We have found no British data bearing directly on the point. But in Sweden – where the ratio of individual to corporate ownership of share capital is much the same as in Britain – the directors of the average company with quoted stock individually owned about 4 per cent of the company's stock in 1963, but *represented* 31 per cent of the stock when the holdings of other companies with which they were associated were taken into account. (Finansdepartementet, *Ägande och inflytande . . .* , op. cit. Part 2, ch. 8, note 1 above: pp. 19–20, 105–109.) It is worth noting that in Sweden the economic predominance of a small number of large corporations is still greater than in this country; and no more than seventeen 'owner-groups' in 1963 held majority or large minority holdings in firms accounting for well over a third of the total output of Swedish industry – one of these groups, the Wallenberg familyal one, involved closely in firms with nearly 15 per cent of all output. (Ibid., p. 23 and chapter IV.) The pattern of shareholding and company-interlocking has much the same shape in the United States as in Britain; and both countries show more 'anonymity' of control in big business than Sweden. For the U.S.A., see, e.g., D. Villarejo, 'Stock ownership and the control of corporations', *New University Thought*, Autumn 1961, Winter 1962; R. J. Larner, 'Ownership and control in the 200 largest non-financial corporations, 1929 and 1963', *Amer. Econ. Review*, Sept. 1966.

committed to a plurality of aims with continuity and growth in first place. The two categories, in this view, take on the shape of distinct classes, divided because one has capital and the other has not.

The division is a myth. There is certainly none visible between owners and top controllers, the directors of companies. For directors in general are themselves large owners of share capital. Only crude average figures are available. Some directors have only small holdings of stock; but others have very large ones, and as a group they rank at the top of the list of share-owners in the society. The average board member of the ninety-odd giant corporations in 1951, for example, owned ordinary stock within his own company to the nominal value of nearly £21,000.[14] That figure was a substantial sum at the time. But it understated the market value of these shares; excluded holdings of preference stock and debentures; and also left out of account ownership of shares of any kind in other companies. A special sample survey taken from directories for London and the Home Counties in 1954 showed directors – drawn from companies of all kinds and sizes – to be by far the wealthiest of the various élite and professional groups covered, with average security holdings to a value of £28,000: more than twice the average for the next group on the list – members of the 'peerage, baronetage, knightage and companionage' – and five times the averages for professional accountants and doctors.[15] There is no later information of this sort; but the corresponding sums today would, of course, be very much larger. The point is not that company directors, of the biggest corporations especially, have control by virtue of the stock they own. Usually they do not: their holdings make up too small a fraction of all capital – colossal figures in aggregate – for that. The point is simply that their ownership still amounts to very large sums in absolute terms: it puts them well within that minority of a minority who (as table 19 shows) between them hold the overwhelming share of private corporate capital. The notion that they are likely to give low priority to considerations of profit, because they have little personal stake in it through share-ownership, simply does not square with fact.

The distinction between the dividends which most directors and top executives receive from shares, and the salaries, fees and expenses which they draw from their positions of office, is in any case a rather

14. Estimated by Nichols, op. cit. (note 9 above, pp. 72–4) from data in Florence, op. cit. (note 11 above).
15. L. R. Klein, et al., op. cit. (Part 2, ch. 2, note 2 above).

formal and artificial one. A considerable part of their incomes from office is of the nature of profit. For directors and top executives are able – collectively rather than individually – to determine their own remuneration within fairly wide limits of tolerance, so long as profits are maintained. Take the salaries drawn by chairmen of the giant corporations, which usually run into amounts equivalent to the interest or dividend on capital sums well into the six-figure range. To list those for a few household names in 1969/70: Shell paid its chairman a salary of £73,000; I.C.I. and Rank Xerox, each about £63,000; B.P., British Leyland, Rio Tinto Zinc, Tube Investments, Unilever, General Electric, £40,000–£50,000; Ford, Distillers, Esso, Marks and Spencer, around £30,000; some lower, a few only nominal figures.[16] Add substantial unrecorded extras in the form of expenses and special fees. It is difficult to argue that these sums – and for that matter the apparent variations among them – are the result just of nice calculations of directorial productivity and the anonymous pressures of a chairmen's labour market. The reality is that these top men and their closest colleagues have their hands on the till: they control the funds from which they pay themselves. Of course there are limits to the sums they can draw – limits set perhaps in the first instance by rather elastic conceptions of business propriety and the

16. A. Sampson, *The New Anatomy of Britain*, Hodder & Stoughton, 1971 (between pp. 590 and 591). A 1973 court case illustrates the point, while the comment which it aroused at the time suggests the degree of ignorance or naïvety which is common on the subject. A number of the directors of a major mining company (Lonrho) brought an action in the High Court seeking dismissal of their chief executive. One of the complaints against the latter was that he had appointed a former Conservative Cabinet Minister to a post of consultant to the company at an annual salary of £50,000 for six years. The contract had been prematurely ended and compensation of £130,000 paid to the ex-minister, though he was then offered appointment as chairman at £38,000 a year. It is clear that salaries or honoraria of these levels are common practice at the top of big business. And the complaint in the High Court action was not that payments of such magnitude were unreasonable in themselves; nor that a substantial part of the payments had been made through an associated company in the West Indies to reduce taxation; but that the arrangements had been made, like several others, without reference to the full board. (Though the image of the chief executive which emerged in press commentary was that of a brash tycoon, it is worth noting that two members of the board, no less respectable than the ex-minister, were reported as having shared in the arrangements criticized – a high-ranking Conservative M.P., former chairman of the Conservative Party; and a member of the royal family by marriage.) Public comment led to the announcement of a government enquiry, though it was not made clear with exactly what issues it would be concerned. (*The Times*, reports on 15 May 1973 and during preceding week; *Sunday Times*, 20 May 1973.)

practices of other boards; beyond that by the risk – real enough in recent years – that large shareholders who may not be represented on the board, or an outsider assembling stock for a take-over bid, may step in if dividends suffer; ultimately by the level of profits over time. Even apart from their stake in ownership, top controllers therefore have a common interest with shareholders in profitability, because their benefits of office depend on it.

V

It may still be argued that the boards are not the real seats of control; that effective power over policy has drifted into the hands of management down the line, who are able to pre-empt the decisions of their superiors through their everyday conduct of affairs and the central role of their advice. If in fact executive and technical managers are the real controllers, they certainly show a startling tolerance in allowing very large salaries and perks – usually well above what they get for themselves – to directors who, by that very argument, are little more than rubber stamps. The point may not be decisive. But it is a reminder of the simple fact that financial control, at any rate, is still centred at the top. And that is crucial. For a distinction must be drawn between 'operational' and 'strategic' policy. The former is without doubt firmly in the hands of executive and technical management. It involves not only the everyday running of business but also, for example, the development of new technical and commercial initiatives and the preparation of periodic plans. It is in these latter areas that the potential for 'middle management control' lies. Yet, extraordinarily flimsy though concrete evidence is on the nature and locus of policy-making in business, the signs that can be found are fairly clear that such control does not extend to decisions on those issues of finance and market position which are central to profitability and growth. It is precisely these issues – of investment, funding and the allocation of profit; of market alliances, mergers and take-overs; of relations with government, and possibly of labour relations recently, as profits have appeared more at risk – which are 'strategic'. They are determined at the top – by chief executives and on the boards, if not effectively by all members of the boards. And it is no doubt the crucial role of finance in these matters which helps to explain the common presence of bankers among the part-time directors of the large industrial and commercial corporations.[17] Again, there seems to be little leeway here for a distinctive managerial control relatively unconcerned with profit.

The argument for benevolent managerialism has altogether an air of striking unreality. For it assumes that decisions are actually *made* on a matter which is not a subject for decision. It assumes that somebody – directors, executives, managers of this level or that, or some or all of these in a tug-of-war among themselves – makes a choice between profit maximization and a number of competing objectives: growth or just continuity for its own sake; the well-being of workers, consumers and so on, for theirs. But by every sign no choice of this kind is made by business, because there is no choice to be made. The aim of profit is simply taken for granted. Other objectives may well be recognized, genuinely or by way of lip-service. But they are subordinate, or just assumed to be in natural harmony with the axiomatic goal of profit. Certainly when questioned about their work, and in public statements on behalf of their corporations, businessmen will often assert a sense of responsibility to society at large, to employees, customers and perhaps the local communities in which they operate. But they see no conflict between profitable and socially responsible business activity. For they subsume the latter within the former. Business is assumed to serve the public interest best by being business-like; profit to provide both the measure of, and the opportunity for, private enterprise's postulated contribution to social welfare.[18] There is nothing very new about this view. It is the

17. There have been very few studies to show where and how, within business corporations, policies on issues of different kinds are initiated, developed and determined. See, however, Pahl and Winkler, op. cit. (ch. 1, note 5 above), a preliminary report on a study of directors and their work in 15 British companies, the results of which point in the directions indicated in this paragraph. (We are grateful to the authors for an opportunity to discuss their findings with them.) Florence (op. cit., note 11 above, pp. 81–3) also points to the importance of the role of directors in financial and related matters. He draws on both his own and some American work. The most relevant and detailed American study is R. A. Gordon, *Business Leadership in the Large Corporation*, Brookings Inst., 1945. Some Swedish work similarly indicates the central role of the boards in financial decisions, and the representation of banks in board membership. (Finansdepartementet, *Ägande och inflytande* . . . , op. cit., Part 2, ch. 8, note 1 above; chapter IV.) See also Brown, op. cit. (note 13 above).

18. See especially Nichols, op. cit. (note 9 above), chapters XIV–XVII, a perceptive discussion of the results of an enquiry among directors and senior managers in a northern city. F. X. Sutton *et al.*, *The American Business Creed*, Harvard University Press, 1956, showed that representatives of large corporations often referred in public statements to the social responsibilities of business. But to

contemporary version of a classical argument of economic liberalism: thanks to the hidden hand of the market, public benefit follows
naturally from private profit. So there is no choice to be made
between the two.

There are, similarly, no choices for business to make between profit
and growth, or usually between moderate and maximum profit. There
are certainly choices to be made between short-run and longer-term
profitability. But these are choices with which business has always
been confronted. Neither before nor now have they included the
option of continued growth without reference to profit. For business
cannot survive without profit; and successful growth is both directed
to profit and – as capital requirements grow and internal funding
becomes more important – increasingly depends on prior profit. In
practice, again, profitability must normally mean profit maximization. Deliberate limitation of profits to a continuously modest level
is not a realistic alternative. It might be so in situations where a
corporation had achieved complete and lasting monopoly over its
markets – and then only if its controllers had less interest in full
exploitation of their monopoly than in merely keeping things ticking
over. But monopolies are rarely guaranteed against all risk of future
competition; and the effort to maintain monopoly itself requires
funds. Moreover, straight monopoly is an exceptional situation. The
uncertainties of that, and of the future on other scores, make profit
maximization the only practical yardstick of policy. There is no level
of profit below that to which it is safe to fall back.[19]

VI

None of this is to say that business is fully efficient and dedicated in
its pursuit of profit maximization; or that those who direct and
influence policy always agree about the best way to achieve the

demonstrate the existence of a managerial 'public ideology' is not to prove the
displacement of profit as an operational yardstick. See also Child, op. cit. (note 9
above), especially pp. 47–51.

19. For one of many debates on the question 'profits versus growth' and related
issues, see S. Peterson, and the reply by C. Kaysen, in *Quarterly Journal of
Economics*, Feb. 1965 (cf. note 9 above). The persistence of the profit imperative
has been strongly argued, in this country, by R. Blackburn, 'The new capitalism',
in *idem* and P. Anderson, eds., *Towards Socialism*, Fontana, 1965. R. Marris,
The Economic Theory of Managerial Capitalism, Macmillan, 1964, by contrast
presents a model based on 'managerial' assumptions.

highest profit. It is probable, for example, that taken as a whole British productive industry has been relatively inefficient by capitalist criteria since the last decade or two of the nineteenth century. Arguments to that effect have certainly had a recurrent place in public debate for a long time; and they became prominent not least from around 1960, when the Labour Party unfurled the banner of 'modernization', and supporters of British entry into the European Common Market built their case in part on the proposition that exposure to wider competition would help to 'cut out dead wood' in British industry. Overall rates of economic growth have indeed been slow in this country by comparison with other capitalist countries since before the turn of the century; and this may reflect inhibitions within British business to the introduction of technical and organizational innovations.[20] Some other 'British peculiarities', it has been argued, fit in with this diagnosis, whether as symptoms or causes of a syndrome of low efficiency: an apparent reluctance of industry to admit technical specialists to positions of control, even though there are more professionally qualified people on and near the boards now than there used to be; an alleged inclination of top management to recruit and promote executive staff by criteria of social background and personal contact rather than by criteria of tested ability for the job.[21]

It is not easy to establish the diagnosis with reasonable certainty; nor, if it is correct, to trace through the causes. The pattern as a whole may involve distinctive national features both of economic structure and of managerial style. The fact that industrialization came early meant that British industry carried into the twentieth century a large heritage of nineteenth-century capital equipment, and perhaps also of nineteenth-century organizational forms and practices, which it was not possible simply to write off at a stroke. British capitalism, moreover, responded to the emergence of competition

20. See, e.g., Phelps Brown and Browne, op. cit. (Part 2, ch. 1, note 3); D. H. Aldcraft, 'The entrepreneur and the British economy, 1870–1914', *Econ. History Review*, vol. 17, no. 1, 1964.

21. For brief summaries of evidence on recruitment and backgrounds of business managers and directors, see Nichols, op. cit. (note 9 above), Chapter VIII and pp. 113–18; and D. C. Coleman, 'Gentlemen and players', *Econ. History Review*, vol. 26, no. 1, 1973. For a recent study of the recruitment of company chairmen, see P. H. Stanworth and A. Giddens, 'An economic elite', in *idem*, op. cit. (ch. 1, note 5 above). M. Burrage, 'Culture and British economic growth', *Brit. J. Sociology*, June 1969, ascribes major importance to 'particularistic' orientations on the part of British businessmen.

from abroad, in the last decades of the nineteenth century, in part by specialization in export of capital and an associated financial imperialism.[22] It is likely that this had long-lasting effects on the general climate of business enterprise: on the availability of capital for domestic versus overseas investment, for example; on the relative power of the interests associated with international banking – of the City of London – versus those associated with productive industry within British business; on the relative influence of these interests in the formation of public economic policy, as the role of government in setting the frame of business enterprise has increased.[23] Again, if British styles of management – in public as well as in private enterprise – display something of a gentlemanly suspicion towards innovation, technical expertise, enthusiasm for initiative and selection of colleagues by criteria of measured job performance, the roots of this are probably long and tangled. Much of the weight of explanation may fall on the nature of the process by which, during the nineteenth century, the centre of economic gravity shifted from land and trade into industry and finance – not through a revolutionary displacement of one dominant group by another; but through a gradual interpenetration of old and new interests, in the course of which the rising industrial bourgeoisie absorbed part of the cultural outlook of the older landed and commercial élite.[24]

The complexities and uncertainties which surround these questions are not relevant here. The point is that, for whatever reasons, business enterprise in this or that capitalist country, this or that sector of the economy, this or that corporation, may well display distinctive features of organization and style of management which make for more or less efficiency in the pursuit of profit. Performance may fall short; but profit maximization remains the operational yardstick of capitalist enterprise for all that, because there is no other. It is probable, moreover, that modern corporate business in general is more, rather than less, efficient in maximizing profit than its predecessors. The individual nineteenth- and early twentieth-century owner-entrepreneur may have been more liable than the board of a modern corporation to be diverted from profit maximization by a concern

22. See, e.g., E. J. Hobsbawm, *Industry and Empire*, Weidenfeld & Nicolson, 1968 (especially chapter 9).

23. Cf., e.g., M. B. Brown, 'The £ and the 1%', *New Reasoner*, no. 6, Autumn 1958.

24. For a useful recent contribution to this long-standing debate, see Coleman, op. cit. (note 21 above).

with personal prestige and self-aggrandizement.[25] The technical aids to efficiency are in any case more highly developed now – including the means of cost- and profit-accounting – and sometimes require very large-scale activity before their introduction pays off. For these and other reasons it may well be that idiosyncrasies of organization and management style, of the kind that for long seem to have inhibited the profit-efficiency of British industry, will lose significance. The very recent history of mergers and take-overs certainly points that way; not towards a market climate tolerant of gentlemanly restraint.

VII

In the picture as it is often painted by the managerial school, corporation policy is the outcome of a plurality of pressures among which management, itself divided, balances and mediates. That is certainly how 'decision-making' looks from the inside; and it is real enough up to a point. But it is not relevant to the issue. For whatever their differences, the various groups and factions which can bring some effective pressure to bear upon policy have one thing in common: the objective of profit maximization. Shareholders and executives alike, for example, may be divided among themselves between policies that would yield high dividends now and policies which would hold back profits for investment to yield high dividends later. If the 'growth faction' in that situation has its way, this may encourage a take-over bid from outside, because share prices tend to reflect current rather than future dividend yield. The conflict then becomes public and acquires a character of drama. But there is no conflict over the principles of capitalist enterprise: only over how the yardstick of profit is to be applied.

Again, the very complexity of corporate organization is likely to encourage divergences of outlook and policy promotion within management. But any policy proposal, whatever its source, has to be

25. It has been pointed out, for example, that while 'managerially-run' newspaper corporations have shown rising profits in recent years, the family- or tycoon-run newspapers have faced losses. (G. Murdock, 'Besitz und Kontrolle der Massenmedien in Grossbritannien heute', in D. Prokop, ed., *Massenkommunikationsforschung – I, Produktion*, Frankfurt, Fischer, 1972: p. 50). It needs to be stressed, however, that losses can be sustained in more than the short run only if they are subsidized by profits from other sources.

so presented that it can pass the acid test of profitability. The scientists, technologists and other professionals employed by corporate business are often seen – in the perspective of the managerial school, and even in some left-wing interpretations – as a potentially powerful element, capable of transforming capitalism from within: a small, but strategically placed and growing army of saints or saboteurs, committed to an ethic of service in conflict with the business ethic of profit. The picture is romantic and implausible.

For one thing, business tends to attract those graduates and professionals who see no conflict between profit and professional commitment. Indeed, to take a crucial case, academic engineering schools usually have close links with business; and the young engineer from the outset is likely to define engineering as the business of applying technology to practical use, where practicability is equated with profitability. The point has still more force in the case of graduates of business schools – the *raison d'être* of which, however useful their contribution to managerial efficiency, is in part to polish the public face of capitalism without questioning its profit drive.

For another thing, promotion to executive posts with an effective say in policy almost certainly goes primarily to those professionals who accept the money-making goals of the corporation with appropriate dedication. Direct evidence on the point is thin. But there are plausible hints to suggest the existence of two fairly distinct career patterns for scientists and technologists in business. In one, the professional stays in the kind of work for which he is technically qualified. Jobs at the top of that ladder may be well-paid. But they confer little or no influence over 'strategic' policy; and even if they sometimes carry a seat on the board, the professional director's role in that capacity is limited to giving specialist advice. The other – and rarer – career pattern involves transfer to the executive ladder, usually at a fairly early point, and requires precisely that sort of commitment to the corporation and its profit which will justify a share in strategic policy-making. So, whatever potential problems the employment of professionals may pose for private enterprise, they are minimized by processes of selective recruitment and promotion and an associated insulation of specialist departments.[26]

26. On these points, or for hints to them, see, e.g., S. Cotgrove and S. Box, *Science, Industry and Society*, Allen & Unwin, 1970; C. Sofer, *Men in Mid-Career*, Cambridge University Press, 1970 (e.g., p. 303); E. Layton, 'Science, business and the American engineer', in R. Perrucci and J. E. Gerstl, eds., *The Engineers and the*

On all scores, therefore, the thesis of benevolent managerialism turns to dust when one touches it. Profit maximization has not been replaced as the main motor of business by a 'social ethic', by growth maximization, or by a concern merely to 'tick over' and deal with problems as they arise. Indeed, the claim that one or more of these new yardsticks of enterprise has taken over and transformed capitalism is transparently hollow. For no explanation is given how, in any case, growth for its own sake or mere 'ticking over' would contribute to general welfare any more than the pursuit of private profit; or what the content of a new social ethic inspiring managers is. If there is such an ethic, its effects on the distribution of income and wealth – on the division of rewards between labour on the one hand, top executives and capital owners on the other – are certainly remarkably similar to those of the profit-driven capitalism which it is supposed to have superseded. The 'human face' of the new managerialism does not smile kindly on demands for fairer shares, let alone for equality.

Social System, New York, Wiley, 1969 (e.g. p. 67); W. Kornhauser, *Scientists in Industry,* Univ. of California Press, 1962.

3 The state and the public services

I

The power of capital has not been tamed through the internal conversion of business to corporate, managerial organization. But it will still be argued that it has been tamed by an accumulation of external constraints: curbs imposed especially by an increasingly active state. That is certainly a common assumption; and it appears to have a good deal of evidence to support it. Thus changes in the law – in this country mainly from the end of the nineteenth century onwards – have cut into rights of property at a number of points. Minimum standards, for example, have been set and extended for safety, space and facilities at work; for sanitation and building; for purity of food; more recently, to guard against false description of goods. All but small-scale building activities and minor changes in the use of land have been subject to public control under planning legislation since the 1940s. Business control over markets has come under the scrutiny of a Monopolies Commission from 1948 and a Restrictive Practices Court from 1956. Rising taxation has squeezed down effective rights of disposal over profits as well as earned income. Compulsory insurance against unemployment and retirement – partial since early in the century, near-universal since the 1940s – imposes obligation on employers no less than on employees. New limitations on employers' rights to fire labour, and provision for compensation on redundancy, have been prescribed in contracts of employment since the 1960s. Changes of law – in the 1870s and the first decade of this century, especially – as well as of government practice have provided a framework to encourage collective bargaining and, to a varying degree, to allow unions to take industrial action against employers. Counter-inflationary legislation at some times in recent years has set statutory restraints on price rises; and it has curtailed the rights of business to offer wage increases as it sees fit, as well as of labour to demand them.[1]

All this – and the list is condensed – has been accompanied by a vast expansion of the physical and economic scale of government activity. Central and local government between them employed about 2 per cent of the civilian labour force in 1891; some 5 per cent in the years shortly before World War I; around 8 per cent during the inter-war period; over 11 per cent in 1950; and 17 per cent by 1971. Add the labour force of the nationalized industries, and the total in the early 1970s came to about 25 per cent.[2] Public expenditure on wages and salaries, other services and goods (both current and capital) had grown to much the same order of magnitude – some 29 per cent of gross domestic product in 1971.[3] When one adds the money for transfer payments – such as pensions and other cash benefits, as well as interest and repayment of debts – total public revenue came to nearly 48 per cent of gross domestic product in 1971. Not all of this – only 41 per cent – came in the form of taxes and national insurance contributions.[4] But taking all sources of revenue into account, the state in one way or another has passing through its hands nearly one-half of the funds generated by economic activity in the country. The public sector's contribution to capital invest-ment for the future is on much the same scale. Almost 43 per cent of the money for gross domestic capital formation came from public funds in 1971; and the figure had been as high as 48 per cent in 1967.[5]

1. For a general review of all but the most recent of such changes in the law, see W. G. Friedmann, 'The function of property in English law', *Brit. J. Sociology*, Sept. 1950; and chapter 3 'Property', in *idem, Law in a Changing Society*, Stevens, 1959 (abridged edition, Penguin Books, 1964).

2. Calculated from M. Abramovitz and V. F. Eliasberg, *The Growth of Public Employment in Great Britain* (Princeton University Press, 1957) and *Economic Trends*, Oct. 1968, June 1970, June 1972.

3. Estimated (at factor cost) from *National Income and Expenditure 1972* (pp. 9, 14–15) and *Financial Statistics*, Feb. 1973 (p. 4).

4. Calculated from *Financial Statistics*, Feb. 1973 (p. 14) and *National Incomes and Expenditure 1972* (pp. 14–15). To take a different measure, total public expenditure grew from some 9 per cent of gross *national* product in 1890 to about a quarter and more in the inter-war years, and around 45 per cent in the late 1960s and early 1970s (A. T. Peacock and J. Wiseman, *The Growth of Public Expenditure in the United Kingdom*, Princeton University Press, 1961; *National Income and Expenditure 1972; Financial Statistics*, Feb. 1973). All figures are at factor cost.

5. Calculated from *Financial Statistics*, Feb. 1973 (p. 4). Estimates from

Here, it seems, is the scaffolding of a persuasive argument that capitalism has been civilized by public control and state provision. The outcome, so that argument runs, is a 'mixed economy'. The mixture has drawn the fangs of private business without eliminating it. There is still conflict between capital and labour – if only, in one view common in public commentary, because inherited prejudices and outmoded patterns of behaviour and organization set up barriers of communication and allow 'agitators' excessive influence. But a fair balance has been achieved, or is near, which can guarantee steady progress and reasonable equity all round. The guarantee may not yet be fully operative. Optimism on that score waned in the 1960s, as economic growth proved unstable, social tension increased and poverty was rediscovered. But the usual prescription to make the guarantee operative is for a rather larger, or better balanced, dose of the same medicine: for reforms within the framework of a mixed economy. The essence of the mixture is a partnership – for all that the partners, like most of their kind, do not always see eye to eye – between business, labour and the state. The role attributed to the state is crucial. Public authority is pressed from different sides, pushed now this way, then that. But the state is seen also as an arbiter between these rival pressures, asserting under governments of different colour a broadly common conception of the 'public interest'. For long, so the usual conclusion runs, the weight of its expanding activities has been thrown into the scales mainly on the side of labour. The long-term growth of public control and government involvement is taken to be synonymous with a steady trend to curb capital and extend the welfare of ordinary people. But today, many adherents of the mixed economy claim, part of the state's weight must be thrown into the scales against organized labour – still in the 'public interest' – because the balance has tipped too far.

This thesis of the growth of a benevolent state is not so much a coherent and readily identifiable theory as a series of assumptions which recur, in different constellations, in much commentary on contemporary society and politics: in the diagnoses and prescriptions of social scientists, journalists, politicians, businessmen and many others.[6] It is the theme, with minor variations, of 'progressive con-

---

National Income and Expenditure 1972 (p. 9) produce still higher proportions (46 per cent in 1971, 49 per cent in 1967).

6. Examples of sophisticated versions of the thesis include T. H. Marshall, *Citizenship and Social Class*, Cambridge University Press, 1950 (part I), C. A. R.

servatism' and social democracy alike. Its message is broadcast by the mass media and probably runs through most teaching of 'civics' and modern history in the schools. The habit of thinking of the state as an instrument – *the* instrument – of 'public welfare' is so ingrained that the thesis may seem self-evidently true.

It is not. For it begs precisely the question of the purposes to which the expansion of state activity has been directed. The reality which answers to that question expose has none of the simplicity assumed by the thesis. In one aspect, state activity indeed appears benign: the outcome of pressures to extend the welfare and security of wage earners; to provide ordinary people with some protection against the vicissitudes of a capitalist economy, and a share in citizenship which their dependent condition would otherwise deny them. In its other aspect, however, state activity has been directed to consolidation of the capitalist economy; to securing its survival and expansion against the risks to which its own character gives rise; and to advancing the interests of this or that section of capitalist enterprise against another. In practice, moreover, the two aspects are intertwined; and the latter conditions and inhibits the former.

II

The welfare face of the state is most visible in the public provision of social benefits, health facilities, housing and education. It is these which are taken as prototypical when the activity of government as a whole is pictured as civilizing capitalism. Government expenditure, of course, involves very much more than that. Nearly a third of it goes on sheer maintenance of the state and of public order: on defence, not least, and foreign relations; on police, prisons and courts; on administration itself; and on heavy regular instalments of interest on public debt. For all that, the social services on a broad definition account for a still larger and, outside the field of housing, growing share of state activity: for about half of all the money spent by Whitehall and local authorities in recent years, when the business of the nationalized industries and similar public corporations is

Crosland, op. cit. (ch. 2, note 9 above) and several of the 'pluralist' interpretations discussed in chapter 7 of Part 3, below.

excluded. (Table 20.) Yet in fact even these services provide only tenuous support for the thesis of state benevolence. Public provision cannot be simply equated with popular benefit.

TABLE 20

Types of government expenditure, United Kingdom 1967 and 1971

	1967	1971
	%	%
Social and allied services		
Social security benefits, personal soc. services, etc.	20·3 ⎫	21·4 ⎫
Health services	10·2 ⎬ 49·6	10·6 ⎬ 50·9
Housing	6·6	5·3
Education	12·5 ⎭	13·6 ⎭
Leisure facilities, environmental protection		
Parks, libraries, museums, arts	0·9 ⎫ 3·8	1·2 ⎫ 4·3
Water, drainage, refuse, fire services, etc.	2·9 ⎭	3·1 ⎭
Productive and allied services		
Roads, transport, communications	5·2 ⎫	4·8 ⎫
Employment services	0·6	0·8
Other services and payments for industry and trade	3·6 ⎬ 12·8	5·0 ⎬ 13·9
Other services and payments, agriculture, forestry, fishing, etc.	2·3	2·2
Research (excl. govt. records and surveys)	1·1 ⎭	1·1 ⎭
Maintenance of the state and the law		
Defence	15·4 ⎫	12·6 ⎫
External relations	1·9	1·7
Police, prisons, courts, Parliament	2·4	2·8
Finance, tax collection	1·3 ⎬ 33·8	1·4 ⎬ 30·9
Miscellaneous other services, central and local	1·9	2·3
Interest on debt	10·9 ⎭	10·1 ⎭
Total* %	100·0	100·0
£m	15,766	22,277

* Expenditure on current and capital accounts combined, central and local government; *excludes expenditure of public corporations* (nationalized industries, etc.) on capital formation, estimated increases in stocks, and current goods and services incl. wages and salaries.
Source: Calculated from *National Income and Expenditure 1972* (pp. 58–62).

For a start, the state's social services are financed largely from the wages of those for whose security they are primarily designed. They make for little redistribution from capital and top salaries: this in contrast with assumptions often embedded in the notion of government benevolence. There is no need to repeat in detail the analysis which we set out earlier on this point. Taken together the various social services result in some narrowing of inequalities of real income. But they reshuffle resources far more within classes – between earners and dependents, healthy people and the sick, households of different composition, from one point of an individual's life cycle to another – then they do between classes. The public welfare services are crippled as a means of cutting down class divisions, for two reasons especially. First, because they co-exist with private welfare provisions for the well-off and the wealthy, financed in part from public funds by way of tax concessions. Second, because in general the tax system that feeds them bears down heavily on ordinary wage earners and even the poor. Moves during the early 1970s towards greater 'selectivity' in the tax-and-welfare apparatus of the state were designed to give rather more help to the poorest – or some of them – at the expense of the broad masses a little way above them; not to tap the resources of the rich. On the contrary, wealth was given greater leeway to grow. And it was likely to accumulate still more in the hands of that 1 per cent minority who already before then took as large a share of all real income as the poorest 30 per cent; who owned some three-tenths of all private property; who held over 80 per cent of the value of all personally owned stock in private corporate business.

The sheer scale of the economic privilege of that minority is enough to explode the myth that workers must pay for their 'welfare state' themselves because there is too little wealth on top of them for anything else. The fact that they do pay for it themselves has not come about by accident or mismanagement. It is the outcome of well-managed design. The lack of progression in overall rates of tax up the scale of income; the perforation of the system by loopholes that allow capital and top business rewards to slip through little trimmed, on a scale unrecorded in official figures; the significant fact that corporate enterprise was able to duck, or at least postpone, the impact of falling profits in the 1960s through a shift of taxation further on to wages – these are the hallmarks of a tax machinery tailored, in the context of large-scale state activity, to the interests of business, property and the high professions. They reflect the needs of a capitalist economy and the continuing power of these groups: a power which does not, on the whole, have to be actively asserted, because it is effective through uneventful routine. The public welfare services bear the imprint of that distribution of power.

For all that, workers do of course benefit from the social services: they would be a good deal worse off without them. A limited amount of redistribution between classes apart, the state in effect acts as an agent for the collective self-security of earners and their dependents. In reallocating resources from one stage of individual life cycles to others and in giving some assurance of bedrock provision for the old, the sick, the unemployed and some of the lowest-paid the state does what individuals and their families could not do on their own; and what even the trade unions, as mutual benefit societies, could do only inadequately.[7] But that, by and large, is as far as it goes.

The social services, moreover, in no real sense 'belong' to the workers and others who draw on them. It is true that, collectively, the labour movement has contributed a good deal to the development of the state's welfare apparatus, in both its main phases of creation. In the first phase, around the turn of the century, the contribution was largely indirect. The previous growth of the unions; the emergence of general unions during the last couple of decades of the nineteenth century, to organize the unskilled and semi-skilled on the militant flank of the established craft unions; the working-class movement's withdrawal from its alliance with the Liberal Party, when the Labour Representation Committee was set up in 1900 and became the Labour Party six years later – these and related developments renewed anxieties among the propertied classes about the stability of the social order, which working-class quiescence from around 1850 until the 1870s had previously dulled. With anxieties came a stirring of consciences and reforming zeal. Here was the sharp point to the rivalry between Conservatives and Liberals for labour support that accompanied the slow admission of slices of the working class to the franchise: in small numbers by the Reform Act of 1867, in rather larger numbers by that of 1884. Out of these pressures – in turn intertwined with the threats posed by the rise of new capitalist economies abroad – grew the distinctive conjunction of imperialism with social reform within the Conservative Party. And the same pressures produced the first substantial instalment of social welfare legislation in the early years of this century. This round of legislation came mainly at the hands of the Liberals, as what proved to be a

7. In some countries – Scandinavia, for example, where the density of union membership is higher than in Britain – the unions have had an active share in administering certain state-supported social service schemes, including housing co-operatives.

swansong before that party sank into decline, unable in a period of widening unrest, world war and revolution abroad either to win back its fading bourgeois support or to maintain its newer working-class support as Lib-Lab'ism dissolved.[8]

The labour movement played, of course, a more direct part in the second, and much larger, instalment of welfare legislation. This was in the late 1940s, when Labour was in office with the first parliamentary majority of its history. But then, too, the programme of social security measures was not an autonomous creation of the movement, forced through in the teeth of Conservative opposition or designed to cut sharply into the privileges of the upper and middle classes. In large part – with exceptions that included the more radical features of the National Health Service Act – it was the product of bipartisan agreement originating in the period of wartime coalition. It reflected the inevitable constraints of such agreement; above all, of the programme's funding through a system of taxation which, then as now, fitted the economic predominance of private enterprise. As wartime restrictions were discarded and the enthusiasm of social reconstruction waned, the continuation of that predominance stood out more sharply.

III

The public welfare services belong to ordinary workers as individuals still less than they do to the labour movement collectively. The great majority of those who use the services have no effective part in their control, and often little understanding of how they operate. Even a small share of popular control and understanding would need organized solidarity of the kind on which workers have otherwise drawn in their relations *vis-à-vis* employers and government. The impact of the social services has tended instead to be divisive: to draw lines between different categories of workers, and to leave individuals isolated in their dealings with the services. Social security provisions distinguish 'the poor' from others; those who are given special help, on special conditions, from those who use only the standard services. That by itself is liable to foster mutual resentments: suspicions about

8. See, for example, B. Semmel, *Imperialism and Social Reform*, Allen & Unwin, 1960; G. Dangerfield, *The Strange Death of Liberal England 1910–1914*, Capricorn Books, 1961 (first published 1935).

'scrounging' of the sort which politicians are happy to attribute to their working-class voters, as postulated evidence of popular opposition to extensions of social welfare. The poor, moreover, meet the welfare services in their most bewildering form, and at the point where receipt of benefits shades into subjection to official control. They, in particular, need collective support to cope with the authorities. Yet they usually receive little or no help of that kind from unions or the Labour Party. The 'claimant unions' which have emerged in recent years to organize the poor, and represent them *vis-à-vis* official agencies and appeal tribunals, have been formed in the main outside and as yet in partial opposition to the established labour movement.[9]

The state's welfare services indeed take on an almost impenetrable complexity as they appear to those who need them most. There are special benefits – in money and in kind – to meet special needs. But need has to be proven. And the proof demanded – the test of poverty or hardship – varies from one such special service to another; in the case of allowances administered by local authorities, also from one area to the next. A count in the late 1960s arrived at a total of some 1,500 different tests of low income used by local authorities for different purposes, with no apparent connection between their variations and any local differences in costs or the character of 'needs'.[10] Only an extraordinarily active itinerant pauper would, of course, encounter anything like that number. But there are today probably over forty separate types of service – national and local, each with its own test or tests of poverty – a considerable number of which may be relevant for an individual family with a low income.[11] Many require the com-

9. Unions will often stand behind unemployed workers, at least those who have recently lost their jobs; rarely behind other claimants for public assistance. On this and some of the preceding points, see Bill Jordan, *Paupers: the Making of the New Claiming Class*, Routledge & Kegan Paul, 1973; and Hilary Rose, 'Up against the welfare state: the claimant unions', in R. Miliband and J. Saville, eds., *The Socialist Register, 1973*, Merlin, 1973. For a general analysis of the operation of the appeal tribunals, see M. Herman, *Administrative Justice and Supplementary Benefits*, Bell, 1972. This author's verdict is generally favourable, though he criticizes, e.g., the dependence of the tribunals on the government department whose decisions they have to judge. But cf. Hilary Rose, 'Who can de-label the claimant?', *Social Work Today*, vol. 4, no. 13, 1973: a brief report on a study showing, inter alia, a tendency for tribunal members to share with the presenting officers an accusatory role *vis-à-vis* the claimant.

10. M. Reddin, 'Local authority means-tested services, in *Social Services for all?*, Fabian Society, 1968.

11. Molly Meacher, *Rate Rebates*, Child Poverty Action Group (Research Series No. 1), 1972.

pletion of forms – sometimes not available at the relevant offices, or even known to their staff; often baffling in content. Tests of need confer discretion on the officials who administer them. And though that discretion is limited by rules – now on paper fairly stringent in the case of services administered by central government agencies – the rules themselves need interpretation, by discretion or from precedent usually unknown to the applicant. The applicant, moreover, becomes a supplicant, just because he has to prove need: liable to be suspected of 'scrounging' by officials who are sensitive to the pressures of an establishment opinion that sees abuse of the welfare services as a significant social disorder.[12] So the poor are exposed to inquiries into the details of their private lives – a woman with no husband, for example, as to whether she is 'cohabiting' with a man.[13] And the testing of claims in one aspect becomes a form of labour discipline: the unskilled unemployed in particular have little effective right to refuse jobs which officials find suitable for them, without risk of losing benefit. (How else deter the work-shy, runs the reasoning behind the practice. The justification displays the skew perspectives of a class-divided society. It plays down the commitment of most workers themselves to the ethic of work which it expresses. And that ethic in turn has the selective application characteristic of a capitalist economy. Property confers immunity from it: there are no penalties for being work-shy if one has money.) So the nineteenth-century distinction between deserving and undeserving poor has a continuing lease of life.[14]

It is hardly surprising, then, that very large numbers of people who would be entitled to special benefits do not claim them. A series of

12. See, e.g., *Report of the Committee on Abuse of Social Security Benefits*, H.M.S.O., Cmnd. 5228, 1973.

13. Cf. Ruth Lister, *As Man and Wife? A Study of the Cohabitation Rule*, Child Poverty Action Group (Research Series No. 2), 1973. As shown by this study, official investigators in practice are at least as much concerned with beneficiaries' sexual relationships as with the financial relationships which can provide the only logically acceptable justification for the rule that a 'cohabiting' couple be treated as man and wife when need for supplementary benefit is assessed.

14. The same distinction is often made by council housing management in allocating older and inferior council housing to tenants judged to be poor, insufficiently respectable, 'problem families' and so on. Cf. Elizabeth Burney, *Housing on Trial*, Oxford University Press, 1967; Centre for Urban Studies, 'Tall flats in Pimlico', in *idem*, ed., *London – Aspects of Change*, MacGibbon & Kee, 1964. There are honourable exceptions: see, e.g. Ruth Glass *et al.*, *Housing in Camden*, vol. 2, London Borough of Camden, 1969. For a general discussion of the ways in which discretionary award of benefit works as a form of labour discipline, see Kincaid, op. cit. (Part 2, ch. 4, note 8; chap. 12.).

estimates and surveys in recent years suggest, for example, that only some 60 per cent of pensioners eligible for supplementary benefits have actually been getting them. Only about 50 per cent of households who might claim rate rebates in fact do so – in some areas far fewer. No more than 20 per cent of those members of low-paid workers' families who should be exempt from health service charges will usually apply for exemption. The take-up for some special allowances is even less. Most often, people fail to claim because they do not know that there is any service to claim or any chance of success; in many cases, too, because they do not understand the procedure, are suspicious of the authorities or afraid to upset a landlord, feel too proud to go begging, are reluctant to expose their poverty, or deterred by previous experience at the hands of officialdom.[15] Their numbers; their reasons; the very limited effect which official publicity campaigns have had so far – all show the width of the social cleavages which insulate the state's welfare services from the people they are claimed to serve.

Such barriers between public services and their ordinary users are evident in all fields of state provision: in health, for example, as well as in social security. Although hard facts on the point are patchy, the health services are probably now used to much the same extent by people up and down the socio-economic scale.[16] That by itself is a noteworthy achievement for the reforms initiated in the 1940s. But sheer quantity of use per head is not an adequate measure. Medical needs, by and large – the risks of illness and death – increase step by step down the scale, and are especially acute among the poor and the unskilled.[17] In fact, therefore, the even spread of use of the state's health services still means unequal access in relation to need. Such inequality arises partly because resources are maldistributed. General practitioners, for example, are thicker on the ground in comfortable

15. Molly Meacher, op. cit. (note 11 above); T. Lynes, 'The failure of selectivity', in D. Bull, ed., *Family Poverty*, Duckworth, 1971; A. B. Atkinson, *Poverty in Britain and the Reform of Social Security*, Cambridge University Press, 1969 (chap. 4).

16. M. Rein, 'Social class and the utilisation of medical care services', *Hospitals*, 1st July 1969 (cf. also *idem* in *New Society*, 20 November 1969).

17. See, in general, Part 2 above, ch. 8, notes 16–17 and the points in the text to which they relate. Butler and Bonham, op. cit., show with respect to perinatal mortality in particular how least effective use is made of relevant facilities by those at greatest risk. Cf. also *Social Trends*, no. 4, 1973. Rates of 'limiting long-standing illness' in 1972 (table 69) showed a marked class gradient, with rates three times as high among the unskilled as among professionals.

middle-class areas than in poor working-class districts; in the more prosperous and economically booming parts of the country – the south, by and large, with its higher social and occupational profile – than in the old industrial cities of the north. Teaching hospitals – superior to others in their facilities, staffing and records of success – are strongly concentrated in and around London, where the élite of the population is concentrated too. Regional inequalities are here, as in a number of other fields, intertwined with class inequalities.[18]

But direct maldistribution is only part of the story. Effective use of the services – medical services like others – requires personal resources on the part of users which are in shorter supply the further down the socio-economic scale one goes. These are resources of a fairly intangible kind. Direct evidence about them is therefore sparse; but there can be little doubt about their significance. They include knowledge of the services available and of recent developments in medicine, as a stimulus to demand; the capacity to talk to the staff of the services in their own language, and with the assurance that can come from equal or superior social position; the self-confidence and insight which it takes to penetrate the layers of junior and intermediate staff – nurses, matrons, housemen – who protect consultants and other senior doctors from hospital patients and their relatives.[19] Middle-

18. For a fairly recent general presentation of regional inequalities in socio-economic conditions and public services, see G. Taylor and N. Ayres, *Born and Bred Unequal*, Longman, 1969. Such inequalities relate in part to differences among regions in their economic structure and occupational composition. But Taylor and Ayres do not deal with the interplay between class and regional inequalities – as shown, for example, in studies of infant mortality. (Regional variations in infant mortality in part reflect the generally much sharper class variations in infant mortality: the high mortality regions have low occupational profiles, and therefore relatively large proportions of their populations in the more vulnerable groups. But only in part – class for class, mortality is still higher in the north than in the south. Cf. Morris and Heady, op. cit., Spicer and Lipworth, op. cit., Part 2, ch. 8, note 17 above.) The metropolitan area, in particular, has a higher occupational profile than the country at large. Its distinctiveness in this respect – as shown by a special analysis of census data since 1921 (see Part 5 below, ch. 1, note 5) – has diminished over time. But Greater London still has a rather larger 'middle class' element in its population, and a disproportionate concentration of the top groups in particular, by comparison with the country at large. With that concentration goes also a concentration of certain services. Thus half the country's teaching hospitals in the 1960s were in the London postal area. (Calculated from *Hospitals Year Book 1966* and Scottish Health Office, *Analysis of Running Costs of Scottish Hospitals*, 1965.)

19. One example which neatly demonstrates class differences in effective access to 'best' current medical practice was given by J. W. B. Douglas and J. M. Blomfield, *Children under Five*, Allen & Unwin, 1958 (p. 143). Routine circumci-

and upper-class people are moving here in a world which is at least partly theirs – familiar in its social contours though not in its technical detail; working-class people in a world to which they are outsiders, recipients of a service over which they have little or no influence.

Much the same applies to most manual working-class parents and children in their contact with the school system. Some of the ways in which this works, and the effective denial of educational opportunity which follows from it, will be discussed later. (See Part Four.) The point here is simply that the benefits which most ordinary people receive from this and the state's other services include no participation in control. Nor do the services work in a way to give such people the kind of everyday familiarity and ease of contact which are needed for power in a more limited sense: the power of individuals and families to make the best use of what is going; to press their demands to the limits of provision, and then beyond; to manipulate the resources of the services in the ways that upper- and middle-class people can – as a matter of course, and often hardly consciously – in their use of state provision for health and education and in dealings with the tax authorities. The barriers between the public services and their rank-and-file clients are not wholly fixed and unshakeable, of course. They may be reduced: by pressure from claimant unions and other organizations, for example, though the relative inactivity of trade unions on this front entails a constant risk of 'middle-class take-over'; by administrative reforms of the services and changes of liberal intent in patterns of staff recruitment, training and professional organization. But the prime source of these barriers is outside the services themselves. It is in the class divisions of the society – in the economic inequalities produced by property and market, in the social and cultural cleavages which go with those in turn. To that extent estrangement between user and service is an inherent feature of public benevolence in a capitalist economy.

---

sion of boys and routine tonsillectomy – fashionable medical practice at one time, but unpopular with the profession by the time of the survey – was found still to be an increasing trend for children of semi- and unskilled workers, but a declining one for those of professional and salaried workers. It was not clear how far this reflected differences in the quality of medical practice available, how far differences in demand from parents; but the latter no doubt played a part.

IV

The point is reinforced when one looks at those state institutions whose functions are a mixture of 'service' with a major and explicit element of active social control: the police, the courts and their associated institutions. Their share of all government expenditure, though growing, is small – under 3 per cent in 1971 (table 20). That is no measure of their importance as the sources of ultimate sanction behind the established order. But the relatively small share of public resources going to the police, courts and prisons could perhaps be taken as a hint of the extent to which maintenance of the social order depends, not on direct enforcement of law, but on widespread routine acceptance of the way things work. It is true, moreover, that the functions of the law – of the courts and to some extent of the police – are mixed. They include restitution as well as repression; the settlement of disputes as well as social control. Indeed it is these functions, coupled with a view of courts and police as guardians of the great majority against a small minority of delinquents, deviants and dissidents, which form the background to the common postulate that respect for the law runs deep in British society.

There is some truth in that postulate. But it is far from the whole truth. It takes no account of the profound ambiguities which permeate relations between the bulk of the population – the manual working class in particular – and the law. Those ambiguities are visible already at a superficial level, when public opinion polls favour the police with a very high degree of popularity in all classes, expressed in answer to abstract questions with no reference to concrete situations; while policemen themselves at the same time complain with some bitterness of a worsening in their relations with 'the public', and are quite conscious of the suspicion they often meet in working-class areas that they are on the side of property against ordinary workers.[20] Suspicion of that kind has long historical roots; and those roots have a solid foundation in the genesis of the police. Old ruling-class and new bourgeois worries played the major part in the establishment of police forces from the late eighteenth century onwards: concerns with riot control and suppression of working-class

20. Cf. M. Banton, *The Policeman in the Community*, Tavistock, 1964, pp. 8–11 and 176 especially.

unrest; with the protection of property and trade.[21] These are still, in changed forms, important police concerns, though most police time goes on other matters. Victorian forebodings of revolution have dissolved. But quite apart from Special Branch surveillance of political dissidents – who may be industrial militants as well – police control of strike picketing is a recurrent source of tension between them and workers. It has come more to the fore as industrial conflict has accelerated: very clearly so during the first few years of the 1970s, with the formation of police 'strike flying squads' to stand by at 'strategic points' and several court decisions that drastically curtailed the possibilities of picketing without falling foul of the law.[22] None of this makes the police simply the strong arm of capitalism. If they were just that, they would be highly ineffective in the role; for they would lack all popular support. But popular support for the police in the role which they like to cast for themselves – as guardians of the peace and friends of the respectable public – is inevitably limited by the fact that the peace and respectability which they protect are those of a divided society.[23]

21. See, e.g., T. A. Critchley, *A History of Police in England and Wales, 900–1966, Constable, 1967.*

22. The establishment of strike flying squads was reported in early 1973; that of an intelligence bureau at Scotland Yard to give advance warning of industrial unrest which might turn to violence, near the end of the same year (*The Times*, 19 March, 13 Nov., 1973). In that year, too, a joint exercise in 'civilian control' by army and police at London Airport, coupled with reports of police as well as army instruction in action against 'urban terrorism', hinted at a possible future use of the police in a para-military role to deal with internal unrest, although these measures in themselves were ostensibly directed against external threats from Irish and Arab armed violence. The crucial cases on picketing were *Broome* v. *Director of Public Prosecutions* (*Times* law report for 20 Dec. 1973) and *Kavanagh* v. *Hiscock* (J. A. G. Griffith, 'The peaceful picket', *New Statesman*, 15 Feb. 1974). In the first, the House of Lords ruled that the right to picket carried no right to stop the driver of a lorry, even briefly, to attempt peacefully to persuade him not to enter a strike-bound site. In the second, the Court of Appeal decided that, in forming a cordon to prevent pickets from speaking to potential strike-breakers, the police were acting in execution of their duty if they 'reasonably' suspected a risk of a breach of the peace. Together the two rulings gave the police almost unlimited discretion to prevent effective picketing. The notorious Shrewsbury trial, in which three building workers were given prison sentences fom nine months to three years on charges arising out of picketing (*Times*, 20 Dec. 1973; appeals dismissed, 5 March 1974) broke no new ground in law. The court found that the three had used violence in picketing. But it was symptomatic of the temper of the time that the main charge against them was the legally elastic one of 'conspiracy' to intimidate: intimidation by itself could not have allowed such heavy sentences.

23. The point, obvious enough though neglected for some time, has been stressed in some of the recent academic work on the police and on 'deviance'. Cf.

Motoring offences apart, it is working-class people who are mainly at risk at the hands of the police. Policemen have considerable practical discretion whether to check up, arrest, prosecute – intervene or turn a blind eye. Their exercise of that discretion is guided by stereotypes that single out particular groups, 'types' – and districts – as deviant: 'roughs', young people who seem scruffy or flamboyant, coloured people, students.[24] The victims here do not include the 'respectable' bulk of the working class. But the line separating 'rough' from 'respectable' is hazy. And, except for students, most of those who are vulnerable are from the manual working class, though minorities within it. Crime as recorded in court convictions is in any case a largely working-class phenomenon; and a substantial minority of working-class youths – even from skilled workers' families – will appear at least once before a court and be found guilty.[25] Their exposure to that risk is still more widespread. Everyday life and leisure, celebration and sorrow, moreover, have a more public character in many working-class areas than among other classes – and, by the same token, are more likely to offend the canons of public 'decency' and 'order' which police and magistrates' courts spend a good deal of their time enforcing. Here, *par excellence,* are offences without victims; and it is easy for policemen to show their zeal by discovering such offences on patrol through the more rewarding areas.[26]

---

the review in Maureen Cain, *Society and the Policeman's Role*, Routledge & Kegan Paul, 1973 (pp. 20–24); for a sharp statement, D. Rosenberg, 'The sociology of the police and sociological liberalism', 1973 (unpubl. mimeo); and on this and several of the following points, S. Box, *Deviance, Reality and Society*, Holt, Rinehart, Winston, 1971 (especially ch. 6). It is well known, to take a further example, that tenants harassed by landlords receive little or no help from the police. And police have stood by passively while private bailiffs employed by municipal landlords have used strong-arm methods illegally to evict squatters (see R. Bailey, 'Housing: alienation and beyond', in I. Taylor and L. Taylor, eds., *Politics and Deviance*, Penguin, 1973; also R. Bailey, *The Squatters*, Penguin, 1973).

24. See, e.g., Cain, op. cit. (pp. 114–19); S. Cohen, *Folk Devils and Moral Panics*, Paladin, 1973; G. Armstrong and M. Wilson, 'City politics and deviancy amplification', in Taylor and Taylor, eds., op. cit.; J. R. Lambert, *Crime, Police and Race Relations*, Oxford Univ. Press, 1970 (especially chapters 5–6).

25. In a large national sample of children born in 1946, 15–20 per cent of the boys from manual workers' homes (skilled to unskilled) had been convicted of at least one offence by 17 (i.e., by 1963); 10 per cent of the boys with 'white collar' fathers; only 5 per cent of those from 'professional and salaried' families. J. W. B. Douglas *et al.*, 'Delinquency and social class', in W. G. Carson and P. Wiles, eds., *Crime and Delinquency in Britain*, Robertson, 1971.

26. Cf. Cain, op. cit. (note 23 above, pp. 67–70).

These are hardly foundations for an unqualified bonhomie between police and large sections of the manual working class. The separation between the two is underlined in other ways as well. Policemen, it is true, are recruited in large numbers from working-class backgrounds; and senior posts have in the past been filled mainly by internal promotion from the ranks – a pattern that contrasts with the tradition and practice of both military and civil services. Indeed, these personnel policies may have been instituted and maintained just in order to reduce the risk of total distrust between police and the common people over whom they are watchdogs.[27] But patterns of promotion are now changing; and police recruitment within the manual working class in any case draws almost entirely on the skilled layers. Very few policemen come from semi- and unskilled workers' families; a very large minority at least – perhaps even a majority – are from white-collar homes.[28] Policemen and their families are altogether rather cut off from companionship with people outside the force. But their links – in styles of life, friendships and social outlook – are closest with the petty bourgeoisie and the most secure, respectable and aspiring ranks of manual workers.[29] The nature of their work; their place on a ladder of promotion, rather rickety though that may be; the criteria by which their capacity for the job are judged; the dependence of lower ranks on their superiors in a hierarchy of command – all can be expected to lead the police to identify with the social order as it exists. The same things lead also to their separation from the bulk of the ordinary working-class population: separation of a kind which characterizes all the agencies of the state.

The break between rank-and-file public and state authority is still sharper, and runs at a higher point of the socio economic scale, in the

27. Cf e.g., Critchley, op. cit. (note 21 above) on recruitment for the metropolitan force set up by Peel's act of 1829 (pp. 49–55); see also pp. 192–99, e.g., on subsequent attempts to ensure recruitment from the respectable skilled and white collar strata, and pay and other conditions in line with this aim.

28. In the city police force studied by Cain (op. cit., p. 101), one third of the men had fathers in Registrar General's Social Class II (intermediate non-manual); nearly three-fifths were from III (routine non-manual and skilled manual, without distinction between the two, including 6 per cent who were sons of policemen); only 9 per cent had fathers in IV and V (semi- and unskilled). The county police force showed fewer from II, more from III (including more policemen's sons), hardly any from IV and V. (B. Whitaker, *The Police*, Penguin 1964, p. 96, gives similar – not identical – figures for a city and county force; whether unrevised figures from Cain's survey or data from another source is not stated.)

29. See Cain, op. cit. (e.g., pp. 82, 87); Banton, op. cit. (note 20 above, pp. 176–214, 246–50).

case of the courts. In principle institutions to settle disputes as well as to exercise penal control, in practice they are not open for people to use readily as a service. Legal aid and some decentralization of jurisdiction, especially since World War II, have widened use of the courts. But legal aid – granted only on fairly stringent tests of financial need – is no more than a concessionary exception from the principle which still stands: that access to justice in civil disputes should be rationed by the purse.[30] That principle is symptomatic of a class-divided society; the state's adherence to it symptomatic of the state's class affiliations. Except on matrimonial matters, even comfortably placed middle-class people rarely resort to litigation: the risks and complexities are too great. The clientele of the higher courts in civil cases must be very largely drawn from the same economic stratum as the judges and barristers whom they meet there: often, indeed, from one or more levels higher up, since businessmen and their companies are prominent in litigation. The restitutive functions of the law are essentially a matter of bourgeois privilege.

Legal aid has, it is true, brought working-class people into the courts as litigants: mainly in cases of dispute between husband and wife. Divorce now runs at more or less the same rate in all classes of the population, whereas it was earlier a privilege of the upper and then the middle classes. But access does not yet seem to be equal in relation to demand, though the chief barrier is probably no longer the cost of divorce proceedings. There are still many broken marriages in the working class which go no further than the magistrates' courts, where their dissolution is recognized by separation and maintenance orders without legal right of re-marriage.[31] So this lowest flight of

30. The upper income limit for free legal aid was raised to about £7 per week, after certain basic expenses, from 1 January 1974, that for legal aid in the form of a limited contribution from public funds to about £22 per week. An official committee found these limits 'still much too low'. (Comments and Recommendations of the Lord Chancellor's Advisory Committee, *Legal Aid and Advice 1972–73*, H.M.S.O., March 1974.)

31. O. R. McGregor *et al.*, *Separated Spouses: a Study of the Matrimonial Jurisdiction of Magistrates' Courts*, Duckworth, 1970 (pp. 138–47). See also N. H. Carrier and G. Rowntree, 'The resort to divorce in England and Wales, 1858–1957', *Population Studies*, March 1958. The Divorce Reform Act 1969 may increase the number of broken working-class marriages that will end in full divorce, since it should reduce the need for those kinds of collusive arrangements between marriage partners and solicitors – no doubt more available to upper- and middle-class couples – that were encouraged by the former dependence of divorce on commission of a 'matrimonial offence' by one party. A government committee in 1974 recommended abolition of the de facto class divisions in matrimonial law and jurisdiction, and establishment of a single system with a new 'family court' for all

courts in their civil jurisdiction still specialize in working-class litigation, as they have done since they acquired the first of their current
powers in matrimonial cases in 1878. And their litigants, characteristically, often appear before them without the help of a lawyer to
represent them.[32]

Indeed the difference between civil and criminal jurisdiction –
between the courts when they act as service agencies and when they
act as institutions of penal control – can be hard to see for most
ordinary people who come into contact with them. Financial settlements when marriages break down, for example, come up against the
dull, hard facts of working-class life. A magistrates' court maintenance order gives the wife a legal claim on part of her husband's
income. But often it cannot be enforced to the full amount. And to
the man, likely to run into arrears, it may seem no different from a
continuous series of fines. He may find the sum taken, by 'attach-
ment', from his wages; he may even go to prison for persistent default.
Most, moreover, are bewildered by the court proceedings; they complain that the atmosphere prevents a fair hearing, and that court
officials are unhelpful.[33] So, too, in penal cases, where the great
majority of defendants are manual working class, and where the
safeguards intended to protect prisoners are often denied them. Those
held first at police stations are usually, if they ask, refused access to a
solicitor at the time. Magistrates rarely grant bail against police
objections, although the case on subsequent trial often proves not to
result in a jail sentence; and most of those refused bail are not told of
their right to appeal on the point. Legal representation is uncommon
in these courts, even when defendants plead not guilty; and at least a
large minority of those sentenced to prison by magistrates have had
no lawyer to put their case. Advice about, and help in making, an
appeal are often inadequate.[34] So, whether the proceedings are civil

litigation in matrimonial affairs. See *Report of the Committee on One-Parent
Families*, Cmnd. 5629, H.M.S.O., 1974.

32. McGregor *et al.*, op. cit. (p. 58): in half the post-legal aid matrimonial cases
examined, at least one of the parties was not represented; in 11 per cent, neither
party was.

33. McGregor *et al.*, op. cit., pp. 87–117; 127, 133. The Committee on One-
Parent Families (op. cit., note 31 above) in 1974 recommended that the Supplementary Benefits Commission should no longer encourage women to take their
husbands or their children's fathers to court to enforce maintenance payments,
and that a new guaranteed maintenance allowance from public funds should be
instituted.

34. See M. Zander, 'Access to a solicitor in the police station', *Criminal Law*

or penal, working-class people in court are victims of procedures they do not understand and for which they receive little of the help that is formally prescribed; often sheer indifference or direct hostility.

The unequal confrontation is very much, of course, a confrontation between classes. Magistrates – all but a handful of them laymen – are still recruited overwhelmingly from among professional people and employers. In the late 1960s, as twenty years earlier, only one in seven or eight were wage earners.[35] The judges and barristers who staff the high courts are members of what is still the most tightly closed profession in the country; and this is reflected in their biographies. The path to the high court bench runs from a professional, business or landed home through a 'public' school and on through Oxford or Cambridge.[36] The point is not that magistrates and judges necessarily turn a harsher face to working-class offenders and litigants than to others, when cases are the same.[37] But most offenders are working class; and the law handles 'white-collar crime' differently from the kinds of offence in which working-class people are typically involved.[38]

Review, June 1972; M. King and Christine Jackson, *Bail or Custody*, Cobden Trust, 1972; M. Zander, *Lawyers and the Public Interest*, Weidenfeld & Nicolson, 1968 (p. 170); *idem*, 'Legal advice and criminal appeals', *Criminal Law Review*, March 1972.

35. R. Hood, *Sentencing the Motoring Offender*, Heinemann Educational Books, 1972 (pp. 51–3).

36. Nearly nine out of every ten judges of the high courts and the courts above them in 1963 had attended a public school and Oxford or Cambridge. (M. Zander, *Lawyers and the Public Interest*, op. cit., p. 40.) The corresponding proportions among the élite of the judiciary – the Lords of Appeal in Ordinary – were much the same for those appointed 1948–1969; and recruitment to the legal benches of the House of Lords has, if anything, become a little more uniform by those criteria since 1876. (Calculations from a list in L. Blom-Cooper and G. Drewry, *Final Appeal*, Clarendon Press, 1972, which shows also occupations of fathers.) There are no data on the social origins of barristers as a whole since the inter-war years. (See M. Ginsberg, 'Interchange between social classes', in his *Studies in Sociology*, Methuen, 1932, p. 171 – who showed a more or less constant 80–85 per cent intake from social class I families to Lincoln's Inn from the 1880s to the 1920s.) No data are available at all for solicitors, the junior branch of the legal profession.

37. R. Hood, op. cit. (note 35 above) reports no evidence of such a bias in respect of motoring offences – one of the few types of offence with a wide class span. In another study he found signs that magistrates in predominantly non-industrial, middle- and upper-class towns adopted a relatively harsh sentencing policy towards working–class offenders compared with magistrates elsewhere. (*idem, Sentencing in Magistrates' Courts*, Stevens, 1962, e.g. p. 78.)

38. So far in this country, differences in treatment between white-collar and other crime at the hands of the law seem to have been discussed more than they have been studied. But see W. G. Carson, 'White collar crime and the enforce-

What matters here, however, is just the simple fact of the abyss that separates the world of bench, bar and law from the world of ordinary workers. It is no accident that working-class people often do not use even those sources of everyday legal advice – in short supply though they are – to which they might turn in need.[39]

V

So state service shades into class control. The agencies of the state in no real sense belong to the common people, but are outside them and in others' hands. There is no contradiction between that and the fact that a variety of pressures have contributed to the growth of the public services. Working-class discontent and labour demands were indeed a force for change – as in the period of 'imperialism and social reform', and with the 'social reconstruction' of the 1940s. But the pressure of labour behind those series of reforms did not amount to a power that could be translated into continuous and active popular control of the new public services. And other motives played a large part in reform as well. Calculations of economic efficiency have been a continuous thread in arguments for social improvement. Victorian reformers mixed philanthropy with business sense, and often justified proposals for better sanitation, health and housing by the returns which they would yield in productivity. Alarm at the rise of foreign competition, and over military weakness shown up by the Boer War, was among the influences which made for reforms of education and medical services early in this century. The revived clamour for 'modernization' in the 1960s – a recurrent theme in British debate ever since the country's world economic predominance began to slip away – set the climate for a boom in higher education; and for legislation to improve terms of employment and provision for redundancy, in order to smooth the way for a 'shake-out' of labour between industries.

The story of the growth of public education, even in crude outline, is a case study in the mixture of pressures that have swollen state activities. Direct public provision of popular education was delayed

---

ment of factory legislation', in *idem* and Wiles, op. cit. (note 25 above); cf. also notes 21–22, ch. 4, below.

39. See especially B. Abel-Smith *et al.*, *Legal Problems and the Citizen*, Heinemann, 1973.

until 1870, though state aid to 'voluntary' schools for working-class children had grown over the previous four decades. Opponents stressed the dangers that might come from educating tomorrow's workers 'beyond their station' in life. Supporters stressed the opposing risks that political power would spread to people uneducated to political responsibility; but above all the need for a capable, industrious and dutiful labour force. Public provision from 1870 was first confined almost entirely to elementary education; and there was no bridge between those and other schools. But with the turn of the century state provision was extended to secondary education, though only for a minority of children. The notion was accepted to use the publicly supported secondary schools in part as a 'ladder' up which the ablest working-class children might climb to higher positions in life. Behind that crucial change were concerns with economic efficiency in general; with recruitment of skilled and white-collar labour in particular; but also with the need to make concessions to a labour movement now more conscious of itself as a political force. The 'ladder' was not designed for equality of opportunity. Only some of the state-supported secondary schools' children were free-placers, chosen for their exceptional ability; the rest were there because their parents could afford the fees. But as the public sector of secondary education was expanded over the following decades, more of its pupils – including middle-class children, in competition with workers' children trying to climb the ladder – were given free places.

In 1944 secondary education was made available to all – an aim first asserted by the labour movement in the 1890s – and fees in state schools in England and Wales were finally abolished. The idea of a ladder had been discarded. Instead, public education was now seen as a sieve which was to sort all its pupils by merit, regardless of social origin and parental means; and on that basis steer them towards different destinations in the socio-economic hierarchy of adult life. The goal, in principle, was equality of opportunity; the justification, both economic efficiency and benevolence to meet rising social demands. But the private schools – untouched and flourishing – were immune from the principle. In practice the state school system was given a hierarchical form, crudely paralleling the society around it. From an early stage its children were sorted into streams, which offered different grades of education and sent them out into the world at different ages and on to different levels of the adult class structure. Resources were, and are still, concentrated on a minority, successively reduced in numbers as they grow older. One consequence, almost certainly, has been to add weight to the many obstacles to effective recruitment of talent, since most children have only a short run before they are tested and found wanting. Another, no less probably, has been to hamper changes in school curricula which might help to make tomorrow's workers more versatile and adaptable to changing technological circumstances, because the schools instead have been geared to selection of a minority. Neither consequence, it can be argued, serves the interests of business enterprise best. But both derive from class-tied limitations on common conceptions about the possibilities of popular education; and both give rise to pressures for further change.

The agitation and measures taken in recent years to delay and modify the process of educational grading, by reducing streaming in primary schools and by turning secondary schools 'comprehensive', have been inspired partly by considerations of equity and by the worries of parents – many middle-class parents not least – whose children were liable to fall foul of the process. But anxieties about the inefficiency of early selection – about the 'wastage of talent' associated with precipitate labelling of children – have added a strong utilitarian impetus to reform. On the other hand, class-free conceptions of educational purpose, advocating a common schooling for all irrespective of their future destination, have in practice made little of the steam that has turned the wheels towards some form of comprehensive reorganization. Such ideas cannot pull much weight so long as the society into which the schools feed their children is itself deeply divided, and offers very different rewards for jobs of different kinds. There is no 'common culture' to which a common education could be directed. The notion implies a remodelling of schools, colleges and their curricula in an egalitarian mould that would contradict the pattern of the society at large.

There is no such fundamental contradiction between the society at large and an educational system which has adopted the formal ideal of equality of opportunity. That ideal presents no challenge of principle to the inequality of condition in so far as the aim is only to secure equal access by 'merit' to places – in schools and colleges, and thence in the world of work – which are themselves very unequal. The notion of equity involved is quite limited. And it has been the more easily accepted by the powerful because the threat which it might pose is still more limited in practice. The growth of public education has raised levels of schooling and training all round. Its formal dedication to selection by merit alone, however, has so far done little to cut down the privileged opportunities of the children of the privileged. Economic efficiency is seen to be impaired by the consequent wastage of talent. And that again adds impetus to the further expansion of state education. Concern with both efficiency and equity was similarly behind the multiplication of places in higher education in the 1960s. Anxiety to 'modernize' the economy triggered public policy; the rising demand from secondary school children and their parents set the numerical targets of growth for colleges and universities.

This is a very summary sketch.[40] But it should be enough at this point to dispel the assumption that public education is essentially a welfare service designed wholly or at least primarily to enlarge the horizons and opportunities of its children. Preoccupations with political pacification, industrial discipline, and above all labour recruitment and proficiency, have both joined and clashed with more liberal concerns to expand state activity in this field; and they do so still. The mixture of motives that have gone into expansion of the public educational system varies, even among capitalist societies. In the United States, for example, determination to Americanize the children of millions of working-class immigrants, and attach their loyalties firmly to their new society, came together with older concerns to give opportunity to talent, to produce a formally 'comprehensive' system long before this became the trend in Europe. Any future socialist society, too, will no doubt set its schools and colleges to promote efficiency and popular support for its own order by its own terms of reference. In Britain now the demand for the schools to act as agencies of social control is asserted a good deal less overtly than it was earlier, though echoes of that demand are still to be heard in the contention, for example, that it is the job of the schools to instil in their pupils a 'sense of community', of the absence of which working-class delinquency is taken to be a sign. But the hierarchical organization of schools, and the processes of competitive selection to which the children are subjected, may well serve to familiarize pupils

40. Some of these issues are discussed again later; see Part 4. For a cogent historical analysis of the development of the English educational system, see D. V. Glass, 'Education and social change in modern England', in A. H. Halsey et al., eds., Education, Economy and Society, Free Press, 1961. (The Scottish educational system has a different history, and even now differs from that of England and Wales in some respects.)

with the logic of inequality that pervades the society at large; to reduce potential opposition to that inequality through such early familiarity; and to make many or most children breathe a sigh of relief when they are released from school, into subordinate positions in adult life, after long experience of educational rejection. Such indirect support from the school system for the established order may be much more important than direct indoctrination: another example of the power of anonymous institutions through the uneventful routine of their everyday operation.

The pressures and motives behind the growth of state education have been mixed, in short. So is the direction of the outcome. But property and private business are certainly among the main beneficiaries in a society such as Britain, directly as well as indirectly. Industry draws large, though not easily measurable, subsidies from public education. It would have to pay heavily if it were to take over from the state the groundwork of adapting, training and sorting its future labour.

VI

The educational system provides just one example of the ways in which the shape of the class structure and the weight of private capital are imprinted on the services of the state. These are the forces that set the broad limits of the public services. Within those limits there is room for some diversity of development; for controversy about the scale and direction of expenditure; for rivalry between more and less generous definitions of policy objectives; thus also for pressures towards modest reform to have some effect.

The professions which make their living out of the public services may be one such source of pressure, in so far as they have a vested interest in expanding the demand for their skills and in widening official conceptions of their jobs. But the professions with strongest potential interests of that kind – those which cannot readily adopt the alternative tactic of restrictive practices, because they lack the market power to define their own work and to control recruitment to it – are also for just that reason the least able to exert pressure successfully in any direction. Teachers, nurses and social workers are the prime examples. The professions with well-established monopoly and autonomy in their own fields – notably lawyers and doctors – by contrast can exercise pressure much more effectively. But their very market strength enables them to adopt tactics, in their self-interest, with social effects opposed to those of expansion of the services in which they work. Their organizations have hardly shown great dedication to an ideal of popular welfare; more to defence of privilege.[41] Neither their record nor as yet on the whole that of the 'lower' professions – prototypically petty bourgeois still in their socio-economic marginality – supports the notion that the public service professions can be expected to tear away state social provision from its class moorings. They are not a kind of 'third force', as that notion implies. They are tied – in different ways at different levels of the professional hierarchy, and the marginal professions least securely so – to the structure of class dominance which sets the framework of the services.

So, in summary, the growth of state social services marks no significant shift of power into the hands of wage earners. The services help to provide elementary security and, in the case of public education, some institutionalized opportunity for advancement of individuals of low or modest social origin. Even those benefits are noticeably ragged; and they are paid for largely by wage earners themselves. The public services are outside the control, and very often the comprehension, of those whom they are supposed to serve: shaped and run from above, tailored to fit with the interests of capital and wealth. In general, though not in every detail, the social and allied services of the state are essential to the maintenance of the complex capitalist economy and society of today. Their effects are to help contain working-class unrest by smoothing off the rougher edges of

41. The medical profession strenuously opposed the introduction of the National Health Service, despite earlier support for the principle and the increased security which it promised (and in fact has given) many general practitioners. The profession pressed successfully for consultants to be allowed to use public resources for private patients; persuaded an official committee in 1957 to recommend a cut in the intake to medical schools; and have in general been more vociferous in pushing their monetary claims than in pressing for measures to make the health services fully available to all. Cf. H. Eckstein, *Pressure Group Politics: the Case of the B.M.A.,* Allen & Unwin, 1960; R. M. Titmuss, *Essays on the 'Welfare State',* Allen & Unwin, 1968, ch. 9; *Report of the Committee to Consider the Future Number of Medical Practitioners* (Willink Committee), 1957. On restrictive practices maintained by the legal professions, see especially M. Zander, *Lawyers and the Public Interest,* op. cit. (note 34 above); cf. also B. Abel-Smith and R. Stevens, *Lawyers and the Courts,* Heinemann Educational Books, 1967. For an excellent sociological history of one of the 'lower' professions, by contrast, see A. Tropp, *The Schoolteachers,* Heinemann, 1957.

insecurity; to provide a semblance of justice without the reality of equality; to educate, sort out and maintain a labour force to a tolerable standard of efficiency – not on the whole to a very high standard, by ideal criteria of a capitalist economy, since the internal contradictions of the society militate against that. The barriers to any significant liberalization of the social services are strongly embedded in the continuing structure of class dominance. For all the resources it handles, the service arm of the 'benevolent state' is frail.

4 State economic activity and private business

I

State involvement in economic production has no more displaced capitalism than has state provision of social services. No sizeable shift of power from capital to labour has resulted; let alone the abolition of capital. The crucial question again concerns, not the magnitude of public sector activity, but its direction: the purposes at which it is aimed, the interests which it serves, its effects.

There is no substance to the idea that state intervention in economic affairs is inherently inimical to private enterprise. The *laissez-faire* model of a capitalist economy on which that idea is based had some reality at one time and place – in mid-nineteenth-century Britain, before the rise of large-scale corporate enterprise and the emergence of capitalism abroad in serious rivalry with British business. Even then the model fitted reality imperfectly.[1] It does not fit the twentieth century at all, when the growth of business and government, hand in hand, has eroded competition, but left private profit intact as the prime motor of the economy and private property intact as its institutional foundation. The notion of an inherent conflict between private enterprise and state involvement in economic affairs implies, moreover, that capital creates a single interest among its owners; that there is no rivalry among different factions of property

1. See, e.g., J. B. Brebner, 'Laissez-faire and state intervention in 19th Century Britain', *J. of Econ. History*, Supplement VIII, 1948. (Even the late nineteenth century U.S. economy was further from the laissez-faire model than that of Britain in the mid-nineteenth century, in so far as tariffs protected domestic industry.)

sufficient for one faction to invoke the state in aid against another. In fact, part of the story of the growth of public economic control is the story of just such conflicts – from the first steps towards factory legislation, sponsored by representatives of the old 'landed interest', and supported or tolerated by some of the larger manufacturers who could bear the costs which their weaker competitors could ill afford. Another, and large, part of the story concerns the use of the state and law to reduce the risks which capitalists face so long as there is competition in their markets. Often here, too, conflicts between rival business interests have been involved: between industries highly vulnerable to foreign competition and others, as over the tariff issue which helped to shift business support from Liberals to Conservatives from before the turn of the century onwards; between large corporations and smaller-scale enterprise; between banking and manufacturing interests.

For long – in Britain for seventy years at least – the state has also been called upon to set a legal and administrative framework for the peaceful settlement of disputes between employers and workers. These arrangements are of indubitable benefit to capital, whose profits depend on normal continuity of production. They have no such certain advantage for labour, except on the assumption that private appropriation of profit is as sacrosanct as state-encouraged collective bargaining assumes it to be. Unions cannot negotiate to abolish profit: it is on that unspoken premise that the wheels of conflict resolution in industrial relations turn. More recently – since World War II especially – state-activity has been more and more consciously directed to control of the economic environment: to establishing conditions of general business prosperity and growth. The benefits again are plain for capital, but at best only conditional for labour. 'Full employment' policy in the 1940s and 1950s clearly and significantly reduced working-class insecurity. But the mixed economy's theme song of a natural harmony between worker and employer rang steadily thinner in the 1960s, as official diagnoses of national needs promoted rising unemployment, to discipline workers and 'shake out' labour between industries; and as governments of both colours moved to legislative action to repress shop-floor militancy. Even when the refrain of public policy is conciliation rather than confrontation, however, it is conciliation always on terms that take the maintenance of private profit for granted. Whatever the pay-off for labour, it is within those fixed limits.

The state, in short, is not neutral in economic affairs. It cannot be, for there is no neutral ground for it to take up between acceptance and rejection of the principle of private profit. There is no social vacuum in which public authority can float unattached, in a society divided by the profit principle between those who gain and those who lose from it. Capital and labour have both invoked government aid; and the state has grown in consequence. But its economic activities have been directed throughout to maintaining a society in which capital lives on labour; not to transforming it into one in which labour would live free of capital. The history of government economic involvement in the twentieth century is that of the evolution of an alliance between business and state agencies, with organized labour encouraged to accept a place as a third partner provided that it agrees to the essential preconditions of the alliance: the maintenance of private property and profit as the mainsprings of the economy.

II

The forces out of which this alliance grew began to make themselves felt in Britain from the last decades of the nineteenth century onwards – in this as in other respects a watershed in British social history. The growth of corporate enterprise gave big business increasing power in the market, and both opportunity and incentive to use the state to entrench its position. Competition from abroad destroyed the world pre-eminence of British capitalism, and encouraged public intervention to create conditions within which business could survive and expand. Obsolescence in British industry by comparison with its competitors – the heritage of early foundations in coal, iron and cotton – added to the severity of the business climate which the state was called on to temper. The rise and new militancy of organized labour around the turn of the century required either drastic repression – a very risky undertaking in an unfavourable situation – or the evolution of an apparatus of accommodation, which would give recognition and some influence to labour without conceding the routine power of capital to shape economy and society.

Collective bargaining between workers and employers received positive state support from the early years of this century; and the pressures for protection of British business against foreign competition had set in a little earlier. More direct government intervention in economic affairs was delayed until World War I. That war was a major stimulus to the process. State agencies were set up to co-ordinate the shift of production to military objectives. Official union acceptance of labour direction and of legal prohibition from strikes was bought cheaply, at the price of increased recognition for the unions in collective bargaining and minority representation of the Labour Party in the wartime government. But these major steps towards institutionalization of class and industrial conflict also provoked, extensive unlawful strikes, and gave a new temporary impetus to work place militancy and syndicalism of one shade and another.[2]

During the inter-war years government involvement in the affairs of private industry was directed especially to 'rationalization' – to co-ordination of production, development and marketing, particularly through mergers between companies and enforced elimination of small producers. It was the older industries – doubly hard hit by economic recession because they were declining anyway – that were the main object of these efforts. Some new industries became the first to be nationalized, in a form that set an organizational model for nationalization after World War II – broadcasting, the electricity grid, the main overseas airways. But 'rationalization' of older industries was pursued without abrogation of private ownership. Coal-mining, of course, was a recurrent source of conflict; and the government's refusal to accept a royal commission's majority recommendation in 1919 for nationalization of the industry was a major element in the genesis of the general strike of 1926. The railways were merged by statute in the early 1920s into four large companies, still private though under public supervision. Extensive government assistance during the 1930s went into reorganization of shipbuilding, cotton and fishing – a process which meant amalgamation of firms to the advantage of large producers and against generally ineffective opposition from small producers.[3] In the period after World War II, again, cotton, shipbuilding and aircraft manufacture have received

2. See, e.g., N. Harris, *Competition and the Corporate Society*, Methuen, 1972 (chapter 2); R. Miliband, *Parliamentary Socialism*, Merlin, 1973 (2nd ed., chapter 2); G. D. H. Cole and R. Postgate, *The Common People 1746–1938*, Methuen, 1938 (chapter 41); B. Pribicevic, *The Shop Stewards' Movement and Workers' Control 1910–1922*, Blackwell, 1959.

3. Cf. Harris, op. cit. (chapter 2); R. Brady, *Business as a System of Power*, Columbia Univ. Press, 1943 (chapter 5).

substantial public aid contributing to concentration of private production and control.

The 1940s, of course, saw a considerable extension of government economic activity. Yet this took place broadly within the patterns for which there are already precedents: there was no radical change of direction. Wartime controls to militarize the economy – such as rationing of raw materials for industry – were almost certainly a good deal more effective than during World War I. But they followed the earlier model of setting businessmen to watch over business. The Labour government which came to office in 1945 – with a commitment to national economic 'planning' that proved both vague and rather nominal – gradually relaxed and eventually scrapped most of these regulations. So long as the new government kept wartime controls in force, however, their exercise remained largely in business hands. Labour's Chief Planning Officer in the economic field was a former director of British Aluminium. The ministerial advisers, commodity directors and controllers of materials were typically business executives, often drawn from the largest firms in the relevant industries or from the trade association of this or that industry as a whole. So, too, were many of the lower-level staff of the controlling agencies, whose salaries might still be paid by their firms. Individuals shuttled between posts in those agencies and jobs in the companies from which they were seconded. In some cases, control was delegated direct to the relevant trade association, to one large firm in the industry or to a specially formed consortium of firms.

No conflict was seen between this pattern of staffing and the purposes of control. Nor was there ground to see serious conflict, since control was never designed to achieve purposes hostile to the predominant interests of business. Indeed, after the original purpose of winning the war had been achieved, it became increasingly unclear why regulations should continue. Both that fact and the business connections of the controllers themselves encouraged the eventual abandonment of controls. While they lasted, their exercise by representatives of business – of big business in particular – appears to have worked in much the same direction as government support for 'rationalization' before the war. The position of large companies, monopolies and cartels was strengthened; and price levels were probably set higher than would otherwise have been possible. The notion of re-directing controls to a policy of radical redistribution of income, wealth and power was no part of Labour's programme in

office after 1945. The only important new element in the objectives of
government economic policy was a bi-partisan commitment to a high
level of business activity and full employment. There was no major
clash with the interests of industry as a whole inherent in that at the
time. Memories of pre-war recession still veiled the risk to profit
from worker indiscipline associated with a strong demand for
labour.[4]

III

Nationalization of industries, however, may seem to involve a fundamental breach in the alliance between business and government.
There were a few examples of nationalization under Conservative
governments during the inter-war years. But Labour after the war
considerably extended the scale of public ownership by taking over,
for the state, the coal-mines; the railways and much of road transport; steel; electricity and gas, though the transfer here was in part
only from local to central government ownership. There were certainly left-wing pressures, fired by socialist objectives, behind this
programme. A shopping list of industries for nationalization had
been forced on a reluctant Labour Party executive at a wartime party
conference; and the unions in the relevant industries themselves
pushed for public ownership. Many Labour supporters then still saw
the nationalization programme as the first major instalment in the
party's official long-term policy of appropriation of the means of
'production, distribution and exchange', although so-called moderate
demands to keep the mix of the 'mixed economy' as it was now
became increasingly explicit and dominant in party policy. The
Conservative Party in opposition resisted the nationalization programme, although it was committed to some form of extensive public
control at least in the case of coal and rail. It made a full-scale on-
slaught on Labour's measures only in the case of steel, over which the
government itself had been divided. In office after 1951, the Conservatives put through legislation to return road transport and steel –
but not coal, railways and public utilities – to private ownership.
They also gave back to landowners the right to future increases in the

4. The points in the last two paragraphs are drawn very largely from A. A.
Rogow, with P. Shore, *The Labour Government and British Industry 1945–1951*,
Blackwell, 1955 (especially chapter 3).

value of their land arising through development, which had become nationalized under the Town and Country Planning Act of 1947.

So there were radical motives among those that led to the nationalization programme of the 1940s, as to the re-nationalization of steel by the Labour Government of 1964–70. And there were grounds for business opposition on that score. But socialist objectives were mixed with, and in practice repressed by, many others. And the effects of nationalization have in no way been to shift British economy and society perceptibly away from capitalist dominance.

For one thing, public ownership of sections of industry has done virtually nothing to diminish the concentration of private wealth. Compensation has been paid in each case to the former owners. Where nationalization is piecemeal, that indeed appears only reasonable by conventional criteria of formal equity. Otherwise owners of assets singled out for public appropriation would lose, 'arbitrarily', by comparison with those fortunate or foresighted enough to have their property in other fields. Of course, compensation might have been paid at less than full rates, either by design or by accident. Inadequate account might have been taken, for example, of long-term future increases in the value of the assets taken over by the state. That could well have been so in the case of prospective development values in the land, taken into public ownership in 1947. For on any plausible prognosis land is bound to appreciate progressively in value, since there is a fixed upper limit to its supply. It is no accident that those values were returned to private hands in the 1950s. And it is symptomatic of Labour's deference to private appropriation of profit even in this field – where gains are sheer windfall by any criterion – that the party neither opposed the crucial stage in that process of de-nationalization nor re-appropriated development values for public benefit when in office from 1964 to 1970. (In an ostensibly more radical mood in opposition in the early 1970s, the party's policy-makers suggested public ownership of land itself, not just of the increments in its value. But even this proposal was limited to land deemed to be needed for development within ten years.[5]) In general,

5. See 'Programme for Britain', *Labour Weekly*, 9 June 1973 (a draft by a party working group). Full compensation would not, however, be paid according to this draft: land would be taken over at existing use value, excluding additional development value. The principle of public appropriation of land needed for development was adopted by the Party Conference in October 1973, though the terms and the period over which 'need' would be anticipated was left indefinite. (*The Times*, 4 Oct. 1973.)

Labour has prided itself on paying full and 'fair' compensation. Not least in respect of coal-mining and the railways – wasting assets with every prospect of mounting losses when they were taken over by the state – the terms have been distinctly generous. Nationalization has thus given the former owners secure and marketable public stock in return for share-holdings of sometimes even diminishing value. Private wealth has remained, in broad terms, as massive and concentrated as before.[6]

Once established, moreover, the nationalized industries have pursued policies in no way designed to help towards a significant shift in the structure of power and wealth. Even had that been intended, it would be difficult or impossible to achieve, so long as the publicly owned sector makes up only a small fraction of all industry. (Its net output was estimated at less than one-eighth that of private firms in the second-half of the 1960s, for example.[7]) In fact this was never the practical intention. Left-wing pressures helped to sway Labour to adopt public ownership as a device to meet problems in some crucial industries which might otherwise have been met by government aid for 'rationalization', cartelization and joint planning, with ownership still in private hands.[8] But left-wing pressures have had virtually no effect on the actual conduct of business by the nationalized industries.

Indeed, there has been no clear and distinctive role conceived for public sector industry by governments of either colour. This is not surprising. Socialist objectives would have set public enterprise a distinct and ambitious line of policy. Their absence as any influence in practice has left what seems, at first sight, a policy vacuum. The effective purposes of nationalization have differed from one case to another, with no single and explicit overriding aim. Coal-mining and the railways, for example, were distressed industries. Nationalization transferred their heavy losses from private to public hands. With these losses the state also took over the special strains of that process of rationalization – involving heavy cuts in employment – which was taken to be essential whatever the precise contribution of coal and rail to the economy in the future. Electricity supply, by contrast, was a booming industry, and proved steadily more so. The public was not saddled with any losses here. But the need for

6. Atkinson, *Unequal Shares* (op. cit., Part 2, ch. 7, note 2 above), pp. 210–14.
7. R. Pryke, *Public Enterprise in Practice*, MacGibbon & Kee, 1971 (p. 15).
8. This indeed was the pattern adopted for the steel industry between de-nationalization in the early 1950s and re-nationalization in the late 1960s.

co-ordinated development of this increasingly important source of energy – vital for business at least as much as for domestic consumers – had already brought about the first step of nationalization in this field during the inter-war years. The process was merely completed after World War II. Co-ordination of investment, production and marketing in fields essential to the economy as a whole again provided a rationale for nationalization in other cases. This was so especially in the case of road transport and steel, though both were de-nationalized in the 1950s and only the latter was restored to public ownership by Labour in the 1960s.

Here, after all, is something of a common theme in the patchwork of purposes of nationalization: the need for a central framework for the long-term development of services and supplies on which the business economy at large depends. The more complex that economy and the more interdependent its different parts, the greater the need for some sort of common framework of this kind in the interests of private industry itself. And the argument for public control of monopoly – an element in the case for nationalization of railways and public utilities especially – is an argument in the interest of business consumers no less than domestic consumers. The case for using public enterprise – nationalized industry as well as other state agencies and devices – to provide the preconditions of 'modernization', economic growth and business prosperity came to be stressed increasingly during the 1960s, with Labour as the main spokesman for state stimulation of private capitalism.

IV

Even so, to say that is not to say that public policy and the affairs of nationalized industry have been directed very effectively and single-mindedly to this end. There are too many contradictory influences at work for that.

For one thing, public ownership of this or that key service may be successfully resisted by the business interests most immediately affected, even when other business stands to gain from it. On the whole, moreover, however geared to the maintenance of a private enterprise economy, nationalization arouses business fears that it may be extended beyond those limits. There is no thick socialist end to the thin wedge of pro-capitalist public ownership; but business is inclined to see one. So selective state appropriation for co-ordination and growth remains a last resort in a capitalist economy, and is normally opposed by business and its political representatives. North Sea oil, to take a very recent example, might well have been nationalized in the interests of industry at large. Instead, concessions for its exploitation were handed in the main to some of the established giant oil corporations. The use by these firms of a legal device to make their profits from this new source virtually immune from taxation, moreover, is hardly of direct benefit to other business.[9] But other business can console itself that parallel benefits come its way from the same system of taxation and the same system of private ownership of resources. Business entrepreneurs, like entrepreneurs in organized crime, stand to gain something from public action against their competitors; but to lose far more if it should be extended against themselves. The balance of interests can be delicate, but on the whole dictates caution in business support for state enterprise. The case for co-ordination has to be very strong, and the surrounding circumstances exceptional, for businessmen to accept state curtailment of any source of private profit, even if the direct gain is theirs while only their rivals suffer.

Within the public sector of industry, furthermore, there has been no clear line of common policy to translate the rationale of co-ordination and growth into full and effective practice.[10] To take a few examples, the nationalized gas and electricity supply industries compete against each other for custom; and the first government attempt to formulate a national policy for long-term development of fuel and power resources was delayed until 1965, nearly two decades after coal, gas and electricity had been taken into state ownership. A major scheme for 'reshaping' – in effect drastically curtailing – railway services was published in 1963; but it was concerned only with rail in isolation from other forms of transport, and with internal balancing of

9. House of Commons, Committee of Public Accounts, *First Report, Session 1972–73: North Sea Oil and Gas*, H.M.S.O., 1973. The minority Labour government in July 1974 proposed measures to close these tax loopholes, and powers for state acquisition – if the government should so wish – of majority holdings in any new oilfields.

10. The information on which the following paragraphs (and some earlier points) are based derives from a variety of sources, among which the most useful summary accounts are: A. H. Hanson, ed., *Nationalization*, Allen & Unwin, 1963; L. Tivey, ed., *The Nationalized Industries since 1960*, Allen & Unwin, 1973; W. Thornhill, *The Nationalized Industries*, Nelson, 1968. See also M. Shanks, ed., *The Lessons of Public Enterprise*, Fabian Society, 1963.

railway revenue against costs. Later steps towards more comprehensive statements of transport policy still fall a good deal short of the
kind of 'national planning' which might seem to serve the common
interests of capital enterprise best. Again, it might perhaps be
expected that the nationalized sector would consistently favour
private industry by subsidizing sales to business. The requirement in
the early years of post-war nationalization that the public corporations need aim only to balance their accounts one year with another,
without necessarily making a profit, allowed some scope for that.
And coal prices were certainly kept below international market levels
– though to domestic consumers as well as to industry, and with
restrictions on import of foreign coal. But no consistent policy of
subsidization in favour of private industry was followed even then.

Since the 1960s, moreover, the nationalized industries have been
required in effect normally to pursue a commercial profit. Subsidization is not ruled out; but it has to be identified as a separate element
in the accounts, and requires both special justification and government sanction. The general effect of these requirements is to reinforce
other pressures on the nationalized industries each to act as a separate
and commercially directed enterprise, chasing its own profit in the
market like any private corporation. That certainly militates against
any use of state-owned industry as an instrument of social policy, a
potential agent of redistribution. There is nothing anomalous in this,
since nationalization was never designed for that end in an economy
which remains capitalist. But it also sets obstacles to full use of
public sector industry for purposes which are in the interests of
business taken as a whole: that is, for long-term co-ordination and
'planning' of essential common services.

The anomaly in that, nevertheless, is more apparent than real.
More precisely, it is an anomaly built into the very nature of a
capitalist economy.

First, business is not a unity. It has some obvious basic interests in
common. But it is also necessarily divided by market rivalries. Quite
apart from uncertainties arising from imperfect knowledge, those
divisions themselves hinder agreement on how best to direct the
activities of state agencies to business interests. Powerful sectional
lobbies obstruct policies for co-ordinated development of essential
services. The road transport interest, for example, can be relied on to
oppose any integrated transport policy that puts its own particular
corner at risk. Such lobbies can usually do so without arousing col-

lective opposition from the rest of industry, because other sectors of business have their own furrows to plough in a similar way on other occasions.

Second, knowledge is imperfect. In particular, forecasts for the future of the kind that policies of co-ordination require are often no more than crude projections or plain guesswork. There is ample room for disagreement there, given even agreement about common interests. What is more important, knowledge in that sense is especially imperfect in a capitalist economy, because the bulk of industrial production is not centralized in public hands. Decisions about investment in industry – hence also, for example, about the pattern of population distribution – will be influenced by public policy. But they will in the main ultimately be taken by a number of separate – or semi-separate – businesses. The point of 'indicative planning' by the state – of the type probably developed furthest in France, or of the half-hearted sort represented by Labour's ill-fated 'national economic plan' in the 1960s – is precisely to reduce the uncertainties of prediction inherent in capitalist economic fragmentation. The essence of such planning is to set mutually compatible targets for investment over the whole range of industry, but without state control of resources. Measures of this kind can limit the effects of uncertainty. They cannot remove them. And with such entrenched uncertainties of knowledge and prediction go also uncertainties about objectives. The requirement that the nationalized industries clearly separate subsidization from normal profit chasing, to take just one example, was introduced partly in order to allow more overt and rational scrutiny of their policies (inherently restricted though the rationality of such scrutiny would be). Yet that objective has been frustrated whenever government, in pursuit of the counter-inflationary objectives to which it has increasingly tried to harness the public sector of the economy, has acted behind the scenes to persuade the nationalized corporations to hold back wages, prices and investment.

Third, private business is trapped within its own mental horizon. Willing enough to take financial aid from the state, and to seek government support to reduce market insecurity, it yet looks with suspicion at any overt and extensive departure from 'sound business principles' on the part of public enterprise, even if designed in the long-run interests of private industry. The anxieties behind such suspicion are partly rational: anxieties, for example, about potential competition from state industry, perhaps especially for capital funds.

Other anxieties border on the paranoid: the fear, notably, that once 'sound business principles' are publicly and explicitly set aside for one purpose, they could be set aside far more widely, for purposes directed against the interests of private property and profit. There is little enough warrant for that fear in the history of state growth in Britain and other capitalist countries. But indiscriminate suspiciousness is a common condition among businessmen, especially when profit margins are insecure. The frightened reactions of City and industry to Labour's electoral victory in 1964, for example, were hardly appropriate to the pro-capitalist zeal of the new government. It is such anxieties, not least, which have inspired the insistence that the nationalized industries should, in normal practice, follow the principles of private commercial enterprise, each pursuing profit maximization for itself.

V

These inherent obstacles to setting public enterprise to work for a single, coherent policy have been accentuated in Britain by the particular constitutional form adopted for nationalized industries. The standard prescription has been for a semi-autonomous 'public corporation'. This is a body outside the ordinary machinery of ministerial government; directed by a board whose responsibility to the appointing minister is in practice loose and indeterminate; and answerable to Parliament in the main only through the minister. The formula – devised to leave each corporation free to get on with the business of running the industry without detailed 'interference' by government or parliament – is a curious one. It assumes that the objectives towards which the running of the industry should be directed are, in normal circumstances, self-evident and non-controversial; or at least that they can safely be left for the board to formulate for themselves. Some general guidelines are provided – until the 1960s, for example, that the corporations should aim to balance costs and revenue, taking one year with another; thereafter – and with more specific prescription of financial criteria – that they should normally aim for commercial profitability. And an indefinite degree of scope is allowed for ministerial intervention on matters of major policy. Yet the expectation built into the formula is that, by and large, political direction of the affairs of nationalized industry would be both undesirable and unnecessary. On that principle, there are no distinctive public purposes to which public enterprise should be aimed; or if there are, board members can be assumed to pursue those purposes with a minimum of direction. The former alternative rules out both socialist policy and pro-business 'planning' of a centralized kind. The latter equally rules out socialist policy; and it makes pro-business 'planning' no easy matter – if the logic of the formula is followed. In fact, that logic has been followed less and less.

It has been suggested that the adoption of this constitutional prescription for the nationalized industries reflects a distinctively British preference for 'professionalism' as a form of work organization. The public interest, so this argument runs, was seen as well protected if entrusted to responsible men on the boards, enjoying an autonomy to act for the 'common good' similar to that of the best established professional bodies. Anti-capitalist sentiment, on this interpretation, was a major force behind nationalization; but it was inspired by distaste for the lack of moral restraint in commercialism, not by egalitarian socialism. The boards were expected to bring a professional moral restraint to the conduct of business, once the element of private profit was removed by public ownership.[11]

There is point to this interpretation. The model for the constitutional form used in post-war nationalization was the B.B.C., where the case for an autonomous corporation had been seen as the need to safeguard broadcasting both from commercial pressures *and* from direct control by the state. The application of that model to other publicly owned industries certainly showed that socialist and egalitarian notions played little part in shaping nationalization in practice. Strong state control of publicly owned industry would have been needed, if the intention had been to direct policy towards equality. But it is doubtful whether 'anti-capitalism', even in the non-socialist but pro-professional form alleged, had much practical influence. For if 'professional' by contrast with 'commercial' modes of conduct are valued so highly in both major parties as the argument implies, it is odd that nationalization should have been pushed no further. To contrast professionalism with commercialism – though the contrast is commonly made both by those claiming professional status and by sociologists – is in any case misleading. Professional

11. M. Burrage, 'Nationalization and the professional ideal', *Sociology*, May 1973. While we disagree with Michael Burrage's interpretation on several points, we are very grateful to him for the opportunity to discuss these questions with him on several occasions and to draw on his knowledge of nationalization.

organization involves regulation of its own work and affairs by an occupational group – or in this analogy, by a nationalized industry and its board in particular – on the basis of an accepted professional assertion of technical competence and commitment to 'public service'. But the conception is morally and politically empty so long as the notion of public service remains undefined; so long as the purposes to which both that and technical competence are directed are left unspecified. So long as that is the case, the public good in whose service technical competence is supposed to be harnessed may well be defined by direct commercial criteria; or it may be defined, more generally, in terms that accept the maintenance of private profit-driven capitalism as the explicit overriding end, or the implicit conditioning limit, of policy. There is then no contrast between professionalism and commercialism.

It is just that situation which describes the nationalized corporations in Britain, as indeed follows from what we have said earlier. Popular anti-capitalist sentiment – in fact with a strong though diffuse element of egalitarian socialism among Labour's rank-and-file – helped to force nationalization on a reluctant Labour establishment in the 1940s. But it played no effective part in shaping the structure and policy of these industries after nationalization. The corporations never – whether trying to balance their books or to pursue profit – asserted a role for themselves directed against the dominance of private capital. Nor could they have been expected to. That was clearly ruled out by the absence of any positive directives to them to take on such a role; by their small share in total production; and by their inevitable practical links in those circumstances with private industry, through the everyday conduct of business as well as through the recruitment of board members.

In fact, top businessmen – major company directors and one or two bankers – made up about four in every ten of the men on the boards in the early days of post-war nationalization; trade unionists and others with labour movement associations – usually from the respectable right-wing of the movement – less than half of that number (table 21). Too much can be made of the significance for power of the precise composition of 'élites'. It matters less who rules than what rulers do with their power – to what ends, in whose interests, under what unspoken assumptions and constraints power is exercised. By the early 1970s, for example, when the policies of the nationalized industries had become *more* clearly business-oriented

TABLE 21

Previous occupations of members of boards of nationalized industries, 1950 and 1972/73

Occupation before board appointment within nationalized industry	1950			1972/73		
	Full-timers	Part-timers	All	Full-timers	Part-timers	All
Company director, banker	13	26	39	13	25	38
Manager, engineer, technical specialist:						
In nationalized industry or public service	} 10	4	14	38	12	50
In private industry				—	—	—
Civil servant, local govt. officer, member of armed forces	7	4	11	2	5	7
Scientist, academic, professional	6	2	8	7	14	21
Trade unionist, Labour Pty. politician, Coop. movement	10	9	19	3	12	15
Not known or not classifiable as above	1	4	5	9	5	14
Total (Number of boards)	47	49	96 (12)	72	73	145 (14)
No. of *part-time members* holding current directorships in private sector companies	} not stated				30	
No. of such directorships held by part-timers					179	

Sources: For 1950, Acton Society Trust, *The Men on the Boards*, The Trust, 1951 (pp. 4–9).

For 1972–73, compiled from *Whitaker's Almanack 1973, Who's Who 1973, the Directory of Directors 1972*, supplemented by latest annual reports for some boards.

Notes: Part-time members serving on two boards are counted twice.

The analysis covers only the relevant national or central boards. Area Boards and the equivalent are excluded, as are the Bank of England, the BBC and the ITA.

'Professionals' in the fourth main occupational category listed include, e.g., lawyers and accountants in practice outside the industry before appointment.

than they were around 1950, top private businessmen had been pushed into second place on the boards, with managers and technical specialists whose main careers had been within the corporations or in other public service in first place.[12] Even so, the pattern of recruitment to the boards – especially in the early years after World War II, when the boards' autonomy was greater than now – clearly has some significance. If 'professionalism' was the keynote, it was hardly a professionalism that could be expected to be hostile to private capital and 'commercialism'. The continuing ties today between the nationalized corporations and business are reflected, among other ways, in the interlocking of the public boards with those of private companies, through the many directorships held by part-time members of the former. (Table 21, last two lines.) Board members with labour movement associations are now a still smaller element than they were initially.

The partial fragmentation of control over nationalized industry among separate and semi-autonomous boards was in fact less anomalous in the early days of nationalisation than it appears now. The problems of the industries taken over by the state were seen then as primarily internal to each industry, and divergent in character from one to another. The requirements of 'rationalization' in the cases of coal and rail, for example, differed from those of long-term expansion in the case of electricity. And government economic policy at large was aimed at avoidance of recession and unemployment, by very general measures, rather than at economic growth through specific measures of co-ordination and 'planning'. In those circumstances a considerable degree of self-regulation on the part of the publicly owned industries made some sense. Even then, their practical autonomy was less than it seemed. The provision in the formula for ministerial intervention on matters of major policy left room for 'much decision-making . . . in that twilight world between the Ministers and the public corporations which is not amenable to public and parliamentary scrutiny'.[13] As government activity to counter

12. The arrival of internal promotees on the boards, though without any obvious implications for policy, may also signify a very slight widening of channels of upward social mobility to top economic positions. Fewer than half the chairmen of the 14 nationalized corporations in 1972/73 had been at public school, compared with three quarters of the chairmen of very large companies of about the same age group (those born after 1900); for the latter figure see Stanworth and Giddens, op. cit. (ch. 2, note 21 above).

13. Thornhill, op. cit. (note 10 above), p. 70; see also pp. 41–2, 56–74. On this question in general and on the role of the House of Commons Select Committee

inflation and create conditions of business prosperity and long-run growth accelerated, ministers increasingly used their discretion to influence board policies behind the scenes, and also to secure more co-ordinated and explicit planning of development across the boundaries between the separate corporations. There remain anomalies and inefficiencies. In no way can they be taken as signs that nationalized industry forms a spearhead of opposition to commercial principles and interests – let alone a spearhead of socialism.[14]

Indeed it is implausible that piecemeal nationalization – even if it were to extend the public sector a good deal further than now, and the intentions behind it were more radical than they have been in practice hitherto – could make for any sizeable shift in the distribution of wealth and power, so long as private enterprise remains the predominant element in production. For one thing, there is no likelihood that a nationalizing government either could or would ignore the pressures to pay 'fair' compensation. It is, by all signs, bound to defer to the demand that it avoid formal inequity between one set of property owners and another. For another, it would be impracticable for public sector industry as a minority element to pursue investment, pricing and pay policies which would put it widely outside the general market conditions set by the predominance of private enterprise. Publicly owned industry would still, as now, have to recruit all levels of its personnel – including board members, executives and managers at high premiums – in the same hierarchically divided labour markets as private industry. It would still have to sell its products in markets the effective demand of which reflects the skew distribution of income and wealth. It would still have to raise its capital, if not from the same immediate sources, then on much the same terms as private enterprise. The pressures on nationalized industries to pursue profit and avoid deficit – to the point where even subsidization of business is held back, let alone

---

on Nationalized Industries – which has exposed the corporations and their relationship with ministers to more public scrutiny than was possible originally, though within quite tight limits – see also A. H. Hanson, *Parliament and Public Ownership*, Cassell, 1961.

14. Characteristically, for example, a well-publicized Fabian Society pamphlet in the mid 1960s argued for an extension of public enterprise as an aid to modernization and growth in business – not in any way as a means of redistributing wealth and power. The argument was squarely in line with the dominant interpretation of the role of public enterprise by the Labour Party's leadership. (M. Posner and R. Pryke, *New Public Enterprise*, Fabian Society, 1966.)

subsidization for popular welfare – would remain as strong as they are now.

The upshot is that nothing short of full-scale public appropriation of the bulk of the private economy – certainly of the big business that dominates it – in a single programme phased over a short period of time could be expected to produce a significant change in the structure of wealth and power. The political prospects of that, of course, are dim at present. Even Labour's left and most of the socialist fringe groups, after all, can press only for a step-by-step extension of public enterprise, although their ultimate objective of total socialization marks them off sharply from Labour's centre and right, who see nationalization as justifiable only on the discrete 'merits of each case'. Yet step-by-step extension of public ownership, paradoxically, entails a risk of discrediting the goal of full public ownership in the eyes of ordinary earners who stand to gain from it, just because piecemeal nationalization cannot produce commensurate piecemeal redistribution. Its effects by that criterion are negligible – and therefore liable to promote disillusion about the socialist goal. Such disillusion is reinforced when – despite indications of a successful overall record of production and technical efficiency[15] – the nationalized sector includes declining industries and once-bankrupt firms, whose losses make public enterprise a ready target for business and press accusations of bureaucratic incompetence. So, limited nationalization not only serves positive economic functions for private business, in rather diverse fashion and with some muddle on the way. In fact, if not by explicit design, it also neatly helps to undermine popular support for the public appropriation of capitalist enterprise at large.

VI

Government, in addition, makes a sizeable direct financial contribution to private enterprise. Of public expenditure on employment services, industry, trade and agriculture as recorded in 1971 – some 7 per cent of all government spending excluding the nationalized corporations (table 20) – nearly two-thirds went on grants and loans to the private sector. Under that and other headings, altogether some £1,400 million were handed out from public funds in the same

15. See Pryke, op. cit. (note 7 above).

year to business and agriculture. All but an insignificant fraction of this went in outright grants, the small remainder in loans on favourable conditions. Farming, in relative terms, was then the most heavily subsidized sector of the private economy: public grants here were equivalent in value to nearly a quarter of gross domestic agricultural product. But industry took the great bulk of government aid in absolute terms – to a value, again to give a rough notion of the scale of business benefit involved, equal to some 7 per cent of total manufacturing output.[16] Much of this – about two-thirds – went on investment grants and on special aid to firms in areas of low development and high unemployment. In so far as public policy pays off, of course, workers should benefit from a consequent increase in job opportunities. But it is characteristic of a capitalist economy that the demand for labour needs special stimulation in the first instance; and that the major route to such stimulation must be through guarantee of private profit. Government subsidization of industrial research and development again is usually justified by reference to its long-term spin-off for all and sundry (even if that may amount, as in the case of the Concorde superjet, to no more than a dubious boost to 'national prestige'). But the immediate beneficiary is private business – nearly 40 per cent of whose expenditure on research and development is borne directly from public funds.[17] There is no ready way of calculating the much larger indirect contributions from government resources to private profit: from investment in roads and environmental services, for example; from research undertaken in universities, polytechnics and other public institutions, directed to business objectives; from the educational system in general, in its role of pre-selecting and training labour. But the direct contribution alone – at 6½ per cent of all government expenditure in 1971, well above the sums spent on public housing by central and local authorities together, and three-fifths of the way to the total spent on all health services – is by itself a heavy subsidy to private enterprise.

Government, it may be argued, intervenes not only to help but also to regulate business. So it does; and in some part such regulation benefits ordinary consumers and rank-and-file workers. But only in

16. These points are based on calculations from *National Income and Expenditure 1972* (pp. 13, 58–62) and *Estimates 1972/73* (*Treasury*), Cmnd. 4921, 1972. It may need to be pointed out that the agricultural subsidies (before Britain's entry into the E.E.C.) were subsidies to producers – not to consumers – designed to allow domestic farmers to sell at prices competitive with those of imported food.

17. Calculated from *Annual Abstract of Statistics 1972* (table 172).

some part. It is not they who are the main beneficiaries of company law, for example, either by intention or in fact. The 'public interest' served by legal provision for audit and publication of corporation accounts, for the procedures by which capital is raised in the stock market, for government investigation of the affairs of individual companies, and so on, is the interest in the first instance of shareholders and creditors, business associates and business rivals; in the second instance of business at large, since legal regulation provides the framework of order and predictability essential for business continuity. The more complex and large-scale business organization and finance have become, the more elaborate this protective apparatus of state regulation. At points, of course, the apparatus stretches beyond that, and is designed also to protect workers, consumers or the public in general. But just because business power is strong, both definition and enforcement of the 'public interest' are usually weak.

Acts of 1948 and 1965, for example, provide for investigation by a Monopolies Commission of business monopolies and impending mergers referred to it by the relevant government department. A study of its monopoly inquiries in the mid-to-late 1960s has shown, not only that the Commission used no consistent criteria by which to judge the 'public interest' in this context, but that the measures which it recommended hardly ever included any to break up the structure of a monopoly business, for instance through compulsory sale of assets or by embargo on future mergers. There was, moreover, no effective machinery to follow through and enforce those recommendations – concerning prices charged and market agreements, for example – which the government accepted. Of some two hundred mergers over a period of forty months, only eight were referred to the Commission and only three stopped as a result.[18] 'More stringent legislation in this field is in any case not likely to be very effective. Thus American, in contrast to British, law makes an automatic formal presumption that business combination is against the public interest. But whatever difference there may be in the degree of actual business concentration between the two countries, it is not sufficiently large and firm to show up consistently in different comparative studies.'[19] The legislation passed here in 1956 and 1968 to counter price-fixing agreements and related restrictive practices of business appears to

18. A. Sutherland, *The Monopolies Commission in Action*, Cambridge University Press, 1969.

19. Sawyer, op. cit. (ch. 2, note 1 above).

have had some effect – and if so has benefited, not just consumers, but some firms as against their rivals. But it has also encouraged techniques of successful evasion – price leadership, for example, and not least mergers and take-overs.[20]

What is clear, above all, is that the agencies of the state – police, inspectorates, commissions, tribunals and courts – act with great reluctance and leniency in respect of breaches of law and 'public interest' committed by business. This contrasts strikingly with their severity in action against 'ordinary', overwhelmingly working-class, offenders; and against trade unions found to be in contempt of court orders to stop strikes, on whom massive penalties were imposed under the Industrial Relations Act 1971. (See chapter 5 below.) Breaches of factory legislation, for example, are formally subject to criminal jurisdiction. They can, indeed, hardly be reasonably regarded as nominal offences, since they usually put the health and even the lives of workers at risk. In fact, such breaches are commonplace. Yet employers are rarely threatened with prosecution, and hardly ever brought to court, on charges under this legislation – even on third detection of the same offence.[21] The justification for the practice of non-prosecution   that conformity with the law is more likely to be achieved through persuasion and negotiation – is not one which is commonly applied when ordinary working-class people are in conflict with the law, especially not a second or a third time round. The argument itself implicitly acknowledges the power of business behind the formal regulation of business.[22]

That power, in this instance, is an outcome of uneventful routine: the example is a small but clear illustration of this theme of our analysis. No examination of 'decision-making' is likely to show employers actively imposing their will on factory inspectors – even putting covert pressure on them, let alone needing to bribe them, though that might perhaps occur on occasion – in order to obtain

20. D. Swann *et al.*, 'The impact of restrictive business practices legislation', *SSRC Newsletter*, June 1973 (a brief preliminary report of a study to be published under the title *Competition in British Industry*).

21. Carson, op. cit. (ch. 3, note 38 above). The following interpretation of non-prosecution as a reflection of 'routine' business power is, we should add, ours and not Mr Carson's.

22. As another example, the average fine imposed on tanker owners for oil pollution of the sea was £200 in 1971; and though provision for the maximum to be raised to £50,000 came into force in June 1971, the level of fines in 1972 was said to be little higher than in 1971. (Annual Report of the Advisory Committee on Oil Pollution of the Sea, for 1972, quoted in *The Times*, 2 July 1973.)

virtual immunity from prosecution. Even the inspectors can hardly be said to 'make decisions' not to prosecute. They make decisions only on the rare occasions when they do prosecute. For the rest, they follow a routine which is set by the assumption that there will, in most cases, be no pay-off from prosecution. That assumption – normally unspoken – marks the limit of such influence as the factory inspectorate can pull as representatives of 'the public interest'. It reflects the power of business that inheres in the property and market institutions of our society without, in this case as so often, needing to be exercised in overt action.

It would be too simple to say that the state here – in its formal regulation of business, as in its diverse other economic activities and its operation of welfare services, education and law – is merely an agent of capital, a committee for managing the common affairs of the whole bourgeoisie. That description certainly has the virtue of combining pungency with incomparably more accuracy than any of the bland and blind conventional characterizations of the 'welfare state' and the 'mixed economy'. The classical form of the Marxist description of the state is not false. But it is incomplete – a point recognized in some recent major reformulations and extensions of Marxist theory on this subject.[23] And being incomplete, it is liable to mislead. The state is as much the prisoner of capitalist assumptions, held to them by a leash that has some elasticity, as it is the agent of capital. The sources of the state's growth are diverse as we have argued; and they have included popular pressures, channelled mainly through the labour movement. Those pressures have clearly made some impact. Capital interests have had to make concessions to contain them: more so in Britain and in most other European capitalist societies than in the U.S.A. That is the prime reason why both worker insecurity and the sanctity of private property on the whole are less

23. See especially R. Miliband, *The State in Capitalist Society*, Weidenfeld & Nicolson, 1969. Our own debt to Ralph Miliband's analysis is evident, and too extensive to be acknowledged by specific references, even though our approach differs from his in emphasis and on some particular points. N. Poulantzas, *Political Power and Social Classes*, New Left Books and Sheed & Ward, 1973 (French ed., 1968) has also aroused interest as a contribution to Marxist interpretation of the state in capitalist society. However, we ourselves have found little guidance from Poulantzas's abstract and obscure discussion, for a concrete and specific examination of the state and of power in late twentieth-century capitalist societies. For a debate between Miliband and Poulantzas about the approaches appropriate to the subject, see J. Urry and J. Wakeford, eds., *Power in Britain*, Heinemann Educational Books, 1973 (chapters 24–25).

institutionally entrenched, solid though their roots are, here than in America. Yet the keyword is 'containment'. Popular pressures, and the state activities in whose growth they have played some part, have been contained within a framework of institutions and assumptions that remain capitalist. Those institutions and assumptions circumscribe the role of state agencies even when public authority is not engaged in active and direct support of business.

5 The state and labour relations.

The history of the part played by the state in collective bargaining and industrial conflict illustrates the character of government intervention in economic affairs once more. It illustrates also two other themes which have recurred at different points of our argument. One is that capital does not generate a single and coherent set of interests, united at all times on how best to put state agencies to its service or on other issues. The point might seem to be so obvious as not to need making, were it not that the fact of disunity among capital interests is often taken as a sign that capital and capitalism are myths. The other, subsidiary theme of the story of the public scaffolding of industrial relations concerns the judiciary. The courts are formally independent of the executive-and-legislative arm of the state. But they cannot be independent in practice, when the issues presented to them – such as the issues of industrial relations – go to the heart of those class divisions which separate judges and employers alike from the rank-and-file of ordinary workers.

From the early years of this century to the 1960s in Britain, the predominant line taken by the state in labour relations was to encourage 'voluntary' agreement between employers and unions from the sidelines. In crises, of course, the weight of state power would be used openly against 'disruption' through labour militancy. Strikes were made illegal – though only with limited effect – during both world wars; and the Conservative government was well prepared in advance to defeat the General Strike of 1926, and to exploit the divisions within the labour movement at the time. But crises apart, the normal role of the state evolved into that of maintaining a legal and administrative framework to promote 'voluntary' collective bargaining and eventual peaceful resolution of disputes between business and labour.[1]

This normally 'soft' line of conciliation was coupled with a relatively passive role for the law, which was distinctive in British industrial relations during much of this century. These developments had their origin in an intensification of union organization and labour conflict around 1900; and in consequent divisions within the establishment of government and parliament, courts and business, about how to meet this challenge. The courts then represented a rearguard of opposition to the concessions required by a policy of conciliation. Legislation in the 1870s had removed the main liability of the unions to criminal prosecution. But the courts around the turn of the century – in their *de facto* law-making role – brought to a high point a concept of civil liability for conspiracy, which would have drastically impaired union action unless new legislation had been passed. The crucial judicial decision was made by the House of Lords in the notorious Taff Vale case in 1901. This decision made unions financially liable for the losses sustained by an employer in consequence of a strike – and would, of course, have made strike organization virtually impossible. The 1906 Trade Disputes Act – passed by a Liberal government in agreement with organized labour – reversed the effect by giving unions, their officials and other labour organizers 'immunity' from legal liability in tort in respect of 'trade disputes'. The Act did not – as has so often been claimed – put unions and strikers 'above the law'. All it did was to remove a device evolved by the courts to attach crippling penalties to the organization of industrial action against employers. It did so only where there was a 'trade dispute'. And it did nothing to remove the probable liability of individual strikers in law for breach of contract on their own part – a point never fully tested by the courts, since employers in the interests of workday relations with their employees and for other practical reasons have rarely been tempted to take large numbers of workers to court in individual suits, each for only a small sum.

The 1906 Act – which gave no legal guarantee of a right to organize a strike, but made it practicable to do so without a grave risk of court

1. The following summary account of legal developments with respect to industrial relations to the end of the 1960s draws in large part on K. W. Wedderburn, *The Worker and the Law*, Penguin, 1st ed., 1965 (2nd ed., 1971); O. Kahn-Freund, 'Legal framework', in A. Flanders and H. A. Clegg, eds., *The System of Industrial Relations in Great Britain*, Blackwell, 1960; *idem*, 'Labour law', in M. Ginsberg, ed., *Law and Opinion in England in the 20th Century*, Stevens, 1959.

action – remained a cornerstone of employer–labour relations till the 1960s. Some exceptions apart, it put the courts out of business for years as a source of law directed against the normal line of state encouragement for voluntary collective bargaining.[2] And it allowed the main public agency concerned – the Ministry of Labour – to evolve a distinctive role of conciliation.[3] The institutionalization of industrial conflict through an elaborate apparatus of centralized collective bargaining – first triggered by union militancy in the early years of the century – was reinforced by the weakness of labour during the depression and near-depression years of the inter-war period, especially after the decisive union defeat of 1926.

II

This established 'system of industrial relations', however, started to crack at the seams by the 1960s. It was now increasingly challenged from both sides – first from within the ranks of labour, no longer kept passive by gross market insecurity; then, in reaction, from business and the press, governments of both shades, the courts, and also sections of the union leadership who found themselves caught between rank-and-file militancy and the routine of compromise which had become their *raison d'être*. Steady inflation, coupled with generally high demand for labour during the first two decades after 1945, gave a semblance of weight to wage pressures. This encouraged firms that were best placed in boom conditions to exceed centrally settled pay bargains, following local negotiations and disputes. That was one factor which contributed to the growth – after a near-standstill for thirty years or more – of an 'unofficial' pattern of labour organization close to the shop floor. Other factors helped this process along. One was the inherited complexity of particular payment systems, to which industry-wide agreements had to be fitted: there was plenty of scope for local bargaining and conflict in that. Another was the multiplicity of unions often represented in the same work-

2. Among exceptions were the Osborne judgment of the Law Lords in 1909, which ruled out the use of union funds for political purposes until the Trade Union Act 1913; and the statement in court by Mr Justice Astbury in 1926 that the General Strike, since it was directed against the government, was illegal – a statement which has been seriously questioned by lawyers since then. (See also ch. 7, note 31 below.)

3. See, e.g., Royal Commission on Trade Unions and Employers' Associations, *Written Evidence of the Ministry of Labour*, H.M.S.O., 1965.

place: shop-floor organization cut across the divisions between them. Still another, and crucial, factor, was rank-and-file disillusion with the slow pace of established procedures and the moderation of union officialdom. The result was that a pattern of negotiation and conflict emerged in strength side by side with, but for practical purposes largely outside and in part opposed to, the centralized order of accommodation between labour and capital.[4]

Establishment reaction – on part of much of the labour movement leadership, as well as of top business and the Conservative Party – was one of intense concern, mounting to hysteria. The ostensible reasons for that were unconvincing. The most relevant measure of the immediate impact of strike activities on production – the proportion of working time lost – remained fairly stable until the late 1960s, at a low or modest level by any standards.[5] Far more cogent in stimulating establishment fears, clearly, was the threat to the old order which the 'anarchy' of shop floor organization represented. This threat was underlined by a shift of strike intensity away from coal mining into new and expanding industries: engineering and the car manufacturing branch of it in particular. Strikes, hitherto largely contained within a fast declining industry, were thus spreading to key growth sectors of the economy: a disturbing omen for the future. Shop-floor organization, moreover, was obviously not readily amenable to the policies of wage restraint increasingly actively pursued by the state. Rank-and-file pressures on the union leadership to withhold co-operation in such policies were rising; and they came to fruition during the last few years of Labour government, at the tail-end of the 1960s. In short, one of the prime conditions of the routine power of capital now looked a good deal shakier than before. The tight institutionalization of industrial conflict, on terms implicitly accepting the priority of profit and property in the economic order, no longer seemed secure. And this, whatever causal connection there might be, came in a period when falling pre-tax profits and mounting uncertainties about the route to business prosperity made capital's need for labour discipline steadily more imperative.[6]

There were two possible lines of response, between which official action has fluctuated since. One was to try to adapt the 'normal'

4. See especially the *Report* of the Royal Commission (Cmnd. 3623, H.M.S.O., 1968) and some of the associated research papers, Nos. 1 and 10 in particular.

5. Strike trends are examined in more detail in Part 5 below.

6 Cf. Part 2 above (e.g. ch. 1, notes 5–6, ch. 2, note 7, ch. 8, notes 27–8).

policy of accommodation to the new situation. This would involve taming shop-floor organization by allowing it some formal recognition – beyond the practical everyday recognition which it already received from local management at the workplace – and incorporating it in the settled order of conflict institutionalization. The other was to take a tough stance: to try to crush shop-floor organization, if not by eliminating it totally – an impossible task – then by so drastically circumscribing the functions of shop stewards and convenors on the workplace floor as to produce much the same effect. The choice between the two was never entirely clear-cut. In practice it came to be conditioned increasingly by government and business relations with the official unions.

Trade union co-operation in the three-cornered partnership of the mixed economy – state, capital and labour – could no longer be taken for granted by the mid-1960s. The unions were under growing pressure for more militancy from their rank-and-file and from the sheer growth of shop-floor organization, which was eroding the unions' hold over their members. Those pressures in turn made union leadership increasingly conscious of the incompatible duality of roles imposed on them by institutionalized collective bargaining in general, and by co-operation in official policies of wage restraint in particular. The clash was underlined between the unions' role as agents of government and business to enforce labour discipline (adherence to agreements and to incomes policy) on their members, and their role as representatives of their members' interests in the jungle of a capitalist market. A tough line aimed at repression of shop-floor organization would clearly now involve government confrontation with the unions, who would be forced into defence of the 'unofficial unionism' of the factory floor. This was all the more certain since measures directed against the latter would be liable to spill over to hamper official unionism as well. In fact, government policy from the middle 1960s – and the policy proposals of others associated with government – vacillated between trying to tame and trying to repress shop-floor organization. Elements of the former line were strongest when the overall direction of policy went towards enticing labour into co-operation 'against inflation'; elements of the latter line, strongest when overall policy turned instead to more reliance on *laissez-faire* forces and market testing of the strength of capital and labour, with a new framework of law to weight the dice more heavily against labour.

The courts showed their sensitivity to the new climate of establishment hostility to labour early on, before either major party had even come near to deciding on a line of policy. In their decision on a leading case in 1964, the Law Lords virtually invented a new tort for which those instigating strikes could be sued. Strike organizers – whether union officials or shopfloor representatives – were now exposed to an apparently almost unlimited risk of legal liability for 'civil intimidation'. That court ruling seemed to drive 'a coach and four' through the 1906 Act.[7] Though the Labour government, which came to office in 1964, soon after passed an act to restore the main 'immunities' which for six decades had made strikes legally practicable, the strike phobia expressed by the Law Lords in their abortive reinterpretation of the law was a pointer to things to come. Shopfloor organization was soon to be singled out as the prime target for new measures to enforce labour discipline. That sharpening of focus came especially with the report of a royal commission set up by the Labour government.[8]

On the whole both the royal commission and the Labour government chose to try to tame unofficial unionism by incorporating it in the recognized order of collective bargaining. Labour not least because it was desperately trying to revive its crumbling alliance with the unions in support of policies of wage restraint. But neither opted consistently for this 'softer' line. A majority of the commission – trade union and academic members dissenting – proposed a measure designed to cripple shop-floor militancy. They recommended that the protection of the 1906 and 1965 Acts for 'inducing breach of contract' (that is, in effect, for organizing strikes) should be available only to unions registered under a new procedure; not, therefore, to the shopfloor representatives of unofficial unionism.[9] The Labour government rejected this recommendation. But it went on in the same breath to propose ministerial power both to delay 'unconstitutional' strikes for twenty-eight days and to require a ballot before an 'official' strike.[10] Neither provision would have been likely to have much practical effect. But they were symptomatic of the shift in the climate of public

7. See especially Wedderburn, op. cit., (note 1 above), chapter 8. The crucial case was that of *Rookes* v. *Barnard*, while a subsequent case – *Stratford* v. *Lindley* – in the same year was decided on similar lines, if with additional confusion of the legal implications.

8. See note 4 above.

9. *Report*, para. 894.

10. *In Place of Strife* (Cmnd. 3888, H.M.S.O., 1969), paras. 88–98

policy towards a tougher line, even when coupled as here with attempts also to maintain accommodation between capital and labour. The twenty-eight-day pause, characteristically, was intended to allow unions 'to intensify their efforts to see that procedures were observed by their members', thus emphasizing the unions' disciplinary role in the interests of industrial order. The proposal for a pre-strike ballot at ministerial discretion – aimed directly at the established unions, in contrast to the 'conciliation pause' – made no provision for a ballot before *termination* of a strike. For all the government's professions of concern for democratic participation, union officials would thus have kept the power to end a strike without reference to their members, but not to begin one. The two proposals sharpened the growing tension between the political and industrial flanks of the labour movement to a critical point; and they were eventually withdrawn by the government, which could not easily go into an election a year ahead in face of overt hostility from organized labour.

III

By 1970, therefore, the unions were no longer – for a time at least – amenable to persuasion from governments of either shade to co-operate in statutorily entrenched counter-inflationary policies, which with union co-operation would put a seal of ostensible consensual approval on the status quo. Militancy had spread from unofficial to official unionism. Large-scale strikes had changed a pattern of industrial disputes for long dominated by the local, short-lived though recurrent incidents characteristic of most shop-floor action.[11] The Conservative Party already in opposition had set its face in favour of more *laissez-faire* economic policies, and of reliance on a combination of market forces and new trade union law to discipline labour. The latter policy meant confrontation with official as well as unofficial unionism. This, following the Conservative electoral victory of 1970, came to a head with the Industrial Relations Act 1971.

One main provision of the Act was to draw a sharp distinction between unions legally registered, after state approval of their constitutions and rule-books; and any unregistered forms of worker organization, which would lack protection of the law for most

11. The break in the pattern of strike statistics in this respect came in 1968: see Part 5 below.

purposes. The Act exposed unofficial – and certain kinds of official – strike instigation to the risk of heavy penalties, by way of financial 'compensation' for 'unfair industrial practice' or even by way of imprisonment for contempt of court. It made unions responsible in law for taking 'all such steps as are reasonably practicable' to ensure compliance of their members (and of anybody else involved, for that matter) with any collective agreement that acquired, under the Act, the status of a legal contract. It allowed the minister power – more extensively than proposed by Labour in 1969, though subject to a procedure of formal judicial approval – to delay a strike for sixty days or to require a pre-strike ballot. And it established a set of first-instance tribunals and an Industrial Relations Court above them to deal with litigation under the new law.[12]

The Act represented a significant shift away from the philosophy of the 1906 Act, and from the hitherto normal emphasis on a government role of ringside conciliation between capital and labour in industrial disputes. It is just for this reason that the story of the Act – though repealed in 1974 under a minority Labour government – needs to be told in some brief detail here. The 1971 provisions for registration involved state vetting of trade unions. Strike organization became – to a wide though uncertain extent – a legally risky business, especially in the so-called wild-cat form associated with shop-floor militancy. The notion of union responsibility to 'the public' – that is,

12. Despite a provision in the original bill to that effect, the Act of 1971 did not make strike instigation by anyone not an authorized official of a registered union *in itself* an unfair industrial practice. But it did so *in effect* by making it unfair practice for any such unauthorized person to induce a breach of contract (sections 96–97); and by requiring that strike action should be preceded by notice, corresponding to that needed for termination of employment, in order *not* to constitute a breach of contract (section 147). This made most 'unofficial' industrial action illegal, since it is typically short and sharp, without prior warning. The Act also placed some, though high, limits on the 'compensation' for unfair practice which registered unions might have to pay (e.g., £100,000 in the case of unions with 100,000 or more members); but no such limits, except those indicated by the losses suffered by the plaintiff (such as a strike-bound firm), in the case of non-registered organizations and unauthorized persons. (Sections 116–17.) The Act, again, did not give all collective agreements the status of legal contracts – with the parties, including registered and non-registered worker organizations, required to seek observance of the agreements even by people who were *not* themselves parties to the contract. (Section 36.) But it gave that status to all written collective agreements which were not explicitly exempted from the provision by the signatories. (Section 34.) In fact, during the Act's first year of operation the great majority of agreements had been so exempted, usually at the insistence of the unions and in accordance with T.U.C. policy. (Commission on Industrial Relations, *Annual Report for 1972*, H.M.S.O., 1973, p. 22.)

for maintenance of industrial order – was given statutory force. And the judiciary was brought back into an active and overtly political role to uphold the class order in industrial relations.

Actual application of the new restrictive framework of law was another matter, and already after one year showed signs of varying with the temper of the time. In any case the main initiative in litigation was placed, not in the hands of government as some business voices had called for; but with those who felt themselves victims of 'unfair industrial practice': in effect, individual companies, as well as individual employees who might take action against either unions or employers. This itself introduced an element of unpredictability into the operation of the Act. Even in a climate of general establishment hostility to unions most firms are still likely to be reluctant most of the time, in their own practical interests, to take workers or their unions to court. The new law for all that was a heavy, blunt weapon in reserve; and it was brought into active use against labour on several critical occasions within a short time after it came into force. The clash between state and labour was accentuated by the fact that the unions, following agreed T.U.C. policy, refused to register under the Act with only few exceptions.

Government and court decisions at first clearly reflected the tough line of confrontation which itself had given birth to the legislation.[13] The design of the Act to confer a stamp of judicial legitimacy on government policy was exemplified early on. If the government wanted to impose a compulsory ballot before a threatened industrial action, this required court approval under the Act. In the first case of this kind – when the railway unions threatened to 'work to rule' over a wage dispute – the Court of Appeal confirmed that the relevant conditions for Court approval of a ballot were satisfied merely when the minister asserted his belief that the industrial action would be in breach of contract, and might be against the workers' own wishes. The court was not itself to question the validity of these views; only to rubber-stamp them once the minister had asserted them.[14] The

13. An excellent summary and analysis of the relevant events till about the end of 1972 is A. Barnett, 'Class struggle and the Heath government', *New Left Review*, Jan./Feb. 1973, on which – together with newspaper accounts and *The Times* law reports – we have drawn for part of the following.

14. By contrast, the court could not accept the minister's word that a threat to the national economy was involved, but had to satisfy itself independently on that score – a plainly political judgment; *in practice* here too, the court had to go by the Minister's word. (*The Times*, law report for 19 May 1972.)

minister's surmise that the workers were not behind their unions in fact proved dramatically wrong in this case. Some 90 per cent of the unionized workers, and two-thirds of those outside the unions, voted for action against the wage offer made to them; and their own claim was then granted.

The 'emergency' procedure thus backfired. But the new Industrial Relations Court – chaired by a high court judge, without union representation among its lay members in consequence of a general policy of non-cooperation in the Act on the part of the T.U.C. – continued the disciplinary line which it had been set up to follow. In the first of a series of disputes over the use by container firms of labour recruited from outside the docks, the Court held the Transport and General Workers Union responsible for some local shop stewards' refusal to comply with an order to stop industrial action. It imposed a penalty of £55,000 on the union for its 'contempt' in refusing to back up the order by removing the elected stewards from office. That decision clearly conformed to the spirit of the Act, with its concern to affirm union responsibility for industrial order. It was by no means clear that it conformed to the letter of the Act; and it was overturned by the Court of Appeal. In retrospect, the Appeal Court reversal may seem the first sign of hesitation within the establishment of government, courts and business about the practical consequences, if the new legal framework were pushed as hard as possible into full confrontation with organized labour.

That was in the spring and early summer of 1972. The signs of establishment hesitation were to multiply during the following months, as a hard anti-labour course threatened industrial strife on a scale unknown since 1926. The Conservative government, moreover, was beginning to toy once more with the idea of trying to enlist union support for wage restraint. The courts again showed a nice sensitivity to the shift in climate, their inconsistencies of judgment mirroring the limited and uncertain nature of the shift itself.

Such sensitivity, however, came slowly to the Industrial Relations Court. Unable to hold the union responsible, pending further appeal of the initial T.&G.W.U. case to the House of Lords, it ordered three London dockers to be sent to prison for contempt in defying an earlier court order to stop 'blacking'. Their actual imprisonment was prevented, against a background of strikes and calls for a nationwide stoppage, by a last-minute decision of the Court of Appeal. That court had been mysteriously convened at high speed without appeal by the dockers themselves, but on the intervention of a government official (the Official Solicitor) and an ostensibly self-appointed defence counsel, who appeared on the scene without the consent of the men. About a month later the Industrial Relations Court again took action and – this time successfully – sent five dock workers to prison for contempt on closely similar charges. The T.U.C. called a general strike. But before the date set for that the dockers were released on grounds that made political, but no obvious legal, sense. The House of Lords, timing its decision neatly, ruled that the T.&G.W.U. was, after all, responsible for ensuring shop steward compliance with a court order to stop industrial action. That ruling promised to have grave long-term consequences for the union movement on any future occasions when it might be invoked; and it reimposed the £55,000 penalty on the union for contempt. But its essential immediate effect was to provide the Industrial Relations Court with a pretext to discharge the five dockers from prison. The Court's argument was not that the men had purged their contempt – for indeed they had not – but that the burden on the unions to meet the responsibilities now imposed on them by the House of Lords would be 'immeasurably increased' if the dockers stayed in jail.[15] That argument, and the whole sequence of events, hardly confirm the notion of judicial independence and concern only with the rule of law. To make this comment is not to allege specific consultation or conspiracy between judges and ministers. But the courts on the whole, clearly, are fairly well attuned to changes of wind in the climate of the establishment to which they belong – perhaps more so today than at the turn of the century.

Indeed the Industrial Relations Court later declared itself a reformed character. It would not, it said, in future send union officials (and it may have implied others of no official status as well) to prison for contempt; and it might prefer to suspend interim orders, to allow unions an opportunity to coax their members into compliance.[16] The degree of reform was modest. It concerned tactics, not principle. The use of the law always at its fullest blast against organized labour now appeared impolitic. It would provoke total industrial disruption, and undermine any attempts by govern-

15. For a caustic account and discussion of these events, on which we have relied in the main, see J. A. G. Griffith, 'Reflections on the rule of law', *New Statesman*, 24 November 1972.
16. Griffith, ibid.

ment and business – even if designed only as exercises in public relations – to hitch the unions to counter-inflationary policy.

Some subsequent court decisions reflected this greater tactical caution, for a time. The Court of Appeal thus refused to rule that a nationwide one-day strike called for 1 May 1973, in protest against government policy and the Industrial Relations Act, was illegal as a 'political strike'; and the Industrial Relations Court itself on one occasion declined to make an interim order to a union to stop action in a particular dispute, on the ground that to do so 'might inflame the situation'.[17] But that Court had been established specifically to enforce the new Act. And in several crucial cases, when there could have been scope for judicial application of the law in a more conciliatory manner, its decisions continued also to express the spirit that had inspired the Act. It imposed penalties of £55,000 on the Engineering Union in late 1972, for contempt, when the union refused to comply with an order to prevent a branch of the union from excluding from meetings a man ruled by the court to be a member, though expelled by the branch for alleged non-payment of dues; and in its first action of this sort, the court obtained the sum by sequestration of a union bank account.[18] It awarded compensation to the tune of some £100,000 from the T.&G.W.U. to a Canadian aviation company, for successful industrial action against the company initiated by stewards of the union, designed to prevent ground handling of aircraft at London Airport by private firms instead of by the state corporation.[19]

By then, in late 1973, government and unions were once again heading for confrontation over a further stage in the former's efforts to enforce wage restraint; and the Industrial Relations Court took the first of a series of decisions against the Engineering Union over a case which, perhaps more than any other, came to symbolize the clash between labour and the law. The union – which consistently refused to be represented in court – was found to be in contempt for

17. *The Times*, law report for 27 April 1973 (*Sherard and others* v. *A.U.E.W. and others*); *The Times*, 25 May 1973, news report of a case brought by Polymathic Engineering against the A.U.E.W.

18. *The Times*, law report for 7 December 1972; see also news reports, e.g., on 9 December 1972. (The case against the union was brought by a Mr Goad. In this, as in other cases brought against it under the 1971 Act, the A.U.E.W. refused to appear or to be represented in court, although the original T.U.C. line of total 'non-cooperation' had been modified to allow unions to defend themselves.)

19. News reports (*Times, Morning Star*) 21 November 1973, *General Aviation* v. *T. & G.W.U.*

failing to call off a strike against a small engineering company which had denied the union recognition. The penalty of £75,000 was backed by court sequestration of union funds to a still larger amount, £100,000, than was required for the immediate purpose. Although another government body, the Commission on Industrial Relations, shortly after this recommended that the company should recognize the union, a second round in the same case was to follow – even after a Labour government had come to office and taken first steps to repeal the Act. The Court awarded compensation to the firm of £47,000, to meet its losses through the strike; and when the union refused to pay, again ordered sequestration of union funds – this time of all its funds, some exceptions apart, until the money had been found. A nationwide strike of engineering workers in response was called off only when an anonymous group – rumoured to include some large businessmen with no interest in perpetuating this particular battle – paid the award and associated costs on behalf of the union.[20]

IV

To sum up, state power has been invoked for long periods during this century in sideline support of a 'voluntary' *modus vivendi* between capital and labour. But at times, especially in the early 1970s, it has been called upon to repress labour militancy: when such militancy has seemed particularly threatening. While the unions came into conflict with the law in its new shape under the Industrial Relations Act of 1971, the courts also during the same years took decisions which made strike picketing highly vulnerable to prosecution.[21] In short, the 'voluntary' character of the *modus vivendi* when most successfully institutionalized is clearly conditional, to put the point mildly; spurious, to put it more sharply. When the voluntary basis of accommodation was not thought to be sufficiently secure – even by the Labour government of the 1960s, most decisively by the Conservative government which followed – legal compulsion was attempted to enforce labour discipline. It was especially significant that the

20. The company was Con-Mech. Details from *The Times* law reports for 10 and 22 October 1973, 3 and 8 May 1974 (also news reports on 2 November 1973 and 10 May 1974).
    21. Cf. ch. 3, note 22 above.

unions then had imposed upon them, by statute and judicial interpretation, a duty to act as agents of discipline on behalf of government and business, which they had been increasingly reluctant to
continue to accept of their own accord. That, the series of restrictions
on strike action, and the thrust against unofficial and shop-floor
unionism – from which the initial threat to the previous pattern of
accommodation had come – were the outstanding elements in the
active use of state power against labour during the early 1970s.

The Industrial Relations Act did not have the effects intended for
it. It helped to raise industrial conflict to new heights, and to add
official union militancy to unofficial militancy, though it was not the
only factor behind these developments. The Act itself was repealed
by Labour in 1974. Even the Conservative Party, after the election
early in that year, expressed reluctance to reintroduce it in its
original form. But that in no way rules out future use of state
force to keep labour in check. The 1971 Act proved ineffective,
not just because the labour movement is able to exercise some negative
influence on policy – a limited power of veto – through persistent
non-cooperation that threatens subversion of the order of capital,
without positive attempts to replace it by a different order. The Act
was ineffective also, and not least, because its specific provisions left
its operation too much to chance. The emergency clause for a
compulsory ballot before major industrial action, for example,
depended for its successful use on the assumption that rank-and-file
unionists would be opposed to militancy. That proved wrong on the
one occasion when the clause was used; and the clause, significantly,
was not invoked again: not, for instance, against the miners' action
in the winter of 1973/4, which in fact gained overwhelming support
in a union ballot of members.[22] Still more importantly, activation of
the ordinary provisions of the Act against labour militancy depended
on initiative by individual employers. Large employers were reluctant
to take such initiative on their own. All the cases which led to crises
of confrontation between unions and the law in its new guise were
precipitated by litigation by small- or medium-sized firms and by
individuals: on grounds and in circumstances not chosen by government and business at large.

22. In an 86 per cent poll in late January 1974, when the miners were already
operating a ban on overtime, 81 per cent of the members of the N.U.M. voted in
favour of a full strike to back a wage claim well in excess of the limits set by
government policy as interpreted by the government itself and the Pay Board.
(*The Times*, 5 February 1974.)

The point illustrates the divisions within capital – of interest as well as over tactics – which we shall discuss shortly. But it is also a reminder that, should attempts following the 1971–74 Act to return to an ostensibly voluntary *modus vivendi* fail, a new use of law to impose labour discipline might well be tried, with provisions more likely to avoid these anomalies and with perhaps heavier resort to state force to back it. The Conservative Party in 1974 had made no commitment to abandon its attempts to find a 'new framework of law', in some form, to control union activity. The Labour Party, though trying hard to reach agreement with the unions, might well again feel pressed in the same direction so long as it tries to run a 'mixed economy' on capitalist premises. By mid-1974 already – only a few months after the minority Labour government had taken office with aspirations to reach a 'social compact' with the unions – press, politicians and businessmen were debating the 'need' for some form of either coalition or dictatorship – or the two in conjunction – to repress labour unrest, cut back wage demands severely and raise unemployment, as measures against 'hyper-inflation'. But even a return to a pattern of accommodation akin to that which grew out of the 1906 Act would still, of course, in no way challenge the entrenched status of private property and profit which is the routine premise of the 'system of industrial relations'. Trade unions try to nibble at profit. They have done so, on the whole, with little impact on the relative distribution of income and wealth outside exceptional periods. And when the share of profit in the 1960s showed distinct signs of decline, the effect was countered by a shift in taxation against labour. Whatever in any case their capacity to bite off bits at the edges of profit, the unions cannot, as we have said before, bargain to abolish profit and property. Those institutions are not negotiable.

6 The state and divisions within business

I

The history of labour relations shows one recurrent line of division among the establishment of business, its Conservative political allies and their immediate political rivals, once the Liberal and now the Labour Party. Policies designed to build bridges of institutionalized accommodation between capital and its workforce have vied with policies of confrontation. It is because the former have prevailed, on the whole, that the organized labour movement – its leadership in particular – have to be seen in part as one member of an 'establishment' triad of business, state and labour. Only in part, because labour acquires a dual character in the process of accommodation. The duality arises from the conjunction of simultaneous acceptance of capital with opposition to it. It is that process of accommodation, not least, which has helped to promote the growth of the state. State agencies have provided the machinery for such concessions – welfare and social security arrangements especially – as business has had to accept to obtain co-operation from organized labour without giving away the routine power of capital and the concentration of wealth which goes with it. But business, like labour, has not been united in pursuit of institutionalized compromise. And opposition to that line of policy among business, the Conservative Party and their socio-political associates, has usually been linked with opposition to the continued expansion of state activity.

Two clusters of capitalist opinion on the role of the state can be identified in rivalry with each other throughout this century. To call them groups would be to attribute more coherence and permanence of form to them than they have. Neither has repudiated the need for substantial state activity. But one has sought to keep it within tight limits and to preserve as large areas of the economy as possible for private profit making. It has sought to reduce the risk of competition from public enterprise and of frustration from public regulation, even when both are designed to promote business prosperity at large. It has favoured cutting concessions to labour, and relying more on a combination of market forces and penal law to ensure labour discipline. The other school of thought has sought both to extend state activity in aid of business – for rationalization, co-ordination, and promotion of an economic climate favourable to growth and prosperity – and to secure the 'partnership' of organized labour for these ends through concessions and through firm institutionalization of ostensibly voluntary collective bargaining.[1]

The line between the two schools can be blurred. It does not coincide with the line between the two main parties. And it does not always fall in the same place. The 1950s, for example, marked a shift away from state economic aid and regulation on the part of the Conservative government, and some cutting back of the welfare system – quite sizeably so in respect of housing policy. But as labour remained quiescent on the whole, there was no resort then to repressive law to maintain industrial and social discipline; and 'voluntary' collective bargaining with state encouragement from the sidelines seemed still firmly ensconced. From around 1960, by contrast, public intervention for 'planning', 'modernization' and 'economic growth' became the order of the day. This began under Conservative government. But it was Labour, from 1964, that became the protagonist *par excellence* of a policy of harnessing the state to promotion of capitalist efficiency. Increasingly, however – for all attempts to maintain a 'partnership' with organized labour – that policy pitched government and unions into conflict. And it persuaded the Labour Party in office to tighten the machinery of law against the labour movement in market-place and factory: first by giving statutory force to incomes policy in restraint of wages; then in its abortive attempt to introduce emergency legislation against strikes.

Against just the same background, the school within the Conservative Party which favoured wider scope for 'free market' forces began to gain support again. The Labour government's dedicated occupation of the ground of pro-capitalist state intervention provided

1. See especially Harris, op. cit. (ch. 4, note 2 above).

the tactical opportunity for that. The uncertain course of economic growth despite 'planning', and the threat of a continuing decline in rates of profit, provided the business rationale for it. The crisis of a squeeze on the return to capital is understandably likely to bring into sharper relief the division between the pro- and anti-state interventionist schools of thought in business; and to enhance the attraction of policies to cut down both public activity and public expenditure, in order to leave the field apparently more free for private accumulation and retention of profit.[2] At least to do so for a time. But business dependence on state aid and services has grown to the point where a lasting shift towards a *laissez-faire* policy is unlikely. That certainly is suggested by the fact that the Conservative government in the 1970s soon returned to practices of state intervention of a familiar kind, after only a short period in which it professed concern to let market forces ride with little public guidance. In both phases of Conservative policy at that time – quasi-*laissez-faire* and interventionist – changes in general taxation and welfare benefits were introduced to bolster the share of profits and top incomes more securely against the squeeze on the return to capital. It is no accident that this was combined with legislation to blunt the teeth of organized labour. The rising militancy of the workforce made some such disciplinary measures an imperative for business, no matter what policies the government pursued otherwise.

II

There is little systematic evidence to identify the sources within business from which the two schools of thought have drawn support. At times the division between the two may have coincided in part with the distinction between big and smaller business. State-sponsored rationalization, for example, has often been opposed by small firms which were eliminated in the process or merged into combines. But the contrast between large and small-scale enterprise, and the evident difference in interests which sometimes goes with it, does not appear to have made for anything like a coherent, visible and durable cleavage of policy orientation along this line. It may be there, under the surface. But if so, its subterranean character is in itself significant.

2. See e.g., A. Gamble and P. Walton, 'The British state and the inflation crisis', *Bull. Conf. Socialist Economists*, Autumn 1973.

For it appears to be a general feature of British capitalism that structural divisions of interest within business are obscure or impermanent. This lends capital and conservatism further strength in face of the evident and long-lasting divisions among labour: between right, centre and left; between political and industrial wings; between sectional and class bases of organization.

The contrast is easily explained up to a point. Labour's strength is in numbers. But numbers are also a source of weakness. To bring them together in any kind of unity requires a bridging of many cracks. Those cracks are accentuated by the dependent status of labour in a market economy. For the exact conditions of dependence vary from one sector of the market to another; and dependence poses an inescapable dilemma of choice between pragmatic acceptance and conscious opposition. None of this applies to business – still less today than in the past, since the concentration of capital gives the strength not only of wealth but of small numbers and close mutual links. Yet there are points of the business complex, for all that, at which one might expect more visible and more durable cleavages of interest than have in fact appeared.

One such potential cleavage would seem to be that between banking and manufacturing interests. Britain's adjustment to the growing competition from foreign capitalism since before the turn of the century, through specialization in export of capital and in world banking, almost certainly helped to hold back the growth of manufacturing enterprise here by comparison with other countries. It reduced the capital available for domestic investment, or at least the certainty with which it could be obtained. It may have diverted skill and initiative from innovation in the technology and organization of productive industry. Among its longer-term effects was, not least, a marked influence of 'banker thinking' on the formulation of overall government economic strategy in the 1950s and 1960s. The priority given then to the maintenance of the international value of the pound, and to the role of sterling as a reserve world currency, reflected the persuasiveness of the City of London: City definitions of national economic interest; City conceptions – right or wrong – of the means required to maintain London as a prime international banking centre. Characteristically, the post-war nationalization of the Bank of England had – until very late in the period at least – led to no significant change in the relationship between the Bank and government. Orthodox banking views continued to shape Bank of England policy, and through the Bank usually found ready acceptance in the Treasury. Governors of the Bank continued to assert a freedom to criticize government policy in public, when they found it out of line with the financial stringency of national housekeeping favoured by conventional banking thought. To this day, they and their fellow directors of the Bank of England have been recruited largely from the City of London and private industry with City associations.[3] The priority given to sterling in economic policy in the 1950s and 1960s might, it seems, have aroused opposition from wide sections of business engaged in productive industry. For its effect was to produce recurrent restrictions on capital investment and market demand – the 'stop-go' pattern which Labour undertook to end, but in fact continued when in office in the 1960s. This in turn must have accentuated the uncertainties of forward planning by business. Yet, though there was plenty of criticism, no clear line of opposition with its source in manufacturing industry emerged; and what there was of that kind was not directed audibly at the banking interests of the City.

That may seem puzzling enough. No less puzzling appears the shift in government economic strategy on this score from about 1970. The priority once given to upholding the international value of sterling was then abandoned – at least for a time; the pound was 'floated'. The arguments in favour of this, of course, are known. What is still uncertain – and indeed little asked – is how this shift occurred without the outcry from the City, and the fervent pressures for reversal, which it would have provoked only a few years earlier. The answer is probably not that the City had lost its central position in British top business: a position suggested both by its strong representation of the boards of industry and by its earlier capacity to get its way on economic policy with little overt resistance from potentially rival interests. It is more likely that the City had diversified its banking activities, and taken advantage of new opportunities in Europe especially, to a sufficient extent for the old role of sterling as a reserve currency to be now much less relevant to its interests. In character and probable sources, this shift of economic policy seemed

3. In early 1973, five of the seventeen members of the Court of the Bank were merchant bankers; seven others were directors of large commercial and industrial companies (several with banking associations); four (including as a rare occurrence the Governor and Deputy Governor) had had careers as officials of the Bank; and one was a 'moderate' trade unionist. (Data compiled from *Whitaker's Almanack* and *Who's Who*.) The Governor retired later that year and was replaced by a merchant banker. (*The Times*, 3 July 1973.)

well in line with the rather earlier swing of predominant business and Conservative Party opinion in favour of Common Market entry, where uncertainty and divided views had prevailed before.[4]

III

There is much that is speculative here: less the fact of divisions within capital than the questions where precisely the roots of such divisions are over one issue and another; what are major and what more evanescent conflicts of interest and tactics; what the balance of forces is which will shape the outcome, when differences of policy and approach can be seen. It is clear, for example, that there was some – and at times quite widespread – business dislike for the hard line of confrontation with labour which became government policy in the early 1970s. Differences of view became partly visible not least when the Conservative administration reduced the working week to three days during the winter of 1973/74, in response to a ban on overtime and the threat of full-scale strike by the miners. That move was almost certainly much less forced on the government by an immediate shortage of fuel supplies than it was adopted as a deliberate measure to defeat the miners, quash wider labour opposition to wage restraint and rally 'middle opinion' in the country behind the government. To business the crisis posed sharply the dilemmas inherent in confrontation policy. Profits clearly would be hard hit by the three-day week; but if labour were put in its place for a considerable time to come, the losses could be worth the price. It seems plausible that business support for the three-day week would come from those firms and sectors of industry best able to weather the loss of profit for a time, the more so if they had good reason to want labour indiscipline sharply curbed. Very large corporations with extensive international connections might well often be in that category. That not only because they would normally have large resources to carry them, while fragmentation of shareholdings would enable their directorates more easily to take a long-term view of costs and benefits; but also because, even should the outcome not be a clear defeat for labour, they might more readily safeguard themselves by diverting new investment to countries at least for the present

4. Cf., e.g., T. Nairn, *The Left Against Europe?* (special issue of *New Left Review*, No. 75), Sept./Oct. 1972; revised ed., Penguin Books, 1973.

less affected by industrial disputes. In some cases, moreover, large internationally ramified companies of this kind seemed to have a clear direct interest in curbing labour, since they had felt the effects of militancy often over the previous years: motor manufacturers were a prime example. Many other companies would have neither comparable resources nor comparable incentives to find a tough line with labour supportable. Yet the divisions of opinion within business over this crisis and the longer-run issue, though they came to the surface from time to time, were never clearly enough visible to show this or even some other sort of pattern to the structural roots of division.

There is room for far more exploration and analysis than has so far been done in this field. Our comments inevitably hang in the air without such a firmer basis of knowledge. In some part, no doubt, the answers will prove to be that differences of interest within capital often do not, in fact, set up clear and durable cleavages between one sector of business and another. There may instead, on many issues, be a patchwork of pros and cons for each sector, to make the balance uncertain and the lines of difference blurred – a pattern to delight social scientists committed to 'pluralist' interpretations, but a pattern that holds within capital, not over society at large. That, however, is hardly the whole story. Another part of the answer must be that the concentration and the power of capital themselves help to obscure internal rifts. Towards the world outside itself, business is able to maintain a front of unity, or of only haphazard differences, because it is a small group, hard for the curious to penetrate, with the resources to back its normal interest in keeping internal conflicts and uncertainties discreetly veiled. The effect of that, of course, is to reinforce the power of capital and its semblance of routine and unruffled legitimacy.

7 Power and pluralism

I

The argument that the growth of state activity has tamed business and converted capitalism into something else does not, then, stand up to inspection. Indeed, its implausibility is suggested from the outset by the variety and vagueness of the labels applied to the 'something else' which capitalism is supposed to have turned into as a result: 'post-capitalism', 'welfare state', 'mixed economy', and so on. But that argument is only one arm, or one version, of a broader thesis which denies that the power of capital is dominant in societies like Britain. This is the thesis of 'pluralism'.

The essence of pluralist interpretations is that there is no longer a concentration of power in the hands of capital, or of any other interest that might have supplanted it. There is instead diffusion of influence among a multiplicity of groups.[1] None of these is dominant. All compete with one another for a share in power. They enter into alliances, of course; but the lines of coalition and division tend to

---

1. The most explicit formulations of a pluralist approach to the study of power known to us are American. See especially R. A. Dahl, *Pluralist Democracy in the United States: Conflict and Consensus,* Rand McNally, 1967; A. M. Rose, *The Power Structure: Political Process in American Society,* Oxford Univ. Press, 1967; S. M. Lipset, *Political Man,* Anchor, 1963; J. K. Galbraith, *American Capitalism: The Concept of Countervailing Power,* Houghton Mifflin, 1956; **and** in application to the study of power in local areas – N. W. Polsby, *Community Power and Political Theory,* Yale Univ. Press, 1963; R. A. Dahl, *Who Governs?* Yale Univ. Press, 1961. Similar assumptions and preoccupations are implicit in much political analysis in Britain, but – characteristically – have rarely been made so explicit. See, however, e.g., S. E. Finer, 'The political power of private capital', *Sociol. Rev.,* Dec. 1955, July 1956; and R. T. McKenzie, 'Parties, pressure groups and the British political process', *Polit. Quarterly,* Jan.–March 1958. Cf. also R. T. McKenzie, *British Political Parties,* Heinemann Educational Books, 2nd ed., 1963.

shift from one issue to another. There is no clear-cut and durable
pattern of confrontation across one major line of cleavage; and
certainly no lasting ascendancy of one set of interests over another.
The outcome of this pattern of multiple competition and shifting
alliances is instead variable, favouring now this group or coalition,
now that, and then another. The pattern is not exactly random, in
the technical sense of that term. The pressures and shifts within the
polygon of forces can be charted and explained. That is precisely the
task of political analysis. But the pattern is random in the sense that
power is dissolved, in the eyes of pluralist observers, into a jumble of
influences from diverse sources and with varying outcome. That in
turn is likely to spell safety for the existing social order – a conclusion
which pluralists generally welcome – because no one group has the
power to upset it, and no alliance of groups is in prospect with a
common interest in doing so.[2]

The trouble with this thesis is twofold. First, in so far as it is right,
what it says is hardly worth saying. Second, its proponents studiously
avert their gaze from questions that do matter. Because they then see
nothing, they draw the conclusion that there is nothing to see.
Clearly there is some truth in the pluralist picture of a fragmentation
of influence. The formal mechanisms of parliamentary government;
the existence of a market-place of pressures on policy in public and
private enterprise; the institutionalization of class conflict in politics
and industry – these rule out an alternative postulate of a total and
monolothic concentration of power. But to rule that out is to rule out
a man of straw. It is to exclude only the limiting case at one extreme.
It tells one nothing more than does excluding the limiting case at the
other extreme: the equally unrealistic possibility of total diffusion of
influence among all and sundry through a 'participatory democracy'
floating in an economic and social vacuum.

2. Pluralist approaches to the study of power have much in common with a
kind of 'grass-roots pluralism' sometimes found in sociological textbooks and
functionalist sociological analysis. This attributes to the 'associational' ties of
modern urban man (in contrast to the 'communal' ties of rural and small-town
man) a randomness of direction unrestrained by those barriers of economic condition and class which in fact constrain most peoples' lives and social relationships
within tight limits. The connection between 'power pluralism' and 'grass-
roots pluralism', as socio-political perspectives, is especially obvious when 'grass-
roots pluralists' welcome their own observations as indicating that major social
conflict is unlikely, because the alleged diversity of direction of people's multiple
ties prevents the formation of common interest groups except on limited ranges
of issues.

There is no value, then, to the point that many pressures go to shape the outcome of events. It is obvious. The crucial questions concern the nature of the pressures and the direction of the outcome. How far in fact do the various formally distinct groups which may compete for power represent, not separate and rival interests as pluralists postulate, but broad clusters of similar interests in different dress? What is their relative strength: where does the balance of power lie between them? These questions in turn raise another issue. This concerns the kinds of information one needs to answer the initial questions, and the criteria by which to assess the information.

It is at this point that pluralists put on spectacles which focus well short of the target. They have, it is true, a case when they criticize those who, for answers to these questions, have looked primarily to information about the composition of 'élites'. The fact, for example, that bankers and Conservative ministers come from similarly exclusive families and schools does not, by itself, say what they do with such power as they have; or how that power is constrained by the power of others. Conversely – though this illustration hits a different ideological key from most pluralist commentary – a government with men of working-class origin may still govern by bourgeois prescriptions. Yet agnosticism on this score can be taken too far. Information about 'élite' recruitment is not irrelevant to the study of power, as current fashion has come close to asserting. For such information suggests the extent of ties of association and common sympathy within ruling groups; the experience and perspectives which are likely to influence policy; the limits on the capacity of rulers to represent others. In the end, however, the test of power is not who decides; but what is decided – and what not.

The formula adopted in pluralist analysis for that test is quite inadequate. It is to examine disputes among rival groups on a number of 'key' issues; and to measure the respective power of those groups by the outcome of the disputes. The formula is inadequate – indeed irrelevant to the central questions of power – because it has nothing to say about those issues which do not come into dispute at all. They may be excluded through the capacity of one group or another to manipulate them off the agenda. That capacity is certainly power – the power of 'non-decision making', as this term has usually come to be used by critics of the pluralist school.[3] But still more important is

3. See Bachrach and Baratz, op. cit. (ch. 1, note 4, above). For other criticisms of pluralist interpretations see, e.g., Miliband, op. cit. (ch. 4, note 23 above);

the power to exclude which involves no manipulation; no activity on or off stage by any individual or group; nothing more tangible than assumptions. For the most part these are unspoken assumptions. They predetermine the range of issues in dispute, and limit it to those in which negotiation, competition or conflict has some practical chance of shifting the balance between the contending parties. It is power of that kind – anonymous, institutional and routine – which sets the parameters of the pluralist polygon of pressures. Pluralist analysis fixes its gaze on what goes on inside the polygon. It is not usually aware – or at least not concerned – that there are parameters; still less how tightly drawn they are. It sees trees, but no wood.

In fact, of course, one cannot see the wood unless one stands away from it. And one cannot see the routine assumptions that keep everyday conflict within tight bounds unless one sets oneself outside those assumptions. One has to look beyond what is familiar in order to understand the force of the institutional premises of our society – the continuing influence of property, profit and market on how things work and what issues make practical matters for dispute and bargaining, without active decisions usually being taken by anybody to that effect. One has to think those premises away, and replace them in one's mind by others. To follow the workings of private property, in short, one must be able to envisage its abolition. That of course comes easier to those – like many critics of pluralism –who have either little moral commitment to private property, or a positive commitment against it. Most pluralists, by contrast, uphold the institutional values of capitalism or take them simply for granted. Their support for those values, it is true, is sometimes reluctant, negative more than positive. Typically they then value liberty more than equality; unlike socialists, see the two as opposed, equality in any case as unlikely to be attainable, and capitalism for all its defects as a bulwark of liberty. But whatever the specific moral positions which they reflect, pluralist interpretations have generally carried an

C. W. Mills, *The Power Elite*, Oxford Univ. Press, 1956; T. B. Bottomore, *Elites and Society*, Watts, 1964; R. Presthus, *Men at the Top*, Oxford Univ. Press, 1964; G. W. Domhoff, *Who Rules America?*, Prentice Hall, 1967, and *The Higher Circles*, New York, 1970; Carol Pateman, *Participation and Democratic Theory*, Cambridge Univ. Press, 1970; J. Urry and J. Wakeford, eds., *Power in Britain*, Heinemann Educational Books, 1973 (contributions by Urry, P. Worsley and D. Lockwood). The approach which we adopt here proved to have much in common with S. Lukes, *Power: a Radical View*, Macmillan, 1974, which we had the opportunity to see in draft after completion of this part of our book.

explicit or implicit endorsement of the 'power equilibrium' which they describe. Just because pluralists on the whole share the routine assumptions which set the limits to any such equilibrium, and just because the assumptions are routine, they often have little eye for them. On both sides of the debate, moral outlook influences empirical perception. There is nothing new or surprising in that. But it is as well to be clear about it.

There are, in other words, two levels to the study of power. At one level the questions concern 'core assumptions'. What are the implicit terms of reference within which conflict about policy is confined for all practical purposes; which exclude alternatives outside that range from consideration? Whose and what interests do these core assumptions favour?[4] At the other, and lower, level the questions concern the conflict and outcome of pressures *within* the boundaries set by the core assumptions. There indeed the picture will look something like the polygon of forces found by pluralist analysis. Trade unions may win one round of wage disputes and lose another. Business and Conservative Party interests are likely to be divided on a variety of issues, and on lines that differ from one issue to the next. Labour interests will certainly often be divided. That is, as we have already argued, inherent in labour's reliance on numbers; in its dependent condition; and in that institutionalization of class conflict which itself helps to fix the constraining framework of core assumptions. Divisions within labour for the same reasons are more durable, and more consistently follow the same lines, than divisions within the business complex. On other issues again, neither business nor labour will be directly involved; or only factions and subgroups among them will be, in varying patterns of alignment with other groups and special interests.[5] It is easy to see a pluralistic pattern here. But no

4. We take for this purpose a 'sociological' conception of interests – i.e., we see interests as the possibilities and potential objectives of action which are inherent in economic positions regardless of whether the incumbents of those positions in fact so define their objectives at any given time. To define interests in 'psychological' terms – to confine labour 'interests' to those objectives which workers in fact recognize and act upon at a given time, for example – would be to ignore the point that part of the power of capital rests precisely on its routine capacity to rule out certain potential labour objectives as impracticable. Our conception of interests – a Marxist conception – is ostensibly open to the objection that it leaves the specification of interests 'arbitrarily' to the observer. But the 'arbitrariness' involved is no more than that involved in any specification of concepts and categories by social scientists.

5. Cf., e.g., C. Hewitt, 'Elites and the distribution of power in British society', in Stanworth and Giddens, eds., op. cit. (ch. 1, note 5 above): an analysis of the

characterization of the fundamentals of the power structure can be inferred from it.

II

At the centre of the core assumptions of our society, clearly, are the institutions of property and market, and the working premises which go with them. These premises can be summarized as follows. Private ownership of economic resources entitles the owners to whatever surplus the resources yield, once costs have been met. Maximization of the surplus is the main motor of economic enterprise. The prime determinant of income for those without property is the pull which they can exert in the markets where they sell their labour. Even in retirement the fall-back incomes now provided are well below working wages; and, above a minimum pension level, they follow gradations set roughly in relation to earlier market income. The quantity and direction of output are governed by the market demands which arise from the distribution of wealth and income determined in these ways.

The growth of state activity has made for modifications of these institutions and premises in their earlier forms. But these are modifications only; not radical changes, important though they have been. Public ownership of some productive assets has reduced the size of the field from which private profit is raised directly. But on the whole – despite a mixture of originating motives and despite ineffici-encies of implementation – public ownership in practice is directed to securing private profit elsewhere. It certainly has little effect on ownership of wealth. Public provision of services has vastly increased, in some fields to remove consumption wholly or partly from the direct blast of market forces. But tight limits are still set to the ways in which tax revenue is raised and benefits are distributed, through the simple fact of the continuing predominance of private enterprise and private capital in the economy.

These modifications of the core assumptions mark limited shifts in the structure of power, whichever party or group took the prime initiative in making them. A Liberal government was the main author of the measures associated with the first notable shift of this kind, in

_____

sources of policy-making on a number of post-war issues, which emphasizes the pluralist pattern among the trees but ignores the non-pluralist shape of the wood.

the years before and into World War I. Labour interests were then given official recognition as legitimate, while still of course subordinate. An initial framework of social security for the wage-earning population was established. State policy in industrial relations shifted to encouragement of 'voluntary' bargaining between employers and unions, and made it practicable for organized labour to strike without punitive legal retaliation. It became standard practice for individual representatives of labour to sit on a variety of public bodies. The working-class movement's acceptance of a status as junior partner in the polity – partial though that acceptance was – was a crucial stage in the process by which class conflict became institutionalized.

The second main set of modifications to the core assumption of British capitalism came during and immediately after World War II, with a Labour government as their principal author. It is easy now to forget the high hopes of major change which accompanied the Labour victory at the polls in 1945; and in retrospect to blur the internal contradictions between radicalism and moderate reform in the post-war government's policies. Some of its measures had a socialist thrust which, if applied consistently and over a much wider field, would have threatened the continuing dominance of capitalist premises. This was hardly the case with nationalization of selected industries, in the form those measures took. But the National Health Service took medical provision almost entirely out of the market. The new system of town and country planning was anchored in public appropriation of future increases in land value, and in allocation of the major role in urban development and redevelopment to public authorities. But no other social service followed the comprehensive and egalitarian pattern of national health. Charges for medicine, dental treatment and certain other services were soon imposed in overt denial of the principle of free and equal access. And the tax system from which health provision was financed retained its essential inequity. Even in its early progressive phase just after World War II, town and country planning lacked a larger framework of national economic planning to give it coherence. Development values in the land were returned to private ownership in the 1950s; the role of public authorities in housing and other building was drastically curtailed; and market principles were given successively more freedom of rein over development in the public and private sectors alike. Planners in practice increasingly narrowed their sights from the generous social objectives characteristic of the early period –

in part egalitarian, in part inspired by a romantic ideal of neighbourly intimacy within local communities – to projection of the trends of urban development inherent in things as they are, and to a fixation on transport and traffic. In short, Labour policy after 1945 was not all of one piece. But the sharp points of its more radical measures were soon blunted or worn off, just because those measures were isolated.

Government restraints on the operation of market forces in the 1960s and early '70s, in association with counter-inflationary policy, involved no departure from the predominance of capitalist premises in the working arrangements of the economy. Their overriding objectives were the control of wages and the protection of long-term private profit. Ostensibly designed to apply fairly to all groups of the population, measures to limit increases in incomes assumed, as a 'fair' base, a distribution of income grossly unequal from the start. The burden of paying for any special increases in the lowest earnings and in social security benefits was placed firmly, and with much establishment moralizing, on the shoulders of better-paid labour. Restraints on rises in managerial and executive salaries are necessarily less effective than those on rises in publicly negotiated rates of pay. Controls on profits have usually been rejected as impracticable. Where they have been introduced in some form, they have commonly involved at most deferment of profit distribution to shareholders; not cancellation of profit increases, let alone their appropriation for redistribution to labour. Business demands for a light application of profit controls, if any, have been conceded in recognition of the 'need' to maintain incentives to private enterprise. Government surveillance of prices, as of profits, has been in all essentials a public relations exercise without effective sanctions, designed to elicit labour co-operation in counter-inflationary policy. There have certainly been divided opinions within business about the efficacy of intensive government intervention in economic affairs to limit inflation and promote the growth and profitability of industry. That in no way signifies a shift of government policy away from the core assumptions which determine the shape of British society.

This is to repeat matters which we have already spelled out in much more detail earlier. The point of repeating them is to underline the conclusion. The core assumptions of our society are firmly in line with the interests of one small group. That group comprises top business and large property owners. It also includes those who derive substantial privilege from their association with this central cluster:

the highly prosperous and well established professions, the senior ranks of officials in public service. This dominant group does not constitute a 'ruling class' in the simplest and most vulgar sense of the term. In order to retain power and privilege, they have had to make some concessions to labour. The labour movement is the only significant source of opposing power. But the threat from labour has been contained through a series of compromises, by which labour has acquired some influence – and accepted responsibility – without gaining power. Labour's lack of power is reflected in the essential continuity of the core assumptions of the society. Capital with its associates is still the effective ruling interest. It is not just one élite among several.

III

It is important to stress the strength which this ruling interest enjoys through its concentration, its consequent small size and close internal links. The key link within the cluster, of course, is the connection between top business and the leadership of the Conservative Party. That link became close from the latter decades of the nineteenth century onwards, as the Tories – earlier more narrowly identified with the 'landed interest' and parts of the old financial bourgeoisie – successfully established themselves as the party of all property. The party drew increasing support from the industrial bourgeoisie and the rising professional groups in the process; and this sowed the seeds of the decline of the Liberal Party.[6]

The very top flight of businessmen and the biggest property owners are now rarely themselves active in Conservative parliamentary politics.[7] Professional people – especially lawyers, in contrast to the lecturers and teachers predominant among professionals on the Labour benches – have long been the largest group in the Conservative parliamentary party, when members are classified by their current or previous occupations outside the House of Commons. Professionals have made up around one-half of the Tories in Parlia-

6. On the shifts in composition of parliamentary parties and cabinets, and in interest alignments involved in this process, see especially J. A. Thomas, *The House of Commons, 1832–1901*, Cardiff University Press, 1939; and W. L. Guttsman, *The British Political Elite*, MacGibbon & Kee, 1963.

7. Cf. e.g., W. D. Rubinstein, 'Men of property', in Stanworth and Giddens, eds., op. cit. (ch. 1, note 5 above).

ment, with only relatively small variations, both inter-war and post-war to this day.[8] Business interests do not need to be directly represented, in strength, in parliament and cabinet in order to find a response within the Conservative leadership. There is a common sympathy of outlook. Even so, the personal representation of business in Conservative politics at Westminster is sizeable. A fairly steady one-third of Conservative M.P.s, inter-war and post-war, have been employers and managers in their main extra-parliamentary occupations. The same group – including financiers and property developers – indeed provided half the membership of the Heath cabinet in 1973: a much larger direct business representation than in the average earlier Conservative cabinet.[9] Counts in the 1960s and early 1970s have shown a rough overall average of two company chairmanships per head among Conservative M.P.s, and well over twice as many other company directorships.[10] Often one individual, of course, holds a number of such business appointments; but directorships in private business are not uncommon, too, among Conservative parliamentarians whose main occupational experience has been professional.

The Conservative Party as a whole, naturally, draws considerable financial strength from its business connections. Its annual income in the early 1960s, for example – central and constituency funds combined – was estimated at £3 million (by comparison with £1½ million for Labour). Two-thirds of that total came from large companies. It is not surprising that nearly all Conservative constituency parties were able to employ a full-time agent, while little more than a third of their Labour rivals did so. In addition, direct Conservative political propaganda is usually supplemented by pre-election publicity campaigns for 'free enterprise', or against nationalization, undertaken and financed by business and associated pressure groups. Before the 1964 election, for example, the privately owned steel industry spent some £1·3 million in this way, one-third as much again as all pre-election expenditure by the Conservative Central Office and four times the expenditure by Labour's headquarters.[11]

The similarities of background, as well as the network of family connections, that tie Conservative politicians to top businessmen and

8. Data compiled from Guttsman, op. cit. (note 6 above) and D. Butler and M. Pinto-Duschinsky, *The British General Election of 1970*, Macmillan, 1971.

9. Sources as in previous note, supplemented by *Who's Who* for 1973.

10. A. Roth, *The Business Background of MPs* (1972 ed.), Parl. Profile Services, 1972.

11. R. Rose, *Influencing Voters*, Faber, 1967.

members of other formally separate 'élites' are well documented. For decades, the 'public' schools and the Oxbridge pair of ancient universities have been the path to parliament for something like three in every four Conservative M.P.s and cabinet ministers. There has been little change in this pattern over time, except that Old Etonians were down, from between a quarter and a third earlier, to about a fifth in the early 1970s.[12] A university education is less common – despite an upward trend – among the élites of finance and industry. But the public schools, with a tiny group of them in special place, have produced most of the top men in British business; and also majorities and near-majorities of those 'distinguished public figures' who are selected to join royal commissions, other government committees of inquiry and such bodies as the B.B.C.s Board, the Arts Council and the British Council.[13] The point is not that this kind of information tells one what these people do with the influence which they wield. It simply shows part of the background from which their sympathies with the core assumptions of economy and society spring; and the closeness of the links between them from common experience, often also personal association and family ties, which add unity to their power.

By these criteria, too, the business and Conservative Party power cluster has close ties with the top flight of state officials. It is a familiar point that a large proportion of the members of the senior civil service are people of similarly privileged background. The range of social and educational origins represented among high ranking civil servants had widened somewhat during this century, it is true. This has been, in the main, the result of some institutionalized provision for recruitment to the top levels – the grades which until recently were known collectively as the 'administrative class' – by promotion from middle-level posts. Among the small élite of officials in very high advisory positions, just over one in four in 1967 was the child of a manual or routine-grade white-collar worker, for example, by comparison with only about one in every eight in 1929. The proportion educated at local authority schools had risen from around a seventh in the late 1920s to a little more than a third in the late

12. Sources as in note 9 above.
13. See, e.g., Guttsman, op. cit.; T. Lupton and C. Shirley Wilson, 'The social background and connections of top decision makers', *Manchester School*, Jan. 1959; H. Glennester and R. Pryke, *The Public Schools*, Fabian Society, 1964; Stanworth and Giddens, op. cit. (ch. 2, note 21 above). Cf. also D. Boyd, *Elites and their Education*, Nat. Foundation for Educational Research, 1973.

1960s. But 'open competition' among candidates with university degrees, overwhelmingly from middle- and upper-class families and to a very large extent still from Oxford and Cambridge Universities, remains the predominant form of recruitment to the upper levels of central government administration. And attempts to widen the social and educational range of the intake, after it had narrowed for a time in the 1950s and early 1960s, appear to have done little more than restore the position to what it was shortly after the end of World War II. Nearly two in every three top civil servants in 1967, of the rank of assistant secretary and above, had been educated at independent or direct grant schools (though the 'public' school contingent came mainly from middle-level and minor schools of this type, rather than from Eton, Harrow, Winchester and the few other élite-within-élite institutions which contribute so sizeably to the highest echelons of finance and Conservative Party politics). One in two had been to Oxbridge. Recent changes in the structure of the civil service, in the formal classification of posts and the procedures of recruitment and promotion, seem to offer little prospect of any significant change in this pattern.[14] The corresponding ranks of the Foreign Service, as one might expect, are drawn from a still smaller and more exclusive circle of the population.[15]

To point to these bonds of social experience between the senior permanent officials of the state and that central cluster of interests

14. For this and other information about recruitment to the administrative class (and equivalent grades) of the civil service, and to top grade posts in particular (above Assistant Secretary for 1929–1950, Assistant Secretary and above for 1967), see R. K. Kelsall, *Higher Civil Servants in Britain*, Routledge & Kegan Paul, 1955; *idem*, 'Recruitment to the higher civil service', in Stanworth and Giddens, eds., op. cit. (ch. 1, note 5 above); A. H. Halsey and I. M. Crewe, *Social Survey of the Civil Service* (vol. 3, pt. 1, *The Civil Service*, report of the Fulton Committee), H.M.S.O., 1969.

15. D. C. Watt, *Personalities and Politics*, Longman, 1965 (pp. 189–91). Army officers, too, have until recently been recruited very largely from among young men with 'public' school education; and in 1971 still, nearly three in four of the army élite with the rank of major-general and above had been at schools of this kind. The contribution of these schools to the intake of new cadets, however, has been reduced since the early 1950s. (C. B. Otley, 'The educational background of British army officers', *Sociology*, May 1973.) But the political and domestic role of the military in Britain – by contrast, for example, with the U.S.A. since World War II and Germany till then – has normally been too limited for it to be important for our discussion here. To say that, however, is not to rule out the possibility that in certain circumstances (protraction of the Northern Ireland crisis, for instance, or a further sharpening of domestic class conflict in an economic situation defined as critical), army officers might try to assert more influence on policy in the future.

whose core is big business, and whose direct political arm is the
Conservative Party, is not to argue that the top civil service is merely
a tool of business and Conservative Party policy. The notion of civil
service 'neutrality', heavily underlined in British government, is not
just a façade. It is real enough in one sense. The civil service undoubtedly, in the normal run of events, observes formal neutrality as
between the two main parties. It carefully avoids any direct or overt
bias against Labour, when that party is in government, by comparison with the Conservatives who are more often its political 'masters.'[16] The story has often been told how top civil servants had
contingency plans prepared to implement some of the elements of
Labour's programme in 1964, before the election of that year which
brought the party to office. It is quite likely, indeed, that many
administrative class officials then privately even favoured an electoral
victory for Labour, as offering a better prospect of efficient prosecution of policies of 'modernization' and 'economic growth' than the
continuation in office of a temporarily demoralized Conservative
leadership. Neutrality vis-à-vis alternative governments – even at
times a covert leaning towards Labour, though Labour is likely to
prove more awkward – is quite consonant with the conservative
sympathies suggested by the social background and connections of
high civil servants. Such neutrality is encouraged by that institutionalization of class conflict which is the hallmark of politics in a country
like Britain. For the result of this process is that the Labour Party has
been converted – for practical purposes, most of the time – from a
potential threat against the capitalist order to the prime protagonist
of one prescription for the maintenance of that order. This prescription – shared in part by substantial sections of business and the
Conservative Party, though opposed by others – is for extensive and
widening state involvement. It is not at all surprising if many top
state officials also sympathize with it. In some countries, in fact,
where class conflict has been institutionalized with the social democratic party as the normal incumbent of office – and where formal
requirements of civil service 'neutrality' are rather less stringent than
in Britain – it is common knowledge that there are officials in key
positions who have overt social democratic leanings. That is so in the
Scandinavian countries. Yet top civil servants there are also drawn

16. The Labour Party leadership has in any case also come to be drawn increasingly from among people of middle- and upper-class occupational experience. See
Part Five, chapter 2 below.

largely from the privileged groups of the population.[17] And they share, in broad terms, the standards and styles of life of businessmen; not of course of ordinary earners.

But the notion of civil service 'neutrality' is misleading in other senses. First, it greatly exaggerates the purely instrumental role of officials. It implies that the job of all civil servants – even at the highest levels – is merely to find the most effective means to implement the policies of their political 'masters'. In fact, the capacity of senior officials both to initiate and to inhibit policy goes well beyond that, although knowledge on this point is more impressionistic and anecdotal than systematic. Second, while their bias in exercising this influence is not normally and certainly not necessarily Conservative with a capital 'C', it is inevitably in the ordinary way conservative with a small 'c'. The higher civil service is often in a position to initiate policy, especially when ministers and cabinet have no very distinctive policies of their own to assert. It is still more often, through the advice which it offers on practicalities, able to exercise a restraining influence on policy: to hold back measures that might otherwise threaten too drastic a break with past practice, to cut them down to 'size'. In either case, de facto official discretion will normally be exercised conservatively. Innovations will be designed to extend, round off, smooth out existing provisions: not to depart from the premises of the established order. The restraining influence which goes with negative advice will be used to reduce the risk of disruptive change. Indeed, this is just the way in which one of the prime tasks of top officials has often been defined: to pour the cold water of practical sense and experience on any 'wilder' features in politicians' schemes. It is the alleged need for 'continuity' which provides the rationale of a system of government in which – as former ministers have testified – the permanent officials carry the advantages of a mastery of the machinery of the state, of connections among themselves, and of access to information, which weighs heavily against any unorthodox leanings on the part of ministers that are not backed by exceptional determination, clarity of purpose and cabinet solidarity.[18]

17. See, e.g., S. Landström, *Svenska ämbetsmäns sociala ursprung*, Uppsala, Hessler, 1954; and also K. Samuelson, *From Great Power to Welfare State*, Allen & Unwin, 1968 (p. 285), quoted in R. Scase, 'Industrial Man: a reassessment', *Brit. J. Sociology*, June 1972.

18. Cf. e.g., Barbara Castle, 'Mandarin power', *The Sunday Times*, 10 June 1973. The fact that Mrs Castle, like some other ministers of the Labour government 1964–70, was concerned to explain the government's lack of radicalism by pin-

A good deal, it is true, needs to be known about how this works in practice; and in what circumstances it may *not* work this way. In the final analysis, moreover, responsibility for the conservative bias built into the role of the civil service rests, not with officials themselves; but with the nature of the political system of which they are part. It rests, in an immediate sense, with the labour movement for its normal effective acceptance of that institutionalization of class conflict on capitalist premises which perpetuates the conservative bias of officialdom. The limited social experience and horizons of top civil servants do not create that bias. They demonstrate it; at most they also reinforce it. A widening of recruitment to the top posts in the state bureaucracy – as has indeed been an object of official policy, to improve efficiency and the civil service 'image', though not pursued very diligently – would do little by itself to change the bias. But if the labour movement were to achieve political power with a programme designed to make a frontal challenge to the established order, it would need top officials and advisers, within the machinery of government, socially and ideologically far more attuned to such radical objectives.

IV

The dominant place in the structure of power, then, is occupied by a ruling interest representing a very small section of the population: those in whose hands large wealth and private corporate property are concentrated. Much the same could be said, in these general terms, of the structure of power in other capitalist countries. The main case in which basic features differ is that of the United States, where labour opposition has not crystallized in political form. But the central cluster of ruling interests in Britain has its own unique features, which mark it off from its counterparts in other capitalist societies. Many of these special characteristics may derive from the long history

---

ning some of the responsibility on the civil service does not weaken the point. The moderating influence of the civil service is powerful especially *vis à vis* a government without distinctive policies of its own or the collective determination to carry them out. By contrast, the introduction of the National Health Service in the late 1940s appears to provide an example of how ministerial determination, backed by the cabinet, may prevail in considerable measure over official caution and opposition from vested – in this case professional – interests. Cf. Eckstein, op. cit. (ch. 3, note 41 above).

and slow growth of capitalism in Britain. The gradual pace at which a capitalist economy emerged here may help to explain the historical capacity of old ruling groups in Britain to absorb ascendant groups which might otherwise have dethroned them: their capacity to adapt themselves to new economic ways, while imposing part of their old culture and life styles on their successors. Other factors may also have played a part in making established ruling strata open to individual penetration from below. Upper-class primogeniture – inheritance mainly by the eldest son – may have encouraged it by creating ties of kinship in each generation between nobility, gentry, the professions and commercial occupations. And it almost certainly helped to promote the advance of capitalism, in turn, by forcing younger sons into careers of their own in business or professional work.[19] Be that as it may, the industrial bourgeoisie of the nineteenth century came to power without a revolutionary displacement of the landed and mercantile interests which ruled before them. And while members of the old establishment often successfully switched investment to mining, industry and the new forms of finance and trade associated with these, the successful strata of the industrial bourgeoisie appear to have absorbed features of the culture and outlook of the old ruling class, which imprinted themselves distinctively on some of the institutions of the new industrial capitalist society. Hence, for example, the nineteenth-century revival of the 'public' schools, with their ethos directed to the cultivation of 'Christian gentlemen', though later also of imperial leaders.[20] Hence probably, too, some of the special features of the British civil service.

The reforms of the two decades after 1850 converted the machinery of central government into what, in many respects, was a model of the kind of bureaucracy described later by Max Weber. An elaborate division of authority and labour was imposed in hierarchical form, for example; standardized open competitive examinations were introduced for the recruitment of all regular staff. These and associated changes can be seen as the application to public enterprise of those principles of utilitarian rationality which the bourgeoisie brought to the conduct of private business. Yet the cultural tone, as distinct from the administrative form, of these changes seemed in

19. H. J. Habbakuk, 'Family structure and economic change in nineteenth-century Europe', *J. Econ. History*, vol. 15, no. 1, 1955.

20. See especially E. C. Mack, *Public Schools and British Opinion*, 2 vols., London, 1938; New York, 1941.

some respects more 'old upper class' than 'utilitarian bourgeois'. The entrance examinations encouraged recruitment, to the higher levels, of candidates with a classical or humanistic education, rather than the lawyers – later economists and other 'specialists' in administration and policy – favoured by most continental government services. Importance was attached in the British Civil Service to critical ability and shrewdness of judgment as the essential qualifications for senior posts, rather than technical expertise. This was associated with a relegation of professionally qualified personnel to relatively non-influential positions; with a practice of moving officials marked out for the higher appointments from one department to another; and with reliance on personal judgment and on measures of general education, rather than tests of specific job competence, in selection and promotion of staff. The development and persistence of these features of the British civil service have been the target of recurrent criticism. They came under fire especially during the period of enthusiasm for 'modernization' in the 1960s.[21]

Whether or not the critics have been right, by their own criteria of efficiency, these administrative practices imply a premium on critical detachment and *savoir-faire*, as distinct from technical specialization and innovating initiative. That premium is likely to have been a product, at least in part, of the 'gentlemanly' culture generated by interpenetration of old landed and mercantile interests with new industrial bourgeoisie around and after the middle of the nineteenth century. This culture has helped to give the ruling cluster in contemporary Britain its own distinctive character. But its values were never anti-capitalist. They incorporated a certain disdain for those forms of business enterprise, in each generation, which were too recent to have proved their respectability. Banking and overseas trade, for example, have a long-established status as socially honorable activities; manufacture in a wide range of fields has gradually acquired it; property development in its newest forms is still somewhat suspect. On the whole, this has been a rentier culture more than

21. See especially *The Civil Service: Vol. I, Report of the Committee* (Fulton Committee), Cmnd. 3638, H.M.S.O., 1968, chap. 1; also, e.g., H. Thomas, ed., *Crisis in the Civil Service*, Blond, 1968; and Burrage, 'Culture and British economic growth', op. cit. (ch. 2, note 21 above). J. Garrett, *The Management of Government*, Penguin, 1972, applies to the civil service the kinds of criteria of managerial efficiency which were also adopted by the Fulton Committee, but is less sweeping and more cautious than the committee (for which the author worked) in criticizing the service.

a pioneer-entrepreneurial culture. That is hardly surprising. The rentier ethos emerged at a late stage of a long development of capitalism; and in an economy which, when it eventually lost its world supremacy, was adapted to the new situation of international competition through renewed development of financial capitalism in association with imperialism. The values of this culture – said to pervade private as well as public enterprise – may have hampered the twentieth-century efficiency of British capitalism: we have discussed this possibility earlier. Its roots in any case, so it seems, are economic, themselves embedded in the particular history of capitalism in Britain. And if its distinctive features are eventually eroded, the result would not be to make this society either more or less capitalist: the core assumptions of economy and polity would not be changed thereby. The result could be to make the management of British capitalism more effective by commercial criteria. Characteristically, one of the changes sought – and now partly in process of implementation – by reformers of the civil service is greater contact, and more interchange of personnel, between government service and private business. The effect will be to underline the unity of shared assumptions and experience which helps to give the ruling interest of capital its power.

V

The power of capital is buttressed further by the main channels through which information, opinions and values are disseminated: the educational system and the 'mass' media. We have already discussed some aspects of the system of education; and we shall come back to the subject later (Part Four). The media, seen in this context, are of two kinds. One group is, on the whole, directly aligned with the central power cluster constituted by big business and the Conservative Party. The press is in that group, together with a variety of other enterprises engaged in the commercial production of entertainment of less immediate consequences for opinion formation. The other group comprises those media which are under some form of public control, whether publicly managed – the B.B.C.; or commercially run but under public supervision. The role of this group is more complex and difficult to characterize with certainty. It has some similarity with that of the civil service. The broadcasting media are formally 'neutral'; required to give 'impartial' expression to a diversity of views and news, in somewhat the same way as the civil service is responsible for impartial implementation of policies which it is not itself supposed to determine. And there is, again, some ostensible reality to the notion of 'neutrality'. Yet the diversity of opinions and perspectives which find expression on television and radio are broadly contained within the limits of a 'consensus' that allows little scope for more than spasmodic questioning of the society's core assumptions. Like the civil service, the broadcasting services in effect thus uphold continuity of the established order. But they do so discreetly. The limits of the 'consensus' to which they adhere are in the main unspoken, the ways in which conformity to them is achieved in the main indirect. Both limits and means have been little studied; and they are therefore difficult to demonstrate except in a loose and impressionistic manner.

There are no such difficulties in describing the character of the press, the central medium among those in the first group. For the press, quite simply, is big business. The story of its growth is well known in outline.[22] The crucial development in this country came with the publication of the *Daily Mail*, founded in 1896 by Northcliffe, the first of the press lords, and designed to appeal to a mass public. It was aimed at the petty bourgeoisie and the artisan strata – written, in Lord Salisbury's phrase, 'by office boys for office boys'. Daily newspapers directed specifically to the working class came much later. But the Northcliffe formula laid the tracks on which the popular press subsequently moved, and became a semi-monopolistic industry. The elements of the formula – unchanged in principle since then, though the early *Mail* looks staid to present-day eyes – were twofold: first, a mixture of news, features, serial stories (later also pictures), all kept brief, designed for casual reading and slanted to entertainment value, intended to attract as broad a cross-section of the potential public as possible; second, a price held low by the reservation of a large proportion of space for advertisements. The dependence of the Press – 'quality' as well as 'popular'·– on advertising revenue has been of overwhelming significance for its development since then. It has made circulation size – at different minimum levels, according to the socio-economic composition and hence the purchasing power of the readership – the essential condition of

22. For a good popular history and analysis of the British press, see F. Williams, *Dangerous Estate*, Longmans, 1957.

newspaper survival. Market considerations have therefore become the prime determinant of newspaper content. And the process of press concentration in steadily fewer hands has been inexorable, as papers have died or merged with others in the struggle to stay in business.

By 1972, the five largest newspaper combines between them accounted for 85–90 per cent of the aggregate circulation of both national morning and national Sunday papers; for half that of the provincial morning papers; and for one-third of that of the provincial evening papers.[23] Several of these newspaper enterprises, moreover, are part of very much larger organizations, with interests increasingly ramified throughout the publication and entertainment industry. Their holdings often include substantial stock in the 'independent' television companies. In seven out of the fourteen regional television companies in 1972, newspapers held large blocks of shares (amounting to between 25 and 65 per cent of all voting stock in these cases), with sometimes a single massive block in the hands of one newspaper corporation. I.P.C./Reed, for example – publishers of the *Daily Mirror*, *Sunday Mirror*, *Sunday People* and a long list of magazines, a concern also with large interests in the paper and newsprint industry – held 30 per cent of A.T.V.s voting stock and 24 per cent of its non-voting stock. The Thomson organization – *The Times* and *The Sunday Times* – owned a quarter of Scottish T.V.s voting stock and 8 per cent non-voting stock. News International – the Murdoch group, with the *Sun* and the *News of the World* – held a third of London Weekend T.V.s non-voting stock, though it shared the 30 per cent newspaper slice of voting stock with several other papers.[24] The list can be extended. It illustrates in any case only one of the sets of links through which control over the whole range of production in communication and entertainment is increasingly concentrated in the hands of a few empires. The concentration of press ownership is now just part of this larger process.[25]

23. Calculated from *The Press and the People: 19th Annual Report of the Press Council, 1972*. No direct comparison can be made with the data of the extensive analysis, nearly twenty-five years earlier, in the *Report of the Royal Commission on the Press 1947–49* (Cmnd. 7700), H.M.S.O., 1949. For the Commission's summary data concerned the five largest 'chains', organizations with predominantly provincial newspaper interests, whose influence is now less important than that of the giants whose interests spread today from the national press to a wide range of other activities. The general trend of increasing concentration is clear, however.

24. Press Council, op. cit.

25. For a valuable discussion of this process, see G. Murdock and P. Golding,

The importance of advertising as a prime source of newspaper revenue is reflected only partly in the disappearance of newspapers unable to achieve sufficient circulation figures to attract advertisers on a competitive scale. Far more significant is the fact that those papers which do survive have to tailor their contents to the demands of mass circulation. The process, moreover, works unequally across the social spectrum. Wealthy newspaper readers – especially if they control corporate property as well as their own individual wealth – count for more in the eyes of advertisers than ordinary wage-earning readers, because they can buy more. A newspaper with a wealthy readership can therefore charge its advertisers more for each reader than can a paper read mainly by people with middle-range or, still worse, low incomes. Advertisers, naturally, are willing to pay more for a given space – a single column inch of advertisement, for example – to reach 100,000 'high-class' homes than to reach 100,000 workers' homes. Calculated in this standard way, in fact, advertising charges show a marked gradient the steps of which correspond fairly neatly, minor quirks apart, with the steps of the socio-economic gradient of the newspapers' readership. (Table 22.) For each 100,000 copies of a single column inch advertisement, the *Financial Times* – many of whose wealthy readers join control over corporate purchasing power to their own private purchasing power – can thus charge more than seven times the amount charged by the working-class *Daily Mirror*; *The Times* over four times the *Mirror's* charge, the *Guardian* well over three times. As a result, a newspaper for 'top people' needs a much smaller circulation to survive than does a 'popular' paper. For *The Times* and the *Guardian*, the critical figure may be near the half-million mark. (Both are in difficulties with circulations below that level, especially *The Times* whose figure has been falling.) For the *Mirror*, it runs into several millions, and even then security is not guaranteed; while the *Sun* could not have survived as a paper directed largely at working-class readers, had it not succeeded in pushing up its circulation far beyond the level shown for 1971.

Two crucial points follow from this. First, head for head, the upper and middle classes have more, and a wider variety of, papers directed specifically to them than does the mass of the wage-earning popula-

'For a political economy of mass communications', in R. Miliband and J. Saville, eds., *The Social Register 1973*, Merlin, 1973. We are very grateful to Graham Murdock for the opportunity both to see this paper in advance and to discuss the subject with him.

TABLE 22

National morning newspapers – class composition of readership,
advertising charges and circulation, 1970/71

Newspaper (in approx. order of class composition of readership)	Per cent of readers in class:					Charge for a single column inch advert, per each 100,000 copies of the paper in circulation	Circulation 1971 (av. number of copies sold of each issue) in 000s
	AB	C1	C2	DE	Total		
Financial Times	50	33	11	6	100	£ 7·44	175
Times	51	29	12	8	100	£ 3·73	402
Guardian	45	36	11	8	100	£ 3·30	303
Telegraph	45	32	14	9	100	£ 1·78	1,402
Mail	21	28	25	26	100	£ 1·20	1,917
Express	15	26	30	29	100	£ 0·91	3,607
Sketch	8	18	38	36	100	£ 1·24	806
Mirror	5	17	41	37	100	£ 0·92	4,697
Sun	4	15	42	39	100	£ 1·13	1,509

Sources: National Readership Survey 1970 (vol. 3, table 6); *Newspaper Press Directory 1971.*

Notes:

(i) The classes (those of the National Readership Survey) are defined in primarily occupational terms, as follows: *AB*, higher and intermediate manag./admin./profess; *C1*, junior manag., etc., supervisory, clerical; *C2*, skilled manual; *DE*, semi-and unskilled manual, state pensioners, etc.

(ii) The *Daily Sketch* closed in 1971. Its fate illustrates one of the points of the table. With a predominantly low-income readership, it was unable to attract advertising on a circulation of only about 800,000. Its advertising charges were then unrealistically high; but even at lower charges, so relatively small a circulation could not be expected to appeal to advertisers given the low average purchasing power of its readers.

(iii) The Communist Party *Morning Star* is not listed, because it carries very little commercial advertising and is financed in part by voluntary contributions raised by appeal among its readers (its circulation was and is about 50,000.)

(iv) Some deviations from a smooth downward gradient of advertising charges in the table – and from a smooth upward gradient of circulation figures – are to be expected: in part because the crude class readership data do not take account of corporate purchasing power controlled by readers (*Financial Times* and *Times*, in contrast to *Guardian* and *Telegraph*); in part because of special circumstances (*Sketch*, see note (ii) above; the *Sun* by contrast was on the point of expanding its circulation phenomenally and by 1972 had reached a figure of 2·6 million).

tion. The non-manual groups – classes AB and C1 of the market research classification used in table 22 – comprise only just over one-third of the population; yet there are four national dailies which draw about 80 per cent of their readership from these groups. (Indeed the same four papers take about half their readers from the top section – businessmen, administrators and professionals, who make up no more than a seventh of the population; and they are primarily oriented to such 'top' and 'near-top' people.) By contrast only three commercial newspapers in 1970/71 had a readership drawn in similarly predominant terms from the manual working class, who comprise two-thirds of the population; and of those the *Daily Sketch* died in 1971. Second, the conditions of survival in the working-class newspaper market impose a prescription for content, style and orientation that varies very little. The formulae by which the *Daily Mirror* and the *Sun* are produced are caricature versions of North-cliffe's formula for the early *Daily Mail*: scattered pockets of news and commentary mixed with feature articles, personalia and advice on private problems, sports, sex and entertainment material, pictures, and of course advertisements. The eyes of editors and the commercial press managers behind them are on what they believe to be the common denominators of interest – if only casual interest – among a 'mass' wage-earning public. 'Minority interests' cannot be catered for, even if the minorities run into six-or-seven-digit figures. The fate of newspapers outside the high advertising-charge 'quality' range, which have died despite circulations of 2 million and more, is an ever-present memory.

The image of the 'mass' reader to which the popular newspapers and magazines work is not totally unreal; but it is drastically selective. Most people, after all – capitalists and intellectuals as well as wage earners – are interested in sex and sensation; personalities and problems of private life; hobbies or home comforts; clothes and cars; entertainment and often sport. It is not – as the spokesmen of high culture disdainfully proclaim – that these and similar interests are the lowest common denominators of outlook in the bulk of the population. There is, in our view at least, nothing low or shameful about them. The point is that they are the only safe common denominators of interest to which press managers who need circulation figures in millions can appeal. The press with a working-class target does not give its readers 'what they want'. It gives them part of what they want; and it ignores whatever else they may want, because it is not securely within the area of common denomination.[26] Half a century or more of this sort of press diet, moreover, generates assumptions on all sides that there are no alternatives. Nor are there – so long as the press remains an integral part of a capitalist economy.

It needs emphasis that the compulsion to work to a selective image of readers and their interests is much greater in the case of 'popular' than of 'quality' newspapers. The content of the former tells one nothing of substance about the distinctive demands, sensitivities and cultural horizons of the readers of the popular press, though their expectations over time may well be coloured by what they have become used to be fed with. It tells one only that their purchasing power is of no interest to advertisers except in massive numbers. The hierarchical cultural structure of the Press is a product of economic inequality in a market system; and directly so, not obliquely. In this, as in other fields, the privileged escape the uniformity of mass production to which ordinary earners are confined.

The consequences for the political character of the popular press are as can be expected. Press controllers – newspaper barons or bureaucratic managers, and the editors whose livelihood is tied up with the commercial success of their business – are no more likely than other businessmen to be critical of the capitalist order. And while they usually take pride in disclaiming party links, most newspapers in the normal run of events lend support, not just to conservatism, but to the Conservative or perhaps the Liberal Party. A paper determined to maintain a predominantly working-class readership, however, has to take a different line. It imports a radical-sounding tone into commentary and reporting; and it may side in a general way with the Labour Party, as a deliberate measure of appeal to its market. It was this modification of the Northcliffe formula which made for the success of the *Daily Mirror* from around 1940, when it made a calculated switch to hunt for working-class circulation. But the *Mirror*'s radicalism does not go far. It is spasmodic, not systematic, and brings no continuity of information and argument to bear on its targets. Its prime targets, in any case, are not capital, property and business, but officialdom. Its ideological slant, such as it is, combines distrust of bureaucrats and large scale organizations – not least militant trade unions – with welfare reformism. The paper's

26. The Pilkington Committee (Committee on Broadcasting, *Report*, Cmnd. 1753, H.M.S.O., 1962) made the same argument strongly against regarding size of audience as an index of demand.

editorial loyalties are firmly within the framework of the 'mixed economy'; vociferously committed to partnership between capital, state and labour, and opposed to strikes as causing economic 'wreckage'; mainly behind right-wing Labour with occasional support for the Liberals. Its pretensions to iconoclasm – inconsistent as they are – are associated with a bluff, 'matey' style of address to readers, which has been well described as imitating the tone of working-class solidarity without its substance.[27]

Yet this – the non-commercially produced *Morning Star* apart – represents the left of the political spectrum covered by the national newspaper press.[28] The point needs qualification, it may be argued. The 'quality' press, though in editorial commitment normally Conservative or Liberal and never left of right-wing Labour, includes papers whose range of reportage and comment can be a good deal more critical than the 'left' of the popular press. That is true. But it is also of little consequence for the bulk of the ordinary wage-earning population. For, by style and language, the quality press is not directed to them; and barriers of style and language are powerful in a society where economic position and education are closely related. As in education itself, so also with respect to the press: liberal diversity is far more real for the privileged than for the majority who might be subverted by it.

One popular daily in the past maintained an explicit commitment to the Labour Party over several decades; allowed a wider range of Labour and radical views some voice, though its predominant leanings were to the centre and right of the movement; and attempted, until fairly late in its career, to mix a larger measure of political coverage into the Northcliffe prescription. This was the *Daily Herald*, jointly owned for much of its life by the T.U.C. and commercial publishers. Its circulation was around 2 million or more. But that still fell short of the level needed to continue to interest advertisers in its working-class readership. Pressed by its business management to trim its mild deviation from the Northcliffe formula, the *Herald* died in the 1960s. Instead there is now the *Sun*, which works to a still more entertainment-slanted and politically still emptier version of the *Mirror*'s variant of the formula.

Opposition to the established order of capitalism is certainly

27. R. Hoggart, *The Uses of Literacy*, Chatto & Windus, 1957.
28. The left-wing *Workers Press* also became a daily in the early 1970s but was then, as yet at least, hardly secure enough to be counted in with the national press.

widespread in the working class and the labour movement. But it is, of course, typically diffuse in character, and shot through with contradictory orientations of resignation or conformity. Active political interest and consistent left-wing dissent are minority phenomena. Even though the minority is large in absolute numbers, there is no secure basis here for a radical press, if it is to run commercially against the peculiar exigencies of the advertising market. And the labour movement in Britain – unlike that in some other capitalist countries – has been unwilling to pay the large and continuous subsidies which would be necessary if it were to maintain at least one clear voice for itself in the press. Quite apart from their natural political loyalties, commercial newspaper controllers have to play safe. And business safety in the low-income market – precarious in any case given competition for advertising from 'independent' television – requires undeviating appeal to what are seen as the common denominators of 'mass' taste. The margin is too slender to allow risks to be taken. When the labour movement opposed the Conservative government's war against Egypt in 1956, the *Mirror* swung from backing Labour to nationalist support of the invasion, as soon as it detected some fall in circulation. Odd exceptions apart, no commercial newspaper normally finds a word to say in sympathy with industrial militancy, however wide at times the support for militancy in the labour movement and the working class. The T.U.C.s solid and reasoned refusal to co-operate in Conservative incomes policy on the government's terms in 1972/73, for example, evoked stony moral disapproval from the press – not least from the *Mirror*. There was, proclaimed a banner headline in that paper, 'NO OTHER WAY' than to accept the government's 'package deal' as essentially fair. 'The public' – from which, plainly, the T.U.C. and most of its affiliated unions excluded themselves in their perversity – 'will not readily forgive anyone – on the Left or on the Right – whose only response is to snipe, jeer, and undermine.[29] The limits of the 'consensus' are tightly drawn when defined by a market-driven press.

VI

In broadcasting, too, the range of views and news given effective expression falls within some conception of a 'consensus'. Indeed this,

29. *Daily Mirror*, 18 Jan. 1973.

together with adherence to 'balance' and 'impartiality' within the consensus, is a formal requirement of either statute or internal written rules. But there is, of course, little in the way of correspondingly formal prescription to define what the limits of the consensus are – to lay down what will, and what will not, 'offend aganst good taste or decency, or be likely to encourage crime and disorder, or be offensive to public feeling'. There is no formula to distinguish impartiality from that neutrality 'between truth and untruth, justice and injustice, compassion and cruelty, tolerance and intolerance' which the rules condemn; to ensure that producers stay 'not only within the Constitution [but also] within the consensus about basic moral values'.[30] Occasional codification of past and current practice offers a few, though ambiguous, guidelines. Republican 'extremism' in Northern Ireland in the 1970s, according to the B.B.C. rules just quoted, was thus well outside the range of views that merit impartial treatment. Interviews with its representatives, for example, could be broadcast only 'after the most serious consideration' and in such form as to make clear the B.B.C.s opposition to their 'indiscriminate terrorist methods'. Deep political and industrial divisions nearer home may be regarded as falling within the consensus – or they may not. Labour's opposition to the Suez war in 1956, the rules point out approvingly, was handled as legitimate, despite government pressure on the B.B.C. to curtail publicity for its critics. But the rules also refer to Lord Reith's refusal in 1926 to broadcast anything which 'might have prolonged or sought to justify' the General Strike, while allowing 'authentic impartial news of the situation'. This is said to illustrate a principle still relevant, though capable of application with more 'latitude' today.[31] The unions placed themselves outside the B.B.C.s conception of the consensus in 1926. It is significant that the B.B.C. still quotes this as a precedent, while leaving its current interpretation ambiguous.

There are similar, if vaguer, rules within commercial television to

30. The phrases are those of an internal B.B.C. circular on 'Principles and practice in news and current affairs', June 1971.

31. As the circular points out, Lord Reith referred to a court judgment in which the General Strike was said to be illegal, in justifying the B.B.C.'s explicit support for the government in 1926. The circular does not point out that this judicial statement has later been seriously challenged by lawyers; nor does it emphasize that Reith's justification relied only in part on the judgment. For a general examination of B.B.C. policy in 1926 and reactions to it from the labour movement, as well as the text of Reith's memorandum, see A. Briggs, *The Birth of Broadcasting*, Oxford University Press, 1961 (pp. 360–84).

underline statutory requirements. But such formal prescriptions set only a few scattered signposts to the boundaries of what is curiously called the consensus. The limits of tolerance are certainly narrower, for practical purposes, than those signposts can show. Producers will generally play safe. They work to formulae – unwritten professional assumptions and modes of practice – that keep the content, tone and perspectives of most programmes within accepted moulds. Occasionally one or other may step outside the ring of orthodoxy – perhaps because constraint is more effective and less visible when a deviation now and then is tolerated; perhaps because the normal off-stage mechanisms of supervision break down. The sharp social critique of a programme on homelessness some years ago – 'Cathy Come Home' – is said, for example, to have slipped through the net because its form was that of a play, not a documentary. But most producers and controllers, most of the time, do not look for trouble. The limits of the 'consensus' are therefore rarely tested. To demonstrate where they lie and how they are enforced in continuous practice requires systematic inside observation of a kind which has yet to be done.[32]

The boundaries of tolerance, the scope for some expression of unorthodoxy, are undoubtedly wider in broadcasting than in the popular press. Commercial pressures are at work here too, of course: directly in the case of 'independent' broadcasting; indirectly in the case of the B.B.C., through its competition with I.T.V. and the compulsions to hunt for large audiences as a test of demand.[33] These

32. Our own very general comments here derive in large part from discussions with Brian Winston, for whose help based on long experience of television production we are most grateful. But see, e.g., A. Smith, *The Shadow in the Cave*, Allen & Unwin, 1973 (especially chaps. 3 and 11) and also S. Cohen and J. Young, eds., *The Manufacture of News*, Constable, 1973. Several points made in these are similar to ours, though the latter symposium discusses the manufacture of news primarily with reference to non-political deviance. J. D. Halloran, P. Elliott, G. Murdock, *Demonstrations and Communication*, Penguin, 1970, is a rare and very relevant example of a case study in news production (using both observation and content analysis of press as well as broadcast news). Cf. also, e.g., H. Gans' comments, from the USA, on the practical selective processes by which news programmes 'tend to emphasize the public activities of the upper and middle class élite, and the deviant activities of the lower classes and younger people', and concern themselves more with protestors' and demonstrators' altercations with the police than' with reporting their demands: 'The sociologist and the television journalist', in J. D. Halloran and M. Gurevitch, eds., *Broadcaster/Researcher-Co-operation in Mass Communication Research*, Kavanagh, 1971.

33. On the competition between B.B.C. and I.T.V. see, e.g., A.C.T.T. Television Commission, *Report to Annual Conference 1972*, A.C.T.T., 1972 (pp. 19ff.).

pressures put a premium on the broadcasting of programmes of safe 'mass' appeal, and on compensation for the expense of some productions through an extensive diet of cheap mid-Atlantic fare – including old films – in which usually no breath of radical social critique stirs.[34] But the prescription of 'balance' on news and current affairs programmes makes for some genuine diversity of expression. Moreover, the dominant ethos among media professionals, of the press as well as broadcasting, may well be liberal rather than conservative; and television and radio allow that ethos a voice, directly and indirectly, more than do the daily mass circulation newspapers. Right-wing attacks on broadcasters especially, for putting 'established' values in question, are not without some substance. Yet the liberalism against which such attacks are directed is just that: liberal. It is culturally broadminded and anti-puritanical. It may reflect both current fashions of intellectual scepticism and generous concerns with personal freedom, with tolerance of individual deviance. It may look critically at authority as it does often at tradition. But the targets of its scepticism do not, and cannot, usually include the unspoken premises of the current economic order. The professional formulae for good journalism and effective broadcasting, moreover, also work against sustained presentation of views critical of those premises. Dramatic incident is 'better news' for mass audiences than argument of a case. So strikes and demonstrations can get into the news, but little in the ordinary run of things about what lies behind them. Personalities are taken to have more appeal than politics. So a left-wing individual may be picked out by the media, made a national or international figure, accredited even with a 'leadership' doubtfully recognized by those who share his views; but the case which he represents is likely to go largely by default.

Our argument is not, in short, that there is no diversity of expression in the media. There is, and in broadcasting more effectively than in the daily press. But this is still diversity within significant limits: within limits set by professional conceptions of what is good journalism, of what 'works' when audiences must be kept large; within the limits, in the main, of a consensus silently defined by broadcasting controllers and routinely practised by producers. To show those limits one needs systematic and qualitatively sensitive content analysis of programmes, as well as detailed studies of what goes into and what is left out of their production. Since these have not yet been

34. Cf. Murdock and Golding, op. cit. (note 25 above).

undertaken, our argument here is impressionistic. But it seems plain enough that, in selection of news and background information, in tone of commentary and camera direction, in the emphases of interviewers and discussion-chairmen, in choice of spokesmen, the broadcasting media are not 'neutral' between those who accept and those who appear to threaten the established order: for example, between militant workers and 'moderates'. The media's common use of the latter label, to describe the right wing of the labour movement, is by itself indicative.

To talk of freedom of communication in these circumstances is to mistake form for substance. There is freedom only for those who can put the effective means of public communication, the mass media, to their own use. Ordinary people certainly cannot do that: the media communicate only one way, so far as the bulk of the population are concerned.[35] Even journalists, broadcasting producers and other professional staff in the industry work within constraints which are not of their own making. They are subject to a censorship that is no less effective for taking place off-stage. There is, of course, censorship of other kinds, closer to the sense in which the term is ordinarily used: in the sense, that is, of restrictions on communication imposed by direct public authority. The government has, for example, discretion to issue so-called D-notices to 'discourage' publication of news on matters which it deems to involve security. It can withhold information normally given to journalists from those who have lost favour with it, by excluding them from press conferences, ministerial briefings, the press lobby in Parliament and circulation lists for material. It exercises blatant political discrimination as a matter of course by refusing to publish government advertising in the Communist *Morning Star*. The law of defamation, obscenity and contempt of court is notoriously elastic; and fear of its application leads to far more restraint in publication than the number of cases taken to court

35. The B.B.C. in 1973 started a television series, *Open Door*, designed to give voluntary groups a chance to broadcast their own programmes (initially late at night for 40–45 minutes a week, though a repeat showing was subsequently provided at lunchtime on Sundays.) Even this tiny breach in the professional monopoly was hedged around with safeguards. Groups given time would not be allowed 'to promote a political party or group, or to pursue an industrial dispute' (*The Times*, 16 February 1973). A B.B.C. spokesman was quoted as saying, in elaboration of this ruling that 'while political people could not advocate their political policies they might get on to talk about something else . . . a group of nihilists might be allowed to put on a programme about the need for more playgrounds but not to preach nihilism' (*Morning Star*, 16 February 1973).

would indicate.[36] But though it is not conventionally recognized as such, the *de facto* power of censorship exercised by press and broadcasting controllers every day is much more important and pervasive. That power is taken for granted. It is legitimized merely by the fact of control. Newspaper editors have indignantly accused printing workers of censorship, on the rare occasions when the workers have refused to print some malevolent anti-labour comment or cartoon.[37] Yet the operative censorship is that, routinely applied under the authority of the media controllers, which effectively limits the circulation of news and views out of tune with the core assumptions of the established order.

All this, it has been argued, may matter very little because communication through the media is ineffective. A mass of socio-psychological research, experimental and quasi-experimental, shows that people select what they read, hear and see to fit in with perspectives and assumptions which are set in their minds beforehand. Ideas and perceptions, it is concluded, are therefore not readily amenable to change by newspapers, television and radio.[38] There is point to this argument, in so far as it underlines the resistances built in from other sources towards persuasion by the media in any direct and immediate manner. The impact of the media cannot be crudely inferred from their content. But that is also as far as the argument goes. No research of this kind can cope with the question of the long-term effects of exposure to the media. While empirical measurement is

36. On these and other forms of censorship, see P. O'Higgins, *Censorship in Britain*, Nelson, 1972. Two illustrations of the effects of judicial powers of censorship may be worth mention. *Private Eye*, a magazine which specializes in news, gossip and caustic comment about public figures and the inside stories of public affairs, is regularly faced with suits for libel. As a result of two such cases, it was compelled to agree not in future to criticize the *Daily Express* and the *New Statesman* or their editors. (O'Higgins, op. cit., pp. 117–18). In July 1973, the Law Lords ruled that publication by the *Sunday Times* of an article summarizing evidence that Distillers Company (Biochemicals) had exercised insufficient care in putting the drug thalidomide on the market, twelve years earlier, would constitute contempt of court, although the litigation against the company had been in abeyance for several years, pending settlement out of court, and was highly unlikely ever to be revived. (*The Times*, Law Report for 18 July 1973.)

37. See, e.g., O'Higgins, op. cit., pp. 120–22.

38. J. T. Klapper, *The Effects of Mass Communication*, Free Press, 1960, though not now up to date, is a valuable and extensive review of research in this field. But see also, e.g., C. Seymour-Ure, *The Political Impact of Mass Media*, Constable, 1974, which argues, by illustration from particular instances in recent politics, that the mass media do exercise influence in a variety of ways, in conjunction with other factors and circumstances: not through some uniformly effective force of their own alone.

impossible on this point, it is implausible that there is no cumulative impact of the media over time: that the media have no influence as one of the sources from which the 'frameworks of perception', within which people see the world, are themselves built up.

The media are the more likely to have such influence because, with their near-monopoly of effective public communication, they have the power to withhold as well as to transmit information. There is considerable social significance to that power. An image of strikes as irrational, for example – other people's strikes, not those in which the reader or viewer has himself taken part – receives cumulative support from the normal failure of the media to explore their sources and background, even to explain their immediate causes and the strikers' demands. Again, to take a recent particular example, the media withheld virtually all news about an extensive though scattered campaign of rent strikes in 1972/73 against the newly introduced Housing Finance Act. No doubt press and broadcasting silence was not a prime cause of the collapse of the campaign. The failure of the official labour movement to support it was a much more important factor. But the almost total silence of the media must have contributed to demoralizing the campaigners. For each group of strikers acted with only rudimentary knowledge, if any, of similar actions elsewhere. And the fact of protest went unrecorded for most people except, where there were rent strikes, as a local phenomenon. So, by simple omission of news, a brushstroke was added to the picture of society as harmonious; a patch in that picture was covered up which, if visible, could have encouraged dissenting views. The maintenance of dissent requires the knowledge that others, too, dissent; and knowledge of why they dissent. The power to withhold such knowledge must be among the most important elements in the influence of the established media. In general, they strengthen the order as it is far more by omission than by transmission.[39]

VII

Predominant power, to sum up, lies with a ruling interest whose core is big business. The strength of business is manifest in its ties with a

39. Another notable example of this is the virtually unanimous and consistent media presentation of the Soviet Union as poised to start military aggression against the West at the time of the cold war, a view for which the evidence – to put it mildly – was not good. Counter-evidence was rarely transmitted.

variety of other influential groups and bodies: directly with the Conservative Party, the commercial press and a range of pressure groups; less directly but none the less effectively with the machinery of state and the broadcasting media. These links are formed in part as bonds of common experience among top people. But the power of the ruling interest is founded in the set of common assumptions which govern the routine workings of economy, government and mass communications. Those assumptions – the core assumptions of the society – indicate the central place of business, because they are business assumptions: principles of property, profit and market dominance in the running of affairs.

The relationship of the labour movement to this cluster of power is crucial. We discuss this in more detail later, when we take up the question of the character and sources of working-class response to capitalist dominance (Part Five). But the ambivalence of that response needs to be underlined already here. Labour's interests are inherently opposed to the business interests that prevail; dissent is inherent in its place in the order of things as they are. But labour's dissent in fact has a dual character. For the most part in practice – in the normal activities of the Labour Party and the bargaining of unions with employers – it is conservative dissent. It is aimed, not to overthrow or disrupt the core institutions of capitalism, but to moderate their operation within terms of reference that assume the continuity of private property and market mechanisms. The movement, in this predominant role, plays the part of loyal opposition and occasional alternative government; of principal protagonist for policies designed to improve capitalist efficiency through extensive engagement of the state in affairs.

But it is a fundamental misconception to believe that this, for all purposes that matter, exhausts the part played by labour. Labour dissent has not been fully tamed by the institutionalization of conflict. There is always a risk to capital that the elaborate structure of compromise may break down, which normally contains dispute and labour counter-pressure within capitalist terms of reference. The structure of compromise in fact crumbles at the fringe in small ways all the time – whenever workers refuse to abide by agreements; or when they press demands for wages and job control to a point where, if multiplied, those demands might break the system. At times the risk of breakdown appears to become critical. It did so in the late 1960s and early 1970s when, with pre-tax profits continuing to fall or showing uncertain prospects, the established union movement began to join shop-floor militants in strikes, while government measures to hold back wage increases and to discipline labour gave a political content to every industrial dispute. The institutionalization of class conflict is central to the continued predominance of capital; the possibility that it may disintegrate an ever-present threat – mostly latent, sometimes manifest.

PART FOUR

INEQUALITIES OF OPPORTUNITY

1 Social mobility: significance and measurement

I

It is a widespread assumption that Western societies today allow a great deal more movement of individuals up and down the socio-economic ladder than they used to, say, a hundred, fifty or just thirty years ago. This is a common belief at least about European countries, including Britain. In the case of the United States, it has quite often been suggested, social fluidity in that sense was at a peak during much of the nineteenth and perhaps into the twentieth century. It may then have declined after the opportunities to acquire new land on the frontier of settlement had dried up; and as the growth of big business in the cities cut into the chances of 'make or break' from small beginnings in independent enterprise. Be that as it may, the usual image of America is still that of an 'open society' where individual movement up and down the scale is more free than in the older countries of Europe, especially when a blind eye is turned to the mobility handicaps of black Americans. And on both sides of the Atlantic, it is commonly believed, improvements in educational opportunity are making for a new trend towards higher rates of social circulation. True, the complacency on that score characteristic of the 1950s and early 1960s has given way, by and large, to a more realistic recognition of continuing obstacles to 'equal opportunity' in education; and to a series of attempts to direct policy to reducing them. Yet that recognition has generally only moderated the assumption of increasing social mobility; not removed it.

The premise that individuals are markedly less tied to a particular socio-economic level from birth to death than they were a generation or two ago, is built into a great deal of commentary about contemporary society – professional and lay commentary alike. Inferences of different character and tone are drawn from that premise. In some, the emphasis is negative. One consequence is said to be a loss of personal anchorage, for example, from which in turn a variety of 'problems' are believed in part to flow: from neuroses and 'identity crises' to drug addiction and student unrest. In others – and there is no necessary contradiction – the emphasis is positive. Capitalism is taken to lose a good part of its sting in so far as wage-earning dependency is not a fixed and inherited condition. Class barriers are seen as dissolving, the more individuals can move across them in the course of their lives; as people at different socio-economic levels in consequence acquire ties of family and acquaintance across the face of the social structure; as the possibility of movement helps to generate personal aspirations among workers that either they, or at least their children, may be able to reach the security of supervisory, managerial or professional positions. Classes in this view are replaced by 'strata', fluid at the boundaries and interlocked by a steadily gathering flow of people between them. The basic premise that mobility has been and is increasing in this way is itself rarely examined, except by professional sociologists. And even many of these are inclined to forget the question marks which research results set against this picture, when they pronounce upon the general condition and prospects of modern Western societies.

II

There are important issues here. But they are not so central as the attention which they often attract may suggest. The questions which they raise are necessarily of a secondary kind. They concern the recruitment of people to classes; not the brute fact of the existence of class. It is that which is primary. If there were no inequality of condition and power – no privilege and no contrasting dependence – there would, plainly, be no questions to ask about who becomes privileged and who dependent. Conversely, when there is such inequality, the answers to those questions tell one little by themselves about the nature of privilege and dependence. Capital is concentrated and carries power in Britain, whatever the proportions of the wealthy who have inherited their wealth or, by extreme and uncommon contrast, have come straight from rags to riches. The labour market and a class-skew system of tax and welfare provision dictate the conditions of workers without property, whatever the precise mixture of social origins among them. Subsidiary though it is, however, the question of recruitment has come to take an often over-riding place in discussion about class, especially when discussion is directed to policy. Sometimes this preoccupation goes to the point where the rate of social circulation appears to be regarded as the main test of class. Low mobility is then seen almost as the identifying mark of a class-divided society; high mobility as the hallmark of a state of near-classlessness. What matters in practice, from this restricted viewpoint, is the extent to which power, privilege and their opposites are inherited. Never mind if these contrasts of social condition persist as sharply as before, it is implied, provided that advantage and disadvantage are achieved by personal 'merit' rather than acquired and retained by accident of birth. Indeed, some sociologists who take this line have applied the label 'egalitarian' to deeply divided capitalist societies, because one traditional stand in the public ideology of those societies pays lip-service to an ideal of equal opportunity and free circulation of talent.[1] So entrenched inequality of condition is pushed out of mind by an overriding concern with questions of personnel recruitment. And even the realities of recruitment may take second place, from this kind of perspective, behind a dream of 'opportunity'.

The dream, of course, is distinctively American, though it has spread. 'Equality' has come to mean different things in America and in Europe. In the United States the notion for long has been conventionally thought of as 'equality of opportunity'. The ideal then is seen as a state of affairs where each individual would find his own level in the hierarchy of inequality, according only to his abilities and drive, regardless of his parentage and the circumstances of his early life. There is no challenge in that notion to the existence of hierarchy itself. The European conception of equality, by contrast, incorporates just such a challenge. In some interpretations here, too, equality has

1. The United States is thus often described as egalitarian (or 'equalitarian') for this reason and the related one that everyday deference to social rank is said to be less in America than in Europe. Cf. the work of S. M. Lipset, e.g., 'The value patterns of democracy', *Amer. Sociological Rev.*, August 1963; and K. B. Mayer, 'Social stratification in two equalitarian societies: Australia and the United States', *Social Research*, Winter 1964. There is, of course, a mass of evidence – some of which we refer to elsewhere in this book – to show the depth and tenacity of substantive inequalities in American society. For Australia, see S. Encel, *Equality and Authority: A Study of Class, Status and Power in Australia*, Melbourne, Cheshire, 1970.

been narrowly defined, to mean only equal opportunity. But other interpretations have pushed the definition well beyond that. The ideal then is 'equality of condition': the eradication of all significant divisions of power, wealth and security.

The cross-Atlantic contrast in conceptions of equality is associated with fundamental differences of political complexion. It is the labour movements in Europe which have given the ideal of equality of condition its political and organizational impetus. The ideal, on the whole, has been only inchoately expressed by the social-democratic wing that has dominated labour politics in North-Western Europe; and it has not been translated into policy when social-democratic governments have been in office. But it has had, and still has, force as a hope for the indefinite future. As such, it helps to prevent a total encapsulation of labour in the politics of compromise on capitalist premises. The continuing emotional appeal of socialist egalitarianism within the British labour movement, for example, was evident when even the staid Labour Party centre and most of the established unions in the early 1960s set their face against right-wing proposals to abandon the party's formal commitment to full public ownership as a long-term objective. It was evident again in the pressures that led the party conference in 1973, reacting against Labour's record in office in the 1960s, to adopt a programme which, on paper at least, promised further nationalization and measures to redistribute wealth. In Britain, as elsewhere in Europe, labour has thus given at least hesitant voice to a fraternal conception of equality: to an image of some future society where resources would be shared, and their product distributed according to need – not according to 'merit' as established by competition, let alone according to the possession of property. Hollow though that conception may look in practice, its survival even in symbolic form provides something of an ideological springboard for a radicalization of dissent and militancy. It may at the same time reduce the appeal of the alternative and more restricted conception of equality: that of equality of competitive individual opportunity. If British by comparison with American workers seem less concerned with personal aspirations to 'make good' – as American commentators often say, for example – at least part of the explanation lies in the political contrasts between labour here and there. Their ambitions in practice usually restricted to far more mundane concerns, workers here have nevertheless been influenced by a folklore of hope for some future transformation of society, through collective political struggle, towards a condition of structural equality in which the very notion of competitive rivalry for privilege would make no sense. Not so in the United States. Organized labour there has not formed a political movement; and it has not therefore given collective support to a socialist definition of equality, to challenge a capitalist conception of 'equal opportunity'.

Paradoxical though it may sound, the notion of equal opportunity has indeed capitalist inspiration. And it is quite compatible with capitalism, provided that it remains an ideal the implementation of which is not too diligently pursued. Historically, the ethos of bourgeois enterprise asserted the right – and also the duty – of individuals to make their own way in the world, free of old restraints on trade and movement of labour, and in defiance of inherited privilege and handicap. Opportunity and corresponding risk were to be renewed in each generation. The justification was not only equity, but efficiency as well. Society at large would gain, in aggregate wealth no less than in aggregate individual freedom, from an unhampered deployment of talent and initiative in open competition. Yet the conception, of course, was shot through with a contradiction inherent in the nature of capitalism. Wealth and power accumulated in one generation – poverty and dependence too – would be transmitted to the next generation by direct descent. The young would never start from scratch, each with only his 'natural' endowment of ability and drive to place him in the race.

Apologists for capitalism point out that some transmission of privilege and handicap from generation to generation is inevitable, so long as there is any kind of inequality at all. And indeed they are right. Only equality of condition would make full equality of opportunity possible – and would then make the whole notion of equal opportunity irrelevant. But capitalism's liberal defence counsel are unconvincing when they go on to suggest that public policy has at least symbolically disavowed inequality of opportunity, by removing all formal and legally sanctioned barriers to free competition among individuals for position; that what now remains to be done is to cut down a residuum of real but informal barriers of culture, influence, know-how and so on that still impede the achievement of equal opportunity. In fact, restrictions on free circulation – barriers to equal opportunity – remain legally entrenched in capitalist societies. Private property rights are the foundation of capitalism, and are solidly protected in law. They include the right to transmit wealth by inheritance and gift from one generation to the next; and the right of parents to use wealth, if they have it, to buy private education for their children. Inequality of opportunity – the inheritance of competitive advantage and handicap – is not just an obdurate fact of life, to which the letter and spirit of public policy might be said to be opposed. It is a principle of law. The state in capitalist society explicitly affirms the right of privilege to breed privilege, through its legal sanctification of property.

Of course the call for equality of opportunity – an ostensible objective of official educational policy in this country since 1944, and the focus of much reforming zeal and research effort – is not usually intended to be taken literally. The goal in reality is more modest: to open the routes through school and college to an easier flow of talent. In all logic this requires encouragement of a two-way flow: upwards for children of high ability but low social origin, downwards for those of low ability but high origin. And, in principle, the public educational system is now supposed to act more as a sieve through which all its students are sorted according to capacity, than just as a ladder for the most able pupils of humble background to climb. But an emphasis in reform on encouraging the downward flow evokes understandably vehement opposition from the privileged groups of the population, whose opportunities to transmit their privilege to their children would be impaired thereby. Hence, for example, the survival so far of private education with state protection; hence, too, much of the resistance to 'comprehensive' reorganization of secondary schooling. The upward flow of talent is then correspondingly inhibited: the consequences of capitalist privilege are at war with the demands of capitalist efficiency. So long as they are formulated with the modesty which this tug of war necessitates, however, measures to make better use of the 'pool of talent' in each generation, by stepping up social circulation, make good practical sense for the smoother working of economy and society. No serious challenge to the present order is entailed.

III

High and rising rates of social mobility would thus in no way signify a dissolution of capitalism, an erosion of its class structure. But the issues involved still need to be explored, even though they are not so crucial as is often implied. Inequalities of prospective opportunity between those who are born and brought up, or start their working lives, at different levels of the socio-economic hierarchy are one among the many sets of inequality that characterize a class-divided society. To map the contours of the society one needs also to map such inequalities of opportunity: their range and extent; the points of the social structure at which they are most evident; the degree to which the major barriers to mobility may fall along the same prime dividing lines as are set by inequalities of wealth, income, security and power; trends of change, if any, in these and related respects. A central focus of interest must be the possible implications of social mobility and immobility for people's responses to their class situation: for class consciousness and class organization. There is a long-standing and widespread idea that circulation of individuals and families among the different levels of an otherwise divided society acts as a kind of safety valve to keep the pressures of discontent low. Hopes among the unprivileged may then, it is assumed, be centred on personal achievement rather than on collective resistance, rebellion or revolution. Anxieties may be focused on the risk of individual failure; and failure itself may be ascribed by those who experience it to adversity, shortcomings or 'bad luck' peculiar to themselves, rather than to 'the system'. The sense of shared experience and common prospects among the victims of inequality could thus be weakened, and a precondition for radical mass dissent undermined. Internal fragmentation of labour as a political force could be accentuated further in so far as social circulation makes for ties of kinship, personal acquaintance, cultural emulation and social sympathy across the lines of class division.

The numerical facts of social mobility and immobility will not, by themselves, provide a test of the 'safety valve' hypothesis. Popular perceptions may diverge from reality. There is, for example, by some important measures no more fluidity of social circulation in the United States than in Britain. But Americans and others commonly believe there to be; and American beliefs to that effect, whatever their sources, have no doubt helped to hold labour there back from political opposition to the capitalist order. The empirical arithmetic of social mobility must nevertheless set some broad limits to ideologies and perceptions of mobility. Working-class hopes of individual achievement could hardly survive, for example, if they were practically never realized. The first job, therefore, must be to see whether they are; in general, to pull together evidence from a variety of sources about the scale and modes of personal movement up and down the class structure. There is now, in fact, a good deal more information available about this than there was just twenty-five years ago. There are also limitations on the data which need to be outlined before a summary picture can be put together.

The first limitation concerns the time span for which comprehensive evidence can be obtained. Official records – censuses, population registers and the like – rarely contain the information from which social mobility in the population at large could be reconstructed for long periods in the past.[2] Data can often be assembled to show historical patterns of recruitment into particular élite and professional groups. But studies of social circulation in the wider population usually have to rely on information – mainly through sample interviews – from living respondents about their own, and in part their parents', experience. Since most of the relevant research is recent, changes in general patterns of mobility cannot normally be traced far back beyond the turn of the century. More important perhaps, while much debate implicitly turns on the issue of emergent trends of mobility, the information obtainable necessarily relates to past experience: to the experience of those who are at least well set in their working lives when they are interviewed. What will happen to those who are then still too young cannot, by definition, yet be known – though some inferences may be drawn from their educational experience; the more so, the more formal educational qualifications come to set the normal limits of occupational achievement. In that sense, hard facts about social circulation always tend to lag behind current controversy. The main sources on which we can draw for the British population at large, moreover, are national studies undertaken in 1949 and 1959: the results of a large-scale survey in 1971/72 were not yet available in any detail at the time of writing. For all that, the main features in the pattern of mobility are unlikely to have altered drastically over little more than a decade; and the limited evidence already available suggests just that.

The second limitation concerns the definition of groups or cate-

---

2. A few studies have drawn on official records for data on social circulation in the population at large. Cf. G. Carlsson, *Social Mobility and Class Structure*, Lund, Gleerup, 1955 (Swedish population registers) and B. Benjamin, 'Intergeneration differences in occupation', *Population Studies*, March 1958 (census schedules and birth registers, used in conjunction, for this country).

gories between which movement is measured. Not least for practical reasons, mobility research has concentrated on circulation of individuals between broad occupational categories. To attempt instead to trace the movement of people over time between categories of the population defined, for example, directly in terms of property ownership and market earnings would hardly be feasible. Few respondents could give reasonably accurate information in retrospect about their own and their parents' financial histories; and the translation of monetary data for different periods to a common standard would present great difficulties. The result is, however, that the tiny minority in whose hands large wealth and concomitant power are concentrated cannot normally – except in one or two special studies of the transmission of property by inheritance – be separately identified.

There is still the question of how the occupational categories between which individual movement is traced are defined. The convention in post-war research has been to distinguish between occupational bands of different 'social status' – that is, of different 'public' esteem, however that in turn then is assessed. In our view, this practice is dubious both in value and validity. There is a risk entailed of combining, within one 'status' band, groups with quite different positions in the apparatus of production: small entrepreneurs of the 'old middle classes' with salaried managers and with professionals deemed to enjoy equivalent prestige, for example. Issues connected with the historical transformation of the economy – and with possible differences in the ideology and culture of such different groups – may thus be obscured.[3] In so far as classifications of occupations by their relative 'status' have been based on popular opinion as assessed in surveys, moreover, it is doubtful whether the gradings produced in fact reflect 'social esteem'. It is more likely that the people questioned by and large have ranked the occupations listed for them in order of a whole range of advantages and disadvantages – earnings, security and others – seen to be associated with each job. 'Prestige' in practice seems to be only one criterion among several which people use in such ratings, and is not readily

3. T. Geiger, who with D. V. Glass played a major part in promoting research on social mobility on a comparative scale after World War II, put this point among others in a general argument against categorization of occupations in a 'status' (or any other 'vertical') scale in connection with analysis of social circulation. Cf. his *Soziale Umschichtungen in einer dänischen Mittelstadt*, Aarhus University, 1951.

identifiable as a separate element.[4] In so far as it does come into the picture, moreover, ostensible public agreement about the 'status' of different occupations implies no consensus about moral values: there is no agreement that the hierarchy – whether of esteem or for that matter of material rewards – is as it should be.[5]

All this matters little by itself in this context, provided that the occupational groupings distinguished in social mobility studies are recognized for what they are. It certainly makes more sense, in our view, to trace the movements of people during their lifetimes between positions generally regarded as offering this or that net balance of advantages and disadvantages than between positions unequal just in 'honour'. That still often leaves the definition of socio-economic categories between which movement is measured a matter of opinion polling. Relevant though that can be, it may frustrate examination of mobility between groups objectively distinct by reference to their place in the structure of production and power, regardless of how people 'in general' see them. But the dominant minority with massive wealth and influence – at most a few per cent of the population, to take the evidence which we have underlined earlier – is in any case too small a group to be separately identified, for detailed inquiry, through sampling on the normal scale. For the rest, the occupational classifications used in most mobility research are serviceable as a rough and ready guide to overall differences in socio-economic position, so far as the bulk of the population goes.[6]

4. Cf. J. H. Goldthorpe and K. Hope, 'Occupational grading and occupational prestige', in K. Hope, ed., *The Analysis of Social Mobility*, Oxford, Clarendon Press, 1972.

5. Cf. M. Young and P. Willmott, 'Social grading by manual workers', *Brit. J. Sociology*, Dec. 1956; R. H. Turner, 'Life situation and subculture', *Brit. J. Sociology*, Dec. 1958.

6. We do not take the view that the term '*social* mobility' should be reserved for movement as assessed consistently in several 'dimensions' of inequality and accompanied by cultural absorption of the mobile individuals into the group of destination. The prescription is impracticable, and confuses questions of objective class position with questions concerning interpersonal acceptance and rejection. But whatever the terms used, it should be clear that movement from one level of the occupational hierarchy to another does not necessarily entail cultural absorption – indeed perhaps rarely does so fully. We should also underline the point that we are concerned in the discussion that follows with individual mobility – not with movement of whole groups from one level to another of the socio-economic hierarchy (as in the case, for example, of clerical workers, who have come down the scale by some measures; or of successful establishment of a claim to the privileges of 'professional' status on the part of an occupational group, often an example of collective upward mobility).

Two further points follow. First, just because the occupational classifications adopted are rather rough and ready – as well as for practical reasons, relating not least to sample size – the number of socio-economic bands distinguished may vary from one study to another. Because of that in turn, the sheer quantity of movement up and down the scale recorded will vary, too: the more finely graded the scale, the larger the apparent volume of mobility. There is, on that score alone, no single measure of 'the rate' of social circulation. Second, velocities of circulation may well differ from one point of the scale to another; and their significance may differ still more. One might find, for example, that a large amount of circulation between skilled and other levels of the wage-earning population went together with little exchange of personnel between these and 'higher' groups. If so, the pattern of mobility might reinforce a sense of identity and common experience among wage earners, rather than undermine it. By contrast, marked barriers to movement between one level and another within the wage-earning population, especially if accompanied by a low threshold of mobility between its top stratum and the groups above them, would lend weight to the 'safety valve' hypothesis. So, again, there can be no single, simple measures of mobility. Social circulation is not a uniform phenomenon, measurable in aggregate volume or by counts that equate a step up or down at one point of the scale with a step in the same direction at another point of the scale.

Finally, there are factors of an arithmetical kind which set limits, both upper and lower, to the range of movement that can occur. For example, there have long been variations between socio-economic groups in their rates of natural reproduction. From the 1870s – perhaps earlier – to the middle years of the twentieth century, married couples in the non-manual strata on average had fewer children than those in the manual, especially the least skilled, groups. These class differentials in fertility were sufficient, moreover, to outweigh the fact that working-class children were – as they still are – more exposed to the risk of dying before they grew up than other children. So, unless the ratio of non-manual to manual jobs had been shrinking concomitantly, some upward movement from the manual working class had to occur in each generation to make up for the relatively low rate of natural replacement among non-manual families.[7] In recent years, however, the pattern of class differences in

7. See D. V. Glass and J. R. Hall, 'A study of inter-generational changes in

fertility appears to have been changing. Married couples of the skilled working class show signs now of having smaller families than the current average, semi-skilled manual couples following them at a level only little over the average. By contrast, the professional groups now have higher than average fertility, and may be heading a trend in that direction on the part of many other non-manual couples as well – those in the managerial and executive groups, though not routine-grade and low-paid white-collar workers. Already among couples marrying in the 1940s, average family size can now be seen to be less than 20 per cent larger in the case of manual than of non-manual couples, whereas the manual 'surplus' had been of the order of 40 per cent in marriages of earlier decades.[8] With a continuation of these trends, the overall differential may be evened out, and could even be reversed. If so, upward mobility will no longer get the boost which it has had before from the relative shortfall of births in the professional, executive and supervisory groups of the population. Indeed, downward mobility might get an extra push instead.

The earlier boost to upward movement from differential rates of natural replacement reinforced – and the emergent new trend may partly counteract – another set of influences on the parameters of social circulation. In Britain, as in other industrial countries, the shape of the occupational structure has shifted fairly steadily over time. With a growth of 'tertiary sector' economic activity – of distribution, sales and sales promotion, of non-domestic services, of administrative, supervisory and ancillary work, including the effects of the extension of state activities – non-manual jobs have increased their share of the total. That of manual jobs, unskilled and casual jobs in particular, has been contracting. By conventional criteria, the process represents an upward shift in the weight of the occupational structure; and that shift in turn has then added to upward social mobility, since new positions in the middle and upper ranges of the scale have had to be staffed in each generation.

status', in D. V. Glass, ed., *Social Mobility in Britain*, Routledge & Kegan Paul, 1954 (pp. 197–8).

8. D. V. Glass, 'Components of natural increase in England and Wales', *Population Studies* (Supplement, 'Towards a Population Policy for the United Kingdom'), May 1970; and calculations of our own from Census of England and Wales 1961, *Fertility Tables*.

IV

This process has often been described in terms which imply a significant contribution on that score to an alleged conversion of society to a 'middle class' shape. A characterization of this sort both distorts and exaggerates, to a degree familiar from other lines of argument to similar conclusions.

First, the shift towards white-collar work has affected women far more than men: it has, in effect, been predominantly a shift toward 'white-blouse' work. The share of non-manual work in all jobs rose from under a third in 1921 to well over half by 1971 in the case of women – an increase by a factor of about three-fourths over fifty years. (Table 23.) But the increase was much more moderate in the case of men, both absolutely and proportionately: from roughly a quarter in 1921 to somewhat over a third in 1971 – a rise in the white-collar ratio by a factor of only one in two or so over the half-century. It is true that in recent years, as the figures from 1961 onwards show, the shift has been rather faster on the male than on the female side of the labour force. Yet the process has gone nowhere near so far as is often implied. It is quite misleading to point – as so many commentators do – to the fact that nearly half the working population now are in non-manual jobs. For while a majority of working women have jobs that can be so described, over three in every five men are still manual workers, 'blue-collar' workers in American terminology, even by conventional definitions of job boundary lines. And it is still men's occupational positions far more than women's that set the essential circumstances of life for most households, however much one may deplore this. True, it is conceivable that a manual worker's wife who has a secretarial or clerical job may bring home some of the outlook and values of the 'white-collar world' in which she works. But that possibility is so far pure speculation. It slides lightly over the point that she is often only a part-timer; and it begs a whole series of questions – including questions concerning the character and level of work into which office-employed wives of manual workers usually go – to which the answers are not known. The more routine, standardized, and devoid of promotion prospects and contact with superiors the job is, the less likely is any such transfer of bourgeois social perspectives from work to home. By contrast, the continuing preponderance of manual work among men – the chief earners in most households still – is hard fact. And it needs to be underlined in the face of glib references to an alleged shift of the job structure into a 'middle class' mould.

Such references are misplaced for a second, and more important, reason. This is that they imply acceptance of the conventional distinction between manual and non-manual work at its face value. They thereby equate all non-manual work, attaching an implicit or explicit 'middle class' tag to all such jobs without regard to their level and character, their pay, prospects, security, power and its obverse. In fact, as we have stressed earlier (Part Two, chapters 5 and 6) routine non-manual jobs now generally offer men worse pay than skilled and even semi-skilled manual work. How far low-grade white-collar jobs may still retain some of the other advantages which in the past helped to mark men who held them off from the world of 'blue-collar' work, is not at all clear. But promotion prospects have almost certainly declined over time for those who start their working lives at this level. Women clerical workers have not slipped down the occupational scale in the same way that their male colleagues have; and in London, in recent years, their labour has been at a premium in the market. But overall, the distance – in terms of pay and probably also chances of advancement – between them and women in supervisory, executive and semi-professional positions has widened. In short, by objective criteria of market circumstances and work conditions, routine non-manual jobs are now closer to manual wage-earning jobs than they were. In some crucial respects, the conditions they offer rank below those in many manual jobs. While that leaves open the question how low-grade white-collar workers may respond to this progressive proletarianization of their condition, it plainly makes no sense to label them 'middle class' in the way that convention still does, and as many occupational classifications do by implication; let alone to turn a blind eye to the very marked differences in circumstances between them and the wide range of intermediate and higher levels above them.

The point is crucial. For much of the shift into white-collar work has involved an expansion of just this kind of routine labour. This is particularly evident in the case of women. The share of clerical, secretarial and related low-grade non-manual jobs among all jobs held by women more than doubled over the fifty years from 1921 to 1971. But the share of jobs above that level – mainly minor executive

TABLE 23

Changes in occupational structure, 1921–1971

23A. *England & Wales, 1921–1961*

Occupational Groups (special classification)	Occupied Men		Occupied Women		Change in ratio
	1921 %	1961 %	1921 %	1961 %	*1961 share expressed as per cent of 1921 share*
					Men — Women
NON-MANUAL					
Major profess., senior admin./ manag.	4·2 ⎫	4·8 ⎫	2·0 ⎫	0·9 ⎫	⎫
Minor profess., other intermed, non-manual	10·9 ⎬ 15·1	13·5 ⎬ 18·3	13·4 ⎬ 15·4	15·3 ⎬ 16·2	⎬ 121 105
Routine non-manual (clerical, sales)	9·4	12·2	16·3	37·3	130 229
All non-manual above	24·5	30·5	31·7	53·5	124 169
MANUAL					
Skilled (inc. foremen)	40·3	38·3	24·4	9·4	95 39
Semi-skilled	14·8	16·1	9·8	16·6	109 169
Personal service workers	2·4	3·2	28·7	18·8	133 66
Unskilled	18·0	11·9	5·4	1·7	66 31
All manual above	75·5	69·5	68·3	46·5	92 68
TOTAL ABOVE	100·0	100·0	100·0	100·0	— —
Excluded above (as per cent of grand total)					
Agricultural jobs, etc.	9·9	5·1	1·7	1·1	
Unclassified	0·8	2·0	0·6	1·8	
Armed forces	1·7	1·6	—	0·2	
All excluded above	12·4	8·7	2·3	3·1	
GRAND TOTAL %	100·0	100·0	100·0	100·0	
000's	12,113	14,649	5,065	7,045	

Sources for tables A and B

England and Wales, 1921–1961: Analysis of census occupational data using special classification designed to allow approximate comparability over time.

England and Wales, 1961–1966: Socio-economic group tables of 1961 census and 1966 sample census.

Great Britain, 1966–1971: Socio-economic group tables of 1966 sample census. For 1971, Office of Population Censuses and Surveys, *The General Household Survey: Introductory Report*, HMSO, 1973 (p. 195).

Notes for tables A and B

(i) The occupational classification devised for analysis of the changes from 1921 to 1961 is not exactly comparable with the official, published classification by socio-economic groups used to show changes since 1961 (but not available for earlier years). The changes from 1921 to 1961 are therefore shown separately in table A above, while the changes from 1961 on are shown in table B opposite.

(ii) The special analysis for 1921 to 1961 was undertaken only for England & Wales, and could not be extended to Great Britain (including Scotland) without very considerable additional work. The data for 1961–1966 are therefore also shown for England & Wales to provide continuity. But since no census data for 1971 were available at the time of writing, only those from the General Household Survey of that year for Great Britain as a whole, the 1966–1971 figures are shown for Great Britain.

(iii) In the classification by socio-economic groups from 1961 on, farmers are included with employers and managers or, if own account workers, with others so described in the category of skilled workers. Agricultural workers are included with the semi-skilled. (These distinctions within the agricultural category cannot be made for the period 1921–1961.)

23B *England & Wales 1961–1966; Great Britain, 1966–1971*

Socio-Economic Groups (census classification)		ENGLAND AND WALES, 1961–1966			
		OCCUPIED MEN		OCCUPIED WOMEN	
		1961 %	1966 %	1961 %	1966 %
NON-MANUAL					
(1, 2, 13)	Employers and managers	10·9 ⎫	11·1 ⎫	4·2 ⎫	4·1 ⎫
(3, 4)	Major professions	3·9 ⎬ 18·8	4·7 ⎬ 20·4	0·8 ⎬ 14·3	0·8 ⎬ 14·5
(5)	Intermediate non-manual	4·0 ⎭	4·6 ⎭	9·3 ⎭	9·6 ⎭
(6)	Junior non-manual	13·1	13·0	37·6	37·9
	All non-manual above	31·9	33·4	51·9	52·4
MANUAL					
(8, 9, 12, 14)	Skilled (inc. foremen, own a/c wkers.)	40·9	40·1	11·9	10·6
(10, 15)	Semi-skilled	17·7	17·2	17·1	15·9
(7)	Personal service workers	0·9	1·0	12·1	13·6
(11)	Unskilled	8·6	8·3	7·0	7·5
	All manual above	68·1	66·6	48·1	47·6
TOTAL ABOVE		100·0	100·0	100·0	100·0
Excluded above (as per cent of grand total)					
	Unclassified	1·7	0·6	1·8	1·0
	Armed forces	2·0	1·5	0·2	0·1
	All excluded above	3·7	2·1	2·0	1·1
GRAND TOTAL	%	100·0	100·0	100·0	100·0
	000s	14,649	14,491	7,045	8,023

NA = no answer.
For other notes, see under table A.

and semi-professional jobs in teaching and nursing, for example –
grew by only a small fraction. (Table 23.) Working women in the
course of this half-century, in fact, moved from domestic service jobs
and skilled manual work into semi-skilled jobs in offices and factories.
It is misleading to describe this as a contribution to some uniform
process of 'embourgeoisement'. In the case of men, too, many of the
new non-manual jobs have been routine in character. Only in very
recent years – from 1961 or 1966 – has the share of white-collar jobs
above the purely routine level increased faster than that of low-grade
clerical and sales jobs.[9] The ratio of low-level white-collar jobs to jobs

9. Moreover, the figures for 1966–71 used here may not reflect the changes over
that period entirely accurately. The 'census' of 1966 was a sample with some

CHANGE IN RATIO		OCCUPIED MEN		OCCUPIED WOMEN		CHANGE IN RATIO	
1966 share expressed as % of 1961 share		*1966 %*	*1971 %*	*1966 %*	*1971 %*	*1971 share expressed as % of 1966 share*	
Men	*Women*					*Men*	*Women*
102 ⎫ 121 ⎬ 109 115 ⎭ 99	98 ⎫ 100 ⎬ 101 103 ⎭ 101	10·8 ⎫ 4·6 ⎬ 20·0 4·6 ⎭ 12·9	14·7 ⎫ 4·9 ⎬ 25·1 5·5 ⎭ 12·3	4·1 ⎫ 0·8 ⎬ 14·6 9·7 ⎭ 38·0	4·7 ⎫ 0·6 ⎬ 16·0 10·7 ⎭ 38·3	136 ⎫ 107 ⎬ 126 120 ⎭ 95	115 ⎫ 75 ⎬ 110 110 ⎭ 101
105	101	32·9	37·4	52·6	54·3	114	103
98 97 111 97	89 93 112 107	40·3 17·3 1·0 8·5	41·2 15·7 0·8 4·9	10·5 15·7 13·6 7·6	9·0 13·7 14·3 8·7	102 91 80 58	86 87 105 114
98	99	67·1	62·6	47·4	45·7	93	96
—	—	100·0	100·0	100·0	100·0	—	—
		0·5	NA	0·4	NA		
		1·5	NA	0·1	NA		
		2·0	NA	0·5	NA		
		100·0	—	100·0	—		
		15,994	NA	8,595	NA		

of intermediate and higher levels in fact hardly changed between 1921 and the early 1960s so far as men were concerned; and for women it became noticeably less favourable. (Table 24.) For men starting their working lives in routine kinds of non-manual work, therefore, the prospects of promotion suggested by these ratios have not improved over time, at least until very recently, even if no account is taken of the fact that positions in the middle and higher levels of non-manual work increasingly require formal educational qualifications of a sort which many potential promotees do not possess. And the changes in

known bias, though slight; and the figures shown here for 1971 derive from a relatively limited national sample survey. Corresponding 1971 census figures had not been published at the time of writing.

the corresponding ratios for the female non-manual labour force suggest a sharp deterioration in opportunities for advancement from clerical, secretarial and sales jobs. In summary, if routine non-manual work is bracketed with the manual work with which it has now so many conditions in common, at least three in every four men and five in every six working women are in jobs of an essentially wage-earning character. There is little in this to support the notion that the occupational structure has been fundamentally recast in a 'middle class' mould.

TABLE 24

Composition of non-manual groups 1921–1971

	England and Wales 1921–1961		England and Wales 1961–1966		Great Britain 1966–1971	
MEN	%	%	%	%	%	%
Intermediate and top grade	62	60	59	61	61	67
Routine grade	38	40	41	39	39	33
Total non-manual	100	100	100	100	100	100
WOMEN						
Intermediate and top grade	49	30	28	28	28	29
Routine grade	51	70	72	72	72	71
Total non-manual	100	100	100	100	100	100

Source: Calculated from Table 23.

2 Patterns of social mobility

I

Low-grade non-manual work has, nevertheless, in the past certainly given those who entered it a distinct advantage, in respect of their own and their children's chances of social climbing, over those who went into manual work even at a skilled level. There is no doubt about the historical relevance of the line between routine white- and blue-collar jobs; or, for that matter, about its continuing presence as at least something of a mobility barrier. For that reason, and because the data on which one can draw sometimes leave no choice in the matter, an examination of social mobility has to focus in part on movements within and across this once clearly marked crack in the occupational structure.

There is in general, however one measures it, a quite considerable amount of movement up and down the occupational scale from one generation to the next. This was clear already from the results of the first nationwide survey of social mobility in Britain in 1949. We shall draw on data from this study in the next few pages. An inquiry in 1959 to which we shall also refer was too small to provide so detailed a picture; and most results of a new comprehensive survey in the early 1970s had not yet been published at the time of writing. But though out of date, the 1949 material illustrates features of the pattern of social circulation which will hardly have changed much since then in their general character. Moreover – as we discuss later – it is unlikely that rates of circulation have substantially increased over the last twenty to twenty-five years.

With a classification distinguishing eight different bands of jobs, fewer than one-third of a sample of men interviewed in 1949 proved to be in a job of the same level as their fathers. (Table 25.) Even when

TABLE 25

Inter-generational mobility among men in Great Britain, 1949 sample

Father's occupational group (ranked as in original classification)	Per cent of sons who –									All sons (aged 18+)
	Stayed in father's group*	Moved, but stayed on same side of non-man./manual line				Moved, and crossed the non-manual/manual line				
		To adjacent groups	To non-adjacent groups		Sub-total	To adjacent groups	To non-adjacent groups		Sub-total	
			Up	Down			Up	Down		
I Professional, high admin.	39 (3)	15	—	31	46	—	—	15	15	100
II Managerial, executive	27 (5)	33	—	19	52	—	—	21	21	100
III Inspect., supervis., etc. (higher)	19 (9)	29	4	10	43	—	—	38	38	100
IV Inspect., supervis., etc. (lower)	21 (13)	19	6	—	25	—	—	54	54	100
VA Routine non-manual	16 (7)	15	14	—	29	29	—	26	55	100
VB Skilled manual	41 (34)	17	—	13	30	7	22	—	29	100
VI Semi-skilled manual	31 (17)	50	—	—	50	—	19	—	19	100
VII Unskilled manual	27 (12)	24	32	—	56	—	17	—	17	100
All sons (aged 18+)	31 (19)	24	6	8	38	4	13	14	31	100

Source: Calculated from S. M. Miller, 'Comparative social mobility', *Current Sociology*, vol. IX, no. 1, 1960 (p. 71). The data are those of the national sample survey the results of which were analysed in detail in D. V. Glass, ed., *Social Mobility in Britain*, Routledge & Kegan Paul, 1954 (especially chap. VIII). But the figures reproduced in Miller's paper are used here, because – unlike the original published figures – they distinguish between occupational categories VA and VB above.

* The figures in brackets in the first column show the percentage of sons from each group of origin who *would* have stayed in the same group (i.e., their father's group) if there had been 'perfect mobility'; that is, if a son's destination in life were in no way influenced by his parental origin. (These figures are equivalent to the percentage distribution of all sons among the different job levels, in terms of their own jobs. Thus, 12 per cent of all sons had unskilled manual jobs; and if parental origin did not affect chances in life, 12 per cent of the sons of each particular origin – including the sons of unskilled workers – would have gone into unskilled jobs. In fact, 27 per cent of the sons of unskilled workers did so – over twice as many as would have done so if there were 'perfect mobility'.)

those who had moved only one step away from their fathers' position are excluded, some four in every ten had clearly either improved upon or slid down below the circumstances of their origin: roughly equal numbers in either direction. Since the steps on the scale are rather arbitrarily defined, and there are far more people on some than on others, these figures themselves are crude in character. But they are sufficient, for a start, to dispel any notion that Britain is a society in which individual position in the hierarchy of inequality is fixed at birth. Capitalism here as elsewhere allows – indeed in some respects encourages – a fair degree of fluidity of circulation.

But to say that circulation is fluid is not to say that it is free. Inequality of condition sets marked limits to individual opportunities and risks of ascent and descent. People are a good deal more likely to stay at roughly the same level as their fathers than they would be if there were 'perfect mobility'. That is true especially of those fortunate enough to be born at or near the top of the scale. Men in the established professions and in high administrative jobs – including the business élite – are a tiny group of the population. If parental origin played no part in determining life chances, whether directly or indirectly, only some 3 per cent of their sons in the 1949 sample – as of men born on any other rung of the ladder – would have found jobs of a kind to secure them a place in this privileged minority. In fact, nearly 40 per cent did so. Here is inheritance with a vengeance, even though it is not guaranteed. Unskilled workers, right at the other end of the scale, are a considerably larger group. The sheer arithmetical risk of getting no more than an unskilled job is therefore also substantially greater: about a 12 per cent risk regardless of social origin, if circulation were entirely free. But the risk in fact was much larger for those who had the bad fortune to be born into an unskilled worker's family: over one in every four of these men themselves became unskilled workers.

Movement right across the face of the social structure – from rags to riches, or riches to rags – is rare, and inhibited by very severe inequalities of opportunity. To take the results of the 1949 survey again, only about 1 per cent of the men from semi- and unskilled workers' families had achieved jobs of an executive, managerial or at least equally privileged level. The corresponding proportion among those born at those levels was some forty to fifty times higher: the top and near-top groups were marked by a large degree of self-recruitment from one generation to the next. (Table 26.) Conversely, while about one in every two men from homes in the two lowest categories themselves found no more than semi- or unskilled manual jobs, only 6 to 7 per cent of the men from managerial or still more favoured family backgrounds came right down the scale to jobs in those grades. Even when all manual jobs including the skilled are bracketed together – with well over 60 per cent of the men interviewed in 1949 falling into this broad blue-collar category – no more than 15 to 20 per cent or so of those born into the two top groups were subsequently counted down there. (Table 25.) Many others were in lower jobs than their fathers had been – not surprisingly, since jobs

TABLE 26

Access to managerial and higher jobs; to all jobs above the routine white-collar/skilled manual level; and to semi – and un-skilled manual jobs, Great Britain 1949

Per cent of sons who, when interviewed were in –	Sons whose fathers were in following occupations								All sons
	I	II	III	IV	Va	Vb	VI	VII	
Prof., admin., manag., exec. jobs (I, II)	54	37	14	6	6	2	1	1	8
All jobs above routine non-manual (I–IV)	80	72	52	38	29	22	14	13	30
Semi- and unskilled manual jobs (VI, VII)	6	7	13	19	26	30	47	51	29

Source: As for table 25. The occupational categories are as listed there.

of their fathers' level are relatively few. But social descent from executive and professional backgrounds usually stopped short of the conventional line of division between the white- and the blue-collar worlds.

That line, in fact, has something of the character of a barrier against mobility; at least it had so still in the experience of the men interviewed in 1949. It is true that many of them had moved across it – altogether nearly one-third of the total sample: about one in four or five of the manual-born moving 'upwards' into white-collar work; proportions as high as 40 to 50 per cent of those from low- or middle-level white-collar homes (groups III to VA) moving 'down' into manual jobs. (Table 25.) The terms 'up' and 'down' in any case have to be taken with a pinch of salt because, as we have stressed, the objective circumstances of routine non-manual work were deteriorating in relative terms over the decades to which the experience of the sample relates. But to be born as the son of a clerical or other low-grade non-manual worker still offered better chances in life than to be born into the skilled stratum of the manual working class. Some 6 per cent of the men from routine-level white-collar homes thus managed to climb to executive or higher position – a very small proportion, but three times the figure for those from skilled manual homes. Altogether, 29 per cent of the 'white-collar proletariat' sons, but only 22 per cent of the skilled blue-collar sons, achieved jobs of at least supervisory level; and rather more of the latter than of the former slid down the scale into semi- or unskilled manual work. (Table 26.)

One should not make too much of the exact figures. Data from another nationwide study at about the same time suggested bigger differences in the chances of ascent to executive and professional jobs, as in the risks of descent to the lower levels of manual work, between men from very modest white-collar backgrounds and those whose fathers were skilled manual workers. There was here a quite distinct gradation of life chances, in these terms, from clerks' through shop assistants' to skilled workers' sons.[1] The trend, though it cannot be traced in the data published from these sources, may well be towards a gradual erosion of these traditional advantages of 'petty bourgeois' origins for prospects of advancement. Those advantages were already quite limited in the overall experience of the 1949 sample, to take those figures as they stand. But they were still visible

1. Benjamin, op. cit. (ch. 1, note 2 above).

then. The persistence of some mobility threshold along the line dividing manual from non-manual labour, even if it is now lower than before, may help to explain the continuing reluctance of many sections of the routine-grade labour force in offices and shops to align themselves politically and socially with industrial workers to the degree which their 'wage proletarianization' might otherwise induce them to.

So, to summarize the picture of social circulation between generations to this point, there is a good deal of movement up and down the steps of the occupational scale. This is a common feature of contemporary Western societies. There is, as we have argued, no incompatibility between that and the nature of capitalism. Allowing for international differences in the shape of the occupational structure, Britain indeed showed rather more inter-generational mobility across the line between manual and non-manual labour, according to survey data from around the middle of this century, than other capitalist countries including the United States. Recruitment to the small élites at the top, at the same time, was tighter and more exclusive than in several other comparable societies, America among them.[2] So far as the impact of mobility opportunities and risks on the bulk of the population are concerned, the former point may be more significant than the latter. But, here as elsewhere, moderate fluidity of movement is accompanied by sharp inequalities of opportunity. Those born into the top strata have enormous advantages in respect of their job prospects – as in respect of so much else – over all others; not least in this country. Long-distance movement especially – from bottom to top, as well as from top to bottom – is uncommon. Most individual mobility is far more modest; and much of it stays on one side or the other of the conventional dividing line between white- and blue-collar work.

II

That point is important, since many questions concerning the consequences of social circulation turn upon it. It is therefore worth exploring further, with the help of information about mobility in the

2. S. M. Miller, op. cit. (note to table 25 above).

course of working life as well as mobility from one generation to the next.

Job changing, of course, is a fairly common phenomenon. About two in every five people in the working population moved from one employer to another at least once during the ten years 1953–63, for example. But only one in five – much the same proportion among both men and women – changed job level in the process, if jobs are classified into six grades from high level professional and administrative work at the top to unskilled manual work at the bottom. And fewer than one in twelve jumped the fence dividing manual from non-manual jobs in either direction. The advantages of routine-grade clerical and similar work as a platform for social ascent were again visible. Some 12 per cent of the men in jobs of that sort at the outset were in middle or higher level non-manual posts ten years later; only 5 per cent of those who started from skilled manual jobs. The ratios were more or less reversed between the two, when it came to the risk of sliding down the scale into semi-skilled and unskilled work. In the case of women, promotion chances were more limited; the risks of descent greater; and the relative advantages associated with a start in clerical work, by contrast with skilled manual work, more marked.[3] So the great bulk of everyday job changing involves either movement without a change in job level; or circulation from one level to another of manual or of non-manual work, not across the line between the two.

There is nevertheless, cumulatively, a good deal of movement across that line if account is taken of job changes over the whole, or over a long stretch, of individual working lives. This is so even when one considers only two points of time in individual careers: the time of entry into employment and a much later stage when people are well set into their working lives, nearing retirement or have actually reached retirement. From the results of a national sample survey in 1959, about one in every three men who started work in a manual job had moved into non-manual work of some kind by the time they were in their mid-thirties or older. There was fairly little difference in that respect between those whose first job was a skilled one and those who had begun in semi- or unskilled work. (Table 27, p. 304.)

3. From data in A. Harris and R. Clausen, *Labour Mobility in Great Britain 1953–1963*, Government Social Survey, 1966 (especially table 52). In the figures quoted here, we have combined semi-skilled 'non-manual' (mainly personal service) jobs with other semi-skilled jobs, and classified both as manual.

TABLE 27

Career mobility of men aged 35 and over, Great Britain 1959

| Job (or last job) at interview was: | MEN AGED 50 AND OVER | | | | | | | MEN AGED 35-49 | | | | | | |
| | First job was – | | | All | | | First job was – | | | All | |
	Non-manual %	Skilled manual %	Other manual %		%			Non-manual %	Skilled manual %	Other manual %		%
Non-manual	81	38	30		41			83	39	29		43
Skilled manual	12	46	27		31			9	45	31		31
Other manual	7	16	43		28			8	16	40		26
Total: %	100	100	100		100			100	100	100		100
no.	58	117	176		351			105	145	244		494

Job (or last job) at interview was	MEN AGED 50 AND OVER								MEN AGED 35–49							
	First job was –						All		First job was –						All	
	Non-manual		Skilled man.		Other manual				Non-manual		Skilled man.		Other manual			
	Born		Born		Born		Born		Born		Born		Born		Born	
	NM %	M %	NM %	M %	NM %	M %	NM %	M %	NM %	M %	NM %	M %	NM %	M %	NM %	M %
Non-manual	92	60	54	29	43	26	62	30	86	77	54	31	44	23	62	32
Skilled manual	3	30	31	54	24	28	19	37	12	5	33	52	26	33	23	35
Other manual	5	10	15	17	33	46	19	33	2	18	13	17	30	44	15	33
Total: %	100	100	100	100	100	100	100	100	100	100	100	100	100	100	100	100
no.	38	20	39	78	42	134	119	232	66	39	54	91	70	174	190	304
	58		117		176		351		105		145		244		494	

Source: Data from the Population Investigation Committee's Marriage Survey of 1959. (We are grateful to Professor D. V. Glass for making these data available; and to Dr Savitri Thapar for her help in extracting them from the other material collected in the survey and in initial tabulation of the data.) For a description of the design of the sample, see e.g. Griselda Rowntree and Rachel Pierce, 'Birth Control in Britain', *Population Studies*, July–November 1961.

Note: Since it was necessary to confine an analysis of mobility between three points of time in individuals' lives (birth, for which socio-economic position was indicated roughly by fathers' occupation; the time of the first job; and the time of the interview, 1959) to men who were at least well established in their careers (here taken as men 35 years and older), and also to distinguish between two age groups among them, the limited size of the sample allowed only a crude classification of jobs into three (and for some purposes two) categories as shown in the table. Even so, the base numbers for some of the distributions above are very small.

Yet career chances are less fluid than this might seem to suggest at first sight. For one thing, many of the 'promotees' from non-manual work may have gone no further than to white-collar jobs of quite modest rank and earnings: perhaps as many as half of them, if the data quoted earlier on job mobility over a ten-year period can be taken as offering any clues. There is no direct information on the point from our analysis of the 1959 survey itself. For another, some four in every ten of the promotees from blue- to white-collar work were men of white-collar origins. The chance of moving to non-manual work after a first job in manual work was, in fact, very much greater for those born in a white-collar family than for those born as the sons of blue-collar workers. (See table 27, p. 305.) The advantages associated with non-manual circumstances in early life – in terms of education, money, know-how or whatever – thus continue to play a part in individual life chances, even after men have started work at a particular point of the scale; and those who come from unskilled or semi-skilled families are particularly handicapped in their job prospects, by comparison with others starting work at the same levels. Much of the 'career flow' from manual into non-manual jobs, in short, is made up of people who are thereby returning to the side of the fence on which they were born. (Some of them, no doubt, started in jobs that were only nominally manual – as trainees, for example, destined for early promotion from the outset.) Finally, there is very much less 'downward' movement from non-manual into manual work in the course of working life than there is movement across the line in the opposite direction. Fewer than one in five of those who began their careers in a white-collar job had dropped later to a blue-collar job; and the risk of such 'demotion' was still slighter for men of non-manual birth than for the small number of manual workers' sons whose first job was a white-collar one.

III

This is not to say that social descent is rare. Shifts in occupational structure over time, and class differences in rates of natural replacement, may generate a larger upward than downward flow between generations. That apart, however, there must be as many people coming down the ladder as there are people going up it, from one generation to the next, though downward mobility has aroused rather little interest in public and even professional discussion of social circulation.[4] But most downward mobility appears to be an experience of adolescence or early adulthood. It usually occurs at the point of entry into employment or, for that matter, in the course of the educational process which leads to that point; much less commonly in the course of working life. This was so, at least, in the case of the men included in the survey of 1959; and when, as in the analysis of their experience, jobs were graded crudely into only three levels. About two in every three of the white-collar sons among these men started work in ostensibly blue-collar jobs – roughly equal numbers in skilled and in semi- or unskilled work – although their chances of moving up again to white-collar jobs were much better, as we have shown, than were those of their first workmates from blue-collar homes. Skilled manual workers' sons, too, quite often began work in jobs below their fathers' level. Some two in every five of these took semi- or unskilled work when they first joined the labour force, while only one in seven or eight found white-collar work to begin with. (Two in every three of those from non-skilled homes started in non skilled jobs; only one in ten or so in non-manual jobs.) So entry into employment for men born above the bottom rung often involved a fall down the scale from their circumstances of origin. But while many moved up later, few experienced downgrading – at least as a permanent or long-lasting state of affairs – in the subsequent course of working life. Downward mobility, by this evidence, is thus not usually a matter of job demotion: it occurs mainly at an early stage in life. Upward mobility, by contrast, takes the form primarily of promotion or job changing in the course of working life. (Table 28.)

These are only crude indications. The figures are not detailed enough, for example, to show the kind of sliding down the job scale – into caretaking, cleaning or other low grade jobs – which is probably not uncommon among manual workers at the tail end of their working lives. Nor can they confirm – or refute – the supposition that an increase in the importance of formal educational qualifications, as preconditions for entry to executive and supervisory

4. Miller (op. cit., note 2 above) has underlined the large volume of downward mobility recorded in the 1949 survey as a notable feature of the pattern of social circulation in Britain, The frequency of downward movement shown there follows, as an arithmetical necessity, from the frequency of upward movement (across the manual/non-manual line) in conjunction with the large and, as the occupational categories were defined, fairly stable share of manual workers in the male population over time.

positions, has been shifting the weight of upward mobility somewhat away from promotion through experience on the job. For the main impact of that trend would be to change the balance between early mobility and career mobility *within* the category of non-manual work – to reduce promotion prospects for those who start work in routine clerical jobs and the like, without special educational qualifications.

TABLE 28

Stage of life of movements up and down the occupational scale: men aged 35 and over, Great Britain 1959

Stage of life at which move occurred	Moves between skilled and non-skilled manual levels		Moves across manual/non-manual line		All moves recorded	
	Down %	Up %	Down %	Up %	Down %	Up %
A. for men aged 50 and over						
By entry into employment	74	37	87	17	81	25
During working life	26	63	13	83	19	75
Total moves: %	100	100	100	100	100	100
no.	74	76	86	117	160	193
B. for men aged 35–49						
By entry into employment	71	34	86	23	80	28
During working life	29	66	14	77	20	72
Total moves: %	100	100	100	100	100	100
no.	79	115	131	166	210	281

Source: As for table 27.
Note:
   (i) The totals shown are *movements* from one level to another, not individuals. An individual may have moved twice – once 'by entry into employment' (from his socio-economic level at birth, as suggested by his father's occupation, to a different level in his first job) and again 'during working life' (from first job to job when interviewed at the age of 35 or older, with retired men classified according to their last jobs). Only moves between these three points of time are taken into account.
   (ii) There were, in aggregate, more upward than downward movements recorded on this basis. This reflects, in part, a shift in the occupational composition of the respondent population (including men under 35, though these are excluded from this analysis) by comparison with that of their fathers; in part also the exclusion of those under 35 (whose inclusion would increase the volume of downward movement shown more than the the volume of upward movement, because they were still in the early years of their working lives when interviewed).

The different grades of non-manual work are not separately distinguished in the data to show how far this in fact has been occurring. The
general contrast between downward and upward mobility in their
phasing over the individual life cycle is still very striking – and
suggestive in its implications.

The infrequency of demotion in the course of working life – especially of demotion from white- to blue-collar work – may isolate
those who experience it as a minority of individuals: personal
resentment or resignation seems a more likely response on their part
than any consciousness of a common fate. Moreover, in so far as
people are aware of the risks and chances in life to which the pattern
points, adults' anxieties about losing position are likely to focus on
their children, rather than on themselves once they are set in their
working lives. There is reinforcement here for the trend towards
enhancement of the significance of formal education – and towards
turning the spotlight of social and individual concern on education.
The concentration of upward mobility in the working phase of life,
on the other hand, may help to keep a carrot of promotion prospects
in front of many employees, for some years at least. Socio-political
resentment among young workers may be kept at a lower pitch than
would otherwise be the case, by the fact that about a third of those
who start work in a manual job – even in a non-skilled job – are likely
later to move to non-manual work. And it may not be evident to the
manual-born majority of these young workers that their own chances
of making such a move are only about half as good as the chances for
the minority of their workmates (a quarter to a third of all young
manual workers) who come from white-collar homes. The pattern of
social circulation, in these features of its timing in life, lends some
support for the thesis that mobility may dampen class solidarity
among wage earners.

Yet these inferences are speculative; and there are associated
features of the pattern of social circulation which suggest that the
view of mobility as a 'safety valve' needs considerable qualification.
It is not clear from the evidence referred to here at what stages in
working-life advancement – in so far as it is real advancement – from
blue-collar to white-collar work usually occurs. But it seems probable
that much of it takes place fairly early on. This is not to deny the
existence of a familiar process of promotion – by slow steps, over
many years, to junior or middle level management from the wage-
earning ranks. But even there the step across the line between manual

and non-manual work may often be made early. Certainly, some broad similarities in experience of social circulation between men over 50 years old and those between 35 and 49, in the data from the 1959 survey, suggest that fairly little movement from blue-collar to white-collar work occurs after the mid-thirties or so.[5] And the effective barrier to promotion from the shop floor may, in fact, for most manual workers come well before that.

Moreover, the majority who remain manual workers, and who are probably fixed in that condition after an early stage in their working lives – when they still have thirty years or more to go before retirement – share a pattern of common experience which is in marked contrast to the diversity of experience evident among non-manual workers. From the results of the 1959 survey again, only one in every four men who end up in white-collar jobs – of all grades – have spent their entire lives on that side of the conventional class fence; and, including these, only three or four in every ten have been in non-manual work from the start of their working lives (Table 29, part A.) The rest – a clear majority – have moved to white-collar work after first having some kind of manual job. But these in turn are of different kinds. Many – over a quarter of all those who end in non-manual work – are men who are thereby coming back to the white-collar world in which they were born: helped in their careers by their circumstances of origin, despite a start in manual work. Still more come from manual homes, by contrast, though only about a quarter of all men born and starting work in the blue-collar world eventually go into white-collar jobs. Here are people following an old pattern of social climbing, even if many of them achieve no more than the dubious status of a routine grade office job.

By comparison with this diversity of origins and career paths among non-manual workers, there is a striking homogeneity of experience among those men – the majority – who are in manual jobs when they are in their mid-thirties or older. Some three in every four of these belong to the blue-collar world by birth and first job as well as by their present position. Only one in four or five was born on the non-manual side of the fence; and almost all of these have still spent their working lives on the manual side. Just because downward

5. This is a reasonable deduction unless a marked and new upward trend in social mobility is postulated, which will result in many more manual workers who were in their thirties and forties in 1959 reaching non-manual jobs in their fifties and later, than was the case in the generation before them.

mobility across the conventional line of division typically occurs early, some 95 per cent of the male manual labour force aged 35 and older have been in blue-collar work from their first jobs. (Table 29, part B.) At the same time they show a fair amount of circulation between one level and another of the manual world, even when only the crude distinction between skilled and non-skilled work is made. On average, only one in every three has stayed at the same level

TABLE 29

Mobility profiles of non-manual and manual men aged 35 years and older: Great Britain, 1959

Mobility experience – with respect to level at birth (father's occupation), first job and job at time of interview in 1959	Men aged 50 and over			Men aged 35–49		
	%			%		
A. Those non-manual at interview						
Same level (non-manual) at all three times	24 ⎫			27 ⎫		
Born manual; non-manual during working life	9 ⎬ 33			14 ⎬ 41		
Rose to non-manual during working life:						
Born non-manual and returned after manual first job	27 ⎫			28 ⎫		
Born manual, first job manual	40 ⎬ 67			31 ⎬ 59		
Total: %	100			100		
no.	144			214		

B. Those manual at interview	Skilled	Other	All manual	Skilled	Other	All manual
	%	%	%	%	%	%
Same level (skilled or other) at all three times	25 ⎫	41 ⎫	33 ⎫	18 ⎫	47 ⎫	32 ⎫
Manual at all three times, but moved between manual levels:	⎬ 77	⎬ 76	⎬ 77	⎬ 75	⎬ 72	⎬ 73
Same level during working life	15	22	18	16	12	14
Moved during working life	37 ⎭	13 ⎭	26 ⎭	41 ⎭	13 ⎭	27 ⎭
Born non-manual, but manual during working life:						
Same level during working life	6 ⎫	14 ⎫	10 ⎫	5 ⎫	16 ⎫	10 ⎫
Moved during working life	10 ⎬ 16	6 ⎬ 20	8 ⎬ 18	13 ⎬ 18	5 ⎬ 21	10 ⎬ 20
Fell to manual level during wkg. life*	7	4	5	7	7	7
Total: %	100	100	100	100	100	100
no.	109	98	207	151	129	280

Source: As for tables 27 and 28.
* Of the 5 per cent among manual workers aged 50 and over who had come down the scale into manual work during their working lives, under 2 per cent were non-manual born. The same was true of about 3 per cent of the corresponding 7 per cent among manual workers aged 35–49.

throughout – at birth, on entry into the labour market, and again at the age of 35 or more. And though a majority have spent their working lives at one level – whether skilled or non-skilled – another one in every three has moved between the two since starting work: more often from the lower to the higher level than in the reverse direction. There is considerable mobility here; but it is mobility within the manual wage-earning class. Taken together with the relatively small contribution to the established blue-collar labour force made by men from white-collar homes – and the fact that so few of these in turn began work in a white-collar job – this internal circulation within the world of manual work is likely to strengthen ties among earners on that side of the old crack in the occupational structure; not to weaken them.

IV

So, in summary, there are no simple inferences to be drawn from the pattern of mobility up and down the hierarchy of jobs. There is a good deal of such movement, in both directions. This, and the fact that downward mobility generally occurs early in life while mobility in the course of working life is mostly upwards – at least by conventional categorization of the occupational structure – may well in various ways help to reduce the sense of collective dissent and solidarity among ordinary earners. Yet movement up and down the ladder is inhibited by sharp inequalities of opportunity. There is certainly no automatic inheritance of position; but inheritance is a powerful influence on the life chances of individuals. There is thus a conflict built in with the ideal of free opportunity to which capitalist societies pay lip-service – and with the aim of efficient use of human resources to which implementation of that ideal would conduce. On that score, the facts of mobility are a potential source of social tension, rather than of social quiescence.

The persistence of some mobility barrier between manual and low-level non-manual work also has implications that cut both ways. On the one hand, it no doubt helps to keep up the long-standing ideological separation of routine white-collar workers from blue-collar labour: it is a force for fragmentation of the wage-earning population to that extent. On the other, it is associated with features that may reinforce ties among the manual majority of the wage-earning population. Manual workers probably have little chance of promotion out of their condition after the early years of their working lives. Even before that, their chances of promotion are much smaller if they are manual-born – as most are – than if they have the advantages of a white-collar background to help them out of a start in blue-collar work. Just for that reason, manual wage earners who have reached the point where they are settled in their work – though not tied to a particular job – are people who have much in common in experience and background; and these bonds among them are likely to be the firmer because there is a good deal of circulation within the manual labour force, from one level to another. The arithmetic of social mobility thus, by itself, points to no clear conclusions about its significance for the polical stability of capitalism. These are issues which we shall discuss again later. But before we do so, one further question about social mobility needs to be taken up: is there more of it now than there was earlier in this century?

3 Trends of mobility and educational opportunity

I

It is a common belief that rates of social circulation have accelerated to make Britain, and other capitalist countries in Western Europe, much more 'fluid' societies than they were half a century or a century ago. The barriers that remain to equal opportunity receive greater recognition now than in the 1950s. But they are still widely assumed to have been reduced a good deal: confident references to increasing social mobility ring loud in contemporary commentary, and have done so for twenty years or more. In fact, however, the evidence from the surveys of around 1950, 1960 and 1970 does not confirm these assumptions. It suggests no change of substance in the amount of movement up and down the social scale till about the time of World War II. And there seems now to have been little increase in social circulation after that either, leaving class disparities in individual opportunity sharply marked. The complacencies of conventional wisdom again turn out to have weak foundations.

The national sample inquiry in 1949 showed a remarkable stability in the pattern of mobility over time, when the experience of the oldest men interviewed was compared with that of the youngest generation of respondents who were far enough into their working lives for the comparison to make sense. (Table 30.) The proportion of sons in jobs at, and close to, the same level as their fathers was much the same in both generations; and that right across the occupational range. Indeed, rather more of the young than of the old proved to have stayed close to their father's position; but some of the young – then in their thirties – might still move up or down later in life. The

TABLE 30

Mobility experience of two generations of men: Great Britain, 1949 sample

Mobility experience of sons	Father's occupational group									
	A Profess., admin., manag., executive		B Supervisory, etc: higher grade		C Supervisory, etc.: lower grade		D Routine non-manual and skilled manual		E Semi-skilled and unskilled	
	Sons born:		Sons born:		Sons born:		Sons born:		Sons born:	
	Before 1890	1910–1919	Before 1890	1910–1919	Before 1890	1910–1919	Before 1890	1910–1919	Before 1890	1910–1919
Per cent of sons who, when interviewed in 1949, were	%	%	%	%	%	%	%	%	%	%
In same occup. group as father	40	43	14	20	25	28	42	48	58	47
In same or adjacent group	63	70	44	57	72	81	90	89	90	86
In top group (A, profess., etc.)	40	43	12	17	4	5	4	3	1	1
In bottom group (E, non-skilled)	12	7	17	10	24	14	35	27	58	47

Source: D. V. Glass, ed., *Social Mobility in Britain*, 1954 (chapter VIII, by D. V. Glass and J. R. Hall, p. 186).

Notes:

(i) The occupational groups are the same as those distinguished in tables 25 and 26 above, except that Groups I and II of those tables are here combined to form A; VA and VB are here combined to form D; and VI and VII are here combined to form E. (Details have not been published to allow the table above to be presented for the eight separate groups of tables 25 and 26.)

(ii) We have chosen, as the younger of the two generations for which information is summarized here, men born 1910–1919, who were in their thirties when interviewed and thus fairly well set in their careers.

risk of getting a job in the lowest grades – in semi- or unskilled work – had diminished for all over time. But that shift in occupational structure had benefited those of privileged backgrounds as much as others: the inequalities of opportunity and risk between men of different origins remained as distinct as ever over the generations. Old and young alike, sons from the top group thus had forty times as good a chance of getting a top job as did sons from non-skilled manual homes; and a five to seven times smaller risk of finding themselves in a non-skilled job. There were no signs here of a trend towards greater spread of opportunity.

Of course, the younger generation in these figures were men who left school in the 1930s or before. The pattern might have changed substantially since then. But there was no evidence of that as yet by 1959: ten years after the first major survey of social mobility in Britain, and fifteen years after the Education Act of 1944 which established free secondary education in England and Wales for all children. Comparison of the 1959 survey results with those for 1949 – for all men included in each survey, irrespective of age, since this is necessary to make the data comparable – suggests some narrowing over those ten years in class disparities of individual opportunity and risk; but no change sharp enough to weaken the link between father's position and son's destination in the occupational hierarchy more than fractionally. With a broad classification of jobs into two or three levels – all that the data allow – the men included in the 1959 survey proved to have followed in their fathers' footsteps to much the same extent as the men interviewed ten years earlier. Indeed a simple statistical measure of the tie between the socio-economic levels of fathers and sons – the index of association, which sets aside changes that occur merely because the occupational structure shifts over time – gave almost identical values in both years. There was only one modification of this pattern: men from unskilled and semi-skilled manual homes were less likely in 1959 to have gone into jobs of that level themselves than their predecessors of 1949. (Table 31, first four columns.)

Disparities between men of different origin in their chances of getting white-collar jobs, and in their risks of getting semi- or unskilled jobs, remained of much the same general order from one survey to the next. Sons of non-manual fathers, for example, proved to be more than twice as likely as sons of manual fathers – skilled and non-skilled taken together – to turn up in white-collar jobs in both

TABLE 31

Indices of mobility for men interviewed in surveys of 1949 and 1959, Great Britain

Father's occupational level	Occupational level of son when interviewed in 1949 or 1959											
	Per cent of sons at same level as father		Index of association		Per cent of sons in non-manual jobs		Index of inequality of opportunity		Per cent of sons in non-skilled jobs		Index of inequality of risk	
	1949	1959	1949	1959	1949	1959	1949	1959	1949	1949	1949	1959
Non-manual	58	61	156	156	58	61	234	221	15	15	100	100
Manual	75	72	120	119	25	23	100	100	37	31	243	202
Skilled manual	41	44	121	125	29	32	118	116	30	24	196	155
Non-skilled manual	49	37	167	147	18	24	72	86	49	37	318	244
All sons*	49	48	145	144	37	29	—	—	29	26	—	—

Sources: For 1949, as for tables 25 and 26 above.
For 1959, as for tables 27–29 above. Unlike the data in tables 27–29, however, the 1959 figures shown here relate to all men included in the sample (not just those 35 and older), for comparability with the 1949 data.

Notes: The indices are as follows:
(i) *Index of association* – a measure of the extent to which the actual number of sons following in their fathers' footsteps exceeds the number to be expected if there were 'perfect mobility' (i.e., if a son's position were unaffected by his father's position, in which case the index would be 100).
(ii) *Index of inequality of opportunity* – a measure of the extent to which the chance for a son of a given home background (non-manual, skilled or non-skilled manual) to achieve a non-manual job exceeds (values over 100) or falls below (values under 100) the chance for a son from a manual home (skilled and non-skilled combined) to achieve a non-manual job.
(iii) *Index of inequality of risk* – a measure of the extent to which the risk for a son of a given home background (manual, skilled or non-skilled) of getting a non-skilled manual job exceeds the corresponding risk (set at 100) for a son from a non-manual home.
* The first four figures in the line for all sons are calculated on the basis that skilled and non-skilled manual constitute two separate levels of a three-level occupational hierarchy.

years; about three times as likely to do so as the sons of non-skilled fathers alone. And again, in both years, a non-manual home background proved to give a far smaller risk of work at the semi- or unskilled level than a non-skilled background itself – by a factor of over three in 1949, about two-and-a-half in 1959. (Table 31, last eight columns.) The inequalities of opportunity and risk in these respects had become rather smaller over these ten years, it is true. Sons of semi- and unskilled workers, in particular, had benefited proportionately more than others from a shift in the occupational structure involving a contraction of the number of low-grade jobs and an expansion of white-collar jobs. So there were signs of a mild increase in social mobility over the 1950s; but not such as to make for any marked alteration in the pattern of unequal opportunity, of partial inheritance of position from one generation to the next.

Ten years is a short period over which to measure any changes in the velocity of circulation. If an upward trend were to have set in around the 1950s, it would be likely to have affected mainly those who were in the early stages of their working lives then; not so much the middle-aged and the elderly. So the hints of some acceleration of mobility from the 1959 results should have become firmer signs another decade or so later – if the trend had been maintained. In fact, a new nationwide survey undertaken in the early 1970s points to little or no increase in circulation.[1] Even had it done so, this would not have been startling by itself. No refutation of the dominance of capital in British class structure could be inferred. Capitalism, as we have argued, sets up pressures to ease mobility as well as to limit it. The personal interests of the privileged in passing on privilege within their families, the sheer weight of advantage and disadvantage associated with class position – these pull one way: to restrict circulation, to reinforce the institutions that protect inheritance of

1. The main results of the Nuffield College survey of occupational mobility in England and Wales (see Hope, op. cit., ch. 1, note 4 above, for some preparatory studies), and of the comparable survey for Scotland undertaken by M. P. Carter and other sat Aberdeen University, were not yet available at the time of writing. Some preliminary results from the first of these (presented at a conference of the British Sociological Association in 1973 by J. H. Goldthorpe, and kindly made available to us) suggested a general increase in rates of social mobility between 1949 and 1972. But later analysis to overcome problems of comparability between the two sets of data showed no such upward trend, discounting the effects of shifts in occupational structure. Cf. K. Hope, 'Trends in the openness of British society in the present century', 1974, mimeo. We are grateful to the Nuffield College team for information and comments.

social condition. Demands for more efficient use of man- and woman-power in the economy – not just for greater justice by itself, in conformity with a liberal ideal of individual opportunity – pull the other way: towards loosening the inhibitions on free recruitment of labour according to 'talent' and 'merit'. During this century so far, the two sets of pressures appear to have balanced: the outcome was velocities of social circulation which, while sizeable, were fairly constant. We shall discuss some of the probable mechanisms behind this stability shortly. But there can be no presumption that the conflicting pressures must continue to balance in this way. And it is possible that a translation of recent preoccupations with economic 'modernization' into educational policy and managerial practice, for example, could help to tip the scales towards a greater degree of fluidity in class recruitment. If there is such a trend, however, it was still hardly visible by around 1970. And there are no signs that mobility could rise on a scale to produce anything like the state of equal opportunity to which conventional ideology and policy claim to aspire. The obstacles to that goal are deeply entrenched in the divisions of the society.

II

The stability of rates of social circulation during the first half of this century may seem puzzling. It certainly does not square with commonly asserted opinion. Such opinion usually assigns crucial importance to education as a means of mobility. Educational opportunities have widened significantly in the course of this century, it is pointed out. Consequently, the inference runs, there should be more effective reshuffling of the population between different levels of the socio-economic hierarchy in each generation than there was before, despite remaining impediments to free circulation. This argument, however, turns on two implicit premises. One is that the expansion of educational opportunities has benefited children from wage-earning and poor homes proportionately more than children from privileged backgrounds. An equal expansion of educational opportunities at all levels would leave the situation unchanged. The second is an assumption that there has been, over the same period, no corresponding contraction of other channels of mobility. Both premises need to be checked. Even the first is not self-evident, though it is often thought to be. And the second is frequently just ignored, as if there were – now and in the past – only one possible avenue of mobility: through education.

TABLE 32

The trend of class inequalities of opportunity for entry to selective secondary education, England and Wales

Social origin – i.e., father's occupation	Per cent of children, of different social origins, who obtained education in grammar and independent schools: among these born –				
	Before 1910	1910– 1919	1920– 1929	Late 1930s	Approx. 1957/60
Professional and managerial	37	47	52	62	47
Other non-manual and skilled manual	7	13	16	20	22
Semi-skilled and unskilled	1	4	7	10	10
All children	12	16	18	23	25

Sources: For children born before 1910 and up to the late 1930s – J. H. Westergaard and A. N. Little, 'Educational opportunity and social selection in England and Wales,' in Social Objectives in Educational Planning, Paris, OECD, 1967. (Estimates from data in earlier studies by others.)
    For children born 1957/60 – calculated from The General Household Survey (1971), Introductory Report (HMSO, 1973), p. 234, for children 11–14 in secondary schools.
Notes:
    (i) The occupational categories used are roughly, but not perfectly, comparable over the years.
    (ii) The figures for the last generation shown, those born approx. 1957/60, cannot be directly compared with the earlier figures, because nearly 28 per cent of all children born in 1957/60 obtained secondary education in 'comprehensive' (mixed ability) schools, whereas very few in the previous generations did so. See text.
    (iii) Differences between boys and girls in respect of entry to selective secondary education were very slight.

Educational opportunities in general have certainly been stepped up. The expansion of recent years is familiar: the rise in the proportion of children staying on at school to at least 16, for example – from 22 per cent in 1961 to 36 per cent in 1971; of those staying on to 18 or older – from 12 to 21 per cent over the same period; of those going into some form of full-time higher education – from about 8 per cent in 1961 to 19 or 20 per cent in 1971.[2] But the trend is a long-standing one. It was visible, for instance, in a gradual increase in access to selective secondary education throughout this century; and in a more

2. The figures of numbers staying on at school relate to the United Kingdom. (Source: Education Statistics 1971.) Those for entry into full-time higher education refer to young people with homes in England and Wales only. (Sources: R. Layard et al., The Impact of Robbins, Penguin, 1969, supplemented for 1970/71 by estimates from data in Education Statistics 1967 and . . . 1970, adjusted to make them comparable with the series in Layard et al. We are grateful to Richard Layard for advice concerning these adjustments.)

or less parallel growth in size of the small minority going to university. (Tables 32 and 33: figures for all children.) What needs to be recognized is that this was not only, or even mainly, a process by which educational opportunities were extended down the social scale: by which bourgeois privileges were converted into something more like common benefits. It involved an expansion of educational opportunity for the children of wealthy and 'middle class' homes as well as for children of the common people: in some ways more for the former than the latter. Take access to a grammar school or independent secondary school education. Little more than one third of the children born into professional and managerial families in the years up to 1910 went to schools of this kind; over three in every five of their counterparts born in the late 1930s did so. (Table 32.) Children further down the scale gained, too: the corresponding proportion among those from semi- and unskilled homes thus rose from 1 to 10 per cent over the same period. But that still left nine in every ten children of the late 1930s generation from homes of this level outside the grammar schools – although they reached secondary school age several years after the 1944 Act. If exclusion from academic secondary schooling (or from university education: see table 33) is the measure, then 'educational deprivation' was reduced far more at the top than at the bottom of the class hierarchy, over the decades to about the middle of this century.

Still, by another measure, class differences were reduced: inequalities of access became proportionately smaller, so far as entry to grammar schools and the equivalent were concerned. The premium which a child from a professional or managerial family enjoyed over a child from a semi- or unskilled home, in the chance of getting this sort of schooling, fell from something like 37:1 to a ratio around 6:1 over these generations. (Table 32.) And it fell again to some 5:1 in the case of those born in the late 1950s. But by then figures of this sort were no longer very illuminating. For in 1971, when this generation were at secondary school, well over a quarter of the age group were in 'comprehensive' schools – roughly the same proportion among children of all social classes. A number of these were getting an academic education, similar to that offered by grammar schools. But there is no systematic and nationwide information to say *how* many of them, either *in toto* or with respect to the numbers from different home backgrounds. It is clear, from local studies and from general impressions, that the chance of getting a grammar school type education within a comprehensive school is higher, in general, the more advantaged the family background of the child. This is so both because the usual social pressures are at work in the process of selection and self-selection for 'ability streams' within comprehensive schools; and because the character of comprehensive schools varies with the class composition of their catchment areas. Yet if access to an academic secondary education is the measure of educational opportunity, the effect of the spread of comprehensive schooling cannot be assessed without precise figures, on a nationwide basis, about who gets what kind of education in these schools. It is an ironical consequence of comprehensive reorganization – designed in part to reduce class barriers to equal opportunity – that the effects of those barriers become obscured from view.

TABLE 33

The trend of class inequalities of opportunity for entry to university education

Social origin – i.e., father's occupation	Per cent of children, of different social origins, who obtained a university education:			Social origin – i.e., father's occupation	Per cent of children, of different social origins, who obtained a university education:	
	Those born ———				Those born ——	
	Before 1910	1910– 1929	Late 1930s		Late 1930s	Approx. 1953/54
Profess., manag., and 'intermediate'	3	6	$14\frac{1}{2}$	Profess. and technical Admin. and managerial Other non-manual	10	18 { 35 / 21 / $10\frac{1}{2}$
Remaining non-manual and skilled manual	$\frac{1}{2}$	1	$2\frac{1}{2}$			
Semi-skilled and unskilled	—	$\frac{1}{2}$	$\frac{1}{2}$	Manual, all levels	$1\frac{1}{2}$	4
All children	$1\frac{1}{2}$	$2\frac{1}{2}$	4	All children	4	9

Sources: For the first series (generations born before 1910 and up to the late 1930s) – J. H. Westergaard and A. N. Little, op. cit. (see table 32 above).
   For the second series – as above in respect of those born in the late 1930s; with calculations from Universities Central Council on Admissions, Statistical Supplement to the 10th Report 1971/72, 1973, for the estimate in respect of the latest generation shown.
Notes:
   (i) Comparison of the figures for different generations, even within each of the two series, can be made only in rough terms, because the occupational classifications used for the generations born up to 1929, in the late 1930s and around 1953/54 do not fully coincide; and because the figures for the 1953/54 generation relate to the UK, earlier figures to England and Wales.
   (ii) There were and are very sharp differences between the sexes in chances of university entry. More than twice as many boys as girls entered university education throughout the period covered (with a slight increase in the share of girls in recent years), and these disparities between the sexes widened down the class scale.

Probably, class inequalities in access to academic secondary schooling continued to narrow in the 1960s: at least the figures for grammar and independent school entry alone suggest that. And the corresponding inequalities in chances of getting to university – stable or even widening, in proportionate terms, until the 1950s despite university expansion – appear also to have become a little smaller in recent years. But they remain very sharp: the change is marginal. Even when all manual workers' children are taken together – those from skilled families as well as those from poorer homes – these were still, in the early 1970s, less likely to enter a university than children of 'professional and technical' fathers by a factor of nearly nine times. (Table 33.) There are other ways of getting a higher education than to go to university, of course. And class inequalities of access to institutions outside the university sector – polytechnics, colleges of education and so on – are rather less pronounced. Moreover, these institutions – the polytechnics in particular – grew fast from the 1960s. But the impact of their expansion on patterns of class recruitment to higher education has probably been quite limited, although there is no comprehensive information on the subject as yet. The signs, scattered and indefinite though they are, suggest that as in the past the growth of student places in higher education from the early 1960s met a demand which, in effect, came mainly from professional, managerial and other non-manual homes. The scales remain heavily weighted against young people of manual working-class origin, though probably not quite so much as before.[3]

3. The Robbins Report on *Higher Education* (Cmnd. 2154 and appendices, 1963) showed that among the generation of children born in 1940/41, some 19½ per cent of those from non-manual homes had obtained some form of full-time higher education by 1962; only just over 3 per cent of those from manual homes. The class disparity was sharpest in respect of degree-level courses–then mainly in universities – rather less sharp in respect of other courses. (*Higher Education, Appendix One*, pp. 39–40; see also *Appendix Two (B)*, pp. 3–5, 71–2, 92.) We have found no comparable information about higher education as a whole for later years. But local studies of the entry to particular institutions suggest that the new polytechnics – especially their departments of social sciences and humanities – draw their students preponderantly from non-manual homes. If the results of one such study covering a number of institutions – several colleges of education and polytechnics, as well as universities, in the North and Midlands – could be taken to represent the national picture for the non-university sector, then chances of full-time higher education for children from non-manual homes would have risen from the 19½ per cent of the early 1960s to around 30 per cent in the late 1960s; those of children from manual homes from some 3 per cent to about 8½ per cent – i.e., rather faster in proportionate terms. (Calculated from sample data in N.J. Entwistle *et al., Educational Objectives and Academic Performance in Higher*

III

So the expansion of educational provision has not involved a major redistribution of opportunities between children of different classes. The benefits went to children of all social levels. As in the case of material standards of living, the average rose fairly steadily; but disparities between the classes remained sharp. Nevertheless, some element of redistribution followed in the process: the range of inequalities of educational opportunity became rather less extreme. This was still only barely visible by the early 1970s, so far as access to university and other higher education was concerned. But a gradual and modest narrowing of class differences in the chances of admission to secondary schooling of an academic type can be seen at work throughout the century. The fact that this trend goes back over many decades is important. For it could have been expected, by itself, to make for some limited increase in social circulation between the generations. Yet there was apparently no such acceleration of mobility at least till about the 1950s; nor even by the early 1970s, except by very uncertain and short-lived signs. It seems, then, that the moderate widening of education as an avenue of mobility was counteracted, at least for long, by a concomitant contraction of other channels of circulation.

That is inference. But it is plausible inference which fits in with other hints of change in patterns of class recruitment. Formal

---

Education, Lancaster Univ., 1971.) But though the university students in this sample were nationally representative with respect to class origins, one cannot know whether the same was true of the college of education and polytechnic students. And since the polytechnic sample included no social science and language students, the disproportionate opportunities for children with non-manual background may be understated. It is also worth noting that some 80 per cent of the first entrants to part-time study under the auspices of the Open University (excluding housewives and others without paid work) had non-manual jobs, over 60 per cent as administrators, managers and professionals, including teachers. (*Early Development of the Open University: Report of the Vice-Chancellor,* 1972.) It may well be true that analysis of these students' origins by reference to their *father's* occupations (as in other studies of educational recruitment) would have shown a higher share for the manual population. But this is not relevant if the issue is the contribution made by the Open University to inter-generational mobility from manual to non-manual status, since those with managerial, professional and similar jobs but manual family origins had crossed the threshold *before* joining the Open University, even if the qualifications they acquire there may give an additional boost to their careers.

educational qualifications have increasingly become a prerequisite of appointment to jobs in the middle and upper reaches of the occupational scale. The expansion of educational provision at secondary and higher levels is both product and, in turn, reinforcing cause of that trend. One probable, and logical, result is to make it more difficult for those who start their working lives in fairly low-grade jobs, and without special certification from school or college, to climb the ladder of promotion. As thresholds of educational qualification for managerial, executive, technical and professional posts are raised over time, opportunities for advancement on the basis only of job experience and patronage from superiors are probably curtailed. Those who begin their careers in clerical and similar work are likely to have been most vulnerable to this process of promotion blockage. There may be counteracting influences. Union pressure in the civil service, for example, has helped to institutionalize provision for promotion up the grades. But this is an industry exposed to public scrutiny; low-level white-collar employees, moreover, are weakly unionized in most of the private sector. Male clerical workers may, again, have been able to evade some of the pressures making for promotion blockage, because so many women have been recruited into office work; and they especially are concentrated in routine jobs. But we do not know how far job segregation and reservation by sex may have allowed men to retain chances of advancement which were otherwise contracting. Men who stay in rank-and-file office work have certainly not been able to evade a relative deterioration of their earnings in the market, to figures now generally well below those of skilled manual labour.

It is probable, in short, that social mobility through promotion – and perhaps demotion – over part of the range of occupations has become rather rarer; while the acquisition of formal educational qualifications outside work, and usually before entry into work, has become more important as a precondition of occupational success. Too little is known about this shift to set figures to it. But there is some direct evidence, in addition to impressions and inferential reasoning, to confirm its existence; and to suggest that it follows earlier changes in the channels of social circulation of a different kind.[4] Throughout much of the nineteenth century, while the scale of

4. There is direct evidence for this country, though of limited coverage, on the historical shifts in mobility patterns discussed in this paragraph. See Charlotte Erickson, *British Industrialists: Steel and Hosiery, 1850–1950*, Cambridge Univ.

business enterprise remained fairly small, entrepreneurial activity was no doubt a significant source of mobility: upwards, through business success from small or modest beginnings; downwards, through business failure and bankruptcy. Later, as the scale and complexity of organization in both private and public enterprise grew – especially from the last few decades of the nineteenth century onwards – promotion up the rungs of bureaucratic hierarchies gradually displaced independent entrepreneurial activity as a means of mobility. Demotion in the course of working life may already have been fairly uncommon then, at least for non-manual employees. It certainly rarely occurs now, to judge by the evidence we presented earlier; and downward mobility from one generation to the next usually takes the form of entry into work at a lower level than that of parental origin. But the typical pattern of advancement in large-scale organizations itself changed over time: from promotion primarily on the basis of job experience and patronage, to appointment and promotion for which formal certification in schools and colleges was the first and increasingly essential condition. The trend set in early in the public sector – in Britain, with the standardization of civil service recruitment and promotion by competitive examination from around 1870. But it has spread to private enterprise in the course of this century, though at a rate and on a scale which cannot be traced in any precise way.

Press, 1959. Data on the careers of owners, partners and directors of the steel companies studied show the virtual disappearance from the scene of the 'self-made man' (who built up his own firm alone or in partnership, as over half the steel company heads of the 1860s had done) by the mid-twentieth century; and the rise of people who followed 'administrative' (and later, as yet in much smaller numbers, 'professional') careers to the top. Those who had, directly or indirectly, inherited their top positions increased their share over time – from 30 to 40 per cent, when steel bosses for whom no information was available are ignored. The fraction contributed to the steel élite by men who started work in manual jobs dropped from 13 per cent in the late nineteenth century to nil in this; and that of men who started work as clerks, from 15 to 8 per cent – although in the population at large employment in clerical work was growing during the same period. Data for the heads of the hosiery companies studied show similar trends – but at each point of time a larger representation of self-made men and of men who climbed from a start in low-grade work, in this older industry with its smaller firms. (Cf. in this connection S. J. Chapman and F. J. Marquis, 'The recruiting of the employing classes from the ranks of the wage earners in the cotton industry', *J. Royal Statistical Society*, vol. 75, 1912). There is also evidence consistent with, though not positive proof of, a decline over time in the proportion of managers who started work near the bottom of the ladder, with little formal education, in Acton Society Trust, *Management Succession*, 1956, and R. V. Clements, *Managers*, Allen & Unwin, 1958.

These historical shifts in patterns of mobility are significant on several scores. In particular, they present a corrective to a common – if rarely explicitly formulated – impression that there was little social circulation in nineteenth-century Britain. On the contrary: industrialization and capitalization may well have made for high rates of mobility then, up and down the scale, as they certainly made for high rates of geographical migration and movement of labour from old to new sectors of the economy. There is a widespread and naïve sort of ahistoricism which attributes to Victorian Britain a 'traditional' character it never had; which is half-blind to the fact that the fundamental economic transformations from which the society we have today emerged took place mainly in the nineteenth century, and earlier. Britain is no longer 'industrializing': it did so long ago. And that process of necessity entailed a great deal of movement in the population, vertically as well as horizontally. The educational system was not a prime channel of mobility in the Victorian era; it had not yet been institutionally geared to the business of social selection. But independent business activity, and then career experience in bureaucratic enterprise, provided means of circulation which are often neglected in present-day stereotypes. Even now, education is far from being the only avenue of social mobility.[5] But it has undoubtedly become more important in that role. What is more – while the educational channel has widened, earlier channels of circulation have contracted: and at a roughly matching rate. So, at least, the stability of velocities of social circulation until the 1970s suggests. A similar stability – or only modest increases – apparent in several other Western countries for which there is information may have the same explanation.[6]

5. The point is evident from the data presented earlier on 'career mobility', as well as from the results of the 1949 social mobility survey. The latter showed that, while education certainly helped to shape job chances, the outcome was actually poorer for grammar school boys from semi- and unskilled homes than for elementary school boys from professional, executive and upper grade supervisory homes. (J. R. Hall and D. V. Glass, 'Education and social mobility', in Glass, ed., op. cit., ch. 1, note 7 above.) Cf. also C. A. Anderson, 'A skeptical note on education and mobility', in A. H. Halsey et al., eds., Education, Economy and Society, Glencoe Free Press, Ill., 1961; and Blau and Duncan, in the study referred to in the following note.

6. Findings to suggest that mobility rates changed little in a number of countries during the first half of this century or so, though with a few exceptions, are summarized in Carlsson, op. cit. (ch. 1, note 2 above, pp. 110–13) and S. M. Lipset and R. Bendix, Social Mobility in Industrial Society, Heinemann, 1959 (pp. 33–8, 90, 121–43). A major recent American study, P. M. Blau and O. D. Duncan,

IV

The enhanced importance of education in social mobility is often misunderstood. It evokes, for example, catchy and vaguely phrased postulates that 'class is now a matter of educational achievement' – not, it is said, of 'birth' or 'wealth'. The contrasts posited in this sort of formulation are false. For one thing, they imply a recent or ongoing transition from a 'closed' to an 'open' society. But capitalist societies like Britain have been half-closed, half-open for long. The heightened influence of formal schooling on the levels reached by individuals in the socio-economic hierarchy of adult life does not, *ipso facto*, change this balance – both because other ways of climbing or slipping down the scale are less common now than they were before; and because a child's education is itself very much influenced by his or her social origins. Beyond that, however, the fashionable formulation in any case involves a conceptual confusion. It confounds the character and causes of class inequality with the processes by which individuals find their positions in the structure of inequality. Wealth and power still go with 'top jobs', whatever the routes by which 'top people' get to those jobs; low income, insecurity and dependence still go with 'bottom jobs', whether escape from those conditions requires certification from schools or the hard use of elbows. Moreover, a poor educational record on the part, say, of a company director can raise eyebrows here and there in the circles where he moves – though he may now acquire some kudos from it, just because the conjunction is less common than it was. But establishment contempt for 'upstarts' is no new phenomenon; and the man's wealth is not diminished thereby; his influence probably not much either. Conversely, there is little to be gained from a good education as such, by way of pull or prestige, unless it is translated into occupational success and wealth. School and college qualifications, in short, no more confer privilege in themselves than they ever did: they are just more important as preconditions for access to positions of privilege. The foundations and even the status trimmings of class inequality are not altered merely because the modes of recruitment to particular positions have changed.

The American Occupational Structure (Wiley, 1967), drawing on its own new date together with the results of earlier work, finds no evidence of 'rigidification' over time, but also at most only a moderate increase in social mobility (pp. 97–113).

The channelling of more mobility through the educational system has been fostered, here and elsewhere, by government policy. In England and Wales, direct public provision of elementary education was delayed until 1870, though the state had supported 'voluntary' provision – and exercised increasing supervision over it – since the 1830s. Even when schools for the children of the common people were maintained by public authorities, there was at first no intention to use them as a means of selecting young people for their occupational destinations. From the new and reformed 'public schools' – which of course were private – at the top of the hierarchy, to the state elementary schools at the bottom, there were separate kinds of education for children of different class origin, with no formal bridges between them. It was not the job of the publicly maintained and aided schools to steer their abler children to higher levels of the hierarchy, and thence to better jobs in adult life – except that provision was made, early on, for recruitment of elementary school teachers from the ranks of elementary schoolchildren. But from the late nineteenth century, and in particular after the Act of 1902 and subsequent regulations to establish state supported secondary schools with a quota of free places for selected children, it became part of the business of public education to provide a 'ladder' of opportunity for bright boys and girls from wage-earning homes. The notion was that of a ladder only: narrow – though it was widened over the decades – with intense competition for access to its first rungs; upwards only, with no aim that children from privileged homes should be thrown into competition with working-class children to sink, swim or fly on 'merit' alone. We have already sketched the process by which this conception of a ladder was transformed.[7] With the Act of 1944, the public educational system – primary, secondary and higher stages – was to work as a 'sieve' in which all children would be sorted by ability, educated appropriately, and sent out into the adult world at whatever level their qualifications suggested. All children, that is, apart from those whose parents could avoid this competition by sending them to private and quasi-private schools as fee-payers. With that significant exception, the promotion of social mobility – in half-hearted principle, down as well as up the scale – had become a major and explicit function of education in official policy.

The shape which the post-1944 secondary schools took in practice, though the Act did not specifically enjoin this, was one that imposed

7. See Part Three, chapter 3, section V.

early segregation of children according to 'aptitude'. In form, segregation into grammar, modern and occasionally technical schools usually took place at the point of transition from primary to secondary education, at the age of '11 plus'. In reality, it occurred even earlier, in many primary schools, when children were separated into 'ability streams' at an age of 7 or 8. Much of the criticism directed against the educational system since 1944 has been aimed at this tripartite – or effectively bipartite – division within the schools of the public sector. The gradual postponement of formal segregation by ability which has been in progress in the primary schools since the 1960s, and the more or less concomitant and politically contested conversion of secondary schools to 'comprehensive' organization, may indeed widen educational opportunities in various ways. It should help to delay the process by which resources – of facilities and staff – are concentrated on a successively smaller minority of children, selected and self-selected for academic education as they move up the age-scale. It may encourage a general expansion of the resources available to all children: in so far as the size of comprehensive schools allows economies of scale and specialization; and in so far as the demands of parents and teachers previously met within the segregated grammar schools have to be met in schools with a wider intake of pupils. It is possible that deferment of the pressures associated with selection by ability, which certainly reinforce and may accentuate initial cultural and intellectual differences among children, will allow more children from wage-earning homes to get a foothold on the ladder of academic promotion. Pay-off of that kind, and in part of the former kinds, however, depends upon the extent to which segregation is in fact delayed to a late age. Instead, it may continue on much the same scale: through 'streaming' in a variety of forms; through the impact of residential class segregation on the recruitment of pupils to different schools; through class differences in the effective capacity of parents to choose schools and exercise influence with teachers and authorities in the allocation of resources.[8]

8. On the common, though now slowly relaxing, pattern of early segregation by ability in primary schools, see B. Jackson, *Streaming: an Education System in Miniature*, Routledge & Kegan Paul, 1964. The literature on the division of secondary education in the public sector between grammar, modern and technical schools, and for and against replacement of this division by the introduction of comprehensive schools, is enormous. For an excellent sociological history of secondary education to 1944 and the years immediately thereafter, see O. Banks, *Parity and Prestige in English Secondary Education*, Routledge & Kegan Paul,

To make these last points is not to argue against 'comprehensive' organization of schools and related policies. Their effects cannot be predicted in any precise way; but they are likely to provide at least a framework within which a more equal distribution of educational resources could become feasible. For the present, however, it is doubtful whether they would do very much – especially without measures to eliminate private education – to reduce the ultimate disparities in occupational life chances between children of different

1955. Cf. also, e.g., W. Taylor, *The Secondary Modern School*, Faber, 1963; and for a review and commentary, from a 'pro-comprehensive' perspective, concerning the gradual introduction of comprehensive forms of secondary school organization, Caroline Benn and B. Simon, *Half-Way There* (2nd ed.), Penguin, 1972. Despite the mass of literature, there is little solid knowledge of the effects of 'streaming' by ability, and of its abolition or relaxation, on educational achievement and on inequalities of opportunity in that respect. Joan C. Barker Lunn, *Streaming in the Primary School* (National Foundation for Educational Research, 1970) reviews earlier work in Britain and elsewhere and points to its inconclusiveness. This large-scale study itself (and its sequel, Elsa Ferri, *Streaming: Two Years Later*, N.F.E.R., 1971, in which the sample of children are followed up into the secondary school) suggests no difference between ability-segregation and all ability teaching in their effects on achievement in conventional tests of knowledge and reasoning, but some improvement of results in unconventional tests of 'divergent thinking' when streaming is relaxed. That outcome, however, arises at least in part from differences of educational philosophy and approach among teachers. And the design of the research was such as to rule out examination of the effect (if any) of the organizational form of teaching by itself; while the relevance of these findings to class differences in educational opportunity is not pursued. J. W. B. Douglas and his colleagues (*The Home and The School*, MacGibbon & Kee, 1964: *All Our Future*, Davies, 1968) in a longitudinal study found signs that initial differences in ability were accentuated, with a loss of academic potential among manual working-class children especially, through primary school streaming leading up to selection for secondary education at 11-plus; but a reversal of this tendency after relaxation of the sharp competitive pressures associated with such selection. Two case studies, in particular, have explored in some detail the ways in which segregation by ability within secondary schools contributes to the formation of distinct, and inevitably class-tied, 'subcultures' of children, respectively assimilated to, indifferent to and positively hostile to school and teachers: D. H. Hargreaves, *Social Relations in a Secondary School*, Routledge & Kegan Paul, 1967; C. Lacey, *Hightown Grammar*, Manchester Univ. Press, 1970. Among studies of comprehensive secondary schools, see Douglas *et al., All Our Future*, op. cit. (ch. 9, the data in which suggest a reduction of early leaving, especially in the case of manual working-class children of average ability, as a result of comprehensive compared with selective organization); Julienne Ford, *Social Class and the Comprehensive School*, Routledge & Kegan Paul, 1969 (a case study which emphasizes the persistence of de facto segregation by both educational ability and class within the school studied); and T. G. Monks, ed., *Comprehensive Education in Action*, N.F.E.R., 1970 (a national sample inquiry which, while providing evidence on a larger scale generally consistent with some of the conclusions of the study by Ford, has virtually no material from non-comprehensive schools to allow a comparative evaluation of comprehensive education).

origins. Comparisons with the United States – crude and tentative though they must be – do not suggest that deferment of formal selection by ability to a fairly late stage of education makes, by itself, for a much less class-skew distribution of opportunities.[9] It is more likely that the competitive pressures at work simply set in at higher ages, and at higher overall thresholds of educational qualifications: competition at '7 plus' and '11 plus' becomes competition at '15 plus', '18 plus', and '20 plus'. That change can be well worth having. But it does not of itself alter overall patterns of social mobility and immobility.

To aim to do so is anyway, as we have argued before, to set a quite limited objective: to improve efficiency and equity of personnel selection for positions that remain acutely unequal in the rewards and power which go with them. Advocates of comprehensive education

9. Not only is formal selection by ability normally delayed till a late stage in the United States, but far higher proportions of young people there carry on from school to college or university than in Western Europe. Trends have been upwards on both sides of the Atlantic, but the differences remain marked. Yet circulation between the manual and non-manual groups from one generation to the next has been, in proportionate terms, if anything a little more common in Britain than in the U.S.A. (see ch. 2, note 2 above). And while the range of relative class inequalities in chances of obtaining a degree or the equivalent was rather narrower in the U.S.A. in the early 1950s than here about the same time (J. Ben-David, *Professions in the Class System of Present-Day Societies*, no. 3, vol. 12 of *Current Sociology*, 1963–64), the difference between the two countries on that score were modest. They were quite limited, too, when American class disparities in access to a degree were compared – perhaps more relevantly, with reference to national norms – with British class disparities in chances of staying on at school till 17 or older. (Cf. Westergaard and Little, op. cit., table 32 in text above: U.S. figures, like Ben-David's, from D. Wolfle, *America's Resources of Specialized Talent*, New York, 1954.) Ben-David attributed the cross-national variations in the range of class inequalities of access to higher education which he found, including still wider disparities in some other European countries than in Britain, primarily to differences in the 'flexibility' of educational systems. That is plausible. And a fairly marked rise over recent years in Swedish manual working-class children's representation among university students, probably in consequence of a thorough reorganization of schooling on formally comprehensive lines, may strengthen the suggestion. (J. Israel, 'Uppfostran och utbildning', in E. Dahlström, *Svensk Samhällsstruktur i Sociologisk Belysning*, Stockholm, 1968.) But working-class representation in the universities had been negligible before, and class inequalities of educational opportunity by measures of this kind are still sharp in Sweden. Comprehensive reform of the schools has made a dent; but that so far seems all. And while it is too early to judge, the ultimate impact on overall rates of social circulation (as yet much the same in Sweden as here, and little changed in this century when the effects of shifts in occupational structure are discounted: cf. Carlsson, op. cit., ch. 1, note 2 above; Miller, op. cit., ch. 2, note 2 above; R. Erixon, 'Uppävxtförhållanden och social rörlight', in *Svenska Folkets Levnadsförhållanden*, Stockholm, Låginkomstutredningen, 1971) is hardly likely to be drastic.

have in practice had to set their sights this low. Some, it is true, have been inspired by a vision of a 'common education' for all, irrespective of both social origins and occupational destinations of the children. But to aim for that, without a change in the class foundations of the society, is to try to detach the educational system *en bloc* from its social anchorage: to go flat against its *raisons d'être*. Public provision of education has been expanded to meet in the main utilitarian demands: to encourage social and industrial discipline; to train a diversified labour force; to grade and select future entrants to the labour force by 'aptitude'; to contain popular demands for equity in these processes of grading and selection. Elite education, by contrast, has always set objectives which went beyond this: to bring up children of the privileged in a 'common culture' of a kind – common to the privileged, more or less irrespective of 'aptitude'; to introduce those picked for admission to the élite, from lower origins, to the same culture. Selection by ability has been a condition attached to the growth of popular education; by no means in the same way to the development of education for those born to wealth and position. Elite education – for new recruits as well as for those born to privilege – upholds an ideal of education 'for its own sake', in contrast with the predominantly utilitarian objectives that colour education at other levels. The universities, for example, tolerate a pursuit of 'pure knowledge', 'free inquiry', unorthodoxies of approach and outlook – within limits, yet to a much greater degree than do polytechnics, colleges of education and other institutions lower in the hierarchy of education. The price paid for the expansion of the latter has been further entrenchment of the notion that, except for a minority, education must be seen to pay off.[10]

10. For a history of proposals and measures for 'comprehensive' reorganization of schools in this country, see D. Rubinstein and B. Simon, *The Evolution of the Comprehensive School, 1926–1972*, Routledge & Kegan Paul, (2nd ed.) 1973. Among the many defences of selection in secondary (and other) education, see especially E. (later Lord) James, *Education and Leadership*, Harrap, 1951, in which selection is justified by the argument that the capacity for moral judgment and hence for 'leadership' (rather then intellectual ability per se) is so scarce that it has to be identified early and carefully nurtured; and where a case is made also that religious (and by implication other) unorthodoxy should be tolerated among those selected for education for leadership, while other children should be held firmly to orthodoxy because, lacking the capacity for moral judgment, their respect for the social order might otherwise be undermined. So explicit a distinction between the functions of education for tomorrow's leaders and tomorrow's led is rarely made today, though it was often in the nineteenth century, and there are recurrent undertones of it in contemporary attacks on 'progressive' education

V

The conflict in politics and public debate since the 1950s around proposals to introduce 'comprehensive' education – elsewhere in Europe as well as in Britain – illustrates one outstanding consequence of the larger role which schools and colleges have acquired as agencies of selection. Education has become a major issue of social concern; its organization and workings are subjects now of everyday controversy, flashpoints of recurrent tension. This has been evident, too, in the volume of social research which has accumulated on educational matters. The sheer quantity of material produced reflects the central place occupied by these questions in the public mind today. The themes pursued reflect the anxieties of parents and children, triggered by awareness of the influence of success and failure in school on individual life chances; the worries of politicians, institutional authorities and employers over educational efficacy and order; in some measure also the special preoccupations of research workers and teachers, as members of professions with views, interests and concerns with 'autonomy' of their own to further.

(cf., e.g., C. B. Cox and A. E. Dyson, eds., *Black Papers on Education*, nos. 1, 2 and 3, Critical Quarterly Society, 1969–70). In any case, student unrest from the 1960s weakened any assumption that those selected for the higher rungs of education – now too numerous all to become 'leaders' – would of themselves stay committed to the current order, if unorthodoxy had a loose rein. (For examples of the anxieties aroused by student unrest see some of the contributions to D. A. Martin, ed., *Anarchy and Culture*, Routledge & Kegan Paul, 1969; B. Wilson, *The Youth Culture and the Universities*, Faber, 1970.) There are many histories of educational policy and practice. But for studies concerned specifically with changing and recurrent ideas about the social purposes of schooling, see especially B. Simon, *Studies in the History of Education, 1780–1870*, Lawrence & Wishart, 1960; *idem, Education and the Labour Movement, 1870–1920*, Lawrence & Wishart, 1965; H. Silver, *The Concept of Popular Education*, McGibbon & Kee, 1965; E. C. Mack, *Public Schools and British Opinion*, 2 vols., London and New York, 1938, 1941. The major government reports in the 1950s and '60s reflect both the divisions within English education – there was no report on education as a whole – and the mixture of preoccupations with economic utility and with meritocratic equity which guided public policy: *15 to 18* (Crowther Report), 1959–60; *Half Our Future* (Newsom Report), 1963; *Higher Education* (Robbins Report), 1963; *Children and their Primary Schools* (Plowden Report), 1967; 1st and 2nd *Reports of the Public Schools Commission*, 1968. For discussion of some aspects of the recent expansion of higher education relevant to the points made in this paragraph, see inter al. Layard *et al.*, op. cit. (note 16 above); G. Brosan *et al.*, *Patterns and Policies in Higher Education*, Penguin, 1971; T. Burgess and J. Pratt, *Policy and Practice: the Colleges of Advanced Technology*, LSE, 1970; E. Robinson, *The New Polytechnics*, Penguin, 1968; E. P. Thompson, ed., *Warwick University Ltd.*, Penguin, 1970.

Questions concerning the factors affecting individual success and failure in educational competition have taken first place. The major inequalities of opportunity have been mapped, and mapped again: inequalities by class above all; inequalities by sex, widening the further down the scale of class one goes; inequalities by region and district, often arising from and in turn reinforcing class disparities. Much effort has gone, and still goes, into attempts to unravel the influences at work in the continuous production of these inequalities. 'Natural' differences in intelligence among children explain little. Even if conventional intelligence tests were taken to measure of 'innate' intellectual capacity, the point stands firmly demonstrated that, with the exception only of children at the highest level of measured ability, effective educational attainment falls sharply with class irrespective of intelligence. It is lower, too, so far as access to the more rewarding kinds of further and higher education are concerned, among girls than among boys of the same level of measured ability. There are, in short, large reservoirs of 'wasted talent', even when talent is equated only with performance in orthodox tests of brainpower.[11]

Most relevant research over the last decade or two has concentrated on the ways in which the cultural climates of home and school condition, and interact to condition, the educational progress of children. Children from non-manual homes enter a world, at school, whose outlook and aspirations are on the whole familiar to them. They experience far less of a 'clash of cultures' than do most manual working-class children in their confrontation with teachers, teaching and testing. Lines of division – in principle intellectual, in practice to a considerable extent by class – are at least reinforced by early separation of the promising and amenable minority from the less able, often difficult and reluctant majority. Even if full-blown separation by ability is postponed, the pattern of rewards and penalties, praise and blame, may have a similar cumulative effect of solidifying initial differences, once labelled. It may encourage a self-protective indifference to school in the unsuccessful majority; among many of them, direct hostility. The discordance between ordinary working-class culture and that of the schools – manifest in crude form in survey results pointing to the influence of parental 'interest' on their children's progress up the academic ladder – has been explored

11. See particularly Douglas *et al.*, op. cit. (1964 and 1968, note 8 above); and *15 to 18* (note 10 above), especially vol. II, part II, pp. 116–33.

further in a series of recent studies concerning class differences in uses of language and in habits of communication between parents and children. Their theme – to cut brutally through all subtleties of development and variation – has been a contrast between a 'middle class' empathy with abstraction, a culturally habitual ease in generalizing from particulars; and a working-class rootedness in what is concrete, present, immediately and pragmatically relevant.[12]

Sensitive and imaginative though much of this most recent research has been, there are risks attached to the enthusiasm with which it has been widely received; and that not just because the weight of interpretation placed upon limited data is sometimes excessive, the refinements of interpretation tortured in their obscurity. There is a risk, first, of promoting a caricature image of manual working-class perspectives and life orientations as essentially limited to the here and now; as lacking the vision and the capacity to take off from the particular to the general, from the present to the future, from the known to the unknown. There is plenty in contemporary social commentary – professional and lay – to reinforce such a caricature. Yet it is a caricature. For it leaves out of account those features of working-class life and history which cannot be squared with it: the persistent though diffuse ideals of society-wide equality and fraternity which have given the labour movement a good part of its motive power; the loyalties to unknown others, the sacrifices of present benefits for uncertain future gains, involved even in the most routine and everyday instances of industrial conflict. Working-class culture is shot through with contradictions between particularistic and universalistic orientations, between the pressures of individual

12. The socio-linguistic work on which we go on to comment is that of B. Bernstein and his associates. See especially his *Class, Codes and Controls* (Vol. 1), Paladin, 1971; also, e.g., W. Brandis and D. Henderson, *Social Class, Language and Communication*, London Univ. Inst. of Education, 1970, and B. Bernstein, ed., *Language, Primary Socialization and Education*, Routledge & Kegan Paul, 1970. For some of the other work referred to in this paragraph, concerning the influence of home and school on educational achievement, see note 8 above and some of the official reports listed in note 10 above (especially the Crowther and Plowden reports). Cf. also P. Wedge and H. Prosser, *Born to Fail*, Arrow, 1973. Much else could be quoted. But for some useful summaries or collections of readings, see e.g. O. Banks, *The Sociology of Education*, Batsford, 1971 (chapters 3–5); M. Craft, ed., *Family, Class and Education*, Longman, 1970; H. Silver, ed., *Equal Opportunity in Education*, Methuen, 1973 (a collection of readings which traces the development, in policy and research, of the issue of equal opportunity since the 1920s); R. K. and H. M. Kelsall, *Social Disadvantage and Educational Opportunity*, Holt, 1971.

pragmatism and the commitments and abstractions of collective ideals. And 'middle class' orientations – though there is caricature here too, in contrasts which lump routine white-collar workers with professionals and with the élite of capital – have their own pragmatic and particularistic features: not least the elevation of individual achievement within an unchanged world to a moral virtue.[13]

There is a risk, secondly, of encouraging changes in the style and content of education for the majority of children which, designed to make schooling more 'relevant' to their current and probable future daily experience, could accentuate the place- and time-bound features of working-class culture. Proposals to relate teaching for the rank-and-file of children more closely to the local circumstances and particular situations with which they are familiar may, and sometimes do, have a progressive inspiration.[14] But their effect, if successful,

13. For Professor Bernstein's characterization of the working-class orientations to which he believes the results of his socio-linguistic studies point, see his *Class, Codes and Controls* (note 12 above), especially chapters 8–10. Bernstein recognizes, indeed underlines, the communal identifications and collective loyalties characteristic of working-class outlook, but emphasizes what he sees as their narrow limits of time, place and specific context. By contrast, 'elaborated codes [of speech, and by extension of thought] are less tied to a given or local structure and thus contain the potentiality of change in principles' (p. 200; see also, e.g., pp. 169–71, 199, 219–21). His qualifications are obscure, and do not alter the tenor of the argument. One example illustrates our points both that his data are made to carry a heavy weight of interpretation, and that his contrast between 'working' and 'middle' classes can be extraordinarily crude. In four of the essays reprinted in the book quoted (to date the most comprehensive statement of Bernstein's interpretations and re-interpretations), he draws on the results of a study in which the 'working class sample' comprised only post office messenger boys and the 'middle class sample' only boys at major public schools (a superb example of the common, vacuous use of the term 'middle class' which we criticize elsewhere). Again, in two of the essays he illustrates his characterization of differences between 'class codes' by contrasting two prototypical accounts from five-year-old children of a picture shown to them, where the 'working class' account seems to differ from the 'middle class' one only in that the former uses pronouns which assume (reasonably enough) that the listener can see the picture, while the latter identifies the characters more specifically ('the boys', 'a man', etc.). An elaborate interpretation is said to be exemplified here (pp. 203 et seq., 219 et seq.). For a brief critique of Bernstein, partly in line with these and other comments of ours, see H. Rosen, *Language and Class*, Falling Wall Press, 1972.

14. Bernstein has attacked the concept of 'compensatory education' (op. cit., 1971, ch. 10) for focusing on alleged deficiencies among working-class children and families rather than on deficiencies in the schools (though his own work is open to the same accusation). But while he defines the job of the schools as 'the introduction of the child to the universalistic meanings of public forms of thought' his argument that this must be done in contexts familiar to the children (p. 225) might well in practice frustrate the objective. A. H. Halsey, in an evaluation of government sponsored 'action research' in areas singled out for special aid in

would probably be conservative: to limit working-class horizons; to curtail aspirations – individual and collective; to douse the sparks of discontent which a clash between rising demands and restricted opportunities may ignite; as a result, both to reduce social circulation and to weaken pressures for social change.

The third and perhaps most serious risk is that of stimulating misunderstandings about the causes of class inequality: the sources of inequalities of opportunity as well as inequalities of condition. For one thing, the concentration of interest in research and debate on cultural discordance between homes and schools leads easily to neglect of the effects of crude material factors in maintaining class disparities of educational achievement. Thus, while education in the public sector is now free – and carries a right to means-tested maintenance grants at the post-school level, though not before – staying on beyond the statutory age of leaving school still entails a loss of earnings for a time. This may be a significant consideration in the case of children from homes with low or insecure incomes. Again, children from non-manual families have a disproportionately large share of state resources for education, not only because they are strongly represented among those who are picked for academic training; but also because it is mainly manual working-class children who experience the impact of regional and local variations in the quantity and quality of school provision. Outstanding among material causes of continuing educational inequality, moreover, is the right of parents who can afford it to buy private schooling for their children.[15]

---

education (*Educational Priority*, vol. 1, H.M.S.O., 1972) argues for 'community schools' in which education will be 'relevant to the children's direct experiences' and will equip them 'to meet the grim reality of the social environment in which they live and to reform it in all its aspects'. He recognizes the danger 'of creating a second-class education for second-class citizens through curricula restricted to local horizons. But what we intend is . . . not to fit children for their station in life . . . It is to accept that many children must live out their lives in deprived areas and to inspire them to think boldly about it rather than lapse into resigned apathy' (pp. 117–18). But it is not at all clear that, in practical terms, emphasis on criticism and change would or could prevail in teaching over emphasis on adaptation to circumstances; or that even emphasis on reform and change, when focused on local experience, could avoid the risk of diagnosis and prescription in vacuo – as if causes and remedies were local rather than national and international. Likely effects are not avoided merely by statements of intention to the contrary.

15. Private schools of all kinds accounted for some 8 per cent of children at school aged 14 in 1971 but for 22 per cent of those still at school at ages 17 and 18 in the same year. (Calculated from *Education Statistics for the UK, 1971*, pp. 4–5.)

To put forward these simple reminders is not to deny the force of more complex influences on individual achievement in school and college. But preoccupation with the interplay of cultural factors – perhaps just because those factors work in subtle and intricate ways – has in any case so far left an essential further question virtually unexplored; indeed rarely asked. That question concerns the reasons for the particular kinds of variation in culture, patterns of child-rearing, modes of communication and relations within families, which there appear to be between classes. It is not at all surprising that there should be class differences of sub-culture. It is far from clear why these differences take the specific forms which they do. Attempts to answer this question will, in our view, have to look first to the economic context of life at different levels of the class structure: not least to the barriers to individual 'planning' for the future set, for wage earning families, by relative insecurity and by the flat, non-incremental and non-promotional, character of the typical working-class life cycle. There is no room for confident assertion at this stage. But as long as the question is seldom even raised, there is leeway for conceptions of society in which cultural influences 'float free': in which differences in life style between classes have causal force attributed to them, but themselves are left unexplained and taken for granted.[16]

Among recent studies of the so-called public schools, see e.g. G. Kalton, *The Public Schools: a Factual Survey*, Longmans, 1966; J. Wakeford, *The Cloistered Elite*, Macmillan, 1969; T. Bishop and R. Wilkinson, *Winchester and The Public School Elite*, Faber, 1967; and the Public Schools Commission (op. cit., note 10 above). On geographical variations in state school provision, and their effects, see e.g. Douglas *et al.*, op. cit. (1964 and 1968, note 8 above); and D. S. Byrne and W. Williamson, 'Some inter-regional variations in educational provision', *Sociology*, Jan. 1972. The programme of special aid for 'educational priority areas' which arose from the recommendations of the Plowden Report (note 10 above) of course recognized material deprivation as among the problems involved, though with much emphasis on 'cultural' barriers between schools and children. But in financial terms, the programme was very modest (cf. Halsey, op. cit., note above: chapter 3); and by picking out only a small number of high priority areas, implied a limited conception of policy objectives, analogous to those preoccupations with a reduction of 'poverty' which we have criticized earlier. Access to pre-school education is very much a matter of material resources, and much of the provision is private. In 1971, nearly one-third of all children under 5 years old from professional families were in nursery schools, day nurseries and playgroups; about one quarter of those from other non-manual homes; but only 11–14 per cent of those from various levels of the manual working class. (Calculated from *General Household Survey: Introductory Report*, H.M.S.O., 1973, p. 234.) See also Tessa Blackstone, *A Fair Start: the Provision of Pre-School Education*, L.S.E., 1971.

16. Bernstein (op. cit., 1971, note 12 above) makes some very brief and vague

VI

With the deliberate direction of schools and colleges to the business
of selection, institutional provision has been made for social circulation: the educational system provides a commonly recognized
machinery for the purpose. This in turn may well have consequences
for the ways in which people see their class situation, assess their
chances in life, react to the experience of social mobility or immobility. Such consequences, however, are as yet largely a matter for
speculation.

One may have been to transfer some part of the burden of worries
associated with mobility – and with hopes or fears of mobility in the
future – from the shoulders of the mobile themselves to those of their
parents. The child who is upwardly mobile through educational
success moves upwards in the company of others, in a series of steps
that are well marked and institutionally established. The risk of
failure in the competition is usually with him throughout his schooling. He is not guaranteed a place in the élite from an early age, as one
fashionable characterization of educational mobility in this country
as 'sponsored' implies.[17] Even so, the path to success is more clearly
mapped and visible, even predictable on well-known conditions, than
was that of the man who made his own way in business from modest
beginnings or, say, of a clerk in whose promotion luck and patronage
played a large part. Those who climb through the educational system
may therefore need to use their elbows, and to set a symbolic distance
between themselves and their origins, less than many who climbed by

suggestions about the factors in the work and class situations of manual workers
which may help to promote their 'restricted codes' of language and orientation
(p. 165). But apart from that, a few casual hints elsewhere, and a suggestion (pp.
185–7) that class codes are changing anyway as a result of greater 'affluence', and
for other reasons familiar from the conventional literature about postulated 'embourgeoisement' of workers, his work shows no concern with the question of
causation. His claim to have been inspired in part by Marx (p. 196) is puzzling.
Neither he nor usually other social scientists in this country, however, have postulated that the causes of 'poverty' are cultural, as have some American social scientists. Cf. Part One, note 12.

17. R. H. Turner, 'Modes of social ascent through education', in Halsey *et al.*,
op. cit. (note 5 above) and also in E. Hopper, ed., *Readings in the Theory of
Educational Systems*, Hutchinson, 1971. Among other contributions to the latter,
see also the papers by Hopper (in part a critique of Turner, with suggestions for a
revised and more widely applicable classification of educational systems with
respect to their role in social mobility).

other means in the past. To that extent, the familiar syndrome of the nouveaux riches may be less typical than it was.[18] There is, moreover, evidence to suggest that parents take on a good deal of the load which might otherwise be carried by their sons and daughters *en route* to higher levels of the class hierarchy. Those working-class children who get into, and stay the course of, academic education come disproportionately from families who differ from the ordinary run of manual workers in some of their characteristics. They come from smaller families than the manual average, on the whole; from families in which husband, wife or both not only have fairly high aspirations on behalf of their children, but also have ties in their own past history with the 'middle classes' – by way of origin and education – more often than other manual couples. For all that, however, they may find it difficult to keep up with their children; to understand the world into which these are moving, as they climb the ladder of achievement at school and college.[19] These parents, more than their successful children, may truly be 'marginal': neither fully working class nor 'middle class' except in vague aspiration.

It is possible that, as more mobility is channelled through the educational system, personal failure in life by conventional criteria may be more likely to be accepted by the individuals concerned, as a matter for resignation rather than resentment or protest. Justice might be believed to be done – though it is often not done – because educational testing is ostensibly fair.[20] Moreover, the chances of social ascent may be thought of as greater than they are – and as much greater than in the past, though they are not – because the educational system provides a visible and institutionally established machinery of social circulation. All this is conceivable. But it is again

18. B. Jackson and D. Marsden, *Education and the Working Class* (Routledge & Kegan Paul, 1962) by contrast suggest that successful grammar school pupils from manual homes are inordinately anxious, as adults, to establish their credentials as members of the 'middle classes'. But they have little material about people born to 'middle class' status to compare with.

19. Cf. Jackson and Marsden, op. cit. (previous note), on relations between manual working-class parents and their grammar school children. For systematic evidence on a large scale concerning the characteristics of the families from which working-class children who stay the course in, or conversely drop out from, grammar schools, as well as on parental encouragement as measured by simple indices, see especially Douglas *et al.*, op. cit. (1964 and 1968, note 8 above) and *15 to 18* (note 10 above).

20. Glass ('Introduction', in his *Social Mobility in Britain*, ch. 1, note 7 above) suggests that individual resentment may be *more* acute, just because the selection process seems just.

speculation. And the arguments, without hard facts, can cut both ways.

Just because schools and colleges now are geared to social selection; just because the declared aim of the political establishment is to make that process of selection both fair and efficient – aspirations are likely to be raised: and to levels, perhaps, where their clash with the reality of limited opportunities may become acute. The signs are that working-class parents have a high, and increasing, interest in their children's education – because they are aware of, and may indeed overestimate, the dependence of individual prospects in life on schooling.[21] Typically, however, they lack the means – cultural as well as material, indirect as well as direct – to translate that interest into effective influence on their children's behalf. The result may well be growing consciousness of the ways in which the dice are loaded against their sons and daughters; and such consciousness may be made more potent by the knowledge that they have little chance of advancement for themselves, once they are set in manual working-class jobs without special educational qualifications to help them up. There are many imponderables here, as about other features of working-class consciousness today and tomorrow. But there is certainly no guarantee of a contribution to social order from the routinization of social mobility through education. The effects could well be the other way.

21. Cf., e.g., J. H. Goldthorpe et al., The Affluent Worker in the Class Structure. Cambridge Univ. Press, 1969 (pp 130 et seq.); Halsey, op. cit. (note 14 above, p. 118).

PART FIVE

ACQUIESCENCE AND DISSENT: RESPONSES TO INEQUALITY

1 From class in itself to class for itself: main lines of division

I

It has become standard practice, in the formally agnostic conventions of respectable sociology, to underline the complexity of patterns of inequality in contemporary Western societies. The practice is misleading. There is complexity of detail. But to focus on intricacies in this corner and that is to obscure the simplicity of the picture as a whole. The contours of the class map of Britain – a representative example of capitalist society today – are clear in their substantive features. It is a fairly straightforward matter to pull the threads of our analysis to this point together. We need to do so now; to summarize the hard facts of inequality, before we ask about popular responses to them.

Class inequality is tenacious. Disparities in material conditions and security remain acute, against a background of rising levels of average welfare; and despite some compression of the range of economic inequality in exceptional circumstances, around the time of the two world wars of this century. Ownership of wealth in particular is still highly concentrated. Possession of small property that carries no power – housing for owner occupation, cars and household goods – is more widespread than it was. Not so ownership for profit – property in business shares and securities – some diffusion within families of the rich apart. Public provision for social security has been greatly expanded; so in general have most services and activities of the state. But this has occurred within a framework of policy and practice which leaves the cost of working-class welfare as a charge mainly on working-class earnings, and control of the machinery well away from the hands of rank-and-file labour. Levels of formal education in the population at large have been steadily stepped up by government action. Schools and colleges have been set more deliberately to the business of preparing and sorting young people for their places in the world of work. Yet, limited though the vision which inspires it is, the liberal goal of free opportunity according to individual merit is little nearer achievement. There is a good deal of social circulation, down as well as up; but marked still by sharp disparities of prospects in life according to class origin; and not much more of it well into the second half of this century than by the beginning of the first. As yet, channels of social mobility have changed far more than rates of flow. It is possible that rates, too, could rise: the balance between pressures for efficient use of talent and the restrictions of formal and informal inheritance is not unalterably fixed. But in the pervasive nature of class inequalities of condition and power, the balance is likely to shift only within rather narrow limits.

Private capital is the central force behind the persistence of these and related inequalities of life circumstances. In the simplest and most visible sense: because the concentration of high incomes in few hands arises in substantial part from a still sharper concentration of property in private ownership. Less directly but far more significantly: because the principles which govern allocation and use of most resources reflect the dominance of private capital. The routine assumptions that set the principal parameters of life and policy are capitalist. Ownership of property, however acquired, constitutes an automatic claim on resources and, in sufficient quantity, confers on its beneficiaries an effective right not to work. By contrast, the livelihood of non-owners – the great majority – is set by the terms on which they can sell their labour in the market; or they depend on state support which, at levels generally well below labour market earnings, imposes a penalty for not working, even on those who are retired because of old age or sickness. Production and investment, moreover, are determined by the imperatives associated with the institution of private property: by the search for maximum long-run return to capital in markets where demand itself is shaped by the capital- and market-formed pattern of income distribution.

All this remains in essence unchanged by an ostensible partial transfer of business control from 'owners' to 'managers', associated with the growth of joint stock enterprise. The search for market profit is unaffected in principle, while it may be more efficiently pursued in practice. Top management and substantial ownership of capital in any case go together; and much of the pay as well as the perks of high executive office in business is indistinguishable from profit. The growth of corporate enterprise, moreover, has been associated with a concentration of resources and market influence in the hands of giant companies, which cements the power of private capital across as well as within national frontiers. The growth of state activity has not markedly diminished that power. Public services are financed by a system of taxation which, while it passes a high fraction of national income through the hands of government, takes close account of the profit requirements of business: little redistribution from capital to labour is involved. So too, the purposes to which state policy is directed are defined in terms that are consistent with and in major respects actively promote the prosperity of private business. The formal encroachment of public on private enterprise has gone a good deal further on this side of the Atlantic than in North America. The labour movement has had a substantial part in that process; and public protection of wage earners and the poor against extremes of insecurity is more extensive here than in the U.S.A. But the interests of business and capital retain their predominance – whichever party so far has been in office – over the ways in which government action is conceived, and over the limits which are implicitly set to it. Labour – the party and the unions – have bought some influence, in effect, by practical acquiescence in the routine sway of the working principles of private property, profit and market.

The prospect that containment of class conflict within capitalist premises would remain undisturbed began to appear shakier in the 1960s and 1970s than for at least two decades before. Continuing inflation; recurrent crises for business in this country especially over access to foreign markets and to credit; a decline in rates of profit – these and associated factors combined to threaten the prosperity of capital and to accentuate its dependence on labour acquiescence. Yet labour militancy was mounting – as part effect, part perhaps also cause of the same processes. And it spread from shop floors to union leadership, as the unions tried to resolve – for a time at least – the sharpening conflict between their representative purposes and their *de facto* role as agents of labour discipline, by abandoning the latter. The implications were uncertain. We shall explore them further in this last part of the book. But one immediate consequence was a re-direction of state activity in the field of industrial relations. As union co-operation in wage restraint and labour discipline first seemed increasingly ineffective, and was then withdrawn, law with the sanction of force behind it was brought into use to the same ends. A corner of the veil of 'consensus' was blown aside to reveal the realities of power in a glimpse. Overt compulsion took over from some of the many covert compulsions which uphold the normal order of a society in which class conflict is institutionalized.

II

The continuing predominance of capital makes for deep fissures in the social structure. The economic order draws major lines of cleavage between people whose life circumstances and share in influence contrast, however they themselves may see their position and respond to it.

Extraordinary privilege is concentrated in a very small group. They have wealth; and the near-total security in life, the latitude of choice, the ease in everyday management and manipulation of people and things around them, which all go with wealth. They have power: less because they actively direct affairs – though many of them do that – than because the anonymous regulation of affairs by principles of property, profit and market is in tune with their interests. And they are well placed to pass on their privileges to their children. The core of this group is those who own and those who control capital on a large scale: whether top business executives or rentiers makes no difference in this context. Whatever divergences of interest there may be among them on this score and others, latent as well as manifest, they have a common stake in one overriding cause: to keep the working rules of the society capitalist.

The same is not quite so obviously true of others who nevertheless, by contrast with the bulk of the population, must be counted within the privileged minority. The economic and associated advantages enjoyed by high state officials and established members of the best entrenched professions do not derive principally from personal ownership or control of private capital; they would be greater if they did. But the position of such people still depends on the fact that incomes are determined by market rules and mechanisms over which, in effect, they themselves have considerable influence in their own corners of the market. Their position depends, too, on maintenance of such freedom of expenditure – in housing and education for example – as market mechanisms confer on people who have much money to spend. Moreover, in practice they are often well off, not just because they have high incomes from salaries and fees; but also because they have accumulated or inherited capital, though of more modest dimensions than is usual in business circles. And they have close ties, personal and through common experience, with the élite of private business. The commitments to capitalism inherent in the privileges of top officials and professionals are conditional rather than absolute. But capitalism offers an institutional protection of inequality which it would rarely, if ever, pay them to question.

Wage earners – as well as their dependents and those retired from wage-earning work have no such natural stake in capitalism. On the contrary. Citizens in form, they are subjects in fact: the subordinate majority in a society whose routine rules work to their disadvantage. The institutions of property, profit and market are the prime source of the series of disabilities which go with rank-and-file work, in this as in other Western countries. To make that elementary point is not to postulate an inevitable commitment to socialism on the part of wage earners, 'sooner or later': there is no automatic translation of class 'in itself' into class 'for itself'. It is to say only that there is a predisposition against capitalism, and for some form of socialist order, firmly inherent in the condition of labour.

Again, to talk about 'labour' *en bloc* is not to deny the reality of economic divisions within the wage-earning population. The very fact that those without capital must sell their labour in a capitalist market makes for division: dependence itself conduces to fragmentation. The labour market in effect is a patchwork of markets where skilled and unskilled, blue-collar and white-collar employees, men and women, workers in this industry and that, one region and another, sell their labour on different terms. Moreover, poverty by contemporary standards – once a condition shared by many active wage earners, and their families, with those who were not at work – is now more concentrated among the retired. Here, ostensibly, is a new line of division; or an old one that stands out more sharply today. Yet it is a line of division only on the surface. Most workers will grow old and retire some day; and it is just because far more of them now survive to do so that poverty in old age is a common fate of wage earners today. So, too, many of the former lines of separation within the labour market are less distinct than they were in the past. The gap in earnings between skilled and unskilled, on the whole, has narrowed over time. And there are far fewer unskilled and casual workers in the manual population than there were. There are far fewer household servants, too: once a large group of workers, separated from others by domestic isolation and by personal dependence on their employers. Skilled and semi-skilled – employed in firms of increasing size – now predominate overwhelmingly among manual workers. And among the skilled the craftsman-artisan with some real prospect of setting up in trade as his own master is much rarer than he was a hundred years ago.

There are, of course, new lines of specialization and separation within and on the fringes of labour, clear already now or likely to emerge. 'Technicians' of various kinds, for example; workers with 'polyvalent' skills relevant to a range of jobs; computer operators of different grades: these are among the groups whose numbers are growing with recent changes in technology. Yet it is by no means obvious that new patterns of differentiation in the labour force outweigh, in their effect, the trend toward erosion of old divisions. On the contrary, more likely. Many commentators see a complexity of detail here, in their picture of the present, which only historical insensitivity prevents them from seeing in the past. In fact workers of all grades and kinds, and in all industries, are now more liable than they were to share certain basic conditions in their economic terms of life. The markets for labour are wider and more unified; the consumer market virtually nationwide, except in housing. Collective bargaining in respect of basic rates of pay and related terms of employment covers this and that industry as a whole, though there is considerable scope for variations in application and interpretation between individual localities and firms. Industries, moreover, look one to another in the process of bargaining. And two significant features of contemporary capitalism reinforce and extend these trends towards greater uniformity in the framework of conditions within which workers of different skills and in dissimilar situations sell their labour. One is the continuing growth in scale and concentration of corporate business. The other is the increase of government intervention in economic affairs generally, and in collective bargaining especially.

The crucial common component in the life circumstances of the mass of wage earners is their dependence on market sale of the labour.

How crucial is evident from the wide range of other terms in life which they share and which clearly separate them, by a gap incomparably greater than the internal divisions among them, from the minority for whom the wheels of private capital turn. But the gap is not a vacuum: there are groups in between, with rather indeterminate boundaries. With the eclipse of small-scale business, these are now mainly people who also have to sell their services in the labour market to live; but who do so on better terms than most, and enjoy other advantages concomitantly.

Clerical and similar workers once occupied such intermediate positions of minor privilege, if only precariously so. This was around the turn of the century, when the increasing complexity of organization in private and public enterprise stepped up demand for white-collar staff, and efficiency in literacy was still in relatively short supply. Since then, the earnings of men in routine black-coated work have dropped, in proportionate terms, to put most of them on a par with semi-skilled or even unskilled manual labour. And if they stay in work of that kind, they no longer usually enjoy the regular increments in salary which go with seniority in white-collar work higher up the scale. They still have some special advantages: shorter hours of work, for example; greater security of employment; readier access to employer-provided welfare than manual workers, and on better terms. Low grade office work also still appears to give greater opportunities for social ascent – of promotion for such workers themselves, of upward mobility by one route or another for their children – than skilled blue-collar work; and greater protection against social descent. But some of these benefits, too, may be diminishing: prospects of promotion without special qualifications on paper, almost certainly so. Though a good deal more needs to be known about changes in the situation of these people, the facts of their lives place them more firmly among wage labour – whether they are nominally salaried or not – than before. By criteria relating to material conditions, power and individual opportunity, low-grade office workers and the like are partly within the 'working class', partly on its fringes; not distinctively outside it, as conventional usage still implies.

But by the same criteria, taken in cumulative conjunction, there are others whose place in the economic order puts them outside the ranks of ordinary labour, though they too are employees in fact as well as form. Managers of junior and middling grades in private and public enterprise; executive and technical staff of equivalent levels; members of such lower-tier professions as teaching, trained welfare work, nursing and other medical auxiliary occupations: these and others in similar positions can be crudely described as 'middle class'. They have in common varying advantages in their terms and conditions of employment by comparison with wage earners; prospects of individual advancement over a relatively long course of working life, in consequence both of regular increments in salary and of opportunities for promotion; often some share in everyday authority, though in a subordinate capacity, as agents with little autonomy; a familiarity with the routine machinery and rituals of the established order, which helps them to make their way and to pull small strings on their own behalf; some facility, by the same tokens, in smoothing the path for their children in the competition of an unequal society. Yet the mix of limited privilege varies from one sub-group to another; in degree, in character, and in reliability. It seems least clear and least secure, on several scores, among members of the 'marginal' professions, largely employed in public enterprise; and among technical staff, in both private and public business, who are off the main lines of promotion to higher things.

The use of the term 'middle class' in the singular may obscure such diversity of circumstance among them. The phrase, moreover, is totally misleading if it is used – as so often even by professional sociologists – not only to describe these intermediate groups, *and* the routine grades of white-collar labour; but to embrace also members of the business élite and top professions in whose hands wealth, power and opportunity are concentrated. That small minority, of course, always draws some of its new recruits from the intermediate strata. (Some, indeed, come from the ranks of labour, though proportionately a good deal more rarely.) This, in conjunction with their subordinate share in privilege and authority, may well incline the middle groups in general to accept economy and society broadly in their established forms. But by no stretch of rational imagination can they be seen as members, jointly with the ruling interest, of a single 'middle ciass' – with no 'upper class' above it. The absurdity of this terminology may in part reflect a widespread, misplaced sense of social delicacy. Be that as it may, the common language of class here serves to hide the realities of class dominance in a capitalist society.[1]

1. An alternative use of 'middle class' to describe all non-manual groups *except* members of, and people associated with, the traditional aristocracy and perhaps

III

Arguments have proliferated that inequalities of condition in Western society increasingly cut across each other. They are often said to produce, not a clear division of class resting on economic foundations, but a network of cracks which split the social structure this way and that; or even a pre-eminent division along some line that has little to do with access to capital and market position in themselves. We have already discussed one set of diagnoses of this kind in some detail, and rejected them. This is the postulate, in its diverse forms, that power is no longer strongly associated with wealth: no longer an outcome of property. In fact, managerial control in business is not a new source of power, divorced from and opposed to the interests of large business owners. And bureaucracy cannot be understood as if it were a self-propelled dividing force, splitting rulers from ruled irrespective of the divisions engendered by capital concentration and market mechanisms. Managers, officials, 'bureaucrats' in general – in private enterprise, in the state apparatus, in political parties, trade unions and so on – constitute neither a new single class of controllers; nor a cluster of mutually competing élites who wield power in an economic vacuum. The predominance of capital in private hands sets the context of their activities, their objectives in alliance and conflict, the varying limits of their influence. But there are other arguments which, like the theses of managerial infiltration and of bureaucratic oligarchy, also imply that the cleavages made by capitalist institutions are increasingly blurred or overridden by lines of privilege and dependence in their essence unrelated to class: by stratification based on sex, or age, or region, or colour of skin.

To deny these inequalities a significance of that sort is not to dismiss them as unreal or unimportant. All of them contribute to the totality of inequality. But none of them has the force, the sweeping

---

the country gentry (with the term 'upper class' reserved for these) is equally misleading. It ignores the fact that economic privilege, power and exceptional opportunities are common to members of the latter groups *and* the haute bourgeoisie of capital, top officialdom and the established professions, with variations within this cluster that do not follow the line between nobility-cum-gentry and the rest. It is in any case a long-standing feature of British social structure that this line is blurred and highly permeable; while the distinction between 'old' landed (and commercial) interests and 'new' industrial and professional interests, associated with the nineteenth-century rise of the latter, increasingly lost its relevance after the middle of that century.

repercussions of class inequality. None of them in itself produces the communality of condition which marks class position in the economic order: a common complex of life circumstances shared by the victims; a contrasting set of life circumstances held in common by the privileged; broadly common ambiguities of condition among those who are neither clearly victims nor clearly privileged. The economic divisions of class, moreover, in turn give variations of character and shape to the manifestations of inequality by sex or age, region or colour, at different levels of the class structure. In both those senses, class cleavage is dominant.

The subordination of women to men, for example, has eased a good deal less during this century in real than in nominal terms; and a good deal less as a result of organized pressure and legal reform than of demographic changes: voluntary limitation of family size especially. But increasing awareness of the barriers to change here – of the continuing case for women's liberation after ostensible female emancipation – in no way justifies a diagnosis that women share essentially the same condition, because all are the victims of conventional definitions of sex roles. It is obvious to the point of banality that capital and market make for much the same contrasts in material circumstances, and all that goes with them, among married women and widows as among their husbands; that they draw similar lines among women not dependent on a husband for livelihood. It is perhaps less obvious, but no less significant, that these cleavages of class impose corresponding differences in the patterns of discrimination and self-abnegation by which women are held subordinate.

If women are to achieve effective parity with men with regard to work, for instance, their demands to that end in the working class would focus, in the first place, on pay and conditions at work, on practical opportunities for employment, on job security. They would not, to the same extent as among women of the bourgeoisie, involve assertion of a moral right to work. For working-class women have long had to take that right – hedged as it is by practical obstacles – and must in any case define it as a right to earn. Nor could their demands for parity with men, *tout court*, focus on opportunities for career advancement, for autonomy at work, for a part in authority, since working-class men share their disabilities on these scores. Of course, the demands of working-class women may go beyond a claim for parity with men at their own level of the economic system. But at that point they would become class demands – demands directed against the subordination of labour, not against the subordination of women. And even before that point, demands for parity with men are liable to spill over into class demands. For the penalties in earnings, for example, and educational opportunities, which women suffer because they are women, hit the working class hardest. Sex inequality here, as we have shown, accentuates class inequality. So opposition to it has a radical potential – as yet inexplicit – which could in future come to be difficult to reconcile with bourgeois conceptions of parity between the sexes.

Still less does age divide by lines that dissolve barriers of class. The young of all socio-economic levels may be increasingly inclined to question authority. But the circumstances and prospects in life from which they do so – in work and in education before that – diverge too much for alliances to be likely on the basis merely of common, and inevitably temporary, status as juniors. True, the range of earnings now – with no account taken of direct and indirect support from parents – is narrow when young people first enter the labour market. But it soon widens to separate those with careers marked by incremental advancement from the majority in wage-earning jobs. Again, occupational downgrading near retirement, and poverty after retirement, are not common conditions of old age in general. They are risks – of high probability so far as the latter is concerned – attached to wage earning. Managerial and professional position in working life confers relative immunity from them; property owner-ship of more than small dimensions, total immunity. And it is retired wage earners whose pensions are publicly defined as a 'burden' on the economy. The claim on resources from 'private' managerial and professional pensions, and from those who have capital, escapes that label. Property ownership, moreover, does not divide the old from the young; its concentration is not the result of accumulation over individual lifetimes. It divides class from class, in much the same way at all ages.

The broad pattern of regional disparities of wealth, welfare and opportunity in Britain today is a matter of common knowledge. North and west contrast with south and east; the old heartland of the industrial revolution of the nineteenth century and before, with areas which have a disproportionate share of newer and expanding industries; relatively high risks of unemployment and low rates of economic activity above a diagonal running north-east to south-west, with their converse below it. With these contrasts, by and large, go a series of others: in risks of death and disease; in chances of education within England, though Wales and to some extent Scotland break the pattern; in job opportunities; and so on. It became fashionable for a time in the late 1950s and the 1960s to describe these disparities as a divide between 'two nations'. The description rode rather roughshod over complexities in the geography of inequality. But it was inept above all, because it turned a near-blind eye to the force of class cleavages across and within regional boundaries. Unemployment, to take a simple case, is a contingency of working-class life: a good deal more of a risk still for labour in many parts of the north than for labour in London and the Midlands; but a risk to which executives and professionals are little exposed, wherever they live. Where school resources are poor, and the threshold for selection into academic education high, it is working-class children in particular who feel the effects. The impact on children of the intermediate strata is smaller; and those from wealthy families go virtually free.[2] Though there are geographical variations in mortality and morbidity which cannot be explained by reference simply to class, the higher incidence of infant deaths and stillbirths in the north and west of the country arises in large part from the fact that there are, in proportionate terms, more workers and more poor in the population of those regions than elsewhere. They, everywhere, are more at risk.[3]

In a number of respects regional contrasts have become less pronounced over time. Post-war government support for economic development and industrial diversification in and around depressed areas of the country appears over two decades to have had some, though limited effect, and even at worst has prevented disparities from widening further.[4] Moreover, the metropolitan area of London – often the special target of accusations that it drains resources from

2. Cf. especially Douglas, op. cit. (Part Four, ch. 3, note 8). It is also relevant, though the fact bears on regional disparities only by inference, that when the chances for qualified school leavers to enter university declined for a time in the late 1950s (because the growth of demand exceeded the growth in number of university places) it was school-leavers from the maintained schools who were hardest hit – much less those from the élite direct-grant and independent schools. (Robbins Report, op. cit., Part Four, ch. 3, note 3. *Appendix Two (B)*, p. 14.) The point is consistent with the fact that the overall expansion of education over time has been associated with some gradual diminution in class inequalities of access to academic education – though it needs to be remembered that this diminution has been quite limited.

3. Cf. the references in Part Two, ch. 8, note 17.

4. For a review of government policy and its probable effects, see G. McCrone, *Regional Policy in Britain*, Allen & Unwin, 1969.

the rest of the country – is less a centre of privilege and affluence than the stereotypes coupled with such accusations imply. While expansion of government activities, increasing concentration of business and centralization of collective bargaining have enhanced the pre-eminence of the capital in the network of economic control, never-theless London now stands out less from the country at large as a 'middle-class city' than it did just after World War I. Measured by reference to overall occupational structure, the gap in class composi-tion between the metropolis and the provinces has narrowed: partly because inter-war and post-war industrial development in the outer areas of London has given it more of the character of a manufactur-ing city than it had; not least because the growth of 'tertiary sector' activities involving a good deal of white-collar employment – managerial, executive and professional as well as routine grade – has spread over time from the capital to much of the rest of the country. Class for class, too, metropolitan prosperity is something of a myth. Money earnings on average are higher in the south-east than else-where; but this does not appear as a consistent contrast, when jobs of a similar kind are compared. More importantly, rents and house prices are also higher in the south east. The balance on that score is difficult to assess. And by a variety of indices – multiple occupation of buildings not converted for the purpose, lack of facilities, over-crowding, dependence on furnished accommodation from private landlords – housing conditions on average are worse in Greater London than in other large conurbations. While unemployment was a rather remote contingency for London workers during the first couple of decades after World War II, their exposure to that risk has increased in recent years.[5]

In short, common class situations produce similar – not identical – circumstances in life: in London much as in the provinces, in one region much as in another. And class for class, on a number of scores, geographical variations are probably less than they were. It is the horizontal divisions of class, not the vertical divisions of region,

5. The points briefly summarized in this paragraph derive from a detailed analysis (by John Westergaard, with help from the Centre for Urban Studies, University College London) of the changing place of Greater London in the national class structure, with reference to occupational and industrial structure; the metropolitan concentration of the headquarters of large business companies, trade unions, pressure groups and so on; and some other features. Census data (from 1921 on) and other official statistics were the main sources of information, supplemented on certain points by other material.

which are the crucial breaks in British society by criteria of welfare, opportunity and influence. As when Disraeli first used the phrase, the line between the 'two nations' divides privilege and power from dependence throughout the country; not south from north, or metropolis from provinces.

Immigration from the 'coloured' countries of the Commonwealth is often assumed to have brought a significant new dimension to the pattern of stratification in Britain. The sheer volume of writing and research on the subject since about 1960 suggest the weight which liberal, and sometimes radical, opinion has come to attach to colour discrimination as a divisive force. The effect has been to single out inequality between white majority and black and brown minorities as a distinct and allegedly potent basis of cleavage in British society; to encourage diagnoses, explicit or implicit, that the coloured population is a sub-proletariat, a new dark-skinned under-class beneath the white social order.[6] In fact, there is little sense to such characterizations. They ignore the heterogeneity of circumstances among coloured people, and the concomitant diversity of discrimination in form and impact. They also obscure the overriding common features in the dependent condition of both white and black labour.

Coloured people are not uniformly concentrated at the bottom of the economic order. They are certainly handicapped in the labour market, as they are in a wide range of other respects; but in no way so as to make them, *en bloc*, an 'under-class'. Their occupational distribution is skewed towards the lower rungs of the scale. When only one in twelve of all occupied men in Britain in 1966 had an unskilled manual job, the corresponding proportions were near one in three among men born in Pakistan; over one in five among the Caribbean-born – much the same, it is worth noting, as among men born in the Irish Republic; and about one in nine among the Indian-born. Yet these figures alone square poorly with conventional assumptions: among none of the migrant groups from the 'new Commonwealth' was there anything like a majority of men in unskilled jobs. Even if the semi-skilled are added in – to make, with the unskilled, an aggregate in lower-grade manual work comprising over a quarter of the total male labour force in 1966 – still only the

6. For a theoretical analysis which has such a diagnosis as a lynchpin, see J. Rex, *Race Relations in Sociological Theory*, Weidenfeld & Nicolson, 1970. Cf. also *idem*, 'The concept of race in sociological theory', in S. Zubaida, ed., *Race and Racialism*, Tavistock, 1970.

Pakistani-born showed a clear majority confined to jobs of that kind: some two out of every three in their case. For men from the Caribbean countries, the figure was just under half – not very much more, again, than among the Irish-born; and it was one-third in the case of men born in India. Migrants from Pakistan apart, in short, the majority of men from the coloured Commonwealth were in jobs classified as skilled, or in some form of non-manual work. And the pattern of employment among women born in those countries conformed no better to the familiar stereotypes. True, over half the working women with birthplaces in the Caribbean territories had non-skilled manual jobs – mainly semi-skilled, including service work. Yet such jobs in any case accounted for more than a third of the entire female labour force; and for only one in four of women born in India. A large majority of the latter, and around one in every three even of those born in the Caribbean area, had non-manual work.[7] There is some exaggeration of the degree of occupational diversity in these figures: men and women from India and Pakistan include whites born there in the days of imperial dominion. But distortion on this source is limited; and the qualification has practically no application to those born in the Caribbean countries. The plain point is that professional, white-collar and skilled manual blacks tend to be left aside in the stereotypes of public debate and research alike. The visibility of colour diminishes the higher the socio-economic position of the coloured, in the eyes of liberal reformers no less than the prejudiced.

7. These data are taken from the analysis of 1966 sample census figures presented by S. Castles and G. Kosack, *Immigrant Workers and Class Structure in Western Europe*, Oxford Univ. Press, 1973, pp. 88–90. (Occupational patterns among Pakistani-born women were similar to those among Indian-born women, but there were few of the former at work.) Castles and Kosack explicitly reject characterizations of coloured immigrants in Britain as a sub-proletariat or the equivalent. Though the stereotypes associated with such characterizations persist, their falsity was demonstrated much earlier, by Ruth Glass. Cf. her 'The new minorities', *The Times*, 30 June, 1 July, 1965; and also the references to her work in note 9 below. It follows both from the occupational heterogeneity of coloured migrants to Britain, and from the increasing stringency of restrictions on coloured immigration here (one effect of which has been to give highly qualified immigrants from the new Commonwealth priority of entry), that British policy and practice *vis-à-vis* coloured immigrants cannot be simplistically ascribed to the needs of British business for cheap and readily exploitable labour. Interpretations of that kind, and associated descriptions of migrant labour as an under-class, have much more application to Germany, Switzerland and some other Continental countries which have recruited large numbers of foreign workers into low-grade jobs. (Cf. Castles and Kosack, e.g. pp. 378, 382, 421, 423–5, 476–7.)

To have a dark skin indeed carries a series of penalties; and that, in varying measure and form, at all levels of British society. Coloured people – native-born as well as immigrants – are commonly disadvantaged, often humiliated, sometimes patronized. Official policy has itself been actively discriminatory. While professing distaste for racial discrimination, and eventually accepting legislation designed to give its victims some protection, the two major parties engaged in competition from the 1960s to introduce successively more stringent and unvarnished colour barriers into immigration control. Assumptions of white superiority thus received a stamp of establishment approval. Racial intolerance was made more respectable. The status of West Indians, Indians, Pakistanis and their children as 'outsiders inside' British society was confirmed.[8] But that does not mean that they share, more or less all, the same position in society and economy. What they share is the label 'coloured' and the fact that disabilities go with it.

These are not, in general, disabilities peculiar to coloured people, though dark skin increases the risk of subjection to them. Coloured workers, for example, are more liable than others to be out of work when jobs are short. But they remain a quite small minority of the unemployed. And coloured professionals – doctors and nurses, to take two fairly large groups – are little exposed to that risk: their experience of job discrimination will turn more on opportunities for promotion and access to the more comfortable and privileged sectors of their fields of work. Immigrants from the new Commonwealth pay a 'colour tax' when they rent private lodgings; and they get poor value for their money. But crowding, lack of privacy and

---

8. Cf. Ruth Glass, 'Insiders-outsiders: the position of minorities', *Transacts. Fifth World Congress of Sociology*, vol. III, 1964. Among a very large number of studies concerning the new minority groups, and patterns of discrimination against them, see e.g., *idem, Newcomers: the West Indians in London*, Allen & Unwin, 1960; M. P. Banton, *White and Coloured in Britain*, Cape, 1959; R. Desai, *Indian Immigrants in Britain*, Oxford Univ. Press, 1963; D. John, *Indian Workers' Associations in Britain,* Oxford Univ. Press, 1969; E. J. B. Rose *et al., Colour and Citizenship*, Oxford Univ. Press, 1969; Sheila Allen, *New Minorities, Old Conflicts,* Random House, 1971; Sheila Patterson, *Immigrants in Industry,* Oxford Univ. Press, 1968; P. L. Wright, *The Coloured Worker in British Industry,* Oxford Univ. Press, 1968; P. Foot, *Immigration and Race in British Politics,* Penguin, 1965; W. W. Daniel, *Racial Discrimination in England*, Penguin, 1968; B. Hepple, *Race, Jobs and the Law,* Penguin, 1970. See also J. A. Garrard, *The English and Immigration, 1880–1910*, Oxford Univ. Press, 1971 (in this context especially chapter 1); as well as the references in notes 6 and 7 above, 9 and 10 below.

facilities, at high rents and with a risk of harassment by landlords, are conditions common to many households – migrants from city to city, families with many children, young people – who are forced to rely on the market in private rented housing. Moreover, many coloured people manage to escape from or avoid the imprisonment within these worst of conditions which is often assumed to be their common fate. The majority of coloured immigrants in London in the 1960s, for example, were not concentrated in the districts where colour was highly visible.[9] Rules requiring established residence in the area, and often unfurnished tenure, as preconditions of rehousing keep recent migrants and many others off council housing lists, whether they are black or white. Housing managers for many local authorities up and down the country had made it a routine practice, where they could, to segregate the poorer and less respectable of their tenants in the poorer and older kinds of council property, long before coloured families, if they were rehoused, fell foul of that practice.[10] Local education authorities in the 1960s were officially enjoined to avoid high concentrations of 'immigrant' pupils in individual schools; but high concentrations of working-class children, and children of poor and unskilled parents, are among the ordinary facts of life in Britain. Preoccupied with the disabilities that attach to colour, liberal reformers and research workers have been busy rediscovering what in fact are common disabilities of class: widespread and long-standing conditions inherent in the workings of capital, market and state in a divided society. Such rediscovery may be positive and illuminating if it is recognized for what it is. Too often it has not been so. Colour barriers have been spotlit, the class divisions behind them left in shadow.

Of course, coloured people *might* be an 'under-class'. There might be far more of them than the few per cent of the population which

9. See Ruth Glass, 'Main factors in London's housing needs', in *idem* and J. H. Westergaard, *London's Housing Needs*, Centre for Urban Studies, 1965 (especially pp. 30–44). A far more extensive analysis of patterns of residential segregation by class as well as country of birth in Greater London in the 1960s, by Ruth Glass and her colleagues, underlines the same points: *The Third Survey of London* (as yet unpublished). Concerning housing conditions and residential segregation of minorities outside London, see e.g. J. Rex and R. Moore, *Race, Community and Conflict*, Oxford Univ. Press, 1967; and P. N. Jones, *The Segregation of Immigrant Communities in the City of Birmingham 1961*, Univ. of Hull, 1967. (Cf. also C. Peach, *West Indian Migration to Britain: a Social Geography*, Oxford Univ. Press, 1958.)

10. Cf. Elizabeth Burney, *Housing on Trial: a Study of Immigrants and Local Government*, Oxford Univ. Press, 1967.

they now make up. They might be far more concentrated at the bottom of the economic order than they are. They might be so segregated and so disabled as virtually to monopolize the lowest positions in the society. And things may go further in that direction than they have gone so far in this country. Yet this would still not mean that 'stratification by colour' had replaced 'stratification by class', even just at the lower end of the scale. The poor would be different people. The fact of poverty, the structure of inequality of which poverty is part, the mechanisms of profit and property which produce inequality in a capitalist society, would all be the same. The liberal idea of colour-blindness is praiseworthy; but its aims are limited. Even if it were effectively implemented, and no impediments of condition and opportunity went with dark skin, the result would be only to reshuffle the personnel of classes. Like any other policies designed to remove 'ascriptive' handicaps to achievement by merit, it would increase circulation; but by itself leave the range and roots of class inequality unchanged.

IV

So much, in summary form, for the clefts in British society which are carved out by inequalities of wealth and welfare, power and opportunity. They are clearcut in outline; broadly coincident by different criteria, and thus mutually reinforcing; resistant to change through ameliorative reform; predominant over divisions of sex and age, region and colour, which are sometimes said to cut across them and break up the simplicity of the pattern. But distinct as the pattern proves on examination of a variety of evidence, it does not follow that it is plain also for all to see at a glance. It cannot be taken for granted that the cleavages made by the facts of privilege and dependence mark boundaries between groups whose members have a firm sense of common identity, destiny and purpose. Shared position in the class structure can be expected to generate similarities of outlook and response among the people concerned. But how far and in what forms, against what inhibitions and with what prospects for the future – these are questions which we have still to discuss. Here there are no simple answers.

For all that, it is obvious that the lines of class 'in itself' are also, in some significant part, lines of class 'for itself'. The story of Britain, and of other European countries, would have been very different over the past hundred years and more if that had not been so. The rise of labour as an organized force, and reactions to that rise, are central themes in the political history of industrial capitalism on this side of the Atlantic; a good deal less directly and less clearly so in North America, of course. And support for rival political parties is divided on class lines. The point is taken so much for granted that interest often centres on deviations from the rule: on the minorities who cross class lines to vote for parties 'on the other side'. But the first simple fact is that they are minorities. The Labour Party in this country draws about four in every five of its supporters at the polls from among manual workers and their families. Around 60 per cent of voters in that section of the population cast their votes for Labour; only about half as many for the Conservative Party; the rest mainly for Liberal candidates. This is to strike a rough average for general elections since World War II. There have been fluctuations, of course; and an uneven trend of increase from the 1960s in Liberal voting – as well as in support for the nationalist parties in Scotland and Wales – the significance of which is still uncertain. But despite frequent assumptions to the contrary, so far there are no signs of a long-run right-wing shift in the rough two-to-one split of manual working-class votes after the war between Labour and Conservatives, to take just those two main parties. And Labour's hold on these votes was weaker before World War II, when the party was still a comparative newcomer to competition for government office.[11]

Beyond these elementary facts, there are two especially notable

11. Estimates, from public opinion poll data, of the division of votes within broad occupational classes since World War II are given in R. R. Alford, *Party and Society*, Murray, 1964 (pp. 130–1, 162 3, 348–9) and the studies of D. E. Butler *et al.* of the *British General Election of 1964, ... 1966, ... 1970* (Macmillan: 1965, with A. King, pp. 296–7; 1966, with A. King, pp. 264–5; 1971, with M. Pinto-Duschinsky, pp. 342–3). The latter studies give no figures for men and women separately, of different age, within class. But a re-analysis of data from the same source (National Opinion Polls) for the elections 1959 to 1970 shows that, in general terms, the broad constancy of class voting patterns over time during that period held also for men and women of different ages. (We are grateful to the Social Science Research Council's Survey Archive at the University of Essex for providing us with these special tabulations, and to National Opinion Polls Ltd. for use of their data.) No comparable data for 1974 were available at the time of writing. Concerning the growth of the Labour vote, see especially D. E. Butler and D. Stokes, *Political Change in Britain*, Macmillan, 1969 (chapters 5 and 11); and also C. Chamberlain, 'The growth of support for the Labour Party in Britain', *Brit. J. Sociology*, Dec. 1973, and H. F. Moorhouse, 'The political incorporation of the British working class', *Sociology*, Sept. 1973.

features to the ways in which voting is shaped by class position. One is a broad similarity in the pro-Labour balance at different levels within the manual working class. The second, already implied, is the fact that a main break in the pattern of party allegiance falls along the line between skilled blue-collar workers and routine-grade white-collar workers. The conjunction of the two features is significant, not least because it is repeated in a number of other areas of life which throw light on modes of class consciousness and class culture.

Manual workers, when they vote, give much the same majority support to Labour, whether they are skilled, semi-skilled or unskilled; in relatively well-paid jobs or poor. There are no clear signs, for example, that the unskilled or the very poor *en bloc* constitute a 'lumpenproletariat', distinctly inclined either to support Conservative rule or to stay away from the polls altogether, though particular groups among them – service workers in fairly close personal dependence on their employers, for example – may be pulled in those directions. Nor, conversely, has there been evidence that 'affluent' workers are much more Tory than the less affluent. Of course there are variations in the precise ratios at which votes are divided. The skilled, counted as a whole, are marginally less firm in their electoral support for Labour than are the non-skilled. Union members are certainly, workers with homes in solidly working-class areas and those with jobs in large firms are probably, more faithful to Labour in their voting habits than other manual employees. Unmarried women of the blue-collar world show a larger minority than men in favour of Conservative candidates; elderly and old working-class voters whose party allegiances were formed before Labour became indisputably the main opponent to the Tories have similarly, in elections after World War II, given weaker support to Labour than younger and newer voters in much the same class circumstances. Manual workers of white-collar origin are a good deal more likely than those born and bred in the world of manual work to give their votes to the Conservative Party. And Labour loses more from their defection than it gains from the fact that, on the whole, people who have climbed up out of the manual working class are less committed to Tory voting than others in the strata which they have joined. The swings and roundabouts of mobility between manual and non-manual groups give a net advantage to Conservatism. Yet with the exception of the last, these are all influences of a very secondary kind. They make for only fairly small variations in the pattern of majority support for Labour among manual workers and their families. Differences in skill and income, in particular, matter little.[12] In short, blue-collar earners are not uniformly supporters of Labour. A substantial minority cross class lines when they vote; and more do so in Britain than is usual, for example, in Scandinavia. But this pattern of party allegiance takes much the same form at different levels of job qualifications and earning power. The 'homogeneity' of the manual working-class population in that respect – though it comprises upwards of two-thirds of the entire population – is striking.

There is no parallel repetitive pattern to be seen when one looks at the political allegiances of people of different levels of the non-manual world. Labour support there dwindles stepwise up the scale of occupations and incomes – to small fractions at the top, of course; and Conservative support rises more or less concomitantly. There are variations which cut across this. Independent businessmen are probably more firmly Tory than others with comparable incomes; members of the lower-grade professions – teachers, welfare workers, perhaps nurses – may be more inclined to vote Labour than people who, for the moment at least, are on little better rewarded rungs of the managerial-and-executive ladder.[13] Yet what stands out about non-manual party commitments is their gradation up the socio-economic scale, in contrast to the similarity of pattern at different levels of the manual working-class population. By this criterion, the 'middle' and 'upper' classes – as conventionally defined – indeed appear to be 'strata'; not so the poor, the unskilled, semi-skilled and skilled on the other side of the familiarly acknowledged class fence. The crucial point of division on this score, moreover, comes just there. Not that routine-grade white-collar workers are firm Tories: they are split more or less down the middle. With variations – from

12. The points made in this and the next paragraph derive from the sources quoted in note 11 above, and from a variety of other studies, e.g. M. Benney et al., *How People Vote*, Routledge & Kegan Paul, 1956; J. Bonham, *The Middle Class Vote*, Faber, 1954; J. Goldthorpe et al., *The Affluent Worker: Political Attitudes and Behaviour*, Cambridge Univ. Press, 1968; R. T. McKenzie and A. Silver, *Angels in Marble*, Heinemann Educational Books, 1968; E. Nordlinger, *The Working Class Tories*, MacGibbon & Kee, 1967.

13. See Bonham, op. cit. (note 12 above) and *idem*, 'The middle class elector', *Brit. J. Sociology*, Sept. 1952. Cf. also F. Parkin, *Middle Class Radicalism*, Manchester Univ. Press, 1968. F. Bechhofer et al., in a study of small shopkeepers in Edinburgh (reports on which were due for publication shortly at the time of writing) found that two in every three of these petty entrepreneurs intended to vote Conservative in 1970 (with little variation by social origin) and barely 15 per cent Labour.

time to time, and from one survey to another according in part to
how the group is defined – low-paid non-manual workers seem
generally to vote Conservative and Labour in roughly equal proportions, with an edge to the advantage of the former. But that also
marks them off from manual workers: at least as yet.

To know how people vote, of course, tells us relatively little about
class consciousness. Voting Labour is no index of fiery radicalism.
Yet it is, so far as most of its adherents are concerned, the outcome of
a general sense of class identity: of common interests to be protected
or advanced. Asked why they vote as they do, manual working-class
Labour supporters usually refer to the fact that the party is – or is
supposed to be – the party of the working class. Politics for the
majority of them is a matter of conflict or competition between
classes. The perspective which accompanies this is often passive and
defensive; and it is now also often coloured in various shades of
disillusion about what can be expected from the Labour Party and
from politicians. Yet it distinguishes Labour voters in the manual
working-class population clearly from Tory supporters in the rest of
the population who – whatever consciousness of class interests they
may in fact bring to voting – usually put into words a view of politics
as a matter of choosing rulers fit to rule or of promoting specific
policies for an unspecific general good.[14]

Popular perceptions of class and class structure are difficult to
track down. Simple questions in standard survey form are liable to
produce unilluminating answers. Yet even these confirm the pointers
from electoral research that the conventional line between manual
and non-manual – rather than a line drawn to include low-grade
white-collar employees with other wage-earning labour – remains a
significant division between people who see society, themselves and
others in it, from quite different angles. Most manual workers refer
to themselves as 'working class', either spontaneously or when
pressed to apply some sort of class label to their position. Some do
not; but again, like those manual workers who vote Conservative,
these are a minority. And again, from the results of most relevant
surveys, there is little variation in this respect between manual
workers at different levels of skill. But low-grade white-collar
workers, in broad terms, are more or less equally divided between

14. Cf. Butler and Stokes, op. cit. (note 11 above, pp. 91–4); Goldthorpe *et al.*,
op. cit. (note 12 above, pp. 19–22); McKenzie and Silver, op. cit. (note 12 above,
pp. 106–13).

those who describe themselves as 'working class' and as 'middle class'; while choice of some variant of the latter label (rarely 'upper class', even among the most privileged and powerful) increases stepwise up the scale from that threshold.

The labels do not mean very much in themselves; and probably less now than earlier. The etiquette of twentieth-century welfare capitalism frowns on bare-faced references to class. It takes the façade of common citizenship for reality. It is those who are well off who benefit from commonplace postulates that they, too, like everybody else, 'are all workers now', or – to much the same effect – that 'we are nearly all middle class now'. But the consequent emasculation of language has pervasive influence. All the more telling that crude survey questions still produce consistencies in the pattern of answers: the break in choice of class labels along the line between manual and non-manual sections of the population; a connection between that and the balance of party allegiances. Manual workers who describe themselves as 'middle class' are more likely than the majority to vote Conservative – though not evidently so if by 'middle class' they seem to mean only that they are rather ordinary people, neither privileged nor destitute.[15] People in non-manual jobs are more likely to vote Labour if they describe themselves as 'working class'. This is familiar enough. What may be less familiar is the fact that voting 'across class lines' cannot by any means be equated with – let alone 'explained' by – deviant class identification. Party commitments are not – as is often claimed – determined more by the class position people 'feel' they have than by their actual place in the economic order. For one thing, the position which people 'feel' they have – if we go by their answers to simple survey questions – is itself determined in very large measure by their actual economic position: that much is clear from what we have already said. For another, the 'deviants' – the manual workers who describe themselves as 'middle class', the minorities among executives and professionals who say they are 'workers' – still do not vote across the board as if they really were what they say.

Take the results of a nationwide survey in the early 1960s – the most comprehensive of its kind – to drive home the last point.[16]

15. Cf. W. G. Runciman, *Relative Deprivation and Social Justice*, Routledge & Kegan Paul, 1966 (especially, p. 177).
16. Butler and Stokes, op. cit. (note 11 above, pp. 77–8; see also pp. 66–71). Respondents in this survey were allocated to an occupational category by

About one-half of the manual working-class respondents there who chose the label 'middle class' to describe themselves nevertheless expressed support for Labour as against the Tories; while rather more than one-half of the non-manual respondents who spoke of themselves as 'working class' still preferred the Tories to Labour. The deviants', in short, were not impelled by their ostensibly idiosyncratic choice of class tag into majority support for the party conventionally thought of as appropriate to the tag. And the tags by which people identified themselves were associated with very different patterns of political allegiance in the two main occupational blocks of the population: 'working class' with 75–80 per cent Labour support on the manual side, irrespective of skill, but around only 45 per cent on the non-manual side; 'middle class' with some 85–90 per cent Tory support on the non-manual side, but around only 50 per cent on the manual side. Of course, in a sense, this may reflect little more than the emptiness of the class labels, the diversity of meanings which the people who use them attach to them. But it is significant that there is then a discontinuity in meanings – a break in the political significance of both class labels – between the manual and the non-manual sections of the population. And it is significant that the break comes at just that point. This survey, in fact, had shown a substantial majority of low-grade non-manual respondents describing themselves as 'working class' – some two in every three. On the face of it, and by comparison with earlier work, this might suggest a shift to 'proletarian' identification on their part: perhaps a growing recognition of the decline in their class condition. But the political interpretations which these people put on their professed class identities were still virtually the same as among non-manual respondents right up the socioeconomic scale above them – a marginal preference for the Tories against Labour even among those who adopted the tag 'working class'; overwhelming support for the Tories among the rest; overall, a three-to-two split in favour of the Tories – not, it seems, very different from the pattern general among routine white-collar labour earlier.

Behind the crude class labels and the simple divisions of party political allegiance, there are differences in conceptions of class and inequality which again seem in the main to separate manual from

---

reference to the job of the 'head of household'. But the fact that adult chidren living with their parents, as well as most working wives, were thus not classified by their own jobs is unlikely to affect the essential points argued here.

non-manual workers. True, evidence on this score is patchy. Large-scale surveys can be a clumsy tool for exploring the intricacies and contradictions of class consciousness: highly vulnerable on subjects of this sort to a risk of distortion from the ways in which questions are formulated, the sequence and context in which they come, the unconscious presuppositions which are built into them, the operational assumption that there is a common language in which they can be phrased. And few surveys have attempted to probe very far. Class differences in class images have almost certainly been more than half-masked by the fact, for example, that questions concerning the criteria by which people see classes to be marked off from each other usually, in the first instance, produce many answers that merely define classes in essentially occupational terms. What it is, in respondents' eyes, that distinguishes this occupational grouping from that – money, security, opportunity, power, prestige, or some combination of these – has then often been left unexplored or at least unanalysed: a matter for speculative inference or for no comment at all. Yet fragments from a number of studies can be put together in a rough sketch.[17]

The signs are fairly firm that manual workers – the majority, in particular, who accept the self-appellation 'working class' – are inclined to underline size of income, sometimes ownership of property in contrast to non-ownership, sometimes the capacity or incapacity to exercise power or to pull strings, as essential criteria of class division. Non-manual workers – more or less at all levels – are likely to place relatively little emphasis on such differences of class condition; but instead to give weight to distinctions of prestige and its stigmata, to personal qualities alleged to characterize the members of different classes, to individual virtue and merit as determinants of worldly reward. There are the outlines here of a distinction between some version or another of a 'class' model of society, with conflict at

17. Among British contributions to the exploration of 'class imagery', see especially F. M. Martin, 'Some subjective aspects of social stratification', in D. V. Glass, ed., *Social Mobility in Britain,* Routledge & Kegan Paul, 1954; Elizabeth Bott, *Family and Social Network,* Tavistock Press, 1957 (ch. 6); J. Goldthorpe *et al., The Affluent Worker in the Class Structure,* Cambridge Univ. Press, 1969 (ch. 5); W. G. Runciman, op. cit (note 15 above, ch. 8); as well as some of the local studies discussed by Josephine Klein, *Samples from English Culture,* Routledge & Kegan Paul, 1965, though these are less specifically relevant. Among studies in other countries, see e.g. H. Popitz *et al., Das Gesellschaftsbild des Arbeiters,* Tübingen, 1957 (and the extract from this in T. Burns, ed., *Industrial Man,* Penguin, 1969); and A. Willener, *Images de la Société et Classes Sociales,* Bern, 1957.

least a continuous possibility; and a conservative image of a 'status' hierarchy where individual opportunity is relatively open and class disparity accepted as legitimate. To put it like that is to sharpen lines which the evidence available shows only in rather blurred form; to attribute more consistency to each of the contrasting pictures than either survey data, or probably reality, would justify; to try to guess, from what can be seen, about what cannot be seen because it is veiled by unexplored descriptions of classes as occupational groups *tout court*; and to leave aside – though for discussion later – both contradictions within, and variations of, the 'class' images of society which appear to be characteristically manual. Yet there is enough established fact and plausible interpretation here to allow a conclusion that blue-collar workers' views of the world have a recognizable quasi-Marxist tinge to them – though rarely, in Britain, with any active revolutionary twist. That fits well enough, too, with the fact that politics for the Labour majority among manual workers involves defence or promotion of class interests.

The quasi-Marxist tinge of the 'worker's eye view' may be vulgar Marxist in several ways: among others in dividing the world into only two classes. A two-class image of society is certainly more commonly presented by manual working-class respondents than by others when they are questioned in social surveys. But it is nonsensical to take, as many surveyors and commentators have been inclined, commitment to a two-class image as any kind of test of commitment to a 'class-condition', 'income-property-and-power' model of society. The two no doubt often go together; and since the structural opposition between capital and labour is central to capitalism, there is good reason on the face of it why they should. But the concrete reality of capitalism shows also a variety of rather uncertainly bounded intermediate groups, neither clearly labour nor clearly identifiable with capital. So a picture of class inequality in society as it actually is here and now – popular or academic – would take some account of these. If workers should pick out three, four or more 'classes' when asked to describe the world around them, that by itself is no indication that they have abandoned quasi-Marxist perspectives and see instead a hierarchy of strata, separated by invidious distinctions of status but bonded by opportunities for individual virtue to find its proper rewards. It is simply lazy sociology to assume so: counting classes makes for easy coding.

By all these critieria – political allegiances and conceptions of politics, nominal class identity and conceptions of class division, all taken to this point only in rather superficial terms – the line that separates manual from non-manual stands out more clearly than it does in the structure of wealth and power. Low-grade white-collar workers are not, more or less to a man (and woman), the single-minded aspirants to bourgeois status and humble upholders of Conservative authority epitomized by the Grossmiths' Mr Pooter in the 1890s. They are divided in commitments and loyalties – in a society in which even manual labour's normal dissent from the established order is active only in spasms, and is then in practice reformist or at most subversive, not revolutionary. Their ambivalence of allegiance may reflect differences in circumstance among them: between black-coated employees for whom the benefits of 'staff' status are more than marginal, prospects of advancement real, every-day ties at work stronger with superiors than with colleagues of their own level; and others whose conditions in market and workplace place them more firmly with manual labour.[18]

Union organization among them shows similar ambiguities. Enrolment in white-collar unions has been growing, and in very recent years faster than the size of the white-collar labour force. But despite great variations from one field of work to another – near-universal in public sector employment, low in much of the private sector – it still falls a good deal short, overall, of union enrolment among manual workers.[19] By the kind of signs which might in the past be taken to display some sort of dissent from the order of capital, white-collar unions now seem closer to manual labour and

18. See especially D. Lockwood, *The Blackcoated Worker*, Allen & Unwin, 1958, still the most cogent analysis in English of the position and ambiguous class identity of low grade non-manual workers. Cf. also the evidence for a continuing social conservatism of outlook among even routine white-collar workers in the study by Mercer and Weir referred to in ch. 2, note 50 below.

19. G. S. Bain and R. Price, 'Union growth and employment trends in the United Kingdom, 1964–70', *Brit. J. Industrial Relations*, Nov. 1972, give the following estimates of trade union enrolment as a percentage of all employees – manual versus all levels of non-manual:

	Male employees			Female employees			All employees		
	1948	1964	1970	1948	1964	1970	1948	1964	1970
Non-manual	34	35	43	23	23	32	29	29	38
Manual	64	60	61	25	28	33	53	51	53

No estimates are available, on a comprehensive basis, for low-grade as distinct from other white-collar workers; but it is clear that at all levels there are great variations in union enrolment from one industry to another.

their unions than they were, say, in the 1950s. They are much readier to strike or go slow. Most are now affiliated to the T.U.C. Yet still only few are linked to the Labour Party. And the significance of militancy and some association with the labour movement as signs of dissent – never straightforward in any case – are also less certain: that for several reasons which we shall discuss later.[20] For the moment, the simple point remains that white-collar workers, even those in low-paid and routine grades of work, still stand somewhat apart from the majority of rank-and-file labour.

V

There are class differences of everyday culture – in styles of life and habits of thought – which have no apparent political content and may have no immediately obvious economic source. Yet these, too, need to be noted as features in the background of class consciousness and class identity. They help to mark the boundaries of the separate worlds within which people at different levels of a divided society live much of their lives. They are part of the context in which perceptions of the social order, individual and collective aspirations, stimuli and restraints to organized action, are formed. They may, especially when their patterns change, act as signposts to the future.

There have, for example, been long-lasting and familiar differences in patterns of marriage and child-bearing. Though people in all classes marry younger than they did forty or fifty years ago – and few now remain single – manual workers still typically marry earlier in

20. See the next chapter. Of nineteen major 'white-collar unions' in early 1974, only two (representing professional civil servants and university teachers) were not either currently affiliated to the T.U.C. or seeking re-affiliation (as were the unions of bank officials, actors and airline pilots) after their expulsion because, contrary to T.U.C. policy, they had registered as legally recognized unions under the Industrial Relations Act 1971. But no more than six of the nineteen were affiliated to the Labour Party, though the large and fast-growing Association of Salaried, Technical and Managerial Staff was among these. Of the five main unions recruiting routine-grade black-coated workers which Lockwood (op. cit., note 18 above, pp. 155 et seq.) discussed in detail nearly two decades earlier, still only two were linked to the Labour party in 1974; but the only one of these five outside the T.U.C. in the 1950s – the local government union, N.A.L.G.O. – was now affiliated to the T.U.C. (We are grateful to Mrs Jean Bocock for this information, compiled in the course of research on the political positions and activities of non-manual unions.)

life than others. That is not surprising. They also start work earlier in life; and their prospects next year will not be much enhanced over this year's by the kind of routine opportunities for promotion, and the regular sequence of increments in pay, which go with most non-manual work except now at low levels. Both early marriage, and the inhibitions to individual planning set by insecurity and the character of the working-class life cycle, may have played some part in keeping the fertility of manual working-class couples above that for non-manual couples over many decades. But birth control in marriage came to be practised by working-class people to a steadily widening extent from the late nineteenth century onwards. It is now, in this country, near-universal.

To talk of a 'spread' of family limitation from the upper and middle classes to the working class is probably misleading. It suggests some automatic process of social imitation, and explains little. When the bourgeoisie began to reduce the size of their families, from about the 1870s, one major reason is likely to have been a widening gap between the cost of maintaining what they regarded as a proper style of life – including more expenditure on schooling of their children – and their capacity to do so without increasing strain in a climate of greater business uncertainty.[21] It is not implausible that a clash between rising expectations and limited opportunities may, in a somewhat similar way, have contributed to the gradual adoption of a 'small family' norm by working-class couples from around the turn of the century. Levels of living had been rising for manual workers in the decades before; and mass production for the working-class market – of ready-made clothes, for example – had begun to make an impact. This may well have entrenched expectations of further improvements. The state at about the same time took the first formal steps to adapt schools to the business of selecting able children from wage-earning homes for occupational destinations higher up the ladder: a promise, still pretty thin, of some regular, institutional provision for upward mobility. There were certainly signs of mounting working-class demands on life, in the form of political and union activity. Workers individually may now also have found a modest degree of control over their own lives a more feasible proposition. On all these scores wage earners' aspirations seem likely to have risen significantly around the turn of the century. But actual opportunities remained sharply limited. Average levels of living in fact stayed fixed, or even

21. J. A. Banks, *Prosperity and Parenthood*, Routledge & Kegan Paul, 1954.

fell, during the two decades up to World War I; and though they rose again after that, the inter-war years were punctuated by increasingly severe periods of unemployment.

Be that as it may, while average family size in all classes was falling until World War II, class differentials of fertility in relative terms remained constant from the late nineteenth century to then. The main 'cultural gap' on this score was that again between manual and non-manual sections of the population, with the average number of children born to manual working-class couples some 40 per cent above the average for non-manual couples at any time over those decades. Variations by occupational level on either side of the line were secondary in magnitude; and fertility was lowest of all among poorly paid white-collar workers, hard-pressed by the disparity between their ambitions and the modest realities of their lives. But with the marriages of the 1940s and after, the margin by which manual working-class fertility exceeds non-manual fertility in general has come down to 20 per cent or less. The detailed pattern of variation has changed, too – to show larger families among professional couples than among skilled workers; figures for the semi-skilled little above the overall average; figures for employers and managers little below it.[22] Lower-grade non-manual workers still have the fewest children of all: the dilemmas set for them by hopes and commitments which exceed their circumstances no doubt remain acute. But something of the same kind probably applies also to manual workers; and more clearly than before. Except for the fairly small group of unskilled, they seem now to have much the same kind of ideas as others about what, in some abstract sense, is a 'good' size of family. But more than others, apart from 'lower middle class' couples, they feel forced to have fewer children than those ideas imply.[23] In this as in a number of other fields, manual earners probably share the aspirations of people better placed in the economic order a good deal more than was the case earlier. But by the same token – since inequality persists – their aspirations are more likely to be defeated by their circumstances.

Family relationships became a fashionable subject of research from the late 1950s. Much of the early work in this field focused on

22. See Part Four, ch. 1, note 8, above.
23. Cf. J. Peel, 'The Hull family survey: the survey couples in 1966', *J. Biosocial Science*, Jan. 1970; see also R.–C. Chou and S. Brown, 'A comparison of the size of families of Roman Catholics and non-Catholics in Great Britain', *Population Studies*, March 1968.

the manual working class. The product of a climate of opinion which took it for granted that labour solidarity was becoming a thing of the past, such research was suffused with nostalgia for a cosy intimacy between kinsfolk described as still characteristic of 'traditional' urban working-class districts, but on the wane. Grandparents – grandmothers at least – were rediscovered with a flourish. Married women and their mothers were identified as the key figures in a pattern of regular contact among kin; and this, in 'traditional' circumstances, was shown to go hand in hand with a fairly sharp segregation of domestic roles between husband and wife. Major emphasis was placed at first on the obstacles which suburbanization made to maintenance of this pattern of kin contact: when young families moved – often because they had no reasonable alternative – to housing estates far from 'Mum'.[24] But this emphasis drew attention away from larger features in the circumstances of working-class life which may have helped, both to form kinship ties of this specific character; and then over time to attenuate them.

Mutual aid between relatives as well as neighbours provided some kind of rudimentary social security – highly ineffective, but essential all the same – when public provision was minimal and overtly punitive in character; still so in a variety of ways now, but no doubt less than in the past. The conjunction of many births with no incremental progression in the man's pay plainly exposed working-class marriages to particularly severe strains while fertility remained high. Increasing competition between husband and wife for disposal of the wage packet was a common consequence during the early and middle phases of married life; and still is in similar circumstances.[25] That probably made for growing tension, or just indifference, between the two. And it is likely to have reinforced other pressures for them to lead fairly separate lives: the man away from the home most of the time, if the marriage survived the risks of death and desertion; the woman in everyday charge of the household, with more – if

24. See especially M. Young and P. Willmott, *Family and Kinship in East London*, Routledge & Kegan Paul, 1957. (Having there put forward the rather implausible proposition that local authority housing policy bore major responsibility for an attenuation of kinship ties, one of the authors devoted a later study to throwing doubt on that proposition: P. Willmott, *The Evolution of a Community*, Routledge, 1963.) The connection between kinship ties and domestic relations between husband and wife was first clearly pointed to by Bott, op. cit. (note 17 above), though on the basis of numerically slender material.

25. Cf., e.g., M. Young, 'The distribution of income within the family', *Brit. J. Sociology*, 1952.

enforced – independence of petty authority at home and in dealings with landlords, schools, occasionally police or courts, than bourgeois married women.[26] This in turn must have compelled reliance for her part on whatever help and moral support she could get from her mother and other relatives, if they were nearby. But if, as seems plausible, this syndrome was pushed to its sharpest form by the combination of high fertility with earnings which stayed more or less fixed until the children, and the housewife herself, could add to them, then one element in the combination is now much diminished in force. Manual wages still do not rise much with age or, limited allowances from the state apart, with family size. But manual working-class couples rarely now have more than two or three children.

The salience of ties of extended kinship among the 'traditional' working class has added fuel to characterizations of their cultural world as 'particularistic'. Contact and mutual aid between relatives are seen to join with ties between neighbours – and between work-mates, when homes are near to work and people in similar work live cheek by jowl – to form a close web of local relationships: communities turned inward upon themselves, cut off from the larger society and from wider horizons by their parochial intimacy. Two inferences have been drawn in much of recent debate. First, it is often assumed, the roots of labour solidarity are to be found in conditions of that sort. If so, labour solidarity is weakened as the old bonds of locality – extended kinship ties and others – are attenuated. Second, it is said, manual working-class perspectives on the world are 'traditionally' foreshortened. The local takes precedence over the universal, the immediate over the longer term. Combine the two inferences; and the chances that manual labour can ever play the prime part in creating a new society free of private capital would indeed seem slim. When there is working-class solidarity, it seems, the solidarity is parochially fragmented and lacks vision; when parochial barriers lose their force, solidarity is eroded. In some of the most influential of recent commentary, in fact, the old particularism of localized collective loyalty is seen as being now pushed aside by a new particularism of domesticity. The pivot of working-class life becomes the

26. For some early descriptions of manual working-class family life which pointed to the kind of executive authority exercised by the wife in everyday affairs, see e.g. Lady Bell, *At the Works*, Arnold, 1907; A. Paterson, *Across the Bridges*, Arnold, 1911; M. S. Pember-Reeves, *Round about a Pound a Week*, Bell, 1913.

family of husband, wife and dependent children; aspirations are private, commitments to workmates, neighbours, perhaps even relatives outside the immediate family, are peripheral and individually selective. Parochially solidary or individualistically home-centred, it is implied, manual workers are imprisoned always within narrow social and mental horizons.

We shall take issue with the political conclusions of these arguments in the last chapter. For the moment only one thread needs to be picked out from the tangle: the general assumption that manual working-class culture is distinctively 'particularistic'. Locality certainly ties wage earners down far more than it ties those who are well off. Manual workers have to try to find jobs closer at hand; are up against bigger obstacles if they want to move home, the more so the longer the move; do not have careers in which promotion and assisted acquisition of a new home often go together; have to make do far more with whatever local services are available wherever they live.[27] Public policy especially has made some difference – rehousing by municipal and new town authorities not least. But workers' choice on these scores is limited; and their everyday lives are circumscribed within fairly close geographical, as well as economic, boundaries. A particularism of locality is an enforced, practical concomitant of wage earning, though the labour movement in organization and objectivities collectively transcends this. But particularism of other kinds is a firm ingredient of bourgeois culture as well. Ties of kinship, for example, are no less parochial, in one crucial sense, when their geographical range is wide rather than narrow. They are exclusive in either case, to the extent that they put a premium on loyalties between people who are associated by family relationship: between people who are 'near' to each other by the accident of birth. And ties of kinship are potent among the bourgeoisie; the more so, almost

27. On class differences in geographical mobility, with reference especially to distances moved, see, e.g., D. Friedlander and R. J. Roshier, *Internal Migration in England and Wales, 1851 to 1951*, Centre for Urban Studies, 1966; and recent population census tabulations of migration within and across local authority boundaries. On class differences in daily journeys to work; and on the evident dependence of all, but especially working-class, wives on proximity to jobs if they are to work at all: cf., e.g., J. H. Westergaard, 'The Structure of Greater London', in Centre for Urban Studies, ed., *London – Aspects of Change*, McGibbon & Kee, 1964. R. Pahl, *Urbs in Rure: the Metropolitan Fringe in Hertfordshire*, London School of Economics, 1965, draws a general contrast between the place-bound lives of workers in villages of the outer London area – even those with jobs elsewhere – and the commuting and retired 'new gentry'.

certainly, the higher up the scale of privilege one goes, though they take a different form from that characteristic of the manual working class.

The rich pass on their wealth to relatives. They use money and influence to secure their children's future. They ease the way for their sons and daughters, even when these have left home: by marriage settlements; by loans and gifts – evidently on a rising scale, to reduce the impact of death duties on inheritance; by payments under covenant for their grandchildren's education; by string-pulling in a variety of ways. They may still occasionally use the courts to protect a daughter – and with her, their property and status – from an unsuitable suitor; or bring their resources to bear to help relatives in trouble, perhaps in danger of putting family credit at risk. Wealthy families may have a visible corporate unity, expressed for example in family trusts or in gatherings of the clan, part ritual but also to ensure continuity in common business. Like corporations, they employ professional agents – 'family' solicitors especially – to manage their affairs. An intricate network of ties by blood relationship and marriage within and between the élites of business, conservative politics, senior civil service and high professions strengthens the unity conferred by common wealth and power. There is, as we have underlined before, perennial conflict inherent in capitalism between the demands of economic efficiency and the desire of the privileged to protect their ability to transmit privilege to kin. Overt nepotism has been banned from the public service, and is dubiously respectable– though still practised – in business and in appointment to honours. Restraints on choice of marriage partners in the upper class are no doubt less formal than they were. Yet in other essentials, kinship ties among the privileged have probably not been much attenuated, since privilege itself is still so strongly concentrated. Moreover, men rather than women are the key figures in these family networks because it is they primarily who control property, dispose of money, wield influence; though women may pull strings through men, specialize in enacting the ceremonials of upper-class kinship, and increasingly – as recipients of gifts '*inter vivos*' designed to cut inheritance tax – own wealth in their own legal right.

Once stated, all this is obvious: in general terms at least, if not in the details of its everyday workings, or in respect of precise trends over time. All the more extraordinary that it has figured so little in sociological research and debate. The many hints of strong family bonds among the rich and powerful evident from work in other fields of study – on property ownership, politics, élite recruitment and education – are rarely even pulled together. Similar if less entrenched ties of kinship – cemented by transmission of ownership, money and know-how, with men active in keeping family links alive for those purposes – can be found further down the economic scale, among people born to more modest 'middle class' security; and a start has been made in tracing these.[28] Yet the frequency and specific character even of such an elementary phenomenon as the 'middle class windfall' – inheritance or family aid at critical stages of the life cycle, to reinforce advancement by salary increments and promotion – has yet to be mapped in any systematic way. And much of the last twenty years' work inspired by the 'rediscovery of kinship' has implied or encouraged, if only by omission, a view of extended family networks as somehow peculiar to the manual working class – where in fact such ties are rather ineffective buttresses against insecurity; and a contrasting assumption that kinship links, while not absent, are less regular and more selective in character in other groups. They may be so among people who are moving or have recently moved up the economic scale; not among those who already have some privilege to protect and pass on.

There are other particularistic features of upper class culture which are oddly ignored when anthropologists of class set to work to draw character sketches of the world of manual labour: emphases on a primacy of moral obligation towards those with whom one happens to be thrown together, by accident of propinquity, at least as pronounced and exclusive as the ties of solidarity which can bind

28. See C. Bell, *Middle Class Families*, Routledge & Kegan Paul, 1969. Other British studies which describe and comment on family life among 'middle-class' people, whether in a context of comparison with manual working-class families or not, include C. Rosser and C. Harris, *The Family and Social Change*, Routledge, 1965; M. Young and P. Willmott, *Family and Class in a London Suburb*, Routledge, 1960; *idem*, *The Symmetrical Family*, Routledge, 1973; R. Firth *et al.*, *Families and their Relatives*, Routledge, 1969; Bott, op. cit. (note 17 above). But while much interest in these turned on relationships among 'extended kin', in practice frequency of contact was often emphasized at the expense of purposes of contact, and the economic context and character of family and kin relationships received little attention. This although the firm material interests and concerns with maintenance of status which buttress family networks among wealthy and powerful people were noted at a fairly early stage in the revival of interest in kinship: cf. W. J. Goode, 'The process of role bargaining in the impact of urbanization and industrialization on family systems', *Current Sociology*, vol. 12, no. 1, 1963/64.

'traditional' working-class communities together. The 'public' schools to which members of the old and the new ruling interest have sent their children since the mid-nineteenth century preach loyalty to school, team and house: a blind and mindless obligation to a small, fortuitously constituted collectivity, from which probably only the most securely established of these institutions – Eton and perhaps one or two others – tolerate much individual deviance. The pattern has been emulated further down the scale, in private schools of lesser status and in many grammar schools. And the 'old boy' network established at public school is carried over into adult life at the top. This kind of parochialism – to which an ideal of 'gentlemanly Christianity' in practice gave way – and the associated public school development of a hierarchy of appointed pupil prefects with delegated authority, may well in those forms be peculiar to the British upper class when they educate their young. They are probably best understood as an outcome of the Victorian interpenetration of old and new interests in the upper reaches of British society, and of the assertion of empire in the second half of the nineteenth century. And they have not remained entirely fixed and unquestioned even at the top: loyalties of old school tie can obstruct efficiency no less than loyalties of kin. But the continuing salience of both kinds of particularism in the culture of privilege is in manifest contradiction to those glib social caricatures in which an insularity of working-class allegiances and perspectives is contrasted with a rational and impartial universality of commitment attributed to the bourgeoisie.

No less of a caricature are the common, and closely related, sketches which identify a restriction of vision to immediate situations as the essence of manual working-class culture. We have already discussed the impetus which characterizations of this slant have gained from recent research on class differences in linguistic habits and child-rearing practices.[29] There is a good deal of earlier work, too, which in one way or another has claimed 'short-term hedonism' as a distinctive feature of manual workers' outlook on life. The ordinary child from a manual home, it is said for example, lacks the motivation, in himself and from his parents, to invest the effort and

29. See Part Four above, chapter 3, section V. Cf. also, e.g., J. and E. Newson, *Patterns of Infant Care*, Penguin, 1965; *Four Years Old in an Urban Community*, Allen & Unwin, 1968; 'Some social differences in the process of child rearing' in J. Gould, ed., *Penguin Social Sciences Survey 1968*, Penguin, 1968: the Newsons' data from a longitudinal study in Nottingham suggest some class differences in child-rearing practices similar in character to those underlined by Bernstein.

sacrifices required to do well at school. 'Middle class' children, by contrast, learn to 'defer gratification' in the present for future benefit. This, as it has been pointed out, smartly slides over the facts, both that working-class parents now commonly start with quite high aspirations for their children's education; and that, in a highly competitive school system, immediate rewards in the form of teachers' acknowledgment and parents' praise go to the child who does well. Penalties and disapprobation go to the child who does not. A working-class child who opts out of the competition is not buying present pleasure at the cost of future gain. He is finding other modes of 'gratification' – if the term has to be used – in place of those his experience at school denies him.[30]

More generally, however, our point is not to deny that there are characteristic elements of 'short-term hedonism' in the mental climate of manual labour. The economic circumstances of working-class existence – uncertainties of earnings and about jobs, absence of the kinds of prospects which facilitate investment in the future – virtually force this upon manual workers and their families in their individual lives. They may encourage also a belief in luck – bad and good – of a vaguely superstitious kind, to match the real unpredictabilities of working-class life.[31] But to single out these inhibitions to perspectives and aspirations beyond the here and now is startlingly one-sided. It allows no room for those large commitments to sacrifice the present for the future, to join with unknown people elsewhere, to reform or change the social order – which the labour movement has voiced; and which are expressed, in however limited a form, whenever wage earners strike, work-to-rule, go slow or engage in small-scale sabotage. To say that is not to romanticize the labour movement, or to attribute revolutionary significance to everyday industrial action. But even the most petty withdrawal of labour involves its participants in loss today, for some uncertain gain tomorrow – or much later. And sacrifice of this kind – as well as the solidarity which goes with it, often beyond boundaries of locality and job – is fairly routine among large sections of manual labour: an institutionalized part of their culture. Conventional characterization of that culture as hedonistic neither recognizes this part of the reality of working-class

30. Cf. especially Lacey, op. cit. (Part Four above, ch. 3, note 8).
31. Cf., e.g., F. Zweig, *The British Worker*, Penguin, 1952; R. Hoggart, *The Uses of Literacy*, Chatto & Windus, 1957; Klein, op. cit. (note 17 above); N. Abercrombie *et al.*, 'Superstition and religion: the god of the gaps', in D. Martin and M. Hill, eds., *A Sociological Yearbook of Religion: 3*, S.C.M. Press, 1970.

life; nor gives leeway for exploration of the sources and prospects of labour protest in, and in part against, an order founded on private capital.

VI

There are, in short, well-marked divisions of consciousness, organization and everyday culture in parallel with the cleavages made by inequality of wealth, power and opportunity. But the lines are parallel: they do not fully coincide. Low-grade white-collar workers in particular share many conditions in common with manual wage earners, and more so now than before. But in outlook on society and commitments they still stand half-apart from manual labour. The order of capital cannot depend on their acquiescence or support. But labour protest is weakened by their separatism. It is also weakened by defection to Conservatism even among manual workers, at all levels of skill and earnings; by contradictions in working-class culture, and in the character of the organized labour movement, which encourage conservatism – with a small 'c' – side by side with diffuse radicalism; by the inertia of powerlessness.

Yet in one respect, at least, there are hints that the balance of pressures, so far tipped firmly to secure the maintenance of capital, might tip the other way. Cultural boundaries between the classes in many ways are less distinct than they were: workers have more aspirations in common with people above them in the economic scale than they did. The frustration of those aspirations by persistent inequality may trigger no more than individualized resentment and resignation; or fragmented disorder directed against irrationally chosen targets; or everyday subversion and industrial militancy which still lack the impetus for translation into political radicalism. Or it may build up into a challenge to the order of capital. Of all but the last there are many signs; and the last, as we shall now argue, cannot be ruled out.

2 The challenge from labour: inhibitions and prospects

I

Reform has certainly so far been the dominant note in labour opposition. Working-class organizations maintain allegiance of a sort to a socialist vision of a sort. But the allegiance is mainly rhetorical, and the vision hazy. In practice, union and party efforts have long been directed to a variety of objectives that fall well short of a challenge to the rule of capital: to pressure, through bargaining and industrial action, to defend or raise wage levels and to protect such small discretion as workers and their representatives have over the ways in which they do their work; to mitigating the insecurities of wage-earning life, and modifying inequalities at their margins; to support of measures intended to improve the efficiency of a capitalist economy in the 'general interest', even to the point of co-operation in managerial discipline of labour; to expansion of state activities for these purposes; to ensuring recognition for organized labour, for those purposes again or as an end in itself. Abolition of private capital flits through labour dreams. But it is never on the agenda for today and tomorrow; and labour agendas for the day after tomorrow are rare.

Yet British labour might have been expected to be the first to produce an agenda for revolution. Many commentators at one time – up to the middle years of the nineteenth century at least – feared just that. Manufacture for wide markets transformed the British economy before others: it made of rural labourers and workers in domestic industry, of urban craftsmen and paupers, the first industrial working class in large numbers. Their concentration in the new cities and factories of early Victorian England seemed like 'the slow rising and gradual swelling of an ocean which must, at some future and no distant time, bear all the elements of society aloft upon its bosom – and float them – Heaven knows whither'. There were, it looked clear enough, 'mighty energies slumbering in those masses'.[1] Such energies found expression in the first attempts to unite workers of new industries and old trades in common defence against, and opposition to, the ruling order: the movements for a 'general union' and for 'the Charter'. And the term 'class', with its connotations of antagonistic interests, pushed aside the old terminology of 'order', 'rank' and 'station' in the vocabulary of inequality.[2] True, the early general unions collapsed; and Chartism in turn gave way to a new 'model unionism' of skilled workers, concerned to protect their own particular corners in the labour market. Unrest turned into quiescence for two or three decades from the 1850s to the 1870s and 1880s. But then working-class dissent grew again, and took more active forms. The unskilled and semi-skilled were recruited for unions which began to cut across the barriers of trade and even craft; some of the skilled unions started a gradual process of transformation to admit workers who had not served long apprenticeships. So a common movement of wage earners took shape once more, and in firmer outline. It sought its own political future, moreover, from the turn of the century, when the T.U.C. joined with political organizations of varying shades of pink and red to set up the Labour Representation Committee, forerunner of the Labour Party.

A 'moderate' outcome from all this was not so certain then as has been claimed with hindsight since. The common assumption that Tory electoral successes after the franchise was widened in 1867 and 1884 provide early evidence of a pervasive conservatism in the British working class is misguided. Manual workers are unlikely to have constituted a majority of the electorate until after World War I. As a result of continuing legal restrictions of the franchise, of obstacles to registration, and of class biases in the ways in which constituency boundaries were drawn, the admission of the working class to effect-

1. W. Cooke Taylor, *Notes of a Tour in the Manufacturing Districts of Lancashire*, London, 1842; quoted by Ruth Glass, 'Urban sociology in Great Britain', *Current Sociology*, vol. 4, no. 4, 1955 (p. 16).
2. A. Briggs, 'The language of class in early nineteenth century England', in *idem* and J. Saville, eds., *Essays in Labour History*, Macmillan, 1960.

ive opportunities to vote was in fact a slow and carefully controlled process: in no way a 'leap in the dark'.[3] Elections and parliamentary politics are very dubious pointers to popular sentiment now; still more so then. Other signs suggested a groundswell of radical dissent. A number of unions, from the late nineteenth century, adopted public ownership – of their own industries or of industry at large – as a long-term aim, although the Labour Party did not entrench this objective into its constitution until after World War I. The security of established rule seemed threatened on many sides. Industrial militancy spread in the decades up to 1914. The ruling groups were divided in their response to that; and still more over the Irish issue. Ireland posed a risk of civil war on two fronts: of nationalist rebellion in the south; of armed opposition to Liberal government concessions from high-ranking officers in the north. With this; with an edge of illegality and violence to demonstrations by bourgeois suffragettes; with a new twist to industrial militancy in the prospect of a co-ordinated nationwide strike by the recent 'triple alliance' of miners, railwaymen and transport workers – Britain just before the outbreak of World War I showed rents in its social fabric which may have brought it closer to a revolutionary situation than ever before, or so far since, in its industrial history.

But not close enough: there was no revolution. And it is easier to see now than then that the seeds of compromise between organized labour and capital had been well sown already before 1914. The chances of achieving recognition and some influence became real as the working-class movement grew. Some labour spokesmen had gained admission to Parliament, usually as Liberal members, from the mid-1870s onwards; and to token representation on public inquiries into working class conditions a decade or two later. Neither these men nor, more significantly, the Labour Party in its early years set objectives beyond reform and accreditation to speak for the rank-and-file of wage earners. In the event, the spread of strikes and the attempts of the judiciary both to curb these, and to split the political and industrial wings of the labour movement from each other by force of law, led instead to the establishment of a framework of 'voluntary' accommodation. It was 'voluntary' only with an unstated, contradictory proviso: state power could be called back from the sidelines to try to compel labour discipline 'in the national interest', if wage earners withheld co-operation. So strikes

3. Moorhouse, op. cit., (ch. 1, note 11 above).

were made illegal during the two world wars; the government mobilized large resources of manpower, materials and institutional influence to defeat the general strike of 1926; and courts as well as governments of both parties turned to the law in the 1960s and early 1970s in attempts to enforce labour docility. But the screen of voluntarism could be maintained, in peacetime, through most of the period for the first decade of the century to the late 1960s, because the majority of labour leaders co-operated. They bought admission to minor government office and a weak voice in the making of policy, during World War I, at the price of agreement to public direction of labour and legal prohibition of strikes. They accepted, from the early 1920s, a separation between the political and industrial wings of the labour movement which became a doctrinal premise of class compromise. That separation did not take the form which the judges of the House of Lords had attempted to impose in 1909: a ban on union expenditure in support of the Labour Party, or for any other purposes that might be declared political. It involved instead a voluntary division of spheres of interest between unions and party, with acceptance of the conservative view that industrial action for 'political' objectives was improper and – whatever the legal position – subversive of parliamentary government.

The pattern of accommodation was firmly set in the first decade or so after the end of World War I. The collapse of the 'triple alliance' on 'Black Friday' in 1921 pointed the way to the failure of the unions to prepare for the general strike of 1926, on any scale commensurate with the preparations made by government and business; and to the T.U.C.s abandonment of that strike, after nine days of massive and still solid support, leaving the miners in lonely opposition for another six months till they acknowledged defeat. Even while the general strike lasted, official labour spokesmen strenuously denied that it was 'political'. The Mond-Turner talks between unions and business, which followed this confirmation of labour's recognition of the primacy of capital, set the scene for a pattern of collective bargaining – centralized, routinized, conducted in moderation over a narrow range of initial differences in bargaining positions – that lasted into the 1960s. The Labour Party meanwhile twice took office as a minority government in the 1920s. And while the great bulk of the parliamentary party refused to support their former leader in his formation of a 'national government' in 1931, neither of the two first Labour administrations showed signs, in plans let alone in policies, of looking much beyond assertion of their credentials to govern a capitalist economy.[4]

<h1 style="text-align:center">II</h1>

The story, in such bare bones, is familiar enough, though it has been surprisingly often forgotten in those recent commentaries which have taken official Labour Party conservatism in the 1950s and 1960s as part-evidence of some new trend towards abatement of class conflict. The fact that there was a radical edge to the party's policies in office just after World War II may have helped to suggest that its subsequent modesty of objectives represented a retreat from an older, once well established aggressive line. In fact Labour's programme in the late 1940s – while it served to reinforce the wartime shift in the terms on which capital and labour meet each other – was not designed by the party's main leaders as the first phase of a socialist transformation; but as a set of reforms more or less complete in themselves. And for all practical purposes, the 1940s marked a peak of Labour Party radicalism by contrast with the decades before: certainly so far as its front bench representatives in Parliament were concerned.

So the puzzle of apparent labour acquiescence in the failure of capitalism to fulfil its promises is an old one; especially here, in the country which saw the first clashes between the new classes of an industrial market economy. Indeed, quite a few commentators have seen the puzzle, by implication at least, as one more or less peculiar to Britain. And they, usually, have looked for answers to it in allegedly distinctive features of the cultural climate in which the relations between British capital and labour were formed. Class conflict here, it has often been argued, has been kept in check by common subscription, at all levels of society, to an ethic whose central values are a compound of tolerance, respect for moderation, 'common sense', and deference to authority. This, it is said, is the English version of the 'liberal consensus'; and its hold on all classes, for a century or more at least, has kept back 'extremism' of both left and right.

Several American sociologists have taken up this theme, with a

4. For a penetrating analysis of the process by which the leadership of the labour movement accepted the institutionalization of class conflict, see R. Miliband, *Parliamentary Socialism*, Merlin Press, 2nd. ed. 1973.

twist. They have contrasted the 'particularism' which they identify as distinctive in British culture – expressed especially as a pervasive respect for authority, a general consent to the rule of people born or bred to rule irrespective of demonstrated ability, an acceptance of secrecy in government – with 'universalistic' values of a contrary kind which they claim to be characteristically American.[5] Such comparisons with the United States throw no light on the puzzle. To say that is not to deny them all reality. There may be less popular acceptance of status rituals and status pretensions in America than here – or elsewhere in Europe – though differences in the forms and symbols of social ranking make comparisons on this score hazardous. Business in the U.S.A. probably selects and promotes its managers with more concern for proof of efficiency, and less for evidence of acceptable personal background, than does business in Britain.[6] Government is certainly conducted more in the open there than here; and the traditions of muck-raking and populism have long roots in American politics. But all this goes together with deeply entrenched 'particularistic' features which have been curiously set aside in these characterizations of U.S. society. Discrimination by skin colour and ethnic origin is in flagrant denial of selection by merited achievement: that should be obvious. But divisions based on ascriptive affiliations arising from the accidents of birth and social proximity are much more pervasive than that. City, state and federal politics in the States have evolved in a mould of 'boss' patronage and nepotism – still resilient despite many attacks upon it – in which ethnic and personal loyalties play key parts. It is precisely the fragmentation of class ties by ties of colour, national origin and religious denomination which has helped, in large measure, to give America the almost unique distinction among industrial capitalist countries of having no effective party of labour.[7] Particularist allegiances have

5. Cf. the references in note 14, Part One.

6. Cf., e.g., M. Burrage, 'Culture and British economic growth', *British J. Sociology*, June 1969.

7. This does not mean that individual class position has little effect on political outlook in the U.S.A. A recent major study, using public opinion poll data, shows that the main line of division there in party support and political orientations runs between manual and low-grade white-collar workers on the one hand, and those above them on the other, though another line to some degree splits off white Protestants from others at all levels. This study also shows considerable dissatisfaction among wage earners about things as they are, and support for public welfare measures. It does a great deal to explode the notion of an American 'class consensus'; and the view, alternatively, that the white Protestant upper class is a liberal group thwarted in its hopes of reform by an illiberal, intolerant and autho-

there powerfully overridden the universalist appeals of class and class ideology. And by the same token, populism in the U.S.A. has produced no challenge to the order of capital. Its typical objectives have been, not socialism or social democracy, but defence of a dying world of petty entrepreneurship. If deference to authority is peculiarly British, it is also in this country mixed with its opposite: a diffuse dissent of labour rank-and-file from the rule of business. Deference to capital, by contrast, is peculiarly American, and in its consequences has been a highly conservative force.

Although there is no help to be found from comparisons with the United States, there is clearly an element of truth to the argument that British working-class culture has shown features of respect for compromise, order and hierarchy which have played a part in the institutionalization of class conflict within hitherto quite narrow bounds. And in some interpretations, these are seen as core values of long standing among ordinary British people. The twins of popular moderation and deference are said to explain, not only much of the support on which the Conservative Party has been able to draw within the manual working class; but also the conservatism of the labour movement in action.[8] Even to the extent that this may be so, there is little by way of explanation here. Rank-and-file acceptance of the order in being much as it is – if in fact there is such acceptance – can be the product of institutionalized compromise as much as its cause. Once the main organizations of labour, their leaders and officials, are committed to policies of accommodation, popular dissent finds it the more difficult to make itself heard. Resignation, if not active consent, is then the more likely. But if it is argued that the framework of class compromise itself was built upon acquiescence at the grass-roots – if a popular ethos of moderation preceded the institutions, or the two were locked from the start in a mutually reinforcing cycle of cause and effect – the puzzle would still remain. Why, if so, was a code of restraint so widespread among the workers to whom industrial capitalism seemed to offer promises which it then, of necessity, withheld?

---

ritarian wage-earning class. See R. F. Hamilton, *Class and Politics in the United States*, Wiley, 1972, Cf. also M. Mann, 'The social cohesion of liberal democracy', *Amer. Sociological Rev.,* 1970.

8. For some recent contributions on these lines, see for example McKenzie and Silver, op. cit. (ch. 1, note 12 above); D. Martin and C. Crouch, 'England' in M. Scotford Archer and S. Giner, eds., *Contemporary Europe: Class, Status and Power*, Weidenfeld & Nicolson, 1971.

Some historians have looked to religion for an answer. Methodism, they have suggested, played a crucial role in preventing proletarian revolution in Britain: whether by repressing discontent; or by diverting it into politically harmless channels; or by allowing working-class people in early industrial capitalism to find a new confidence and sense of identity, to express commitments to some kind of equality and reform, without engagement in revolution.[9] But even if Methodism had sufficient support in the wage-earning population to make this thesis feasible as a general – not merely a local or regional – proposition, the ideological diversity of Methodism and the contradictions within it weaken the explanatory force of the argument. Wesleyanism itself enjoined strict respect for authority and hierarchy, condemned political dissent and social unrest. That remained one strand in Methodism. But in other and later forms, Methodism and its offshoots encompassed a range of doctrine. The social philosophies associated with it extended beyond respectful liberalism, in some variants at least, to radicalism and militancy; even perhaps to active subversion. The balance of emphasis on order and on dissent, the mix of contradictory elements, was flexible. The issues are too tangled to be easily summed up in a few sentences. But it seems unlikely that, on its own, Methodism could have set anything like the definite limits to working-class world views which the thesis requires. It appears to have been too patchy in membership, too liable to lose support, too susceptible to divergent political interpretations, for that. Methodism may have had some share in encouraging labour reformism. But if so, this must have been far more through an appeal among leaders and officials than through promotion of a groundswell of liberal moderation among rank-and-file workers; and then only because other and larger factors worked in that direction too.

9. For an important recent revival, in new guise, of the thesis initially advanced by Elie Halévy, see B. Semmel, *The Methodist Revolution,* Heinemann, 1974. Semmel argues, from an examination of Methodist doctrine, that the movement offered the new industrial working class a liberal and progressive ideology which was yet combined with respect for order: so it helped to prevent political revolution, but not by repression. It seems, however, that this argument could cut both ways: the contradictions within Methodism implied a wide range of different political tendencies and possibilities. Among sceptics about, and critics of, the Halévy thesis, see especially E. P. Thompson, *The Making of the English Working Class,* Penguin edition, 1968 (particularly the postscript, pp. 917–23) and E. J. Hobsbawm, 'Methodism and the threat of revolution in Britain', in his *Labouring Men,* Weidenfeld & Nicolson, 1964. See also the references in these three contributions to other relevant studies and discussions.

The very fact that capitalism came to Britain early, and turned to mass manufacture well before other countries in the West industrialized, may have had a part in weakening the forces for revolution. The industrial working class here stood alone, without foreign counterparts in comparable circumstances and numbers, in its formative years. The failure of the first attempts at labour unity, from the 1820s to the 1840s, left divisions by skill, trade and locality which died hard. For centuries, moreover, the ruling groups in each epoch had been open to new membership, just as they also fairly readily switched to investment in new fields when opportunities arose. It is doubtful whether this had much direct effect in deflecting mass opposition from the new wage-earning population of the nineteenth century. True, there were former tradesmen and master craftsmen among the successful entrepreneurs of early industry; and a fair number of men who had started as ordinary workers, among managers and employers in the textile industries even in the early twentieth century. Political moderation appears to have had wide support where manufacture continued to retain a small workshop scale, and journeymen could still hope to set up for themselves, as in Birmingham throughout much of the nineteenth century. But these were not realistic hopes for most rank-and-file wage earners, even at the outset; and still less as the scale of business increased.

Indirectly, however, the relative fluidity of recruitment to positions of power and prosperity in Britain over many centuries may have had more influence in turning working-class protest towards compromise, once it began to make itself felt. For that fluidity had helped to make for a transfer of power in Britain to capital primarily through a repeated interpenetration of old and new ruling groups. The civil war of the seventeenth century, and its aftermath especially, certainly contributed much to securing the conditions in which commercial enterprise could flourish and come to dominate; tensions between rival economic interests, old and new, large and small, were crucial in its genesis. Yet it was not a 'bourgeois revolution', a conflict between a rising bourgeoisie and a dying pre-capitalist order, in any such straightforward terms. Capital, in different forms, was engaged on both sides. The heritage from the civil war, in any case, was one of institutionally supported predilection for the resolution of domestic conflict, within the higher reaches of British society, by pragmatic accommodation. When the industrial bourgeoisie sought power some two centuries later, they acquired it, in instalments, through a process of amalgamation and mutual adaptation with the older interests of land, finance and trade, one result of which was to emasculate their own distinctive spirit of innovating rationalism and to turn entrepreneurs into gentlemen. The effect of that on the working-class movement, in turn, it has been argued, was crucial. When labour organized, this diagnosis runs, it did so without a model of bourgois revolutionary activism to follow, and without a preceding climate of ideological confrontation to sharpen its own critique of society. Hence the defensive character of working-class dissent, its failure in Britain to assert and sustain a direct challenge to capital.[10]

This interpretation has the virtue of offering some explanation – and a forcefully argued one – for a climate of compromise which is often postulated with little explanation or ascribed, no more illuminatingly, to a genius or frailty of 'British character'. But there are weaknesses to it. For one thing, it seems to presuppose that the modes of working-class consciousness are – or were in the nineteenth century – very much the prisoner of pre-existing bourgeois ideology and practice. But it is far from clear that this need always be so. The German bourgeoisie, for example, abandoned revolutionary aspirations and entered into a fateful alliance with the rural landlords of Prussia from the middle of the nineteenth century; yet German labour later produced a strong revolutionary wing in rivalry with social democratic revisionism. Many reasons can be suggested for this, including the pattern of political repression – combined with welfare reforms and imperialism – which arose out of that alliance. Our point here is not to pursue these questions; only to suggest that labour – on occasion at least – can create its own models of revolution. For another thing, the working-class movement in early, and again in late, nineteenth-century Britain took some steps in just that direction. From the days of Chartism and before, labour's response to capital has been a mixture of defence and aggression; of pressures for recognition, to protect wages, to keep work discipline at bay, with assertion of hopes for a society free of private capital; of routine co-operation, with both every-day subversion and principled denial of the legitimacy of business rule. Certainly, defence has prevailed over attack in practice, compromise over brute confrontation. Professions of socialist aims have not been translated into a pro-

10. Cf. P. Anderson, 'Origins of the present crisis', op. cit. (Part One, note 5). See also *idem*, 'Components of the national culture', in A. Cockburn and R. Blackburn, eds., *Student Power*, Penguin, 1969.

gramme, a strategy and set of tactics, for their implementation. In that sense, it is true, organized labour here has not produced a 'model' for revolution. But of radical opposition to the established order – of dissent from its premises – there is much evidence in the history of British labour.[11] There were the makings of what might have become – and might still become – a revolutionary impulse: grumbling at most times under the surface of accommodation, and erupting at some, though to no effect so far. Working-class resistance here is not as ideologically empty as the thesis of 'bourgeois hegemony' seems to argue. But its ideology of dissent indeed lacks coherent form.

We shall take up these questions again shortly. The dual character of labour orientations is as relevant to any attempt to assess the future as it is to understanding the past. But that duality is not a uniquely British phenomenon; and efforts to trace the institutionalization of class conflict in this country to something distinctive in the climate of national culture may well take the wrong tack from the outset. Working-class opposition has so far in no highly industrialized country of Western Europe produced a successful revolution. And even where the labour movement has a strong and organized left wing – with a revolutionary ideology whose formal clarity is sometimes romantically idealized by radicals in Britain – the Communist Party has long shown signs of adapting itself to an indefinite postponement of revolution: the more so, perhaps, as hitherto tenacious divisions between 'advanced' and 'backward' sectors of the economy, in France and Italy, are now giving way to a firmer dominance of big business and large-scale industry overall. It does not follow from this, as it is becoming fashionable to infer, that capital is safe and labour tamed for all time, once 'delays in development' have been eliminated by thorough industrial capitalization of the economy: that the risk of working-class revolution is a passing phase confined to the transition to 'modern' production.[12] The institutional-

11. Cf. especially the critique of Anderson by E. P. Thompson, 'The peculiarities of the English', in R. Miliband and J. Saville, eds., *The Socialist Register 1965*; and also Thompson's seminal study of *The Making of the English Working Class* (op. cit., note 9 above).

12. For two recent books which both adopt the view that left-wing strength in the labour movement is primarily a product of the transition to industrial capitalism, or of a situation in which sectors of the economy hitherto relatively excluded are being incorporated in large-scale capitalist rationalization, while stable and institutionalized class compromise can be expected to prevail otherwise, see M. Mann, *Consciousness and Action among the Western Working Class*, Macmillan, 1973 (e.g., pp. 40–41, 67, 72) and A. Giddens, *The Class Structure of*

ization of class conflict in capitalist societies is, we shall argue, inherently precarious. But the pressures for class conflict to become regulated in some sort of framework of compromise, even though the framework may not last, are clearly powerful throughout the capitalist world. They are not easily overcome.

III

Many commentators have suggested that these pressures are not likely ever to be overcome. Professional sociologists, it is true, have now generally rejected the most glaring *naïvetes* of the notions of working-class 'embourgeoisement' which held sway in the 1950s. But those who have contributed most forcefully to the continuing debate still, in the main, see the *status quo* pretty firmly anchored in grass-root inhibitions to working-class radicalism. The sources of those inhibitions may not be found in 'peculiarities of the English', but in features of wage-earning life common to industrial capitalism; and their character is seen to have changed and to be changing. For all that, according to most interpretations, they make a labour challenge to the order of capital improbable.

There are several threads to these arguments. They are of different authorship and not all neatly in line with each other. Yet there is sufficient overlap among them for something of a composite, current view to emerge about the obstacles to proletarian revolution, in the past and now. From these perspectives, labour radicalism is caught on the horns of an almost irresoluble dilemma. Working-class solidarity is not enough, however intense. If it is to lead to revolution, it must be joined by high collective aspirations; by a critical understanding of the barriers set to such aspirations by capitalist institutions; by faith in an alternative society which could destroy those barriers. Yet working-class subordination itself, and the cultural constraints of wage-earning life, militate against this sort of social imagination. Where it does emerge, it is argued, it is likely to be transient. And when wage earners now raise their demands on life, they are likely to do so in forms, and under conditions, that undermine the first requirement for revolution: collective cohesion.

the Advanced Societies, Hutchinson, 1973 (e.g., pp. 211–14, 285–7). Neither totally excludes the possibility of a general radicalization of the contemporary working class, but the balance of interpretation in both is heavily against it.

Nineteenth- and early twentieth-century industrialization created close-knit communities of workers: cut off from the larger world in their everyday lives, but all the more united within local boundaries by a network of reciprocal ties, by common experience and shared hardship. It is communities of this kind which are seen as the nurseries of rank-and-file labour solidarity: mining districts, shipyard towns, dockside areas, mill towns, and so on – dominated by one or two industries, by a small number of companies or perhaps only one; the population largely of one class and concentrated within a narrow range of jobs. Isolation, the absence of alternative work opportunities, employer paternalism, might keep labour docile; but usually only in small communities, where circumstances prolonged that personal dependence of wage earners on their superiors, in and off work, which also elsewhere made for deferential respect for rank. The prototypical communities of 'the isolated mass', by contrast, bred cohesion of labour in common defence against their employers. Industries mainly located in areas of this sort, in most capitalist countries, for long showed the highest recorded strike rates.[13] And it is in such communities, it has been argued from a variety of evidence and impressions, that working-class consciousness in its 'traditional' form was shaped *par excellence:* consciousness that involves a strong sense of common identity and a shared picture of society as divided in two, between 'us' and 'them'.[14] Such solidarity draws its strength from mutual reinforcement of different sorts of relationship among workers. Companionship at work carries over into life outside work; shop floor, working men's club, pub and street form a single network. Where community and workplace boundaries of the everyday world coincided in this way – and where they still so coincide – they join to make a double roof, to shield workers and their families from the 'official' culture of the larger society. Here is protection against the barrage of exhortation and assumption – preached by business, state, schools and media, reinforced by routine – that the nation is at one and all is well, given only cheerful acceptance of duty and respectable ambitions confined to individual success on the part of ordinary people. Under that protective shelter, a manual working class 'counter-culture' could grow and can stay alive. Without it, the

13. See C. Kerr and A. Siegel, 'The inter-industry propensity to strike', in A. W. Kornhauser *et al., Industrial Conflict,* McGraw Hill, 1954. Cf. also K. G. Knowles, *Strikes,* Blackwell, 1954.

14. See especially D. Lockwood, 'Sources of variation . . .', op. cit.; and J. H. Goldthorpe *et al., The Affluent Worker,* op. cit. (Part One, note 17, above.)

mild deviance even of voting Labour at elections would be threatened.[15]

When the styles of 'traditional' working-class life and labour protest are ascribed to replication of community conditions of this pattern – full-blown or in somewhat attenuated form – in many places, there is a riddle posed which has often barely been noticed, let alone answered. How then could the labour movement become more than an alliance of 'village unions', linked for mutual defence, but with neither wider objectives nor wider common loyalties of class to sustain them? For by itself the solidarity of community-cum-workplace is parochial: particularistic in sociological jargon. It sets off the world of kin, neighbours and workmates against the world outside; the familiar against the unfamiliar; the known past and present against the unknown future. Throughout it favours the former against the latter. It confines the sense of common identity to those who live and work near each other; and it ties down aspirations to what is already at hand. Actual experience – one's own, that of relatives, friends, fellow-workers, people in much the same circumstances – sets a low ceiling to hopes and aims; the yardsticks by which hardship and deprivation are judged are modest, fixed by reference to conditions as they are, or were before. A threat to established levels of living can evoke embittered resistance; and expectations will rise as levels rise – but in line with current 'reality', not ahead of it.[16]

Yet the labour movement has been the voice of hopes a good deal larger than this. Even the social democratic wing has expressed notional commitment to a 'new Jerusalem' and practical ambitions to curb, if not to break, the power of capital in society at large. The organized left – a minority in British labour, but a perennial and active element – has maintained its claim to work for a future

15. See F. Parkin, 'Working class Conservatives', *Brit. J. Sociology*, Sept. 1967; and *idem, Class Inequality and Political Order,* op. cit. (Part One, note 8).

16. Runciman, op. cit. (Part One, note 16 above) has attributed the failure of the British working class to challenge inequality to an alleged limitation of expectations of this sort among ordinary manual wage earners. But his 1962 survey data to back up the argument hardly prove the point. It seems likely that a number of his respondents may have interpreted the relevant questions to mean that they were being *asked* to compare their own economic position with that of people of their own kind, in which case the fact that many did just that would not be surprising. Even so nearly half the manual respondents expressed direct dissatisfaction with their incomes; and the great majority of them thought they deserved more money than they were getting, even by the standards of what was 'proper' for 'people like yourself'.

socialist order when seeking confrontation with the present one. And the movement in all its forms has drawn on a consciousness of class among ordinary manual wage earners which, while often defensive rather than aggressive, goes well beyond the parochial limits of locality, workplace and trade. The history of labour is in part precisely the story of the forging of ties of common action, of recognized common identity and interest, across the boundaries of place and dialect, craft and industry: an uneven process, marked by recurrent setback, still nothing like complete if it ever becomes it; yet, plainly, the 'making of a class' with some sense of its own self over the divisions within it.[17] Community solidarity – occupational as well as local – was often the first stage in the generation of working-class consciousness. Where it survives as an element in loyalties that extend wider, it may strengthen labour tenacity in action.[18] But fixed in its parochial form, it would become a barrier to class unity and to the formation of a radical class perspective. Nineteenth-century reformers had a good eye for this when they made blueprints for 'model communities' and urban villages, designed to fragment the wage-earning population and turn workers' loyalties inwards towards locality instead of class.[19]

Such reformers usually hoped that local loyalties would be deferential: their model was a small community in which workers would be servants, content to accept the authority of their masters. The 'counter-culture' traced in recent interpretations to the overlapping ties of workplace, residence and kinship is not deferential: it turns aside the dominant norms of official society. But such dissent as it reflects is still described as essentially, for all political purposes,

17. See especially Thompson, op. cit. (note 9 above) for the early stages of this process. Cf. also, e.g., Z. Bauman, *Between Class and Elite*, Manchester Univ. Press, 1972: an attempt at a systematic analysis of the evolution of the British labour movement, interesting for the nineteenth century but so much obsessed with the institutionalization of compromise in the twentieth century that every left-wing tendency there is ignored or dismissed.

18. The coal miners, in their two large national strikes in the early 1970s, thus clearly drew much strength from the traditional solidarity of the mining areas. But their success, significantly, was the outcome also of widespread support from other workers, who helped to stop coal deliveries.

19. Cf., e.g., T. Chalmers, *The Christian and Civic Economy of Large Towns*, Glasgow, 1821–26, who advocated a subdivision of the cities into small units in order that the 'unmanageable mass', which would otherwise 'form into one impetuous and overwhelming surge against the reigning authority', could be 'split up into fragments'. See on this subject in general Ruth Glass, 'Urban sociology . . . . . .', op. cit. (note 1 above).

passive and 'accommodative'. The values, loyalties and commitments which go with it, so it has been recently argued, remain imprisoned within the horizons of local community: that despite the larger aims of the organized labour movement, notional or real. The active critique of the established order which lies behind such larger aims, this thesis runs, has not grown from the popular soil of working-class culture. It has been brought to the labour movement from the top and from outside: by bourgeois intellectuals, by leaders and officials of the movement with other sources to draw upon than the local communities which have given labour strength in numbers. In so far as the movement has at times and in part set radical objectives, such radicalism will fade away the more the politicians and men of office in the movement become locked in the compromises of reformist politics and bargaining. The community culture of the working class – now in any case threatened by changes in patterns of industrial location and urban settlement – gave labour organizations solidarity of rank and file support. But it was, and is, incapable by itself of sustaining the political vision, the critical imagination, that larger sense of class identity, which a challenge to the dominant principles of the current order would require.[20]

The argument may seem plausible at first sight; less so on closer consideration. Responsibility for the radical features of labour ideology cannot be neatly assigned to intellectuals and professional politicians – unless these labels are automatically applied, by definitional sleight of hand, to all men of ideas irrespective of their jobs, activities and origins. Well before the circulation of socialist notions, both Jacobinism and radical political dissent of a nonconformist strain found active support among artisans and factory workers in early industrial England, though their modes of expression were riots, demonstrations, petitions, clandestine organization when they faced repression and infiltration by government agents; but not organization for armed revolution. Chartism, later on, was a movement at the grass-roots of the working class. It acquired unity, while it lasted, by agreement on a programme only of constitutional change. But this was by no means a 'moderate' programme: even today we do not have annual parliaments and the direct responsibility of representatives to people which the Charter sought. And the movement spanned a diversity of underlying ideas, in which hostility

20. See F. Parkin, *Class Inequality. . . .* , op. cit. (Part One, note 8): a valuable and important contribution to recent debate, though we disagree with it.

to the power of property as well as insistence on working-class self-reliance were strong elements. Chartist radicalism was in no way a gift from bourgeois intellectuals to the working class. Much later again in the century, when socialist proposals for public appropriation of private industry spread, it was trade unions that led the way in adopting them.[21] The Labour Party did not do so until nearly two decades after its foundation, at the end of World War I. The processes by which once separate working-class communities became incorporated in the labour movement at large, commuted local solidarity into a wider loyalty of class, acquired commitments to changing the total structure of society – the conversion of the South Wales miners from moderate accommodation to a position somewhere on the left, at a surprisingly late stage, to take just one example – are still in many ways obscure. But that these processes occurred there is no doubt. And the accompanying adoption of notions to shift the basis of power in society, however limited their application in practice, made for real changes in popular ideology. At all times, no doubt, the sharpest coherent formulations of radical ideas came from intellectuals and professional publicists, though some of these were men of working-class origin. But popular formulations in any case survive in the record, if at all, only as dimly heard voices in the crowd. No doubt too, at all times, it was a minority of workers who actively propagated radical ideas. But those who took them up, gave them support, absorbed parts of them into their habitual outlook on the world, were many more.

As fragments of an egalitarian critique of society these ideas persist among ordinary British wage earners, though they are mixed with their contradictions. To say that they are the creation of intellectuals is either pointlessly self-evident; or, when the implication is that they have lacked any more than an evanescent popular hold, in the past and now, it is false. It is to mistake the ambivalence of British working-class imagery of society, the co-existence of active dissent, distrust and grudging acceptance of routine, for something like the latter only: for mere passive withdrawal from the values of

21. On the preceding points, from a considerable historical literature including local studies, cf. e.g., Thompson, op. cit. (note 9 above); E. J. Hobsbawm, 'Labour traditions', in his *Labouring Men*, op. cit. (note 9 above); A. Briggs, ed., *Chartist Studies*, Macmillan, 1959; J. A. Banks, *Marxist Sociology in Action*, Faber & Faber, 1970 (with reference to union demands for nationalization); R. Page Arnot, *The Miners*, Allen & Unwin, 1949 (an impressive example of a trade union history).

official society. This last is certainly there. But there is also more: the elements of a mood of subversion, with a half-formed diagnosis of the sources of injustice. We shall discuss some of the contemporary expressions of that mood soon. For the moment, the point to be underlined is that to characterize 'traditional' wage-earner ideology as in essence only a buttress of accommodation, because that seems consonant with the parochial work-a-day features of established working-class community culture, is to fall for a mirage of sociological classification. Reality, historical and current, is a good deal more confused.

One limb to recent interpretations of the class consciousness formed by manual workers in the long process of capitalist industrialization has thus been to give it credit for solidarity, but to deny it capacity for social critique. Another has been to argue that, whether or not there was some fire among the grass-roots in the past – as is conceded by the theory that support for revolution is a phenomenon of 'transition' – the foundations from which a popular radicalism might take off are now crumbling anyway. There would seem small hope for the left whichever way one takes it. The new inhibitions to effective dissent are said to be found, once again, in working-class culture; but this time in emerging changes of everyday styles of life, and patterns of inter-personal relationship, among wage earners and their families who are in the vanguard of contemporary worker 'affluence'. Just because they are in the vanguard – employed in growing and technologically advanced industries, getting relatively high wages, able to change jobs or move homes with more ease than many others, still fairly young – they represent the future.[22]

There is no postulate in this recent thesis that the 'affluence' of such workers has significantly narrowed the gap in conditions of life and power between them and the privileged groups of business and high professions. They are workers still, who put in long hours and awkward shifts for their wages; cannot expect promotion and regular increments; have few fringe benefits and may find their jobs gone if the economic cycle turns down; are subordinates at work and people with little say in how the society around them is run. But they are workers of a new kind, it is argued, who lack the sense of fellowship which once gave the labour movement its impetus. Old connections between work and life outside work are wearing thin; and solidarity

22. The argument summarized in what follows is that presented in J. H. Goldthorpe *et al., op. cit.* (Part One, note 17, above).

evaporates on both fronts in the process. At work these men – the semi-skilled on conveyor belt jobs and the equivalent, in particular – are the victims of repetitive routine. The job carries few or no intrinsic satisfactions. But, it is said, they take it more or less as it comes, shrug off its frustrations by closing their minds to it, recognize a practical need for everyday co-operation between management and shop floor, for one essential reason: to take home the fairly comfortable wage packet which goes with it. That is the limit of their involvement in work; and while they may join with workmates to press, even to strike, for higher wages, the solidarity associated with that has little staying power. Its objectives are too limited and 'instrumental'. Such comradeship as there comes between man and man at work does not carry over into the world outside. These workers live in new areas, where their neighbours earn their livings in a variety of jobs and industries: there is no longer the overlap of relationships in employment and at leisure which gave 'communities of the isolated mass' their distinctive sense of collectivity. The man's central interest – his wife's as well, even though she may well be working too – is in life at home, within the narrow circle of the family. Domesticity and domestic expenditure give existence its meaning, the dull grind of wage-earning its point. Socio-political perspectives come to match this 'privatization' of life, the argument continues. Workers of the new mould do not usually adopt the preoccupations with social prestige characteristic of 'middle class' culture; and they vote Labour much as other manual workers, though with little faith or engagement in politics. They see class divisions, too, as a matter of economic inequality; not of differences in personal character, merit and conformity to this or that code of etiquette. But their diagnosis lacks radical penetration; it goes to the visible signs of economic inequality, not to its sources. Differences of class are seen as differences of income. The picture of society which these workers usually hold, it is claimed, is of a hierarchy of money, of differential capacity to consume, from which conceptions of power and conflict are virtually absent. The quasi-Marxist character of working-class social imagery has been watered down to a mere 'pecuniary' consciousness, with little or no political thrust.

There are echoes in all this of themes which have recurred in much observation and commentary since the 1950s. Workers have long been said to be becoming increasingly 'home-centred'. Their aspirations are rising, it is acknowledged, but are directed to personal goals: to family acquisition of comfort, security and – so it has often been put – social esteem.[23] The consequence inferred is almost always the same: a boost for conservatism, with a small 'c' if not necessarily with a capital. Somewhat parallel shifts have been seen among the substantial minority of manual voters who actually support the Conservative Party: a decline in the numbers who do so out of deference to traditional authority; but an increase in a kind of calculative – and conditional – support for the Tories from workers who decide between the parties from a consideration of their individual economic interest, conceived within a narrow perspective that takes the *status quo* more or less for granted.[24] But the thesis which points to instrumentalism, privatism and pecuniary consciousness as the hallmarks of a new working class has taken a different tack on several counts. Its authors found no evidence of any worker approchement to bourgeois status concerns and political orientations. They recognized also that, in making larger demands on life – including demands for education of their children and for other services from public resources unlikely to expand sufficiently without collective pressure – the wage earners of the new species were liable to experience frustrations that might in time trigger them into some kind of radicalism. The overall assessment of prospects of that sort, nevertheless, was negative. In all probability, it was concluded, nothing much was likely to come of this, because the preconditions for an effective move to the left were missing. The sense of mutual loyalty among workers was slipping away, in all forms except that associated with 'instrumental' militancy for higher wages. The new class consciousness lacked insight into the nature of power. Wage earners' rising demands were in themselves inchoate; and there was little chance that the organized labour movement – party and unions – would knock such demands into political shape, since the leadership is too enmeshed in compromise with the established order to give the lead that would be necessary. So, even without working-class embourgeoisement, the probable outcome would be much the same.

23. Cf. e.g., Runciman (op. cit., see Part One, note 16) who argues that, in so far as workers now set higher aims for themselves than those arising from traditional standards, these new hopes take a status-oriented form. But the survey data which he uses to support the argument are not convincing for the purpose: a manual worker's wish that his son should have a non-manual job, and a desire on his part to move to a different 'kind of district', are not necessarily indications of concern with status rather than with material security, comfort and prospects of job advancement.

24. McKenzie and Silver, op. cit. (ch. 1, note 12 above).

IV

Yet in fact the balance of probabilities can be seen quite differently. The evidence points two ways; and in some respects more plausibly to a drift to the left than to containment of popular frustrations within a continuing frame of institutional compromise.[25] If wage earners increasingly work only for one reason – for the sake of the pay packet – the effect is to confirm Marx's diagnosis of the proletarian condition. Only a single strand, the 'cash nexus', ties the worker to his work, his boss and supervisors, society at large in its present form. Stability of the order hangs by one thread: the market dependence of labour on capital. The thread might hold – if wages were to rise at a pace commensurate with worker demands; if jobs were secure; if those in employment could be relied upon to forget the poverty that threatens them in old age or in consequence of any one of the many accidents of life that can shatter working-class 'affluence'. But these are big provisos, perennially at risk of proving false: the cash nexus is brittle. It is all the more brittle because worker demands are indeed rising. And the arguments that these come now in a shape and in circumstances which make them unlikely to call out a collective radicalism in their support is far from self-evident.

Two crucial preconditions of any such mobilization on the left are said to be absent: solidarity of sufficient scale and resilience, socio-political awareness of sufficient penetration. But on the first of these scores, as we have already argued, the familiar loyalties of locality and kin engendered in communities of the 'isolated mass' are liable to hold back both larger conceptions of class identity and wider social vision, should they remain fixed after their stimulation of early labour resistance to employers and authorities. The gradual demise of these older kinds of working-class communities may therefore prove more a prerequisite of worker radicalization, in effective contemporary terms, than a hindrance to it. There is some direct evidence that can be taken to point just this way. Shipyard towns are prime specimens of the kind of coincidence between the worlds of work and home to which 'traditional' proletarian unity in its firmest version has

25. The following argument takes the same lines as that of J. H. Westergaard, 'The rediscovery of the cash nexus', in R. Miliband and J. Saville, eds., *The Socialist Register 1970*, Merlin, 1970.

been attributed. Yet their populations can be internally divided by stubborn cleavages of craft, trade and place. Community parochialism is replicated within the community. It separates yard from yard, workers of this skill from workers of that and workers of none. Feuds over demarcation issues underline the fragmentation of labour. But the trend is away from this. Local business is absorbed in the wider world of outside capital, 'rationalization' and related measures are imposed in response to market pressures. The effect on labour is both to reduce local fragmentation – and, it seems, to bring workers there closer to workers elsewhere, in a new militancy that transcends the old community boundaries.[26] This, it might be said, is no more than a 'transitional' phenomenon: the protest of wage earners forced reluctantly into the modern world of managerial rationality. But rationalization is a recurrent process, not a once-for-all thing. The market pressures behind it are continuous. It is they that can produce a conscious coherence of labour which grows out of common circumstance and, in the process, sheds the limited loyalties of place and trade born in the microculture of 'traditional' working-class communities.[27]

That indeed could still come to nothing if workers have no insight into the causes of their common circumstances and common frustrations. But the argument that they lack that insight, that their class consciousness looks in all essence only to money incomes, is in conflict with the evidence from which the argument itself derives. Consciousness of class cannot be measured solely by the things people say when they are asked to talk about 'class'. If it could, 'affluent' wage earners would certainly seem to have little more than a 'pecuniary' view of divisions in society. But the conventions of contemporary language emasculate the vocabulary of class, so that conceptions of power and conflict may be expressed – and may have

26. Cf. J. M. Cousins and R. K. Brown, 'Patterns of paradox: shipbuilding workers' images of society', in M. Bulmer, ed., *Working Class Images of Society*, Routledge & Kegan Paul (forthcoming) (several other contributions to this symposium are also relevant to the points made here); and R. K. Brown *et al.* 'The contours of solidarity: social stratification and industrial relations in shipbuilding', *Brit. J. Industrial Relations*, Vol. 10, No. 1, 1972.

27. There is in any case no reason to believe that residential segregation by *class* is much less pronounced in large contemporary cities and suburban areas than in old 'communities of the isolated mass'. And the fact that wage earners who are neighbours in the former often have different jobs in different industries, while sharing similar conditions as wage earners, might if anything help to allow class loyalties to be formed across divisions of occupation and trade.

to be expressed – in other terms. Clothed in such other terms, there are plainly notions that social cleavage goes beyond differences of income, in the minds of both affluent and less affluent manual workers. And those notions are critical of the current order. The pioneer study of the 'new' workers in the 1960s, for example, itself found three in every four of its local manual sample agreeing with the view that there is 'one law for the rich and another for the poor'; three in every five assenting to the proposition that big business has 'too much power'.[28] Much the same support for the latter point was found in a larger and more representative sample of manual workers, 'affluent' and others, a little earlier. One in every two of all these respondents, and two in every three of the Labour voters among them, also agreed that 'the upper classes . . . have always tried to keep the working classes from getting their fair share'.[29] Opinion poll questions may elicit stereotyped answers: off-the-cuff responses to propositions themselves phrased in slogan form. But assent even to slogans cannot be simply shrugged off. There are patent signs here, as from other evidence, of widespread, indeed routine, popular distrust: of a common sense of grievance, a belief that the dice are loaded against ordinary workers, which involves at the very least a rudimentary diagnosis of power and a practical conception of conflicts of interest between classes.

This is not, of course, a clear and consistent ideology of labour opposition to capital. It is an ideology of dissent, but at half-cock. Its weaknesses are several. It is an amalgam, first, of contradictory features. Co-operation with management in everyday work is generally accepted as an ordinary and matter-of-fact necessity. Analogies with 'teamwork' receive assent in a way which they do not appear to do in France, for example. Yet such assent goes along with an awareness of exploitation: firms are seen to get away with paying lower wages than they could afford, the fruits of 'co-operation' to be unfairly divided.[30] Strikes may be questioned in one breath, yet supported in the next as workers' only hope of getting themselves heard.[31] The image which the mass media present of industrial

28. Goldthorpe *et al.,* op. cit. (ch. 1, note 12 above), Vol. 2, *Political Attitudes and Behaviour*, pp. 26–7.

29. McKenzie and Silver, op. cit. (ch. 1, note 12 above, pp. 127, 135).

30. Goldthorpe *et al.*, op. cit. (ch. 1, note 12 above, vol. 1, *Industrial Attitudes and Behaviour*, p. 87). Mann (op. cit., note 12 above) draws on this and several other studies in Britain and France to make the comparative point (p. 35).

31. H. F. Moorhouse *et al.*, 'Rent strikes – direct action and the working class',

militancy is here often at war, no doubt, with wage earners' own experience. But the fact that the media have some success in putting over a negative view of 'other people's strikes' suggests the inhibitions to empathy between workers in one place and workers in another.

Secondly, both the range and the sources of inequality are seen only rather dimly. Most ordinary people probably have little idea, for instance, of the size of the gap which separates their own wages from the salaries and perks of top businessmen; or of the potent part played by interest and profit from property in the making of economic privilege.[32] Many workers again appear to accept the proposition that 'much heavier taxation of the better off and higher-paid' would neither raise extra money nor help the poor and lower-paid. That may, of course, simply represent a healthy scepticism about what could be done in that direction within a continuing capitalist framework. Manual wage earners questioned in the same poll were quite aware, in general terms, of the ways in which loopholes of one kind and another allow the wealthy to avoid taxes; and the majority of them – in unremarkable opposition to the majority of business and professional people in the sample – in fact wanted much heavier taxation of the rich, to share out the country's wealth more evenly, despite their apparent doubts about the practical effects.[33] But there are almost certainly also real contradictions here in the pictures which workers have in their minds about how things work; and ignorance, not least of the sheer magnitude of inequality and of its causes, must play a substantial part in keeping up confusion.

Insensitivity to the role of property in particular may seem to confirm the argument that wage earners, in seeing class differences as disparities of income, fail to see the disparity of power behind these. And it is conceivable – as it is a hope of conservative policy makers – that the spread of owner-occupation of housing among manual workers may detract further from popular criticism of the principles of private property. That, however, is doubtful. Such virtues as wage

in R. Miliband and J. Saville, eds., *The Socialist Register 1972*, Merlin, 1972 (pp. 147-8).

32. These points were strongly underlined in the unpublished results of a small-scale survey of views and knowledge about differences in income and wealth, undertaken in London in 1971 as a training exercise by M.Sc. Sociology students at the London School of Economics.

33. Report of a survey by Opinion Research Centre, *The Times*, 13 May 1974.

earners see in home ownership are probably, in the main, severely practical – lower costs in the long run than for rented housing, a hedge against inflation, freedom from the petty restrictions imposed even by council landlords. None of this would constitute defence of ownership for more than personal use; and even for personal use, ownership of more than one home may be commonly condemned.[34] Workers, it needs to be repeated, accord at best limited legitimacy to corporate business, the crucial form of private property. They see big business as having too much power. Factory occupation by workers threatened with redundancy, like squatting by homeless families, probably evokes fairly widespread sympathy; yet both deny the sanctity of property.[35] And though wage claims by their nature do not challenge the principle of profit from private ownership, the magnitude of many in recent years underlines the fact that wage earners commonly find no justice in the share that actually goes to profit. The point remains that most workers probably have only a fragmentary view of the salience of property in the current social order. That certainly weakens their counter-ideology.

The counter-ideology is weakened, thirdly and not least, by a common sense of incapacity to do anything very effective to change things. Rank-and-file labour's distrust of the current order extends at several points to the representatives, leaders and officials of its own organized movement. Many of the manual wage earners of the 'affluent worker' sample, for instance, expressed agreement with the view that trade unions 'have too much power', though far fewer than had said the same about big business. The great majority were still Labour supporters, but nearly one in three of these felt that it would

34. In a survey of council tenants in Barking in 1972/73, during and after a rent strike, II. F. Moorhouse and C. Chamberlain found nearly two in every three respondents – those refusing to strike little less than rent strikers – in favour of the view that nobody should have more than one home so long as there was a housing shortage. (Reports on this study were as yet unpublished at the time of writing. We are grateful to the two authors for letting us see drafts.)

35. Over two in every three of the respondents in the study referred to in the previous note approved of homeless families taking over empty houses, between 40 and 50 per cent of factory occupations by workers threatened with redundancy – again with little difference between rent strikers and others. For a journalistic account of one workplace occupation that made headline news, see A. Buchan, *The Right to Work: the Story of the Upper Clyde Confrontation*, Calder & Boyars, 1972. (While this occupation like almost all others so far was directed essentially only to preserving jobs, that too goes against the established prerogatives of private property; and there were occasional incidents during the action which may suggest that demands also for direct control could come to be asserted in future instances.) Concerning squatting, see Bailey, *op. cit.* (Part Three, ch. 3, note 23 above).

make little difference which party won the next election.[36] This, significantly, was already in 1963/64, before the arrival in office of a Labour government which was to spread disillusionment about its interest in equality; and at a time when party activists were still generally united in euphoric hopes of electoral victory. Popular criticism of the unions has often been taken to confirm the idea that 'moderation' is widespread. It is more plausible that much of it represents a sullen lack of faith: feelings of powerlessness to achieve fairer shares in society, in the face of the official labour movement's involvement in compromise and tactical bargaining. A sense of chronic frustration of this kind – less of apathy than of resentful bewilderment about what is to be done, when the established channels of pressure for change seem more or less blocked, and the effects of any action prove negligible time after time – rings out strongly in several recent studies of manual wage earners.[37]

The institutionalization of class conflict is liable to evoke a mood of suspicion against politicians and negotiators among the rank-and-file of both right and left; among members of the bourgeoisie who want a firmer line against labour, as well as among ordinary workers who want a better deal. Both flanks may be a prey to xenophobia and racism in response – working class 'Powellites' in Britian because they see blacks singled out for a liberal concern from which they themselves have been long excluded. Or they may turn to parties which, in varying mixtures, direct a deliberate appeal to the distaste for centralization of power that goes with institutionalized class compromise, but steer clear so long as they can of commitment on either side of the clash of class interests. Hence the resurgence of support for the Liberal and Celtic nationalist parties, with their cultivation of class ambivalence, in the 1960s and 1970s.[38] Or again

36. Goldthorpe *et al.,* op. cit. (ch. 1, note 12 above, vol. 2, pp. 26–7).

37. E.g. H. Beynon, *Working for Ford,* Allen Lane Penguin, 1973; B. Hindess, *The Decline of Working Class Politics,* MacGibbon & Kee, 1971; Moorhouse *et al.,* op. cit. (note 31 above; also the study referred to in notes 34 and 35).

38. Developments of this kind do not seem to be unique to Britain. The elections in Denmark in 1973, for example, saw not only a 'liberal' faction split off from the Social Democrats; but also the rise of a new 'Progress' party – to take 16 per cent of the votes – which, while extreme right wing in the ultimate logic of its proposals to whittle down state expenditure and eliminate income tax, still at that time seemed able to put over a front of 'radical' appeal to people, of a wide social and political range, who saw little to expect from the parties committed to the established pattern of class compromise. Those parties lost votes heavily, while the small left-wing parties outside the preceding Social Democratic government maintained or increased their support.

the disillusioned may withdraw from political engagement even of a nominal kind. In a society dominated by capital behind a screen of compromise, it is workers who are most likely so to withdraw; and their movement which is most likely to lose support in consequence. It is hardly an accident that participation in voting showed a general decline over the national elections in Britain from 1959 to 1970, before the partial polarization of class tensions which led to the election of February 1974; and that the Labour Party lost more from abstention than the Conservatives, especially in 1970 when after six years in office it had no record even of mildly redistributionist policy to keep its working-class support solid.[39]

Lack of faith in leaders and officials on the part of many ordinary wage earners is not a matter for surprise. The clash between the stability of inequality and rank-and-file hopes of greater equity is evident. So is the fact of labour movement enmeshment, in Parliament and local council chambers as well as across negotiating tables in industry, in a pattern of accommodation which showed few signs of disruption until the late 1960s. The long-term shift in the social profile of the parliamentary Labour Party has symbolically underlined the widening gap between grass-roots and official representatives. People who had been manual workers or union officers before they were first elected accounted for nearly three in every four of the Labour M.P.s in the House of Commons between the two world wars; for about 40 per cent of the party's contingent in the first three parliaments after World War II; but for only about 25 per cent by 1970. They made up nearly half the membership of Labour cabinets, on average, until 1950, but were hardly represented at all in the Labour cabinet that fell in 1970.[40] While there is no simple correlation

39. Allowances have to be made, in estimates of the 'true' size of the poll, for differences in the age of the register (hence of the proportion of people on it not able to vote because they have moved too far away or have died) between one election and another. We used several different formulae to make these allowances, and with each found a decline in the poll from 1959 to 1970, significantly with a distinctly low adjusted figure for the latter year. The poll was a good deal higher again in February 1974, when the partial polarization of class tensions helped Labour *vis-à-vis* the Conservatives, though the Liberals continued their advance to take support away from both main parties. Our analysis of N.O.P. survey data from the S.S.R.C. Survey Archive, referred to in ch. 1, note 11 above, showed that the poor years for Labour over the period, 1959 and especially 1970, were years in which manual working-class support for Labour dropped primarily through abstention, to a much smaller extent through any switch of working-class votes to the Conservatives.

40. Guttsman, op. cit., and Butler and Pinto-Duschinsky, op. cit. (see Part

among Labour M.P.s between political shading and occupational background, the increasing weight of the professional element in the parliamentary party no doubt helps to weaken sensitivity to the demands, hopes and outlook of ordinary wage earners. But far more important for the blocking of change than the composition of the labour élite is the sheer, compelling logic of institutionalized compromise itself. Leaders, officials, established representatives of the movement, adapt of necessity to routines, and acquire vested interests, which favour the perpetuation of compromise within tight limits. They do so, not through active conspiracy among themselves; but because bargaining, small advances and concessions extracted on retreat, within the practical world as it is, become their *raison d'être* once a pattern of accommodation is established.

V

If this were all, the outlook for the left would indeed be bleak. Popular dissent would continue to be contained, left to smoulder sullenly and to fragment in disillusion. But it is not all. Events in the

Three, ch. 7, notes 6 and 8), supplemented by data for 1970 compiled from *Who's Who*. See also, in general, R. W. Johnson, 'The British political elite, 1955–1972', *Europ. J. Sociology*, vol. 14, no. 1, 1973. Manual workers are weakly represented on council Labour contingents in relation to their contribution to Labour voting strength, especially so at county council level. (Three in every four of the Labour members elected to the Greater London Council in April 1973, for example, had non-manual jobs, overwhelmingly above the merely routine level; only about 7 per cent could be identified as manual workers. Data compiled from *Eve. Standard*, 13 April 1973. For a detailed analysis of the social composition of councils in London at an earlier date, see Centre for Urban Studies, *Statement of Evidence to the Royal Commission on Local Government in Greater London*, C.U.S., 1959; and for a study covering a wider range of local councils, see L. J. Sharpe, 'Elected representatives in local government', *Brit. J. Sociology*, Sept. 1962.) These and other studies do not give comprehensive data on *trends* in this respect within council Labour groups. The share of people in solid middle- and upper-class (excluding routine non-manual) occupations in the Labour group on Birmingham City Council declined until the 1950s, but remained roughly stable at around 40 per cent thereafter, while semi- and unskilled workers were hardly represented at any time. The manual worker element in the Labour group of Wolverhampton City Council fell from a large majority at the beginning of the century to no more than 15 per cent in the early 1960s. (Cf. D. S. Morris and K. Newton, 'The social composition of a city council: Birmingham 1925–1966', *Soc. and Econ. Administration*, Jan. 1971; G. Jones, *Borough Politics: Wolverhampton Town Council 1888–1964*, Macmillan, 1969. Hindess, op. cit., note 37 above, implies but does not document a decline in manual working-class representation on the Liverpool council Labour group over time.)

1960s and early 1970s carried signals that the pattern of accommodation was not as firmly fixed as it had seemed. There was, of course, no build-up to revolution. But there was an unmistakable drift to the left within the labour movement, of a kind for which none of the confident assertions of prevailing social commentary had allowed. It came, moreover, from the lower ranks of the labour movement, not from the top; and from the industrial flank, not from the nominally political wing. There was weakness associated with that: dispersal of opposition in localized action; a continuing reluctance on the part of the unions to abandon the habitual demarcation of spheres of interest between themselves and the Labour Party, and to acknowledge the overt political role which they were acquiring. These handicaps may persist. If they do, they may make the 1960s and early 1970s in retrospect no more than a phase of subversive but inchoate disorder; quite possibly the prelude to a near-totalitarian restoration of 'social discipline' on behalf of business, to which labour resistance will then have been undermined for perhaps a long time to come by its earlier failure. Yet these sources of weakness were inevitable, certainly at the outset. If the mould of institutionalized compromise were to be broken, the pressures for that could not come from the Labour Party in parliament and council chambers. They had to come from the industrial wing of the movement, and from the shop floors of industry in the first instance, just because the 'constitutional' channels for protest and for attempts at social change were ineffective. Industry was the obvious first battlefield for another reason. Rates of business profit were falling; and the threat to their future seemed to come not least from a mounting unruliness of workers and their shop stewards on factory floors: less serious in its immediate impact than for what it was taken to portend.

The trends to be found in the official records of industrial disputes (summarized in the diagrams on pages 411–413) tell part of the story of this crumbling of institutionalized compromise. The records are deficient. The smallest strikes are left out. Others, though above the threshold, may still go unrecorded because employers do not report them. 'Political' strikes, which do not rate as trade disputes, are excluded: several nationwide stoppages in protest against Conservative government policy, and its trade union legislation in particular, do not appear in the figures for the early 1970s. Action falling short of strikes – go-slows, work-to-rule measures, overtime bans – again do not come into the account, though there has been much of this in recent years: in all likelihood a good deal more than for some decades before. Still, the story in outline fits the shifts of the record. Whether measured against union membership or the total size of the employee labour force, the number of reported strikes reached rock-bottom in the late 1920s and early 1930s. It rose thereafter, in a fairly steady upward trend which still seems to be continuing. But the pattern had changed after 1926. The numbers of workers involved in strikes and the numbers of working days lost in consequence – both again taken in relation either to union membership or to employed population – were much below the figures of the years before the late 1920s. Strikes, from the record, were not much less frequent by the 1950s than they had been in the period that led up to World War I. By one of the two measures, indeed, there were now more of them. But they were much shorter and smaller: on average, four to five days in duration and some three hundred workers strong, compared with averages very much larger in the years just before World War I. Industrial action had become localized. As a weapon in the armoury of the established unions, strikes seemed indeed to have fallen into disuse, an institutionalization of conflict in this field to be firmly settled.[41]

But the upward trend in the number of strikes was significant. It reflected a rise in rank-and-file militancy, a spread of shop-floor organization, the expression of which in industrial action still left the great majority of strikes short, small and local, their impact on production negligible.[42] Much of what lay behind this had no necessary radical implications. Shop-floor organization served in part to fill in the holes in the system of collective bargaining left by the competition between different unions within the same firms. Shop stewards and conveners spent – and still spend – most of their time patching up petty disputes which might otherwise erupt into something larger. Local management did not share the view of them as agents of subversion which came to be increasingly adopted by the media, politicians and corporation boards. When shop-floor pressure managed to push up local rates of pay within and beyond the limits of national agreements, this was a 'wages drift' often – at least in the

41. This was one of the conclusions reached, for example, in an interesting comparative analysis: A. M. Ross and P. T. Hartmann, *Patterns of Industrial Conflict*, Wiley, 1960.

42. Cf. H. A. Turner, *Is Britain Really Strike-Prone?*, Cambridge Univ. Press, 1960. The conclusion there that industrial disputes at that time made for only small losses of production, even allowing for their indirect effects, must stand, although there was room for argument about the details of Turner's estimates.

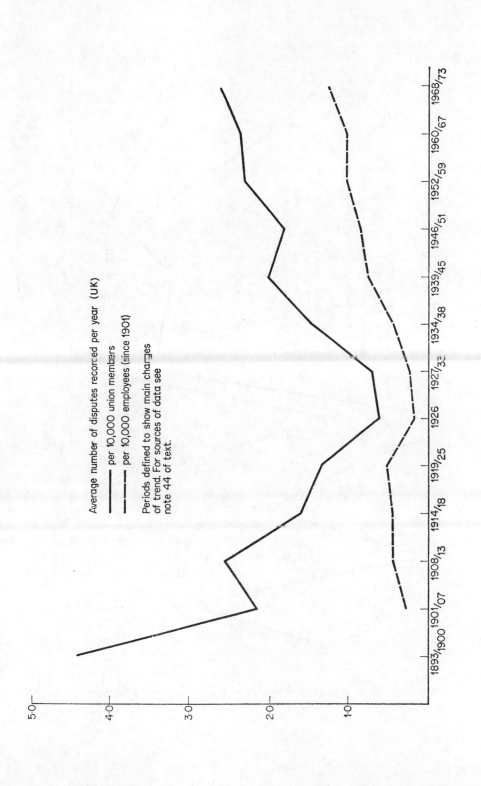

Average number of disputes recorded per year (UK)

——— per 10,000 union members

– – – per 10,000 employees (since 1901)

Periods defined to show main changes
of trend. For sources of data see
note 44 of text.

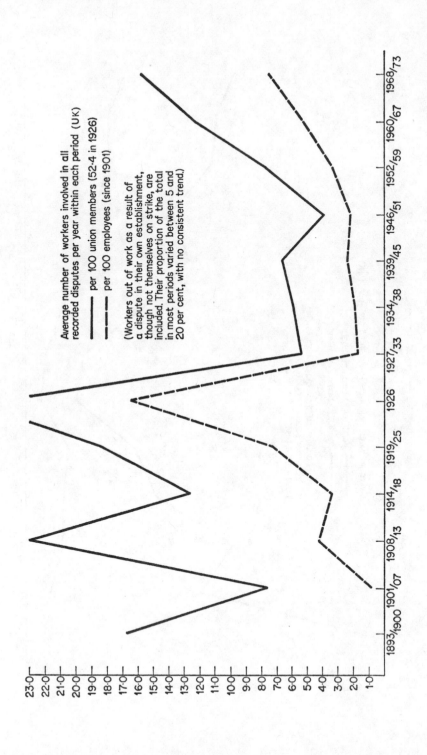

Average number of workers involved in all recorded disputes per year within each period (UK)

——— per 100 union members (52·4 in 1926)
- - - per 100 employees (since 1901)

(Workers out of work as a result of a dispute in their own establishment, though not themselves on strike, are included. Their proportion of the total in most periods varied between 5 and 20 per cent, with no consistent trend.)

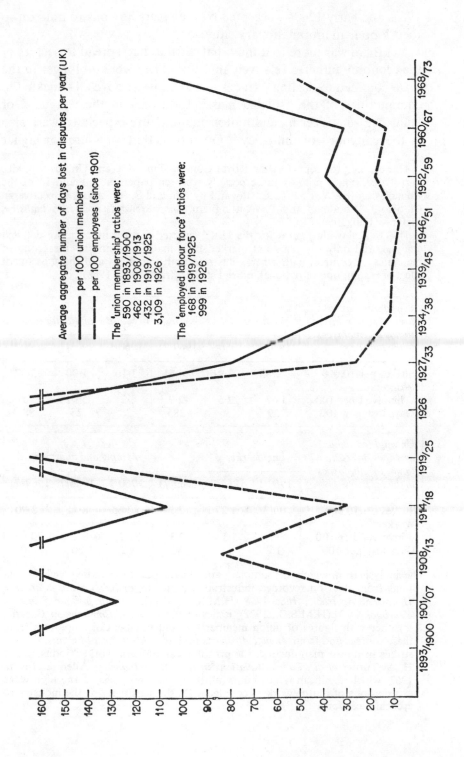

Average aggregate number of days lost in disputes per year (UK)

—— per 100 union members

– – – per 100 employees (since 1901)

The 'union membership' ratios were:
590 in 1893/1900
462 in 1908/1913
432 in 1919/1925
3,109 in 1926

The 'employed labour force' ratios were:
168 in 1919/1925
999 in 1926

1950s and early 1960s – accepted by managers anxious to hold on to their labour in an inflationary situation.[43]

Yet there was more to it than that. Strikes had spread to sectors of the economy hitherto relatively immune. They were no longer in the main confined to declining trades – coal mining above all – located in communities of the 'isolated mass'. Industries in the vanguard of 'affluence'–engineering and motor manufacture especially–were also in the vanguard of militancy.[44] On top of that, pressure for higher

43. See, e.g., the report of the Royal Commission on Trade Unions (op. cit., Part Three, ch. 5, note 4) and especially research papers nos. 1 and 10 of the Commission (by W. E. J. McCarthy and by him and S. R. Parker, respectively). Cf. also J. Woodman and T. Whittingham, *Shop Stewards in British Industry*, McGraw Hill, 1969.

44. The following figures for the U.K., selected from a much more detailed analysis, and only for years not marked by a major eruption in one group of industries by contrast with others, illustrate both this point and the subsequent effect of resumption of national, official strikes (from about 1968).

Unweighted annual averages, in relation to no. of employees in the industry	Vehicles			Metal manufacture		
	1960/1	1966/7	1969/71	1960/1	1966/7	1969/71
Strikes per 10,000 Workers	1·83	2·91	4·51	1·16	1·90	3·97
involved per 100	19·7	22·5	42·9	4·3	5·9	13·2
Days lost per 100	59	56	285	28	25	88

Unweighted annual averages, in relation to no. of employees in the industry	Engineering			Mining and quarrying		
	1960/1	1966/7	1969/71	1960/1	1966/7	1969/71
Strikes per 10,000 Workers	0·87	1·27	2·91	20·65	8·41	3·90
involved per 100	3·4	5·3	10·3	32·2	8·2	22·1
Days lost per 100	16	17	60	82	20	170

The analysis from which this summary and the diagrams derive involved calculations from data on recorded industrial disputes in *British Labour Statistics, Historical Abstracts, 1886–1968* (H.M.S.O., 1971), *British Labour Statistics Yearbook 1970* (H.M.S.O., 1972), issues of the *Dept. of Employment Gazette*, together with figures of union membership and numbers of employees from these sources and from *Annual Abstracts* and *Monthly Digest of Statistics*. (On strikes in motor manufacture, the prototypical 'affluent worker' industry, see H. A. Turner *et al.*, *Labour Relations in the Motor Industry*, Allen & Unwin, 1967, which significantly attributes militancy here not least to the high wage expectations of motor workers coupled with the sensitivity of the industry to cyclical recession.)

wages became more of a threat to capital as profits became more uncertain; and it laid the ground for the massive wage claims of the late 1960s and after. The growth of shop-floor organization, moreover, represented a mounting threat to the apparatus of compromise between unions and employers – indeed to the whole order of tightly institutionalized conflict between the classes. So, too, it came to be seen – by business, by the right wing of labour, by establishment spokesmen at large; less clearly, probably, by ordinary workers, who nevertheless found, through their shop-floor representatives, opportunities for protest and opposition which were otherwise absent.

The pressures from that groundswell came to a head in the late 1960s – with a Labour government in office, increasingly in conflict with its own industrial wing over government efforts to impose wage restraint and restore labour discipline. We have already told the essentials of that story, and do not need to repeat it here. Nor do we need to repeat the details of the process which followed the election of 1970, when a Conservative government took far sharper measures – with little effect – to much the same ends.[45] The outcome was twofold. The first is evident in the record of strikes, though understated: a sharp increase in the scale of industrial conflict (in fact from about 1968) manifest in the measures of days lost and workers involved. Unions took up the strike weapon once more: forced into often reluctant action by shop-floor militancy, and by the incompatibility of their representative role with the pressures of government and business upon them to keep rank-and-file in check. Strikes lengthened – to an average of nearly seven days in the period from 1968 to 1973, compared with only two-and-a-half in the 1960s before that. The number of workers involved rose from figures usually, on average, around three hundred per strike to an average of six hundred between the same two periods. These crude overall averages, moreover, conceal the specific contribution now made by a small number of very large, national and official strikes.[46]

45. See Part Three, chapter 5.
46. For a discussion of the trends of industrial disputes from the 1960s, their context and implications, see R. Hyman, 'Industrial conflict and the political economy', in R. Miliband and J. Saville, eds., *The Socialist Register 1973*, Merlin, 1974. M. Silver 'Recent British strike trends', *Brit. J. Industrial Relations*, March 1973, is a detailed statistical analysis of changes in the patterns of recorded strikes since 1959 (in part parallel to the analysis of ours the main results of which we summarize here in the text, diagrams and notes). Knowles, op. cit. (note 13

The second effect was to thrust the unions increasingly into a role of political opposition, and on the left of the party. Eventually the Labour Party itself adopted a leftward-inclined programe, ostensibly out of line with its policies to promote only capitalist efficiency in the 1960s. It came to precarious government office in early 1974 with that programme in its pocket. But effective resistance to the pressures on wage earners, effective assertion of rising working-class demands, such as it was, came from the unions. It was to them and the T.U.C. – which had previously acquired more formal influence over its constituent unions, paradoxically enough, as an agent of government-imposed wage restraint – that politicians and business looked for labour reactions to official policy designed to safeguard business growth and prosperity.

Union leadership was torn in its response. Every strike, every go-slow and work-to-rule, was now 'political': a challenge to government as well as employers. Yet the unions were markedly loath to recognize this in any overt fashion. At the height of a government-imposed three-day working week, and of the associated miners' overtime ban and strike in defiance of incomes policy which led a Conservative administration to call a general election in February 1974, the T.U.C. remained intent on finding a peaceful resolution which would not appear to flout the principles of government policy – even though the T.U.C. itself had denied the legitimacy of that policy. And they strenuously upheld their assertion that the conflict was no more than an ordinary trade dispute. The climate of commentary on both sides carried a strong whiff of 1926: determination on the part of government and much of business to put labour firmly back in its place; beyond all consideration of tactics, at the same time, a rooted reluctance on the part of the central organization of the unions to commit itself to a struggle for power, and to actions which were castigated by the other side as unconstitutional.

In the event, this particular dispute did not come to a full climax. The February 1974 election intervened, and led to the formation of a minority Labour government which sought a return to the earlier pattern of accommodation. A main objective of that administration

above) is the classic British study of strike patterns; and among more general discussions of the character and significance of strikes, see R. Hyman, *Strikes*, Collins, 1972; V. L. Allen, *Industrial Militancy*, Merlin, 1966; J. E. T. Eldridge, *Industrial Disputes*, 1968. Among accounts of particular strikes see T. Lane and K. Roberts, *Strike at Pilkingtons*, Collins, 1968; Eldridge, op. cit.; Beynon, op. cit. (note 37 above).

was to re-establish 'voluntary' cooperation between capital and labour, with a 'social compact' between unions and government to back this up in return, now, for promises of public policy towards greater equality. But if such a settlement were to be reached, it could still hardly be other than temporary and precarious. Government measures for redistribution, even if implemented, are unlikely to produce striking results so long as property, profit and market principles are left more or less intact. Business pressures to secure a good return to capital and to curb labour indiscipline will persist. Workers' demands on life will almost certainly continue to rise, and to come into conflict with these facts of life in the order of things as they are. Unions will once again be confronted with the dilemmas familiar from their experience earlier.

The analogies between 1926 and 1974 looked ominous for the labour left; but neither quite as ominous or as close as might seem at first sight. The general strike of 1926 came to ignominious failure at a time when wage earners had their backs against the wall, in Britain as throughout the capitalist world: in a period of long-run recession and recurrent heavy unemployment. The economic context of labour opposition in the 1960s and early 1970s was different. Unemployment, it is true, was rising again, in part as the consequence of deliberate government measures to hold back wage demands and keep business profits up. But this was now coupled with continuous inflation on a rapidly rising scale; with market conditions in which the demand of capital for labour failed to respond to counter-inflationary policies by falling to the levels which made workers redundant by many millions in the inter-war years; above all, with increasing aspirations on the part of ordinary wage earners, which resulted both in wage claims of unprecedented size and in an escalation of strikes to support these claims, in other countries as well as here.[47] Labour's stance was a good deal more aggressive now than fifty years earlier.

That aggression, it has been argued, is likely to come to nothing.

47. The annual average number of recorded working days lost per 100 employees through industrial disputes thus rose, from the three-year period 1961/3 to the three-year period 1969/71, by a factor of about twenty-six in Sweden; by one of six in Holland; by factors of about two to four in Belgium, Canada, Australia, the U.K., the U.S.A., New Zealand, West Germany and Ireland; by rather less in Italy; while it fell only in France, Japan, Switzerland, Norway and Denmark (and large strikes erupted in Denmark after this period, in 1973 and again in 1974). (Calculations from data in *Dept. of Employment Gazette*, Dec. 1971 and Oct. 1972.)

Union demands, like the mounting hopes of workers of the new 'affluent' mould, are in all essence no more than monetary: they do not challenge the principles of business rule. Much left-wing commentary joins hands with right-wing, centrist and neutral commentary, in seeing no impulse to radicalism in the 'economism' of union objectives as of rank-and-file aspirations. The point is a very dubious one; and increasingly so. The line between accommodative and radical demands does not run between claims for money and claims for control. Demands for 'worker control' – now in any case more frequently voiced than before – may result in no more than consultation or wage-earner representation on the boards of companies still impelled to pursue profit in capitalist markets. Demands for higher wages may be taken to the point where they challenge the continued viability of private capital. That is exactly what business today fears; and many recent wage claims have been of that order. They acquire political significance, moreover, precisely because business relies on the state to defeat them. That in itself is liable to turn 'economism' into something more; at least where there is a stubborn, though patchy foundation of quasi-socialist counter-ideology within the labour movement to effect the translation.

There were hints to point that way when, for example, miners voted (against an insecure Labour government) to withhold support from any public policy of restraint on wages, 'so long as the capitalist private profit-making character of British society remains unaltered'; or when nurses, in the course of a dispute about pay, withdrew their labour from private wards in public hospitals, in the hope of ending private fee-paid treatment and the associated privileges of consultants within a health service supposedly dedicated to equality of service for all.[48] These were only straws in the wind. But there were others, in the late 1960s and early 1970s, which suggested that demands arising in the first instance out of issues of employment, pay and

48. Delegates to the policy-making conference of the National Union of Mine Workers in July 1974 adopted the resolution quoted by 151 to 131, although it had previously been rejected by a narrow margin on the union's national executive. Opposition to the resolution came from the smaller, politically more 'moderate' coal-fields (disproportionately strongly represented on the executive) and from white-collar workers and several other special occupational groups in the industry. Spokesmen for the resolution emphasized their views that incomes policies set worker against worker and diverted attention from 'the real struggle between wages and profits'. (*The Times*, 29 June, 4 and 5 July 1974.) The dispute over private beds and wards in public hospitals erupted at just about the same time. (*The Times*, 4 July 1974 et seq.)

prices could take a twist to question the principles of societal dominance by property and market. That seemed so, for instance, when
workers occupied factories or shipyards to prevent their closure, even
though rarely to seek their acquisition by the state; when homeless
families once again began to take over empty houses; when some
local councils for a time threatened to resist the implementation of
new legislation to align public housing rents with private market
rents, and council tenants in many districts withheld their increases
in rents to protest against this change in law. All that, it is true, was
scattered resistance, and ineffective for just this reason. That was
significant one way. But it was significant also, the other way, that
each such action set a note of doubt against the working premises of
the order of capital.

Resort to strikes, work-to-rule and threats to that effect spread
beyond the ranks of manual labour during this period. This is a
reminder of the point, repeatedly emphasized in most assessments of
the contemporary condition of Britain, that militancy is not radicalism. Nor indeed need it be. When doctors, for example, threaten
industrial action – or high civil servants and army officers in Sweden
take it – this marks no swing to the left of their part. They are
defending privilege. Occupational solidarity is not confined to wage
earners. It is the more likely to lead to direct action among prosperous
professionals, now that their incomes often come from public
revenue and are, on the face of it at least, regulated by reference to
state policies of restraint on incomes. But the point can be taken to
absurd extremes of sociological agnosticism.[49] Not all militancy is
convertible into radicalism. But much of it may be; and radicalism is

49. Cf. e.g., G. S. Bain *et al., Social Stratification and Trade Unionism,* Heine
mann, 1973. This includes a useful summary and assessment of research on the
relationships between unionization and union 'character' in different occupational
and economic circumstances on the one hand, class position and class consciousness on the other, with special reference to white-collar workers. But the extreme
scepticism as to the existence of *any* relationships of this kind expressed in the
general tenor of the authors' conclusions (notwithstanding qualifications that
formally concede some unspecified relationships) rides roughshod over the elementary facts that unionization is still, in overall terms, more solid among
manual than non-manual workers; and that militancy often (though by no means
always) goes with political radicalism. The authors' discussion of white-collar
unionism, moreover, fails to enquire sufficiently into the question whether specific
groups of non-manual workers whose market circumstances are *least* secure (e.g.,
clerks and some groups of low-grade professionals in public employment) may
have shown signs of *any shift over time* towards militancy with radical connotations in recent years.

unlikely to emerge without a preceding or concomitant militancy. The spread of a willingness to strike among lower-grade professionals, and other salaried groups further down the non-manual scale than doctors, could be an accompaniment primarily of a struggle for recognition in collective bargaining that will prove transient. And even the least privileged of white-collar workers may be hamstrung in any efforts to turn militancy into effective radicalism by the fact that their unions – aggressive or moderate – usually represent a wide range of non-manual staff: from people who are wage earners in all but name, to managers who act for employers and have privileges of their own to protect.[50] Yet low-paid professionals – rank-and-file school teachers, nurses, social workers – have only very limited privileges. Such advantages as they have may well decline further, if pressures to keep public spending in check in order to secure business profitability are maintained; and as the expansion of higher education from the 1960s makes itself felt in a growing supply of formally qualified labour, for which the demand is then inadequate to keep pay differentials between low-ranking professions and routine-grade wage earners at their previous levels.[51] The first response may be militancy to defend and extend privilege. The second, if and when

50. For a recent study of a major, fast-growing and publicly militant but internally divided white-collar union, catering for employees of markedly divergent levels, see B. C. Roberts *et al., Reluctant Militants,* Heinemann Educational Books, 1972. D. E. Mercer and A. T. H. Weir, 'Attitudes to work and trade unionism among white collar workers'. *Industrial Relations,* Summer 1972, found few signs of discontent, or of any more than wage- and consultation-oriented support for unionism, in a fairly large sample of routine-grade white-collar workers in Hull in the 1960s. But this still leaves the question of future possibilities in the air, as further 'rationalization' of non-manual work may make sharper distinctions between staff in fairly well-paid jobs (with prospects of advancement, a share in authority and some diversity of work) and others who lose out on these scores.

51. Cf., e.g., Department of Employment, *Employment Prospects for the Highly Qualified* (Manpower Paper no. 9), H.M.S.O., 1974. We see little, however, in the argument advanced especially by some French sociologists that technological advance is entering a distinctively new phase in which 'knowledge' itself is a major productive force and those who sell their knowledge in the labour market may take over the banner of radicalism. It is very doubtful whether knowledge is more distinctively important now than it has been at any earlier stage of industrialism; and while specific groups of qualified labour may well *lose* past and present privileges if and when their supply exceeds demand for them, it does not seem probable that 'intellectual workers' will develop a radicalism in common (extending also to those able to maintain a distinctive *premium* in the market) arising from the clash between the profit imperatives of private capitalism and a culture of professional and social purpose among these people. (For a recent discussion of these issues, see Mann, op. cit., note 12 above: chapter 7.)

that fails, could be militancy with a more radical twist, to which many clerical workers – scattered over a variety of workplaces, industries and unions – might attach themselves.

That still seems well in the uncertain future, though more of a possibility now than it was just ten or twenty years ago. If there is to be popular radicalization, it is overwhelmingly likely that the main thrust, in intensity as well as numbers, must come from manual labour. A fresh accentuation of conflict between the needs of capital for stable profit and the demands of ordinary people for fairer shares – if not for a deliberate dispossession of capital – is a perennial probability. The next round, and the next again, are imminent: they will not wait until resentments among white-collar workers can coalesce in such a way as to add coherent strength to blue-collar dissent. Manual labour, too, may well again prove unprepared, fragmented, incapable of bringing effective force to their distrust of the established order, to their still diffuse and ambivalent hopes of a fraternal society. Still, the old institutionalization of class compromise showed a vulnerability in the late 1960s and 1970s which was not anticipated in any of the conventional interpretations before that. That vulnerability pointed to the difficulties of forecasting the future: difficulties inherent in a capitalism which survives only by its capacity to persuade labour to accept as routine the breach of promises which capitalism itself appeared to offer. The outcome can be in doubt for a long time to come. While it may go to secure business rule today, tomorrow, the day after, that would not settle the future. Class conflict would still be inherent in the order of private capital, its institutionalization always precarious. The threat of dispossession would continue to hang over it. We ourselves hope that this threat will become reality.

Index of Subjects

Index of Names